Business and Professional Communication for the 21st Century

Deborah A. Gaut
Gaut & Associates

Eileen M. Perrigo
The University of West Florida

Allyn and Bacon

BOSTON ■ LONDON ■ TORONTO ■ SYDNEY ■ TOKYO ■ SINGAPORE

Executive Editor: Paul Smith
Editorial Assistant: Kathy Rubino
Marketing Manager: Karon Bowers
Editorial Production Service: Chestnut Hill Enterprises, Inc.
Text Designer: Carol Somberg/Omegatype Typography, Inc.
Manufacturing Buyer: Megan Cochran
Cover Administrator: Linda Knowles

Copyright © 1998 by Allyn & Bacon
A Viacom Company
160 Gould St.
Needham Heights, MA 02194

Internet: www.abacon.com
America Online: keyword: College Online

All rights reserved. No part of the material protected by this copyright notice may be
reproduced or utilized in any form by any means, electronic or mechanical, including
photocopying, recording, or by any information storage and retrieval system, without
written permission from the copyright holder.

Library of Congress Cataloging-in-Publication Data

Gaut, Deborah A.
    Business and professional communication for the 21st century / by
Deborah A. Gaut and Eileen M. Perrigo.
      p.   cm.
    ISBN 0-13-303579-4
    1. Communication in management. 2. Organization. 3. Management.
I. Perrigo, Eileen M. II. Title.
HD30.3.G376 1997
658.4'5--dc21   97-28091
                                           CIP

Printed in the United States of America
10 9 8 7 6   03

Photo Credits:
Photo credits are found on page 354, which should be considered an extension of the
copyright page.

For our wonderful husbands,
David and Craig,
and our muses,
Boudreaux, Kimo, and Jax

Contents

Preface   xi

Unit One: Overture   1

Chapter 1

Solving Puzzles and Building Communication Competence   1

From Classroom to Boardroom—Are You Prepared to Make the Leap?   4

The Puzzle Model of Business and Professional Communication   6

   Elements of the Puzzle Model   7
   Supporting Evidence   11

Workplace 2010: Three Major Orientations to Work   13

   Scientific Management   13
   Human Behavior   15
   Integrated Perspectives   17
   A Tool for Investigating a Company's Orientation to Work   19

The Communication Process   20

   The Message   20
   The Source   21
   Field of Experience   21
   Communication Competence   21
   Encoding/Decoding   21
   The Channel   22
   The Receiver   22
   Feedback   22

   Shared Meaning/Reality   22
   The Effect   23
   Noise   23
   The Relationship   23
   The Context/Situation   24

Plan for the Book   25

■ Summary   27

■ Knowledge Check   28

Unit Two: Managing Relational Life in the Workplace   31

Chapter 2

The Art of Listening   32

The Benefits of Effective Listening   34

Hearing versus Listening   35

A Model of Listening   36

   Practical Application of the Listening Model   39
   Characteristics of Poor Listeners and Other Barriers to Effective Listening   40
   Typical Verbal Characteristics of Poor Listeners   40
   Typical Nonverbal Characteristics of Poor Listeners   41
   Other Barriers to Effective Listening   43

Gender Differences and Listening   44

Assessing Your Listening Effectiveness   44

   Identifying Your Listening Preferences   46

   Other Variables That Influence Listening
      Effectiveness   48

Improving Your Listening Skills   49

   Tuning into Your Listening Behavior   49

   Learning All You Can about Effective
      Listening   51

   Perrigo and Gaut's Top Ten List of Listening
      Tips   51

How to Talk So Others Will Listen   52

■ Summary   56

■ Knowledge Check   56

Chapter 3

The Care and Feeding of an Interpersonal Network   58

Defining Interpersonal Communication   60

The Impact of Conversations on
Relationships   61

Formal and Informal Communication   61

   Formal Communication   62

   Informal Communication   63

Vertical versus Horizontal Organizations   64

Communication Styles   66

   What Is Communication Style?   66

Communication Climate   68

   Open versus Closed Communication   69

   Defensive versus Supportive
      Communication   69

Aspects of the Workplace That Affect Job
Productivity and Satisfaction   71

   The Crazy Mixed-Up World of Office
      Politics   71

   Humor in the Workplace   73

   Romantic Relationships   76

   Sexual Harassment   77

Building Interpersonal Skills in the
Workplace   80

   The Value of Networking   80

   Mentoring   81

   And Then, There's Old-Fashioned
      Friendliness   82

■ Summary   85

■ Knowledge Check   85

Chapter 4

Successful Communication in Groups and Teams   88

The Elements of Successful Group
Communication   90

   A Definition of "Small Group"   90

   Advantages of Groups   90

   Disadvantages of Groups   92

Types of Small Groups Operating in an
Organization   94

   Formal Groups   95

   Informal Groups   97

Demographic Variables That Affect Group
Life   97

The Group Decision-Making Process   99

Tools for Effective Problem Solving   100

   The Single-Question Procedure   101

   The Reflective Thinking Process   101

Performing Effectively in Teams   104

   Qualities of an Effective Team
      Member   105

Managing Meeting Mania   107

   Establish Shared Agreement   107

   Circulate an Agenda in Advance   107

   Arrive Early   108

   Layout and Design of Meeting Rooms   109

   Six Golden Rules for Meeting
      Management   111

How to Stand Out at Someone Else's
Meeting   112

■ Summary   114

■ Knowledge Check   115

Chapter 5

Managing Workplace Diversity   118

Gender Issues in the Workplace   121

The Development of Gender Differences in
Communication   121
Report Talk versus Rapport Talk   122
The Emergence of Three Language Styles in the
Workplace   123

Benefits of Using Nonsexist Language in the
Workplace   124

Interruptions   125
Differences between Male and Female
Managers   127
How to Create Harmonious Relationships in
the Workplace   128

Other Forms of Diversity in the Workplace   129

Implications of a Diverse Workforce   130
Barriers to Valuing Diversity   131
Overcoming Barriers to Valuing Diversity   132
Implementing Diversity Programs in the
Workplace   132
Developing Your Own Diversity-Management
Profile   133
How to Work with People from Different
Backgrounds   133

Coworkers with Disabilities   135

Communicating with Physically Disabled
Individuals   136
The Language of Sensitivity   137

The Future of Workplace Diversity   137

■ Summary   139

■ Knowledge Check   139

Unit Three: Managing Work Life in the Workplace   141

Chapter 6

Interviews You Will Encounter in Your Work Life   142

Introduction to Resumes   144

Topics to Be Included on Your Resume   144
Topics to Be Excluded from Your Resume   146
Resume Structure   147
Electronic Resumes   149
Resume Formats   149

Cover Letters   150

Mechanics of the Cover Letter   151

The Employment Interview   153

InterviewER Preparation   153
InterviewEE Preparation   156

Surviving the Group Employment Interview   160

The Informational Interview   162

The Performance Appraisal Interview   163

The Coaching or Counseling Interview   164

The Exit Interview   165

■ Summary   167

■ Knowledge Check   168

Chapter 7

Leadership   170

What Is Leadership?   173

Leadership versus Management   173
Effective Leadership Characteristics   174

Leadership Styles   176

Relating to the Leadership Style of Others   178
Two Variables That Influence Leadership
Style   179

Leadership and Power   182

Sources of Power   182

Power and Empowerment   183

Developing Your Leadership Competencies   184

Profiling Your Current Leadership Traits   185

The Role of a Leader and a Sense of
Purpose   186

Developing Your Leadership Skills   187

Cultivating Your Visionary Proficiency   189

The 21st Century Leader   190

■ **Summary   192**

■ **Knowledge Check   193**

Chapter 8

Managing Stress and Conflict   196

Stress in the Workplace   198

Causes of Stress   198

Positive and Negative Responses to Stress   199

Stress Management Tips and Techniques   204

Conflict in the Workplace   205

Causes of Conflict in the Workplace   206

Symptoms of and Tactics Associated with
Workplace Conflict   208

Conflict Management Strategies   209

The Beneficial Results of Conflict   213

■ **Summary   214**

■ **Knowledge Check   214**

Chapter 9

Etiquette for the 21st Century Workplace   216

**Making a Positive Impression in Business and
Professional Communication   218**

Why Etiquette Training?   218

Managing First Impressions   221

Making Your First Ten Words Count   222

Using Body Language That Communicates the
Desired Message   224

Etiquette and Your Relational Life   225

Greetings and Good-Byes   225

Four Rules for Making Introductions   226

Names and Titles   228

How to Avoid Awkward Moments and
Etiquette Gaffes   229

Etiquette and Your Work Life   229

Making Appropriate Entrances and Exits   229

Extending Office Courtesies   231

Handling Appointments Appropriately   232

Receiving Guests   233

Public Life: Podium Etiquette   234

**Techno-Life: Minding Your Electronic
Manners   236**

Telephone Manners   236

Fax Mail and Cyber-Sensitivity   239

■ **Summary   241**

■ **Knowledge Check   242**

Unit Four: Managing Public Life in the Workplace   245

Chapter 10

Making Effective Business Presentations I: Advance Work   246

The Many Faces of Business Presentations   248

**Understanding Your Audience and the Speaking
Occasion   250**

Identifying Your Audience   251

Understanding the Speaking Occasion   254

Accomplishing an Analysis of Your Audience
and Occasion   254

Establishing Your Presentation Goals 259

Net Effects Goals 260

Substance Goals 260

Image Goals 262

Selecting the Best Format for Your Presentation 262

Impromptu 262

Extemporaneous 263

Prepared Manuscript 263

Memorization 264

A Word about "Stage Fright" 264

Causes of "Stage Fright" 264

Methods for Managing Communication Apprehension 266

■ **Summary** 269

■ **Knowledge Check** 270

Chapter 11

Making Effective Business Presentations II: Creating and Delivering a Compelling Message 272

Brainstorming 274

Developing Logical Sequences for Your Messages 277

Chronological Pattern 277

Spatial Pattern 278

Topical Pattern 279

Cause-Effect Pattern 280

Problem-Solution Pattern 281

Climactic Pattern 281

Motivated Sequence Pattern 282

Developing Your Outline 282

Supporting Your Ideas: Generating Appeals and Gathering Evidence 284

Types of Appeals 285

Forms of Evidence 286

Introductions, Conclusions, and Transitions 290

Introductions That Grab an Audience's Attention 290

Conclusions That Make a Difference 292

Transitions: Smoothing Out the Rough Edges 292

Ethicality of your Message: The Litmus Test for Determining If You're Ready to Go 293

Practice Makes Perfect 294

Setting and Achieving Your Image Goals: Optimizing Your PERC-Quotient 295

■ **Summary** 299

■ **Knowledge Check** 300

Unit Five: Managing Techno-Life in the Workplace 303

Chapter 12

Successfully Managing Your Techno-Life 304

The Changing Role of Communication Technology in the Workplace 306

Intense Competition 306

Globalization of Business Operations 306

Organizational Changes 307

The Technology Revolution 307

Communication Technology and You 308

Communication Competence and Life-Long Learning: The Keys to Successfully Managing Your Techno-Life 308

Communication Competence 308

The Philosophy of Life-Long Learning 309

Communication Technology Today 310

Teleconferencing 311

Facsimile (Fax) Communications 311

Electronic Mail (E-mail) 313

Groupware 315

The Internet 316

Intranets 318

Videoconferencing and Business Television 319

Humans, Technology, and the Virtual Office 322

Types of Virtual Offices 323

Three Tips for Maximizing Techno-Life Competencies 327

Tip #1: Select the Appropriate Channel 327

Tip #2: Be Sensitive to Others' Abilities 327

Tip #3: Realize the Importance of the Personal Touch 328

Techno-Life in the Year 2005: What Will It Look Like? 328

A Final Note 329

■ **Summary** 331

■ **Knowledge Check** 332

Appendix I

The Visual Impact of Your Message   334

Appendix II

Case Study Solutions   339

Index   349

Preface

To the Student

Why Should You Read This Text?

As we approach the 21st century, your life will be transformed into a new era of opportunities, a new beginning, a fresh start. Every time you begin something new, you experience changes that affect your life on a daily basis. In our ever changing, diverse workplace, you need to know how to cope with factors affecting your work environment.

Business and Professional Communication for the 21st Century focuses on communication skills that are critical for optimizing success in the 21st century workplace. In addition to classic communication challenges, the text addresses many contemporary issues, including the global nature of business communication in organizations today, diversity in its many forms, business etiquette and protocol, and innovative communication technologies that are changing the way we do business.

The text is written primarily for communication and business students, although business professionals will find the material useful. We hope you find this book to be engaging, captivating, and fun to read.

The Puzzle Model of Business and Professional Communication

The model we developed to guide you through this book evolved from a need to identify a common element to which most people could relate. We believe that the process of searching for a job and moving up the corporate ladder is similar to solving a puzzle. You need to know the rules of the game and how to play before proceeding to your ultimate goal: putting the pieces together to formulate a total picture. Likewise, business and professional life is analogous to puzzle solving. You need to know the rules of the game and how to succeed before you embark on your career path in the business world.

We also believe the four areas of business and professional communication that you must master are associated with your relational life, work life, public life, and techno-life. We have organized the book around these four themes.

To the Professor

Special Features

What makes our book unique when compared with other textbooks is the special attention we have given to topics that will interest you, and our provocative approach to the subject matter. For example, we offer students a crash course in business etiquette that crosses the four areas of business and professional life. We examine diversity issues with an eye toward detail, especially as they relate to gender, multicultural diversity, and persons with disabilities.

We also present a comprehensive outline, in Chapter 12, of current communication technologies that students may be required to manage in the workplace, including teleconferencing, fax communications, E-mail, groupware, the Internet, intranets, videoconferencing, and business television. Throughout this chapter, we emphasize the importance of maximizing communication competence and adopting a philosophy of lifelong learning as the keys to mastering any technology!

Each chapter opens with an actual business narrative that relates to the chapter topic. These stories introduce readers to the chapters and are designed to capture attention.

Distinctive features of the text include:

- ■ a two-color art program
- ■ extensive use of photos and graphics
- ■ "How Do You Measure Up?" boxes that provide opportunities for self-assessment
- ■ ToolBoxes that offer practical guidelines about topics addressed throughout each chapter
- ■ a variety of figures and tables that add depth and understanding to concepts learned

At the end of each chapter, you will find a comprehensive list of "Key Concepts and Terms," which highlights important terminology, set in boldface in the text, with which the student should be familiar. "Putting It All Together" provides thought-provoking questions about material that was discussed in each chapter. Finally, to aid students in applying key concepts, we offer a Case Study based on a "real-life" situation in the business world. Developed by people representing a variety of U.S. and international companies, the cases are designed to enhance the students' knowledge by providing challenging questions that pique their curiosity as well as test their critical- and analytical-thinking skills. Among the companies that are represented are AT&T, Hewlett-Packard, Marriott, Shell Oil International, and Sony, to name a few.

Appendix I provides current information about the visual impact of a message and serves as a primer on designing and creating compelling visuals for presentations. We provide solutions to each of the cases in Appendix II. Each solution was formulated and presented to us by the original case study developer.

Supplementary Materials

An Instructor's Manual accompanies this text and includes:

- ■ chapter objectives and overview
- ■ sample test items
- ■ activities and exercises that help students apply key concepts
- ■ resources that you may contact for further information

We believe you will find the Instructor's Manual to be both helpful and instructional.

Full-color transparencies illustrating chapter concepts are also available from Allyn & Bacon.

We hope you will find our book useful, interesting, and enjoyable to read. If you would like to contribute ideas, constructive feedback, or suggestions for the next edition, please contact us at our E-mail addresses. Deborah can be reached at dgaut@gulf.net, and Eileen at eperrigo@uwf.edu/

Acknowledgments

When we first decided to write this book, we knew that many special individuals would be involved. However, we had no idea that so many extraordinary people would ultimately contribute.

For example, the following individuals spent countless hours in the library and on the Internet conducting research for the book:

Irina Andrushenko, University of West Florida
Susan Avanzino, University of Southern California
Heather Donofrio, Florida State University
Misty McElroy, Georgia State University
Sandy Frank, University of West Florida

Gayle Houser, one of the best minds at Florida State University, contributed the first draft of our chapter on stress and conflict management.

Likewise, a very special friend in Los Angeles, Carrie Coyle, helped us design The Puzzle Model of Business and Professional Communication, as well as our communication model. Without Carrie, Art Aston, and the support of the International Right of Way Association, the completion of this book would not have been possible.

The Pensacola Chapter of the Florida Public Relations Association also deserves a special note of thanks for allowing us to borrow the Toolbox concept.

Case studies always challenge readers to think in new ways about theoretical concepts, especially when those concepts come to life in the "real world." To the following individuals, we owe a debt of gratitude for developing such creative and challenging case studies:

Melissa Crooke, Sony Music Entertainment, Inc.
Jan Flynn, Auburn University
Henry Hanson, Hanson & Associates
Debra Jacobs, Jacobs Consulting Group, Inc.
Patrice Johnson, Spectra, Inc.
Dan Knasel, Hewlett-Packard
Jim Knasel, AT&T
John Lickvar, Shell Oil International
Sheila Reed, Gannett/Pensacola News Journal
Steven Siler, Marriott Corporation
David Sims, Network USA

In addition, the staff at Allyn & Bacon have been extremely helpful and supportive, especially Paul Smith, our editor; Carol Alper, our developmental editor; Andrea

Geanacopolous, former editorial assistant; and, the following reviewers who contributed thoughtful comments and insights:

Steven Ralston, East Tennessee State University
David W. Worley, Indiana State Unversity
Brian Polansky, University of Arkansas, Little Rock
David D. Hudson, Golden West College
Susan Opt, University of Houston, Victoria
Mary Lyn Neuhaus, Loras College
Sandra Ketrow, University of Rhode Island
Bette Brunsting, Central College
Phyllis B. Bosley, Towson State University
Lois Einhorn, Binghamton University
Anita C. James, Ohio University
Richard E. Crable, California State University, Sacramento
Charles Fuller, Texas Southern University
Ralph R. Sisson, Emeritus, SUNY Brockport

Perhaps our greatest thanks go to our family and closest friends who have sacrificed and supported us the most. We love you, David and Craig, Bob and Flora, Betty and Tad, Pat and Squiggles, Gayle, Linda L., Falen, Linda F., Margaret, Anne, Carol, and the "usual suspects."

Whenever you open a book and begin to read, you are instantly transformed into a world of the author's making. For that moment, you see the world as he or she sees it—sense the universe as seen through the author's eyes! If the book is engaging, your perceptions are colored for that moment by what you read. If the book is compelling and touches some part of your soul, you will be changed forever.

This book is about life—business and professional life; a world full of excitement, adventure, and success for those who master its challenges; a house of horrors for those who are unable to deal effectively with day-to-day problems, or who sell their very souls during the process.

To aid you in charting a successful course, we offer you our own personal view of business and professional life and our best advice regarding what it will take to successfully navigate the future. As with any book you read, the assumptions, biases, and world view of any author will impact each step you take. We hope you will find our text to be both engaging and compelling.

In Chapter 1, we begin with an argument for why you should study business and professional communication—not just read about it, but truly study it! From there, we move to a commentary on the subject of puzzles—and the model that drives our view of the business and professional world. As the plot thickens, we talk about four types of organizational life that you must master, and we provide you with cold, hard statistics from corporate America regarding competencies you must achieve. Next, we turn to a discussion about how to attain the "best fit" with an organization. To do so, we talk about three major orientations to work that you will encounter, and we provide our best advice for choosing the organization that is right for you.

The model that we present in Unit One serves as the foundation for the book. Our goal is to increase your awareness, knowledge and understanding of the business and professional world overall, including its nature, pitfalls, and foibles. More importantly, we hope the words we share will help to lighten your load—and make your road to the future a little easier to travel. ■

unit
1

Overture

Solving Puzzles and Building Communication Competence

After studying this chapter, you should be able to

- Understand the importance of obtaining an optimal "fit" between you and your organization.

- Identify the components of the Puzzle Model of Business and Professional Communication and how the model relates to you.

- Recognize the skills you need in order to compete in Workforce 2000.

- Understand three orientations toward work that you will experience in the business world.

- Illustrate and comprehend the elements of the communication process.

The year is 2002 and you have just graduated from college with a marketing degree. You have already conducted an interview via satellite videoconference, and your prospective employer has indicated you are one of two final candidates for the position. The next step in the hiring process is to fly you to the company's corporate headquarters. When you arrive, you will be asked to give a five-minute presentation introducing yourself to the staff. Then you will be interviewed by the vice president and three department heads. Since the company has offices worldwide, you also will take part in a second videoconference, which will be international in scope and will involve brainstorming ideas for a new product marketing campaign. Your final assignment will be to submit a three- to five-page report within the week regarding your own ideas for marketing the new product.

We have just described a hypothetical scenario. However, it may become a reality for many job candidates in the not-too-distant future. Scores of companies like Procter & Gamble, Ben & Jerry's Homemade (Ice Cream), and Microsoft are implementing novel approaches to screening and interviewing job applicants. Their reasons for doing so include increased competition in the global marketplace, increased competition for jobs, and the need to comprehensively assess workplace know-how: from interpersonal to public to intercultural communication.

From Classroom to Boardroom: Are You Prepared to Make the Leap?

In recent years, business schools have come under fire for a growing gap between skills that are taught in college classrooms and competencies that are required for success in today's business world. As a result, a number of organizations have begun to study the problem and make recommendations for bridging the gap. One such study was initiated by the United States Department of Labor in 1990.

To explore the demands of American workers and identify their requisite competencies, the Department of Labor created the Secretary's Commission on Achieving Necessary Skills (SCANS) in May 1990. Results of their research revealed three major skill sets and five major competencies that all employees will need in order to succeed in the 21st century workplace (Secretary's Commission on Achieving Necessary Skills, U.S. Department of Labor, 1993; 1992; 1991). These skills and competencies are presented in Table 1.1.

Of particular importance is the fact that these skills and competencies are required across all industries and occupations in addition to the actual technical skills and knowledge associated with a particular field of study, for example, engineering or architecture.

As Boyett and Boyett (1995), management consultants to several Fortune 500 companies, have noted " . . . the basic skills go well beyond the traditional reading, writing, and arithmetic we associate with American schools. The three R's are still there and are still important, but even they are quite different." According to the SCANS Report, reading today means interpreting blueprints; studying catalogs and manuals; and processing E-mail, faxes, memos, letters, written policies, and formal complaints. Writing also goes far beyond what it did in the past, and includes developing correspondence, reports, policies, procedures, instructions, charts, graphs, proposals, and manuals. Mathematics takes multiple forms from maintaining records, using spreadsheets, applying statistical processes, identifying trends, projecting needs, and reconciling differences between inventory and financial records.

Finally, of the basic competencies proposed by SCANS, listening and speaking play a vital role in job success. Indeed, recent policy reports issued by the American Society for Training and Development, the National Academy of Sciences, and Stanford University also underscore the importance of these and other communication-related skills. Communication skills that are necessary for the 21st century workplace range from developing and maintaining interpersonal relationships, teamwork, and negotiation to problem solving, leadership, public speaking, and multicultural skills (U.S. Congress, Office of Technology Assessment, 1992, p. 38).

Table 1.1	The SCANS Report: Skills and Competencies Required for the American Workplace

I. Three Skill Sets

BASIC SKILLS	THINKING SKILLS	PERSONAL QUALITIES
Reading	Creative thinking	Sense of responsibility
Writing	Decision making	Self-esteem
Mathematics	Problem solving	Sociability
Listening	Seeing things in the mind's eye	Self-management
Speaking	Knowing how to learn	Integrity/honesty
	Reasoning	

II. Five Competencies

Resources	Allocates time, money, material and facility resources, and human resources
Information	Acquires and evaluates information; organizes and maintains information; interprets and communicates information; and, uses computers to process information
Interpersonal	Participates as a member of a team; teaches others; serves clients/customers; exercises leadership; negotiates; and, works well with gender and cultural diversity
Systems	Understands social, organizational, and technological systems; monitors and corrects performance (distinguishes trends, predicts impact of actions on system operations, diagnoses deviations in the function of systems); and improves and designs systems for better products and services
Technology	Evaluates and selects technology to produce desired results; appropriately applies technology to tasks; and, maintains and troubleshoots technology

Sources: Adapted from J. H. Boyett & J. J. Boyett (1995). *Beyond Workplace 2000: Essential strategies for the new American corporation.* (New York: Dutton) and U.S. Congress, Office of Technology Assessment, *Adult literacy and new technologies: Tools for a lifetime,* OTA-SET-550 (Washington, DC: U.S. Government Printing Office, July 1992).

What can you do to continue the process of developing the many skills required for the 21st century workplace? With such an overwhelming number of skills and competencies to be acquired—and we have addressed only the *basic* skills to this point—where can you best begin?

Few business schools in the country systematically address all of the basic skills and competencies identified by SCANS, nor could they do so comprehensively in a four- to six-year period. Instead, you must learn these competencies over time through a variety of life events ranging from college courses, to participation in school and community activities, to on-the-job experience.

As practitioners of business and professional communication with over 40 years of combined experience, your authors also may be able to contribute to your resource file. First, we have written this book with the aforementioned studies in mind. Second, before penning the book proposal, we conducted a survey of 500 North American human resource professionals regarding business and professional communication skills that they consider necessary in order to compete in today's global marketplace (Perrigo & Gaut, 1994). The outcome of this survey was fascinating and offered a glimpse of North American companies we thought would be of interest to you. The results of the study also contributed to the foundation of this book and will be presented later in the chapter.

In the process of researching effective business and professional communication, we have found one analogy to be especially helpful. In a word, we believe success in the business world is a lot like . . . puzzle solving.

The Puzzle Model of Business and Professional Communication

Jigsaw puzzles. Rubic's cubes. Computer mystery games. We have been intrigued by these puzzles since early childhood. They have charmed us, mesmerized us, and stumped us at times. To meet their challenge, we will work until all hours of the night.

Securing a good job and moving up the corporate ladder involve skills and competencies not unlike those required for mastering a puzzle. In fact, the word "puzzle solving" is particularly appropriate for describing the job-seeking process. As the player, you must determine the rules of the puzzle: what to wear, how to act, and what to say—generally "unknowns" when you begin. Hints are available from books on how to get a job, the target company's annual report, literature available on the company, and phone calls or lunches with people inside the organization. Much like studying the rules of the puzzle or game before you begin, doing your homework is ultimately crucial to your job success. Once you begin the puzzle-solving process, every move you make will affect the ultimate outcome.

Similarly, puzzle solving is a useful analogy to describe the process of moving up the corporate ladder. Again, success in this endeavor is a unique combination of sensitivity, knowledge, and skill. To solve the puzzle, you must figure out how the company defines these three aspects of competence, and then use them successfully in order to work your way through the organizational maze. Your ultimate success will be driven by personal goals and expectations as well as by the organization's goals and expectations of you.

To provide you with a framework for thinking about and applying the communication principles presented in this book, we have developed the Puzzle Model of Business and Professional Communication. Depicted in Figure 1.1, this model provides a means of characterizing different types of organizations and the basic business and professional communication skills that are necessary for a successful career.

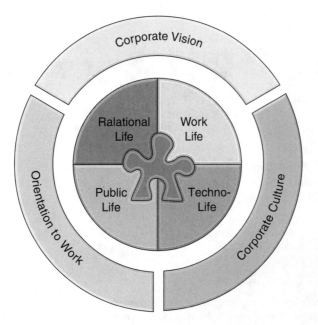

Figure 1.1

The Puzzle Model of Business and Profes- sional Communication

Elements of The Puzzle Model

Generally, a puzzle is defined by three major parts: (1) boundaries that define the puz- zle and distinguish it from other puzzles, (2) components, or working pieces, and (3) one or more solution(s) by which a player may solve the puzzle. To illustrate, con- sider the **boundaries,** or defining parameters, of the three puzzles we mentioned ear- lier: a Rubic's cube, a jigsaw puzzle, and a computer mystery game.

Boundaries that Define and Distinguish the Puzzle. The boundaries of a Rubic's cube are defined by the overall cube itself, the configuration of the smaller mechanical cubes that comprise it, and the rules of the game. Likewise the boundaries of a jigsaw puzzle are distinguished by its physical border as well as the number, shapes, and col- ors of the puzzle pieces. With a computer mystery game, you may be asked to complete a number of sequences, each with its own goals, rules, and distinguishing features. For example, to successfully maneuver through a computer-generated maze like "Seventh Guest," you must look for the beginning and ending points of the maze (i.e., its phys- ical boundaries), and then work your way mentally from one point toward the other to determine the best path.

Similarly, every organization has its own unique boundaries, defined by top man- agement in the form of (1) the company's corporate vision, (2) its orientation toward work, and (3) the resulting corporate culture that emerges.

Corporate vision is defined by Boyett and Boyett (1995) as "the common purpose, mission and values of an organization . . . [as well as its] desired future state" (p. 195). In a word, corporate vision is a company's definition of "success." For example, Anita

When playing chess, you need to know the rules of the game, be sensitive to your opponent's strategies, and be competent at playing the game. Succeeding in the business world is similar. You need to possess a unique combination of knowledge, sensitivity and skill.

Roddick, Chair and CEO of The Body Shop, views "success" as product development tempered by environmental awareness, social consciousness, and ethical business practices (Conlin, 1994). Top management at Scandinavian Airlines believes that "success" means approaching every interaction with a client as a "moment of truth" (Carlzon, 1987). No matter what form an organization's corporate vision takes, that vision will affect both the way a company does business and what organizational life will be like for its employees.

In addition, a company's **orientation toward work** will affect you as an employee and how the company accomplishes its work. By "orientation to work," we mean the way that an organization perceives, approaches, and operationally defines the concept of work on a day-to-day basis. For example, many local, state, and federal governments are known for taking a "scientific management" approach toward work. As a result, these organizations are more bureaucratic in form, and management is in control of both change and decision-making processes.

Other companies, like Hershey Foods, take a different approach, one that strongly endorses the concept of community and team play. Based on the premise that "there is more to life than just work," these "human relations" based companies may offer such perks as flextime; on-site jogging trails, swimming pools, and exercise facilities; annual company picnics complete with company softball or volleyball teams; and annual cruises for everyone in the company when a major corporate goal is achieved.

Other organizations, like Microsoft, reflect a more "integrated perspectives" approach, and integrate human relations and task issues with technology and the needs

> Where there is no vision, the people perish.
>
> —*Ecclesiastes 29:18*

of the larger environment. For example, to offset grueling 80-hour workweeks, employees are given a lot of latitude to release pent-up energy and maximize creativity. Practical jokes, pranks, juggling, hoop shooting, afternoon movies, chess tournaments, and Ultimate Frisbee are just a few of the ways that the employees of Bill Gates, Microsoft's CEO, maintain their incredible pace. Companies reflecting an integrated perspectives approach emphasize shared values and culture, and a balance between work, personal needs, and the needs of the environment in which they work. We will discuss these three orientations to work more completely later in the chapter.

The synthesis of top management's vision and orientation toward work is the **corporate culture** that emerges. The term "corporate culture" first gained prominence in the early 1980's with the publication of *Corporate Culture: The Rites and Rituals of Corporate Life* by Terrance Deal and Allan Kennedy (1982), and Thomas Peters and Robert Waterman's (1982) *In Search of Excellence*. Corporate culture includes an organization's goals, ideals, and resulting values; rites and rituals (i.e., activities and how they are performed); heroes; formal and informal communication networks; norms or ways of doing things; stories, myths, and legends; and organizational climate.

Companies like Ben and Jerry's Homemade (Ice Cream) are famous for the cultures they have created and for their understanding of the role that corporate culture plays in job success. For example, company founders Ben Cohen (now retired) and Jerry Greenfield believe that job success involves "dedication to the creation and demonstration of a new corporate concept of linked prosperity" (Jones & Kahaner, 1995, p. 22). Their mission statement consists of three interrelated parts and is presented in its entirety in Figure 1.2.

Figure 1.2   Ben and Jerry's Mission Statement

Ben and Jerry's is dedicated to the creation and demonstration of a new corporate concept of linked prosperity. Our mission consists of three interrelated parts.

Product Mission: To make, distribute, and sell the finest quality, all-natural ice cream and related products in a wide variety of innovative flavors made from Vermont dairy products.

Social Mission: To operate the company in a way that actively recognizes the central role that business plays in the structure of society by initiating innovative ways to improve the quality of life of a broad community—local, national, and international.

Economic Mission: To operate the company on a sound financial basis of profitable growth, increasing value for shareholders, and creating career opportunities and financial rewards for our employees.

Underlying the mission of Ben and Jerry's is the determination to seek new and creative ways of addressing all three parts, while holding a deep respect for the individuals, inside and outside the company, and for the communities of which they are a part.

Source: P. Jones & L. Kahaner (1995). *Say It and Live It* (New York: Doubleday), p. 22.

Out of this mission statement emerges a unique corporate culture, distinguished by its commitment to environmental awareness, a spirit of fun, and good, old-fashioned team communication. In fact, Ben and Jerry's "Green Teams" and "Joy Gangs" have become as renowned in the business world as their delicious ice creams. The Green Team's responsibility is to ensure that the company is doing everything possible to be environmentally sound. In charge of helping to maintain the company's spirit and sense of fun are the Joy Gangs. Among other things, they are responsible for coordinating theme days (e.g., Elvis Day) and, in general, for keeping everybody laughing.

As you can see, no matter what form a company's boundaries take, its vision, work orientation, and corporate culture play an important role in how that company sees itself and the overall satisfaction of its employees. Much as you begin figuring out a puzzle by determining and understanding its boundaries, or parameters, you will do the same as you make career choices throughout your life. Given an understanding of the first major part of our model (i.e., an organization's boundaries or parameters), we now turn to the second feature of puzzles as they relate to business and professional communication: the components, or working pieces, of the puzzle.

Components of Business and Professional Communication. Consider, for a moment, the crossword puzzle. Its physical boundaries are vertical and horizontal lines that form a unique pattern of black and white squares. Its components are a set of numbers that direct you in making word choices (e.g., one-across; five-down) and a set of clues to guide you throughout the process (e.g., "female pop star, Whitney _____"). Of course, the goal of the puzzle is to fill in all of the squares.

Much like a crossword puzzle, business and professional communication has its own **components,** or working pieces. Within and defined by the organization's boundaries (i.e., vision, orientation to work, and resulting corporate culture), these components are the four communication skill categories in which you must gain competence in order to work and grow in an organization. Based on the SCANS report, our national survey, and other related research, the four skill categories, as represented in Figure 1.1, include: relational life, work life, public life, and a futuristic component we have labeled techno-life. To get a good job, move up the company ladder, and establish yourself as a professional, you must achieve the "workplace know-how" associated with each.

Relational life refers to that part of our organizational lives that focuses on the relationships we build with others through verbal and nonverbal communication. Communication competencies required for a successful relational life include effective listening, interpersonal communication, small group or team communication, and gender and multicultural skills.

The second component, or skill category, in our model involves our business and professional **work life.** Work life competencies that must be mastered include resume writing and interviewing, leadership, problem solving, and decision making, as well as conflict, stress, and crisis management. Your ability to display an understanding of "appropriate" business etiquette and protocol, as defined by the company, also contributes to successful work life in an organization.

Public life comprises the third working component of our model, and involves the creation and management of our public image through effective oral and written presentations. Mastering these public forms of communication begins with the ability to identify goals for a given message, including the overall effect you want to achieve (net effect goals), the means by which you plan to achieve the desired effect (means goals), and the image you must establish and maintain in order to produce the desired outcome (image goals).

The final component of the Puzzle Model involves skills associated with **techno-life.** Techno-life involves your ability to effectively develop and master an ever-growing number of communication technologies that are in the workplace. For instance, how comfortable do you feel with such communication technologies as facsimile (fax) machines? E-mail? groupware? the Internet? intranets? videoconferencing and business television? The list of communication technologies that are available in the business world is almost endless. And yet, mastering them is a vital part of successful business and professional life.

Solutions for Mastering Business and Professional Communication. The third major part of our Puzzle Model involves the solution(s) by which a player may solve the puzzle. For instance, consider the many computer games currently on the market that involve developing solutions to problems. In each instance, you must study the goals, objectives, and rules, and then solve the puzzle within the parameters of the game. If you misinterpret a goal or break one of the game's rules, you may have to start over from the beginning.

In corporate America, developing unique solutions for solving a particular puzzle is the name of the game. That's where you—the center puzzle piece in our model—come into play. To be successful as a professional, not only must you be able to accomplish an assigned task, but you must do so in concert with the company's vision, goals, and objectives. Additionally, you must develop competencies in the four areas of business and professional life as the company defines those sensitivities, knowledge, and skills. How well you accomplish these elusive tasks and the unique choices you make to do so comprise your individual "solutions" to the puzzle. Much as a right move can take you one more step toward successfully working a puzzle, so, too, can a right move take you another step up the company ladder. Conversely, much as a wrong move can slow your progress in completing a puzzle, so, too, can lack of awareness or marginal competence impede your progress in achieving your professional goals.

As you can see, the Puzzle Model offers a simple yet viable approach to business and professional communication that can be used to help you build a successful, satisfying career. To further validate the relevance of the model for your career, consider the previously mentioned 1993 survey of North American human resource professionals regarding the four skill categories which, we argue, constitute business and professional communication (Perrigo & Gaut, 1994).

Supporting Evidence

As you know, to establish the foundation for this book, your authors conducted a survey of 500 human resource practitioners from companies in the United States and Canada. Our questions focused on skills that are necessary to get and keep a job in their respective companies. Survey respondents were members of the College Placement Council (now called the National Association of Colleges and Employers). At the time of the survey, our respondents served as primary interviewers for their respective companies. Of the 500 people who were surveyed, 124 (25 percent) responded. In summarizing the data, we have organized the results around the four skill categories discussed as components of business and professional communication: relational life, work life, public life, and techno-life.

Relational Life.   Five major areas of relational life that we explored in the survey involved (1) ability to get along with people, (2) listening skills, (3) ability to network inside the organization, (4) ability to network outside the organization, and (5) overall communication ability.

For our human resource professionals, the overall ability to communicate ranked the highest of the five variables for getting and keeping a job. In fact, 96 percent of our respondents rated overall ability to communicate as highly important, and only 4 percent rated it as moderate in importance. Ability to get along with people ranked the second highest of the five, with 89 percent rating this ability as highly important, and 11 percent as moderately important.

Listening skills also were rated as very important (75 percent high; 25 percent moderately high). Next in line was networking within the organization (35 percent high; 63 percent moderately high; 2 percent low), followed by networking outside the organization (21 percent high; 71 percent moderately high; 8 percent low).

Work Life.   We also asked questions about skills related to work life, such as teamwork, conflict and stress management, leadership, ability to play by the rules, organizational abilities, and time-management skills. Results of our survey were also interesting regarding these areas. Table 1.2 provides a breakdown of responses from our human resource experts.

Perhaps the most surprising finding was that only 34 percent of our human resource professionals felt that "stress management" was high in importance. This low

Table 1.2   Survey Ratings of Work-Life Skills in Percentages

SKILL OR ABILITY	HIGH	MODERATE	LOW
Teamwork	85.5	13.7	0.8
Time management	67.7	31.5	0.8
Organizing ability	61.3	37.9	0.8
Conflict management	46.3	52.8	0.8
Leadership	60.2	39.0	0.8
Stress management	33.9	61.3	4.8
Playing by the rules	32.0	63.9	4.1

percentage rate is interesting in light of the fact that stress contributes to many life-threatening diseases in our society today.

Public Life.   The third area that we explored with our experts involved skills associated with public life. In particular, we were interested in public speaking and writing abilities. Results of the survey showed that 98 percent of our experts believe that public speaking skills are important to professional success. Writing skills received slightly higher marks, with an impressive 100 percent rating this skill as important.

Techno-Life.   To explore the avenue of techno-life, we asked human resource professionals to identify technologies that their companies presently use or will use in the near future. The top four technologies reported were word processing (97 percent), spreadsheets (94 percent), desktop publishing (91 percent), and electronic mail (89 percent). Comprehensive survey results regarding other exciting aspects of techno-life (e.g., videoconferencing, E-mail, and the Internet) will be presented in Chapter 12.

The results of our international survey also suggested additional skills needed to compete in the global marketplace as we enter the third millennium. These competencies included: (1) skills at using current communication technologies; (2) understanding the implications of, and required skills to manage, diversity in the workplace; (3) knowledge of international etiquette and protocol; and, (4) proficiency in at least one foreign language (Perrigo & Gaut, 1994). Since the focus of our text is on business and professional communication (excluding foreign language), we will also address the first three of these competencies.

As you can see, the four areas of business and professional communication we have targeted are vital to developing a successful career. In fact, the survey we conducted guided us in selecting the skills we address in each of the following chapters.

Before we leave our Puzzle Model, let's explore more completely one aspect of the model: orientations to work that you will encounter in the business world. This area of study has received a great amount of attention in the research literature and contributes substantially to an understanding of the 21st century workplace.

Workplace 2010: Three Major Orientations to Work

The extent to which a positive fit exists between you and the organization for which you work significantly affects your productivity and job satisfaction. In turn, your productivity and job satisfaction seriously affect the bottom line and quality of life in an organization. One way to ensure that a positive fit will exist between you and a company is to learn everything you can about that organization, identify its general orientation to work, and decide if the company is right for you.

Scientific Management

The scientific management school of thought emerged primarily from the research of three individuals: Frederick Taylor (1913), Max Weber (1947) and Henri Fayol (1949). What Taylor, Weber , and Fayol had to say about organizations then impacts life in every organization operating today.

Table 1.3	Characteristics of Organizations with a Scientific Management Approach to Work

CHARACTERISTIC	DESCRIPTION
Organizational goals	Efficiency; maximum use of people and resources
Structure	Hierarchical
Division of work	Based on task specialization
Authority/power	Bureaucratic; management has sole responsibility
Centralization	Yes
Organizational vs. individual goals	Organizational goals—primary; individual goals—secondary
Decision making	Management controlled
Approach to change	Management controlled; top down
Desired channels of communication	Formal; oral and written; carry task messages primarily; interpersonal communication discouraged
Directionality of messages	Vertical; according to organizational chart
Communication climate	Close, personal cooperation between management and workers; no peer communication

Adapted from a discussion by P. Shockley-Zalabak (1995), *Fundamentals of organizational communication knowledge, sensitivity, skills, values.* 3rd ed. (White Plains, NY: Longman), pp. 94–103. Printed with permission of Publisher.

What do organizations which heavily emphasize scientific management practices look like? What approaches to work do they advocate? Consider Table 1.3 for a snapshot.

As you can see, organizations that rely heavily on the scientific management approach to work usually emphasize "proper" chains of command; clear status differences between managers and employees; division of labor among different units in the organization; specialized activities on the part of individual employees; messages flowing primarily in a vertically downward direction; and, decision-making and organizing tasks to be conducted by management. Additionally, communication of a social or personal nature among employees is generally discouraged.

Contemporary organizations that heavily implement scientific management principles come in all shapes and sizes, from government agencies (e.g., local, state, and federal) to small companies (e.g., hospitals, law firms, colleges and universities, and independent department stores) to Fortune 500 companies (e.g., the Tandy Corporation, home of Radio Shack and Computer City). In fact, any organization that implements and enforces communication rules based on a formal organizational chart would fall into this category. If you are comfortable with this particular approach to management, this type of organization is for you.

Human Behavior

In contrast to organizations that reflect a strong commitment to the scientific management school of thought, companies and businesses that are grounded in the human behavior school assume that **people** make an organization successful. As a result, rather than emphasizing efficiency, work design and measurement as the means to maximizing productivity, human behavior managers focus on ways to foster increased participation, cooperation, and job satisfaction. Their general operating principle is: "A happy, committed, and involved employee is a productive employee."

Three individuals who contributed substantially to this particular school of thought were Elton Mayo (1945), Douglas McGregor (1960), and Rensis Likert (1961). To help you better understand the value of information developed by these three historical figures, Table 1.4 describes the characteristics of an organization that is heavily grounded in the management principles of the human behavior school of thought.

Most contemporary organizations embrace principles of the human behavior school at some level. Consider, for example, Intel, the company that invented the microprocessor chip that drives many computers on the market today. Known as an intense, no-frills place to work, the management of Intel still knows the value of its employees.

Table 1.4	Characteristics of Organizations with a Human Behavior Approach to Work
CHARACTERISTIC	**DESCRIPTION**
Organizational goals	Productivity with an emphasis on broad participation by employees in decision making
Structure	More flattened than hierarchical
Division of work	Shared
Authority/power	Dispersed throughout company; individual employees are encouraged to provide creative input
Centralization	No
Organizational vs. individual goals	Equal emphasis on individual and organizational goals
Decision making	Shared
Approach to change	All members encouraged to contribute
Desired channels of communication	Formal and informal; oral and written; carry both task and social support messages; interpersonal communication encouraged
Directionality of messages	Vertical and horizontal
Communication climate	Cooperative, participative, open, supportive

Adapted from a discussion by P. Shockley-Zalabak (1995). *Fundamentals of organizational communication, knowledge, sensitivity, skills, values.* 3rd ed. (White Plains, NY: Longman), pp. 103–109. Printed with permission of Publisher.

A happy, committed, and involved employee is a productive employee.

Despite 50- to 60-hour workweeks and little personal stroking, employees are given the authority, independence, and autonomy to get the job done. As a result, they feel intrinsically rewarded for work well done. Additionally, employees have no problems when it comes to presenting their ideas to management. Intel conducts regular employment surveys and, in difficult times, does everything it can to avoid layoffs. Included in the company's employment package are strong fringe benefits, such as a deferred profit-sharing plan, three weeks of vacation and personal absence time after the first year, an opportunity to buy stock at a discount, and a sabbatical (eight weeks of paid vacation) after seven years of service. To show its appreciation of employees and to celebrate its twentieth birthday in 1988, Intel hired Ray Bloch Productions to put on a 90-minute musical show featuring actors and actresses with Broadway credits. The script was designed to parody many of Intel's idiosyncracies: endless meetings, crazy hours, lack of structure, and use of acronyms. In fact, the three principal executives in its corporate history, Robert Noyce, Gordon Moore, and Andrew Grove, danced onto the stage dressed in "clean room" bunny suits. The company also creates and develops an annual April Fool's Day issue of *The iNTeLNATIONAL iNQUIReR,* which has been published at Intel since 1983 (Levering & Moskowitz, 1994).

As you might guess, carefully constructing questions for a job interview will allow you to determine the extent to which any organization (like Intel!) is committed to human behavior principles, especially if such an organization sounds right for you. We want to reiterate the fact that gaining the proper fit between you and your company is the key to personal and professional productivity and satisfaction.

Integrated Perspectives

Identified by Shockley-Zalabak (1995) as the integrated perspectives approach, this school of thought represents the most current management principles being heralded by business and industry. This approach may be best conceived as the outcome of a super collision between scientific management and human behavior principles—between technological innovation and a heightened awareness of the larger environment in which the organization functions. Integrated perspectives managers are interested in the best way to influence employees by integrating the best of people, technology, and an awareness of the operating environment.

The integrated perspectives approach to management is based on research by a number of writers. Of particular note are Katz and Kahn (1966), Ouchi (1981), and Deal and Kennedy (1982). Table 1.5 on page 18 provides a brief synopsis of this new and innovative approach to work.

Many organizations have turned to a more integrated perspectives philosophy or approach to management due to the rapid change inherent in both the internal and external environments of business today. For example, to meet changing needs, many companies acknowledge the value of cross training and work teams, no matter what level of commitment to hierarchical structure they maintain. Rather than authority and power residing strictly and automatically with top management, power and authority may (or may not) be shared, depending on (1) the needs and goals of the organization, (2) individual needs and goals, and (3) technologies available to them. Additionally, such organizations encourage individual decision making—in effect the "flattening of the corporate structure" that took place for so many companies in the early 1990s. Innovation and productivity are believed to go hand in hand, producing an environment that is conducive and open to positive change. Communication channels (e.g., formal versus informal; oral versus written, etc.) and the direction of messages (upward versus downward versus horizontal) are selected on the basis of individual and organizational needs. (Chapter 3 will provide additional information on these concepts.) Finally, organizations committed to an integrated perspectives approach place an equal emphasis on work and personal needs, depending on the requirements of the environment.

Companies that reflect a more integrated perspectives approach are numerous. One such company that is a household name is Johnson & Johnson, the world's largest maker of health-care products. Although Johnson & Johnson ranks 34th on the Fortune 500 list at the time of this writing, management and employees alike work to keep the "bigness" of their company a secret. To illustrate, business is carried on by more than 160 different companies, each with a high degree of autonomy. Each company employs its own management board; plans, markets, hires, and fires; and makes decisions locally. Although the company prides itself on its level of decentralization, J&J has a set of core

Table 1.5	Characteristics of Organizations with an Integrated Perspectives Approach to Work

CHARACTERISTIC	DESCRIPTION
Organizational goals	Integration of organizational structure, technology, and people with larger environment
Structure	Variable; adaptive; dependent on external environment, organizational goals, and individual goals
Division of work	Variable; cross training and work teams encouraged, with emphasis on group autonomy
Authority/power	Dependent on needs of organization; individual responsibility for decision making probable; innovation and effectiveness are chief features
Centralization	Variable
Organizational vs. individual goals	Equal emphasis on individual and organizational goals
Decision making	Dependent on needs of organization; individual decision making valued, if possible
Approach to change	Based on needs of external environment and possibilities, given access to technology
Desired channels of communication	Variable
Directionality of messages	Variable
Communication climate	Emphasis on shared values/ culture; equal emphasis on work, personal needs, and environmental requirements

Adapted from a discussion by P. Shockley-Zalabak (1995), *Fundamentals of organizational communication, knowledge, sensitivity, skills, values.* 3rd ed. (White Plains, NY: Longman), pp. 112–134. Printed with permission of Publisher.

values, expressed in a document called "Our Credo," which draws the separate companies together into one large family. As for its employees, J&J provides child care facilities, a leading compensation and benefits package, and an extra week's paid vacation (for the honeymoon) if you marry after you have worked for the company for five years.

The company's handling of the Tylenol™ crisis in the early 1980s, when someone laced Tylenol™ capsules with cyanide, killing seven people, is a primary example of J&J's sensitivity and responsiveness to the environment. Immediately upon learning about this devastating event, James E. Burke, CEO at the time, went on nationwide television, accepted responsibility for the crisis, and ordered the immediate recall of all Tylenol™ capsules. Burke attributes the company's weathering of the crisis to their Credo, which emphasizes the company's first and foremost responsibility "to the doctors, nurses and patients, to mothers and fathers and all others who use their products and services" (Levering & Moskowitz, 1994, pp. 208–213).

A Tool for Investigating a Company's Orientation to Work

How can you determine what orientation to work best represents a company or business? What questions can you ask during an interview that will help you determine the "goodness of fit" between you and an organization for whom you think you would like to work? If you are working for a company presently and are unhappy in your job, what questions can you ask yourself that might enable you to make a positive career decision?

Over the many years that we have been teaching, our students have asked these questions on numerous occasions. In response to them, and to help you make more informed career choices, we offer you the first of many "ToolBoxes" that we have developed for your use as you work through this book. In every ToolBox you will find practical tips and techniques for making the most of your business and professional life.

The ten questions presented in Box 1.1 are designed to evoke answers that may help you identify a company's primary orientation to work: scientific management (SM), human behavior (HB), or integrated perspectives (IP). The questions are not foolproof

---

BOX 1.1

ToolBox | *Interview Questions to Help You Determine a Company's Organizational Frame*

As you are preparing for a job interview, consider asking your interviewer the following questions.

1. What would you say is the major driving force behind [company name]: efficiency (SM), participative decision making (HB), or technology and people (IP)?
2. By what means is work most often accomplished at [company name]: task specialty (SM), job sharing (HB), or cross-trained work teams (IP)?
3. On a scale of one to ten (1=low; 10=high), how much would you say the average employee contributes to company decision making? ("1–5"—SM; "6–10"—HB; "It depends"—IP)
4. Who or what would you say most often initiates change at [company name]: managers (SM), employees (HB), or the marketplace (IP)?
5. On a scale of one to ten (1 = low; 10 = high), to what extent does [company name] encourage employees to set and achieve individual goals? ("1–5"—SM; "6–10"—HB; "It depends"—IP)

6. If you could paint a picture of the hierarchical structure of [company name], would it most resemble a ladder (SM), a pancake (HB), or a human cell (IP)?
7. Would you characterize [company name] as more task oriented (SM), interpersonally oriented (HB), or some combination of the two (IP)?
8. Is most communication at [company name] upward (HB), downward (SM), or lateral (IP)?
9. How would you best describe the communication climate at [company name]—close and personal between managers and employees with little peer communication (SM)? open and cooperative across all levels of the organization (HB); or, as having an equal emphasis on work, personal needs, and environmental concerns (IP)?
10. Finally, on a scale of one to ten (1 = low; 10 = high), to what extent would I have an opportunity to provide input into decision making and change in my department at [company name]? ("1–5"—SM; "6–10"—HB; "It depends"—IP

and may elicit entirely different responses from individuals within the same organization. Additionally, most companies will reflect a unique blend of the three perspectives. However, gathering information regarding the ten questions may provide you with insight as to the type of organization in which you would feel most comfortable.

Now that we have more completely addressed three major orientations to work and provided you with a tool for determining a company's predisposition regarding management, we turn to the model of communication that guides this book.

The Communication Process

Effective communication is the key to success in business and professional life. Although each of us would like to think that we communicate well, the complexity of successful communication makes it a challenge at best. To illustrate the intricacy (and puzzle nature!) of the communication process, consider the many elements of communication in Figure 1.3.

The Message

A **message** is the content of a communication, or the ideas and thoughts that we express to others through communication. Generally, we send messages verbally (i.e., orally or in writing) and nonverbally. Verbal messages rely on the use of words and sentences. Nonverbal messages are expressed through our use of facial expressions, eye con-

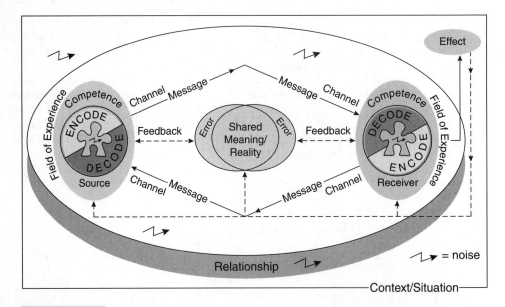

Figure 1.3   Model of Communication

tact, posture, gestures, use of space, dress, and other forms of communication that are neither oral or written. Savvy communicators are aware of the impact that messages can have on others, and constantly work to match their verbal and nonverbal messages with their intended meanings.

The Source

A **source** is the person who formulates a message. As such, he or she determines what message will be sent as well as the best way to send it. A source's perceptions about the object of a message are directly affected by his field of experience. Influencing his ability to accurately relay an intended meaning is the source's communication competence.

Field of Experience

One's **field of experience** encompasses her cultural background, life experiences, and the resulting attitudes, values, beliefs, and perceptual screens through which she views the world. Thus, one's field of experience affects (1) how the object of a message is perceived (e.g., positive versus negative, simple versus complex); (2) the channel that is selected (e.g., face to face versus a written message; and, (3) the relational aspects of the message (e.g., the amount of control, intimacy, and trust that characterize the relationship between a sender and receiver), which are reflected in every message that is sent and received (Millar & Rogers, 1976).

Complicating the communication process is the fact that senders and receivers have different fields of experience. Indeed, one need look no further than the last disagreement with a friend or business associate to see how very differently two people may view the same topic of conversation.

Communication Competence

Communication competence is defined as the sensitivity, knowledge, and skills required to send and receive messages that are both accurate and appropriate for the situation. For instance, a communicator may be highly sensitive and knowledgeable, but unable to skillfully transform his thoughts into words. As a result, he may be less able to communicate effectively. Conversely, if a communicator is low in sensitivity, but highly knowledgeable and skillful as a speaker, she may misread a situation or misinterpret an incoming message, and respond inappropriately despite her eloquence.

Encoding/Decoding

Encoding is the physical process of transforming thoughts and ideas into verbal and nonverbal messages. To this end, encoding involves the conscious (and unconscious!) selection of words and gestures to communicate an intended meaning. In contrast, **decoding** is the physical process of transforming incoming messages into thoughts and ideas (i.e., making sense of a message). The extent to which a receiver decodes a message in the way in which a sender intends determines whether or not the communication process is successful.

The Channel

By **channel** we mean the medium or media through which a sender communicates a message. For example, in face-to-face communication, the channel is air (i.e., light and sound waves). Other channels we use are the telephone, memo, letter, electronic mail, and satellite audio- or videoconferences. Many of us have been the recipients of "Dear John" or "Dear Jane" letters at some point in our lives, and felt the hurt of being told, through such a seemingly "impersonal" medium, that a relationship is ending. Imagine how much more devastated we would be if we received a termination notice through E-mail, an even more impersonal channel of communication than a written letter. Smart communicators take into account both the benefits and costs associated with using a given channel before sending a message. Even the channel that we select communicates subtle nonverbal messages to a receiver.

The Receiver

A **receiver** is any person to whom a message is intentionally or unintentionally sent by a source. As such, a receiver is any person who decodes a verbal or nonverbal message, whether he or she is the intended target of the message. For example, you are talking with a colleague in his office and jokingly tell him to "blow it out his ear." If your boss walks past at the precise moment you say this, without having the benefit of the entire conversation, she may misinterpret your intended meaning.

Like sources, receivers have varying levels of communication competence. In addition, their fields of experience differ from those of the source. Successful communicators take this fact of business and professional life into account whenever they exchange messages with one another.

Feedback

Feedback is the response that a receiver makes to a message, and is generally what is desired by a source when he sends a message. Feedback may be verbal or nonverbal, intentional or unintentional. For example, your boss calls you into her office and asks you to complete a report by noon the next day. She will provide feedback to your response in one way if you smile and say, "No problem." She will interpret your message another way, and respond accordingly, if you say "No problem" through clenched teeth and with white-knuckled fists.

> Grant that we may not so much seek to be understood as to understand.
>
> —*Saint Francis of Assisi*

Shared Meaning/Reality

Shared meaning, or **shared reality,** is the degree of mutual understanding that results whenever a receiver interprets a message exactly the way a sender intended. For instance, if Mike starts to say something and Joy finishes his sentence, meaning has been shared if Joy uses almost the exact words that Mike planned to use. Conversely, if Joy finishes Mike's sentence and she is nowhere close to what Mike was trying to say, the outcome is a high level of **error** (i.e., miscommunication) and very little shared meaning.

In Figure 1.3, shared meaning is represented by that portion of the two individual ovals that overlap in the center of the diagram. The two individual ovals represent the thoughts and ideas (i.e., the meanings) of the source and receiver regarding a particular verbal or nonverbal message. If a message is completely understood (i.e., accurately interpreted), the two ovals would be depicted as completely overlapping. If a message is only partially understood, the ovals would only partially overlap.

The Effect

The **effect** of a message is any outcome that results when two or more people communicate with one another. For instance, if Eduardo, the vice president of an international consulting firm, effectively interprets his client's wishes for an upcoming training program, a number of desired effects may occur: a successful training program (E1), payment for a job well done (E2), and more business in the future (E3).

The two-way arrows, in Figure 1.3, between our concepts of shared meaning and effects represent (1) the extent to which shared meaning in a message ultimately molds and shapes a given effect, and (2) the resulting impact of that effect on the source, receiver, relationship between the two people, and all of their future communications. To continue our earlier example, if Eduardo thought he understood his client's goals, but was wrong, a totally undesirable set of effects might accrue. In turn, these effects would impact Eduardo's and his client's perceptions of each other, future business relationship, and all subsequent communications.

Noise

In general, **noise** is any form of interference that takes place during the communication process. In our model, noise is depicted in the likeness of a lightning bolt in: (1) the heads of the source and receiver, (2) the relationship portion of the model, and (3) the situation or context in which an interaction takes place. For instance, noise may exist in the mind of the source or receiver in the form of mental fatigue, confusion, and so forth. We label this type of noise **intrapersonal noise.**

Relational noise takes the form of questions, uncertainty, or lack of closure regarding the state of a relationship between two people at a given time. Generally, as the level of uncertainty in a relationship increases for a source or receiver, so too does the amount of relational noise. This axiom of communication is especially salient if the two people are significant to one another.

Noise also can exist in the context or situation in which two communicators interact. We term this **situational noise.** For example, you are discussing business with a client over lunch at a busy restaurant, and you can hardly hear what he is saying for all of the talk that is emanating from other patrons. This and other forms of situational noise like ringing phones, humming fax machines, and clacking computer keys may serve to impede the communication process.

The Relationship

Whenever two people meet and communicate for the first time, an opportunity exists for a relationship to form. By **relationship** we mean some level of "coming together" or "coming apart" that exists on the part of two or more people (Knapp & Vangelisti, 1992). Relationships vary in kind (e.g., vendor-client, superior-subordinate, colleague-

Relationships go through various stages of coming together and coming apart. The glue that holds them together is effective communication.

colleague, friend-friend) and move through various stages. By their very nature, relationships are created, molded, and defined through communication.

Just as every interaction molds and shapes a relationship, so, too, does the nature of the relationship impact the messages that we exchange. For instance, if a relationship between two people is mutually rewarding and a conflict ensues, they may communicate very differently than they would if the relationship were disintegrating. Because of the mutual effect that relationships and communication have on each other, we have included "relationship" in our communication model.

The Context/Situation

Every communication exchange that takes place does so within some context and situation. By **context**, we mean "the parts of a written or spoken statement that precede and follow a given word or passage that can influence its meaning or effect" (Random House, 1991). By **situation**, we mean both the physical environment in which a given interaction takes place as well as the circumstances that surround the particular message exchange.

To illustrate how the context of a message can affect its meaning, consider the following interchange between Maria and Carrie:

Maria: Get out of my chair right now!

Carrie: Why don't you just try and make me!

Without additional information, you might think that such an exchange is inappropriate for any business setting. Indeed, in many business situations, your conclusion would be justified. However, consider the same exchange between Carrie and Maria in light of the following conversation, or context:

Maria: I cannot believe we have been working on this project all night, can you?

Carrie: Me either. I am so tired that I could sleep here right on your desk.

Maria: I need to make one final change in the last paragraph of the contract, then we'll be done.

Carrie: Oh, no you don't. That paragraph is perfect; we've already worked on it for hours!

Maria: Get out of my chair right now!

Carrie: Why don't you just try and make me!

Maria: (Laughter) All right. I'll compromise with you. Let's take one more look at that paragraph together tomorrow when we've had a little sleep.

Carrie: You've got a deal. Now let's go—before I drag you out of this office.

Now let's add the following information about the situation, which also should affect how you perceive the initial two-sentence interchange: (1) Maria and Carrie have been close friends since their first year of law school; (2) they have built a prominent firm together over the last 10 years; (3) at the time of the conversation, they were sitting in Maria's office working together on the same computer; (4) our two friends and partners have been working all night to complete a contract that has been in the making for 18 months. How do you perceive the initial conversation now? Do you still think it was inappropriate? Probably not!

As you can see, both the context and situation play vital roles in the communication process, especially when it comes to sharing meanings and "reality" with other people. So, too, do the other elements we have included in our communication model.

> A word is not a crystal, transparent and unchanged; it is the skin of a living thought and may vary greatly in color and content according to the circumstances and time in which it is used.
>
> —*Oliver Wendell Holmes, Jr.*

Plan for the Book

The four areas of business and professional communication that you must master involve sensitivity, knowledge, and skills associated with relational life, work life, public life, and techno-life. To help you gain competencies in each of these areas, we have organized the information in this book around these four central themes.

Unit One has been an overview. It contains the opening chapter and has introduced the two models on which the rest of the text is based.

Unit Two focuses on the first important area of business and professional communication, **relational life.** Included in this unit are discussions of listening (Chapter 2), the care and feeding of an interpersonal network (Chapter 3), small-group communication (Chapter 4), and managing gender and multicultural diversity (Chapter 5).

We then turn to a discussion of three major components of **work life** (Unit Three), the second major area of business and professional communication. This unit addresses resume writing and interviewing (Chapter 6), leadership (Chapter 7); effective management of stress and conflict on the job (Chapter 8); and, business etiquette and protocol (Chapter 9).

Unit Four of this textbook focuses on **public life** and on the competencies that are essential for you to acquire in this area. Chapters 10 and 11 will address the development of effective oral presentations. Because a plethora of texts exist in the area of written communication, and our emphasis is primarily on oral messages, we will not address the topic at this time.

Unit Five then turns to a discussion of the **techno-life** competencies you need to acquire in the area of communication technology (Chapter 12). Given the rapid advances in technology that are occurring every day, these chapters also will help you identify areas of sensitivity, knowledge, and skill that will help you successfully navigate the technological waters of the 21st century workplace.

Throughout the book we will refer to the Puzzle Model of Business and Professional Communication and will show you how all the components fit together. As we move through each unit and chapter, we will present the most current information available, case studies to challenge your thinking regarding the subject matter, and several means of assessing, developing, and cultivating your own unique solutions to problems through the ToolBoxes provided in each chapter. Keep in mind that gaining competence in any area requires knowledge and skill, but even more importantly, sensitivity to other people.

Case Study

Merger of Network USA and A+Communications

David Sims, Manager of Marketing, Network USA

On June 6, 1995, it was announced that Nashville-based A+Communications would merge with its competitor, Network USA, located in Pensacola, Florida. At the time, A+Communications was a publicly owned, regional paging provider, while Network USA was a privately held, national paging company. Up until the announcement of the merger, Network USA had been preparing for its own public stock offering. The merger of the two companies into A+Network, Inc., produced an unexpected set of challenges for managers and employees alike.

On paper, the two paging companies seemed to be the perfect match. Both had enjoyed consistent growth rates that were far superior to the rest of the telecommunications industry. Additionally, both companies operated in the southeastern United States. A+Communications provided local paging and voice mail services, extensive telemessaging (i.e., answering services), and cellular phone service. Through a network of nationally affiliated paging companies, Network USA provided state, regional and national paging coverage. The company also offered its own local paging and voice mail services.

Although both companies marketed their services in some of the same territories, their actual selling areas overlapped in only a handful of cities. The real challenges faced in the merger were not the companies' sales strategies, but rather were the differences in operating philosophies. Since its inception, Network USA had prided itself on centralization, and had conducted support operations from one office in Pensacola. Its sales representatives operated out of their homes and sold from their cars.

In contrast, A+Communications had sales offices in many cities throughout its operating area. Thus, its sales reps were accustomed to both convenient customer service and inventory and management support in the field, where such backing was most advantageous.

Corporate employees of Network USA enjoyed a relaxed work environment and enhanced internal communications. They had an advanced E-mail system, regular social activities, and frequent "town meetings," during which management and line-level employees had conversations about financial issues. Network USA employees also had the opportunity to speak with management on a first-name basis.

Conversely, A+Communications operated with a more traditional management style. The company had a more layered management structure, relied more on formal procedures, and used formal titles. The Nashville office had no E-mail and no intercom system. Employees were notified of changes and happenings via the traditional office memo. Generally, the sharing of financial information was reserved for upper management.

Because of the differences in operating and management philosophies, employees from both companies were nervous about the merger. Additionally, when two companies merge, a duplication in workforce will result. And where duplication exists, layoffs usually follow. As a result, rumors, based in fact and fantasy, spread throughout the two companies.

Questions

1. What two major orientations to work are represented by the companies described in this case? What are the advantages and disadvantages of each?
2. What elements of the communication process would be most affected by this particular merger? Which elements would be most susceptible to noise?
3. How would you handle the corporate communications during the time period between the announcement date and the actual date of the merger between these two companies?
4. What influence do rumors have on morale and production during a merger? In your opinion, what would be some effective methods of rumor prevention specific to this case?

Summary

In order to succeed in the business world, you must gain maximum communication competence. By competence, we mean the requisite sensitivity, knowledge, and skills needed to communicate effectively with others. To aid you in maximizing your communication competence, we developed the Puzzle Model of Business and Professional Communication.

Using the Puzzle Model, we then emphasized the importance of attaining an optimal "fit" between you and your organization's "boundaries." Boundaries include a company's corporate vision, orientation to work, and corporate culture. Second, we used the Puzzle Model as a vehicle to address four communication skill areas to be mastered—relational life, work life, public life, and techno-life—within a given organization. To provide evidence for the salience of the model to your career development, we presented statistics from several surveys that supported our claims.

We then presented three orientations toward work that you will encounter in the business world. Although many organizations can (and probably will) represent a unique blend or mix of perspectives, they generally emphasize one of three management approaches: scientific management, human behavior, or integrated perspectives.

Next, based on information about these three perspectives, we provided a tool that you can use for investigating a company's orientation toward work. Our goal was to aid you in making positive career decisions and, in the process, to raise your sensitivity, knowledge, and skills regarding what is needed to succeed in the 21st century workplace.

Finally, we presented the model of communication that guides this book. Critical elements in the communication process include the message; source; receiver; their respective fields of experience and levels of communication competence; encoding and decoding functions; channel; feedback; shared meaning and reality; effects; noise; relationship; and context and situation. Now that we have given you a solid foundation on which to build, we now turn to a more complete discussion of relational life in the 21st century workplace.

Knowledge Check

Key Concepts and Terms

boundaries	source	error
corporate vision	field of experience	effect
orientation toward work	communication competence	noise
corporate culture	encoding	intrapersonal noise
components	decoding	relational noise
relational life	channel	situational noise
work life	receiver	relationship
public life	feedback	context
techno-life	shared meaning	situation
message	shared reality	

Putting It All Together

1. What expectations does Workplace 2010 present for you in terms of the three Rs (reading, writing, and arithmetic)?

2. Name the three foundations and five competencies associated with the SCANS report.

3. Distinguish between corporate vision and corporate culture. How does the former affect the latter?

4. Why is it important to achieve a proper fit between you and the company for which you work?

5. How do the scientific management, human behavior, and integrated perspectives approaches differ? Include at least five characteristics of each in your discussion.

6. Name and briefly discuss the four communication skill categories associated with business and professional life.

7. Using the communication model presented in this chapter, analyze your most recent conversation with a significant other by (a) identifying each of the elements of the communication process as they operated in your conversation, and (b) discussing how each of the elements affected each other to produce the resulting effects.

References

Boyett, J. H., & Boyett, J. E. (1995). *Beyond workplace 2000.* New York: Dutton.

Carlzon, J. (1987). *Moments of truth.* New York: Ballinger Publishing Co.

Conlin, J. (1994, February). Survival of the fittest. *Working Woman,* 28–31, 68–9, 72–3.

Deal, T., & Kennedy, A. (1982). *Corporate culture: The rites and rituals of corporate life.* Reading, MA: Addison-Wesley.

Fayol, H. (1949). *General and industrial management* (C. Storrs, Trans.) London: Pitman & Sons.

Jones, P., & Kahaner, L. (1995). *Say it and live it: The 50 corporate mission statements that hit the mark.* New York: Currency/Doubleday.

Katz, D., & Kahn, R. (1966). *The social psychology of organizations.* New York: Wiley.

Knapp, M. L., & Vangelisti, A. (1992). *Interpersonal communication in human relationships* (2nd ed.). Boston, MA: Allyn & Bacon.

Levering, R., & Moskowitz, M. (1994). *The 100 best companies to work for in America.* New York: Plume.

Likert. R. (1961). *New patterns of management.* New York: McGraw-Hill.

Mayo, E. (1945). *The social problems of an industrial civilization.* Boston: Graduate School of Business Administration, Harvard University.

McGregor, D. (1960). *The human side of enterprise.* New York: McGraw-Hill.

Millar, F. E., & Rogers, L. E. (1976). A relational approach to interpersonal communication. In G. R. Miller (Ed.), *Explorations in interpersonal communication* (pp. 87–105). Beverly Hills, CA: Sage.

Ouchi, W. (1981). *Theory Z.* Reading, MA: Addison-Wesley.

Perrigo, E., & Gaut, D. (1994, Winter). Is academia in sync with the business world? *Journal of Career Planning and Employment, 54* (3), 58–60.

Peters, T. J., & Waterman, R. H., Jr. (1982). *In search of excellence.* New York: Harper & Row.

Random House Webster's college dictionary. (1991). New York: Random House.

Secretary's Commission on Achieving Necessary Skills, U.S. Department of Labor. (1992, April). *Learning a living: A blueprint for high performance: A SCANS report for America 2000.* Washington, DC: U.S. Government Printing Office.

Secretary's Commission on Achieving Necessary Skills, U.S. Department of Labor. (1993). *Teaching the SCANS Competencies.* Washington, DC: U.S. Government Printing Office.

Secretary's Commission on Achieving Necessary Skills, U.S. Department of Labor. (1991, June). *What work requires of schools: A SCANS report for America 2000.* Washington, DC: U.S. Government Printing Office.

Shockley-Zalabak, P. (1995). *Fundamentals of organizational communication, knowledge, sensitivity, skills, values.* (3rd ed.). White Plains, NY: Longman.

Taylor, F. W. (1913). *Principles of scientific management.* New York: Harper & Brothers.

U.S. Congress, Office of Technology Assessment (1992, July). *Adult literacy and new technologies: Tools for a lifetime* (Publication No. OTA-SET-550). Washington, DC: U.S. Government Printing Office.

Weber, M. (1947). *The theory of social and economic organization* (Trans. A. Henderson & T. Parsons). New York: Free Press.

The "relational life" of an organization is its most personal face. Among other things, relational life is what makes us want to get out of bed and go to work each day. The extent to which we feel valued and heard, informed and nurtured, are only a few of the variables that impact our productivity and job satisfaction. Yet, we often don't consider the nature and impact of our own personal competence in these areas.

In Chapter 2, you will learn more about the importance and contributions of effective listening in an organization and the impact that listening preferences have on your colleagues and you. Additionally, we will show you how to become a more effective listener both personally and professionally, and how to develop messages that will get people to listen to you.

In Chapter 3, the Care and Feeding of an Interpersonal Network, you will learn about the personal impact of formal versus informal communication, communication styles, and communication climate. Additionally, you will find the latest information available on office politics, humor in the workplace, romantic relationships, and sexual harassment. We conclude this chapter with three ways you can build more productive and satisfying relationships in the workplace: networking, mentoring, and old-fashioned friendliness.

Chapter 4, on small-group and team communication, highlights such topics as the advantages and disadvantages of conducting business in small groups; types of small groups (including the most current information available on the subject of teams); and the stages of group development. You also should find our discussions of problem solving, effective team building, and "meeting mania" of interest.

Managing diversity in the workplace is the subject of Chapter 5, with a stimulating discussion of gender issues. We will also provide recommendations on how to create a harmonious relationship between the sexes. As we speed toward the 21st century workplace, organizations have changed from melting pots of cultures to salad bowls—all mixed together. The implications of a diverse workforce will be addressed, as well as how to effectively communicate with physically challenged coworkers.

We hope you will find the information in this unit to be stirring. Our goal is to help you develop competence in managing these four important aspects of "relational life." Strength in the relational life of an organization means a positive, supportive atmosphere in which everyone can work and grow. In turn, such an environment fosters professional success for you and your organization as a whole. ■

unit 2

Managing Relational Life in the Workplace

2

The Art of Listening

**After studying this chapter,
you should be able to**

- Understand the importance of effective listening in business today.

- Differentiate between hearing and listening.

- Comprehend the true complexity of active versus passive listening through the model of listening we present.

- Identify and assess your listening preferences.

- Improve your listening skills by practicing our "top ten list of listening tips."

- Gain your listeners' attention and keep it.

Good listening makes good business sense. Just ask William Malec, Chief Financial Officer (CFO) of the $5 billion Tennessee Valley Authority. For one day each month, he works with one of his 2,000 employees moving office furniture, assembling boxes, cleaning bathrooms—whatever the job description. Malec began his "dirty-hands" project in 1991 as a morale builder to counter the effects of 18,500 job reductions company-wide in four years. As Malec worked with his employees month by month, they gradually accepted him as "one of them." Now they know they have Malec's "ear." He listens to their problems and finds solutions to assist them with their work, which makes them more productive employees (Gutner, 1993).

William Malec's success story is only one of many that are based on an executive's commitment to quality listening. When mistakes are made due to poor listening, money is lost, time is wasted, and productivity in the workplace suffers. Think about it! A simple $10 mistake by each of the 100 million people who comprise the American workforce would yield a loss to business and industry of more than one billion dollars (Steil, Watson, & Barker, 1983). Moreover, many Fortune 500 company executives are no longer willing to pay the price: As of 1991, 51 percent had taken a proactive approach to educating their employees about effective listening, including such companies as Delta Air-Lines, Ford Motor Company, Honeywell, IBM, Pillsbury Company, AT&T, Dun & Bradstreet, General Electric, and Entergy, to name just a few (Wolvin & Coakley, 1991). And many more companies, both large and small, are joining the listening band wagon.

The Benefits of Effective Listening

> Today's successful leaders will work diligently to engage others in their cause. Oddly enough, the best way, by far, to engage others is by listening—seriously listening—to them. If talking and giving orders was the... model of the last fifty years, listening... is the model of the [1990s] and beyond.
>
> —*Tom Peters (1988)*

Why are companies around the world devoting time and resources to listening training? According to Robert Bostrom (1990), a noted listening researcher, how we communicate with others in an organization has "individual, work group, and organizational outcomes. Our degree of success (or failure) is dependent on how well [we] can communicate with significant others within the organization" (p. 12). Results of a study conducted by Bostrom and his associates illustrate the point. Better listeners were found to hold higher-level positions within their respective companies and were promoted more often than those with less developed listening skills. The study also revealed that effective listening can enhance job performance as well as perceived status and power within a company (Sypher, Bostrom, & Seibert, 1989, p. 301).

Increasing corporate profits and lowering consumer prices are two additional benefits of effective listening in a company. As Wolvin and Coakley (1992) have noted, "Business relies on its communications system, and when it breaks down, mistakes can be very costly. Corporations pay for their mistakes in lower profits, while consumers pay in high prices..." (p. 8). Organizational research continues to provide evidence of the need for more effective listening in the workplace. But what about the personal benefits of effective listening? How can you personally gain from increasing your sensitivity, knowledge, and skills in the art of listening? At the personal level, benefits take a variety of forms.

■ You will be more valued by the people with whom you work. Everyone appreciates a manager, employee, or colleague who listens.

■ You will experience improved relationships with your coworkers, supervisor and subordinates. People naturally gravitate to a person who listens well. Effective listeners tend to be more empathic and develop stronger relationships.

■ You will experience greater promotional opportunities. If one of your strengths is effective listening, department heads will want you "on their team." Supervisors and department heads are always looking for more productive team members.

■ You will gain increased knowledge of the subject at hand. By becoming an active listener, you will hear more details and be better able to assimilate information.

■ You will gain greater self-confidence. Listening increases your "likability" quotient and, therefore, makes you feel better about yourself.

■ You will experience improved relationships with family members and friends. You probably have a close friend or family member who you feel is a good listener. By becoming a good listener yourself, you will enhance your relationships both personally and professionally.

And the list goes on. The nature and quality of long-lasting relationships at home and in the workplace are directly affected by your ability to listen. So, too, is the bottom line of the company for which you work.

Now that you have learned some of the benefits of effective listening and the role that listening plays in business today, let's look at how you can begin to effect positive change in your own listening behavior. We'll begin with an important distinction between *hearing* and *listening*.

Hearing versus Listening

An ancient Chinese philosopher once said, "We have been given two ears and one mouth so that we may hear more and talk less." Think about your own listening behavior for a moment. Do you tend to talk more than you listen? If so, you reduce your chances to optimize communication because listening requires the act of "hearing" an incoming message—something we cannot do if our mouths are open.

Hearing is one of the sensory components of listening and refers to the physical act of receiving sounds. Our ears provide the channel through which auditory messages are received. To understand the hearing process more fully, consider the sequence of activities through which a sound must progress in order for us to process it as a message. Figure 2.1 on page 36 diagrams the human ear.

First, your outer ear catches sound waves that are in the environment and sends them through your auditory canal to your eardrum. The sound waves cause your eardrum to vibrate. On the other side of your eardrum are three small bones: the hammer, the stirrup, and the anvil. These bones amplify the vibrations. The sound waves then reach your inner ear where the **cochlea,** a snail-shaped structure filled with liquid, takes over. Inside the cochlea are hairlike nerve cells that convert pressure vibrations to nerve impulses. The nerve impulses are transmitted to the auditory nerve and then to the brain. Then we perceive the sound and "hear" what the other person is saying (Brownell, 1986, p. 31).

In contrast to hearing, which is a passive process, **listening** is an active process that involves hearing as one of its many components. Hearing is passive because it involves little more than receiving information without actively attending to or interpreting the incoming stimuli (e.g., hearing a radio playing in the background while you are studying without actively paying attention to the songs). Hearing becomes listening, an active process, when we attend to, interpret, and respond to incoming stimuli (e.g., when your favorite song comes on the radio and you stop studying to sing along).

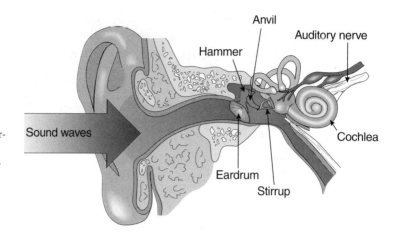

Figure 2.1

Diagram of the Ear: How the Hearing Process Works

Source: Building Active Listening Skills by Brownell, Judi, © 1986. Adapted by permission of Prentice-Hall, Inc., Upper Saddle River, NJ.

To further understand the distinction, consider three current definitions of the word "listening." Wolvin and Coakley (1992), noted researchers in the field, define listening as "the process of receiving, attending to, and assigning meaning to aural stimuli." Sayre (1987) defines listening as "receiving and attending to a message, interpreting the message (i.e., assigning meaning), evaluating the message, and responding to the message." Finally, from the International Listening Association comes the following definition, "Listening is the process of receiving, constructing meaning from, and responding to verbal and nonverbal messages" (M. Fitch Hauser, personal communication, February 10, 1995).

Another means of defining listening in the ethereal sense involves incorporating the way we listen with our entire beings through our ears, eyes, minds, and hearts (Adams, 1987). Listening with our ears entails not only hearing, but also attending to the speaker's vocal intonation and emphasis on certain words and terms. Listening with our eyes involves processing the speaker's nonverbal cues such as facial expressions, hand gestures, and body movements that complement the message. Listening with our minds consists of absorbing words and understanding what is being said. Listening with our hearts provides insight into what the speaker really means. You experience this intangible quality of listening all the time. A definition of "listening with your total self" augments the more technical definitions outlined above.

A Model of Listening

Many different listening models have been developed over the years. One of the most current models was developed by Kittie Watson (1993), whose model presents listening as a five-step process: attending, perceiving, interpreting, assessing, and responding (see Figure 2.2).

The foundation of Watson's model is **attending,** the stage (or step) at which we make differing levels of conscious effort to listen to others. Eye contact, forward lean, use of appropriate facial expressions, and concentration are only a few of the ways we

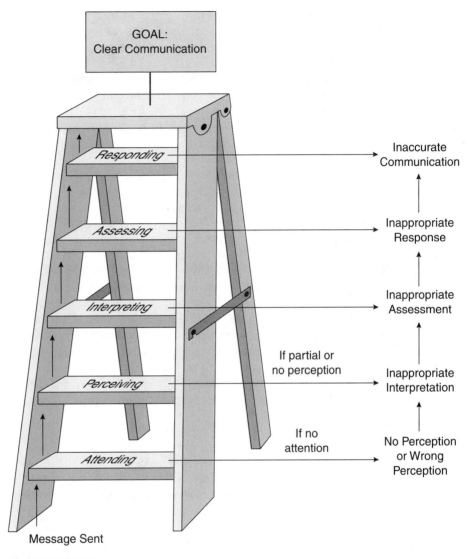

| Figure 2.2 | Watson's Listening Ladder

Source: L. Barker & D. Gaut (1996). *Communication,* 7th ed. (Boston, MA: Allyn & Bacon), p. 48. Reprinted by permission of the Publisher.

attempt to focus on the messages of others. Unfortunately, we often start out by focusing on a message and then become distracted by competing speakers, messages, events, or personal worries. For instance, when you are working on a report and someone interrupts you in mid-thought, you may fail to attend to the message in spite of the fact that you have just responded with a mumbled, "OK, I'll take care of the problem later."

Perceiving is the next step of the listening process and involves use of one or more of the basic senses to receive verbal and nonverbal messages. Hearing and seeing are the two major senses through which we listen, although other senses like taste, smell, and touch can come into play. At this stage, past experiences, personal interests, knowledge, and skills have an impact on what we perceive. Thus, listening errors can occur at this stage as well. For example, consider Raul and Gabrielle, who have been in a relationship for about two years. Raul asked Gabrielle to help him with a writing project, which was due to his boss in one week. Gabrielle trivialized Raul's project when she told him she was too busy learning a new computer game. Raul asked Gabrielle repeatedly to help him think through the project, but she paid little attention to him. The night before Raul's project was due, he exploded and told Gabrielle that she never listened to him, and that she didn't care about his needs. In this scenario, Gabrielle failed at the second level of listening, perceiving. She barely heard what Raul was saying because she was too busy with her own interests to actively process his request.

Sometimes we think the other person is not listening because the expected response is not given. As you have probably already experienced, men and women provide different responses when listening to one another. You will learn more about how these gender differences affect listening later in this chapter.

The third step of the listening model involves **interpretation,** or matching the sender's message with the receiver's message. Interpreting a message means matching your meaning with the speaker's meaning. As you may recall, this is our definition of shared meaning in Chapter 1. For example, after work on Friday, you decide to take a leisurely drive into the mountains for the weekend to enjoy the peaceful scenery. You live for the moment and lose all track of time. Suddenly, you realize you are lost. You stop at the country store to ask for directions. After the clerk in the store determines your destination, he tells you to "go on up the road a piece until you come to the stoplight and then turn right." What is the clerk's interpretation of "up the road a piece?" Does he mean five or six miles, or only a few blocks? To determine his meaning, you will need to ask a few more questions to make sure both of you are on the same track.

The fourth step in the listening process involves the act of **assessing,** during which you make a decision or a judgment about the accuracy and credibility of a given message. At this point, you determine whether to believe the message, agree or disagree with the speaker, and retain or discard the information. Additionally, you evaluate the value of the individual parts of a message as well as the message overall. How you value a message is determined by how much you value the speaker and the content of his or her message. For example, if a professor is giving you information on how to study for the next exam, you probably value what is being said because of the source. In your estimation, your professor is a credible person and has the responsibility for evaluating you academically, so you will listen attentively to what he or she is saying.

Finally, the last step of Watson's listening model involves reacting or **responding** to the sender's message. In the scenario above, Gabrielle "heard" what Raul said and "responded" without adequately interpreting or assessing the value of Raul's message. On some of the most critical occasions in life, we tend to skip the first four steps of listening and respond immediately, without much thought. Then, we regret what we have said to other people, and our relationships with them suffer.

During the assessing stage of listening, we make judgments about the accuracy and credibility of a speaker's message.

As Watson (1993) notes, "The steps of the ladder are hierarchical. Listeners cannot skip steps or proceed effectively to other steps and hope to reach the goal of successful communication" (p. 55). Although we may proceed through the steps in a fraction of an instant, effective listeners deliberately slow the process down and make every effort to avoid listening errors at each step.

Practical Application of the Listening Model

Every listening situation is different, depending on the speaker and the listener. Sometimes we fail to adequately interpret a message because we fail to comprehend the speaker's intent. In other situations, we may inadequately assess a message because we fail to value or respect the person sending the message. To bring the lesson home regarding the value of Watson's listening model, consider another example of the hurt feelings that can result as a function of poor listening. This time the scenario involves a couple that has been engaged for a year.

Karita and Helmut planned to be married as soon as they finished college. One morning after breakfast at their favorite coffee house, their conversation went something like this:

Karita: "Helmut, I'd like to talk with you about some career possibilities I'm considering."

Helmut: "Uh huh, I'm listening, go ahead and talk." (Note: Helmut had his nose buried in the newspaper, as he did every morning after breakfast.)

Karita: "You never listen to me, Helmut. I'm tired of competing with the newspaper when I try to talk with you in the morning. I want more out of our relationship. I have been thinking about this for a long time. I want to end our relationship."

Helmut: Without looking up, Helmut responded, "Okay, sweetie, whatever you say."

It is obvious that Helmut didn't hear a word Karita said. He had tuned her out so often that he didn't hear her plea for attention. Helmut exhibited classic characteristics of poor listening. Let's examine some additional characteristics in the pages that follow.

Characteristics of Poor Listeners and Other Barriers to Effective Listening

Characteristics of poor listeners can be divided into two components: verbal and non-verbal traits. To help you become more familiar with the characteristics of poor listeners, let's take a look at each.

Typical Verbal Characteristics of Poor Listeners

Interrupts You in Mid-Sentence or Finishes Your Sentences for You.   We have all experienced the person who seems to be in a rush and never lets the speaker finish a point. Interruptions are usually the result of a listener's ego involvement or impatience with the speaker or with the topic. For example, consider the following conversation between Isabella and Elise.

Isabella: "You know, this spring weather makes me want to . . . "

Elise: "Go to the beach. I know. Me too."

Isabella: "Actually, I was going to say 'take a walk on the nature trail.' Why do you always interrupt what I'm about to say and finish my sentences for me?"

One of the reasons we tend to interrupt is that we know the other person really well, or like to think that we do. The result is often frustration and anger on the speaker's part and, over time, a breach in the relationship if the interruptions continue.

Poor Use of the Thinking-Speaking Time Differential.   Sometimes a listener and speaker experience communication problems due to effects of the **thinking-speaking time differential.** This differential results from the fact that the average person talks at a rate of about 125 words per minute, while a listener can process information at approximately 450 words per minute (Nixon & West, 1989). Given this ratio, we have plenty of time to think about something else while a speaker is talking. Since we listen at a much faster rate than we speak, our thoughts tend to wander during conversation. For example, while Julie tells Christof about the conversation she had with her girl-friend at lunch, Christof's mind may drift off to Hawaii, where he will be spending his vacation in about two weeks. While Julie tells Christof about her conversation in great detail, he nods and says, "Yes, I heard you," when he is really thinking about parasail-ing in the Pacific Ocean.

Changing the Subject to Fit the Listener's Agenda.   On many occasions, speakers and listeners have different agendas during conversations. While one person may want to do nothing more than chat, another may use the conversation to achieve a specific goal. For example, Charmaine phones Elaine to ask for a favor but knows that she has to talk with Elaine for a while in order to avoid hurting Elaine's feelings. Before long, Char-

Is anybody really listening? It's difficult to listen when both people are talking.

maine gets impatient and interrupts Elaine mid-sentence to get to the point of the conversation—Charmaine's requested favor. Even though Elaine agrees to follow through with Charmaine's request, she is startled at Charmaine's rude interruption. In a split second, without meaning to, Charmaine has become a poor listener.

Talking While the Speaker Is Talking.   If two people are talking simultaneously, obviously no one is listening. This characteristic of poor listeners occurs quite often in business meetings, especially when two people hold opposing points of view. As a result, the person with the loudest voice usually succeeds in getting a point across to the other group members.

Information Overload.   From the moment we get up in the morning until we fall asleep at night, we are constantly bombarded with information. In fact, we have access to more information in one 24-hour day than Abraham Lincoln experienced in an entire lifetime. Television, radio, newspapers, magazines, books, and the Internet all provide immediate information at lightning speed. How we access that information and what we choose to read, watch, or listen to depends upon our lifestyle. Because of the sheer quantity of information that is available in the work environment, we tend to pay the most attention to whatever or whomever interests us at the moment.

Now that we have identified some verbal attributes of poor listeners, let's explore some nonverbal characteristics.

Typical Nonverbal Characteristics of Poor Listeners

Manifests Signs of Impatience.   Sometimes people tend to look at their watches while we are talking, which makes us feel that our message is unimportant. For example, Ted, a marketing manager, is late for the meeting where he plans to unveil his new marketing plan. He knows you have been trying to reach him all day, and he needs to talk with you, too. You catch him in the hall and, as you are talking, he begins to look at his watch. This behavior makes you feel that you are bothering him. His mind obviously is on the report he will be giving at the meeting.

Lacks Direct Eye Contact.   In the Anglo culture, people have a higher level of trust when direct eye contact is shared. If eye contact is less than direct, a sender will perceive a listener to have "more important" thoughts on his or her mind. If a person fails to share direct eye contact, the first impression is that he or she is attempting to hide something or is not trustworthy. A problem with this interpretation emerges when people from different cultures communicate with one another. For example, in many North American Indian tribes, direct eye contact is interpreted as a sign of rudeness or disrespect. This perception also holds true for many other countries, such as Taiwan.

Maintains a Closed Body Position.   Folding your arms and crossing your legs sends a message that you are not paying attention unless, of course, you are cold and are crossing your arms and legs to keep warm. In most cases, this behavior signals lack of interest in the subject matter or the speaker. When the listener taps her foot or crosses her arms and looks away from the speaker, she is sending a message of irritation (or agitation) to the receiver. For example, Becky is the manager of a loan department at a local bank. Her boss has asked her for a report, which is due in his office by 5:00 P.M. She needs to add some finishing touches on the report before she gives it to him. She has had a hectic day and is unable to get back to her report until 4:30 P.M. As Becky begins editing, a customer walks in, and Becky's supervisor asks her to handle the account. The customer, who has her arms folded and is obviously in a hurry to complete all the necessary paperwork, expects Becky to drop everything and wait on her immediately. Needless to say, Becky waits on the customer first but is unable to finish her report before the deadline.

Fidgets Nervously.   Sometimes poor listeners tend to fidget, or play with objects such as pens, pencils, or paper clips while they are communicating. Take Stefan, for example. Stefan has a magnetic widget on his desk, which a colleague gave him for Christmas. Every time you go into his office to talk, Stefan plays with the magnets and manipulates them into all different shapes and sizes. Stefan's habit is frustrating because he is neither looking at you nor (seemingly) paying attention. His behavior makes you feel that what you have to say is unimportant. Such fidgeting is a bothersome habit and tends to interrupt the flow of conversation between two people.

Fakes attention.   Some people are masters at faking attention, or **pseudolistening.** They may share direct eye contact, smile, and nod appropriately, but they are daydreaming or thinking about other things. We have all faked attention at one time or another, especially with people who speak in a monotone voice or deliver boring monologues in meetings. How do you personally handle this type of listening situation?

Other Barriers to Effective Listening

In addition to poor listening habits, a number of other barriers to effective listening exist. For example, we have all experienced situations in which our listening ability has failed us: forgetting an important name at a meeting, a phone number before we can dial it, or a room number at a hotel before we can get from the lobby to the room. According to Day (1980) and Rasberry (1980), what causes these embarrassing moments is listening inefficiency. In fact, we retain only about 50 percent of a ten-minute oral presentation immediately after we hear it, and about 25 percent of the same message after 48 hours (Day, 1980; Rasberry, 1980). Think about everything you have heard in the last two days. How much do you remember? Sensitivity and knowledge about the process of listening can help; however, practicing listening skills is the key to increasing listening efficiency.

Golen (1990) identified a number of other barriers that are frequently encountered by college business students in particular. Results of his survey showed that "laziness" and "closed-mindedness" are two major listening challenges. Table 2.1 outlines these and other obstacles to listening that may impede your own listening effectiveness.

After reviewing the list, how did you compare with regard to your own barriers to listening? You probably have experienced some of these obstacles as your mind has drifted off to the crystal-clear waters of Cozumel or the top of the snow-capped mountains in Colorado. Measure yourself against the yardstick provided by the items included in the list. In which areas do you need improvement? By recognizing these barriers, along with any characteristics of poor listeners that may apply, you are taking the first step toward improving your listening ability.

Table 2.1 — Listening Barriers Encountered by Business Students

Laziness	Avoids listening if the subject is too complex or too difficult. Avoids listening because it takes too much time.
Closed-mindedness	Refuses to maintain a relaxing and agreeable environment. Refuses to relate to and benefit from the speaker's ideas.
Opinionatedness	Disagrees or argues outwardly or inwardly with the speaker. Becomes emotional or excited when speaker's views differ from his own.
Insincerity	Avoids eye contact while listening. Pays attention only to the speaker's words rather than the speaker's feeling.
Boredom	Lacks interest in the speaker's subject. Becomes impatient with the speaker. Daydreams or becomes preoccupied with something else when listening.
Inattentiveness	Concentrates on the speaker's mannerisms or delivery rather than on the message. Becomes distracted by noise from office equipment, telephone, other conversations, etc.

Adapted from S. Golen (1990). A Factor Analysis of Barriers to Effective Listening. *Journal of Business Communication, 27*(1), pp. 25–35.

Gender Differences and Listening

Do women listen differently than men? According to Borisoff and Purdy (1992), the answer is definitively, "Yes!" Women are more likely to understand emotions underlying a message and to communicate empathy, whereas men speak and hear a language of "status and independence" (Tannen, 1990). To illustrate, consider Cyndi and Pierre's conversation at a recent business lunch.

Cyndi: "Pierre, the deadline is tomorrow for the proposal to upgrade the computer system to be in the vice president's office. I can't get Sue and Steve to pull their share of the load. Since I am coordinating the project, the success of it rests on my shoulders. I have talked to both of them, and they seem to be preoccupied with other work in the department. It really makes me angry."

Pierre: "I guess you will just have to do their work for them. You know that the proposal you're working on affects the entire company, so it better be thorough. You better quit talking about it and get back to work. You know how upset the V.P. gets when we don't turn proposals in on time."

Let's analyze this situation. Cyndi is lamenting the fact that she has a project deadline to meet the next day. The people with whom Cyndi works are uncooperative, and Cyndi is pulling more than her share of the load since she is project supervisor. Cyndi is reaching out to Pierre, emphasizing the emotional aspects of her problem and focusing on how she feels. She wants Pierre to listen and show some empathy. Instead, Pierre focuses on the task at hand and the upcoming due date.

Gender researchers have studied the listening behavior of both sexes, but do not yet know whether one sex is consistently better at listening than the other. Best-selling author Deborah Tannen (1990) argues that men and women simply listen differently. While men listen to determine how to solve a specific, recognizable problem, women listen to understand something they did not understand before. This case was acutely illustrated in the scenario between Cyndi and Pierre.

Assessing Your Listening Effectiveness

As you are aware, other people see you differently than you see yourself. While your boss may think you are an excellent listener, your colleagues may think you never listen. How do you perceive your listening skills? Do you think you are an effective listener? How would your friends and coworkers describe you as a listener?

Developing a profile of your present listening skills is the first step toward improving your listening effectiveness. To aid you in developing a clear snapshot of yourself, complete the Personal Listening Inventory in Box 2.1, "How Do You Measure Up?" Although there are no right or wrong answers to the questions, your responses will assist you in better understanding your listening patterns and behaviors.

How do your responses compare with other people who have completed a similar inventory (e.g., Steil, Barker, & Watson, 1983, pp. 46–48)? In general, most people describe themselves as average listeners. Respondents who rate themselves higher tend to

BOX 2.1
How Do You Measure Up?
Listening Skills Assessment

	Poor		Fair		Excellent
1. Overall, how would you rate your listening skills?	1	2	3	4	5

2. How do you believe each of the following people would rate your listening skills?

a. best friend	1	2	3	4	5
b. life partner	1	2	3	4	5
c. supervisor at work	1	2	3	4	5
d. colleague at work	1	2	3	4	5
e. people whom you supervise at work	1	2	3	4	5

3. What words or phrases would you use to describe a person who has excellent listening skills? List four or five here.

4. How many of these words or phrases apply to you when you are listening to your:

a. best friend _____
b. life partner _____
c. supervisor at work _____
d. colleague at work _____
e. people whom you supervise _____

work in an occupation in which listening plays a significant role in their jobs. For instance, psychologists and managers are required to listen in order to perform their jobs efficiently and effectively. Can you think of other occupations that would include listening as a primary communication skill?

How you answered the second question reveals a great deal about your association with others. If you are like most respondents, you indicated your best friend and your supervisor would rate you higher as a listener than you rated yourself. One of the reasons your best friend IS your best friend is because you tend to listen attentively to each other. Effective listening is a natural part of developing a close relationship.

In order to perform your job well, you also need to listen to your supervisor. Thus, it stands to reason that your supervisor would probably rate your listening behavior higher than you ranked yourself. The colleague you considered in the inventory was probably someone you admire. If your score was excellent, congratulate yourself. More than likely, your colleague would rate you in the same manner.

When you answered the third question, what terms did you use to describe an excellent listener? Perhaps some of your selections included good eye contact, empathic, focused, tunes out external noise, leans into conversation, and asks good questions, to name a few. Most of these words describe listeners with whom anyone would like to be associated. When you analyzed your own listening behavior in question four, did you have an "aha" experience? More than likely, if you are like most people, you probably need to work on improving your listening skills.

Identifying Your Listening Preferences

Completing the inventory in ToolBox 2.1 is a first step you can take toward developing your own listening profile. Another way is to identify your primary listening preferences. Kittie Watson and Larry Barker (1992), two distinguished communication researchers, identified four major types of listeners based on their listening preferences: people-oriented, action-oriented, content-oriented, and time-oriented. As you read through the following section, see if you can identify your primary listening preference. Doing so can help you better understand the dynamics associated with listening effectively to others.

People-Oriented.   **People-oriented listeners** generally are caring and concerned about others. They are non-judgmental, easily identify the emotional states of others, and quickly notice moods. Additionally, people-oriented listeners are good at providing clear verbal and nonverbal feedback. Since they are open to others, they may get overly involved, overly expressive, or intrusive. Generally, we seek out people-oriented listeners when we experience personal problems or crises.

Action-Oriented.   **Action-oriented listeners** are interested in getting to the heart of a matter quickly. They give clear feedback about their expectations, concentrate on the task dimensions of a message, and help others focus on what is important. They are organized and concise, and encourage others to be organized as well. On the downside, action-oriented listeners have a tendency to jump to conclusions quickly and are prone to jumping ahead or finishing others' thoughts. They minimize relational issues and tend to be impatient with rambling speakers. Action-oriented listeners are highly effective in meetings. They stay on task, keep meeting times to a minimum, and present information in an organized, logical, and timely fashion.

Content-Oriented.   **Content-oriented listeners** live to process technical information. They are good at seeing all sides of an issue, welcome complex and challenging ideas, and encourage others to provide evidence for their ideas. Negative characteristics of content-oriented listeners include asking specific questions to the point of intimidation, minimizing the value of nontechnical information, and discounting information from sources who are unknown to them. Although they take a long time to make judgments and are highly detail-oriented, they are great to have on your team when you have to process vast amounts of information in a short period of time.

Time-Oriented.   **Time-oriented listeners** are highly committed to managing and saving time. They set time guidelines for meetings and conversations and encourage oth-

Content-oriented listeners welcome complex and detailed information

ers to do the same. When their time is being wasted, they discourage speakers from being wordy and send obvious cues (e.g., religiously looking at their watches). Although their efficiency is to be applauded, time-oriented listeners can go overboard and limit creativity by imposing artificial time restrictions. Their interruptions and impatience also strain relationships with others. Additionally, they limit their own concentration when they let time dictate the way they do business with others.

Although we would all like to think that our own listening preference is best, Watson and Barker (1992) caution that there is no single best listener preference. Our preferences develop over a lifetime as a function of socialization and reinforcement patterns, and they are influenced by our value of time and relationships (Watson, 1993).

How can you use this information about yourself and others to improve your communication effectiveness? Three methods that we advise are: (1) keep in mind that all of us have one of these four listening preferences; (2) identify the preference of the person to whom you are speaking; and (3) develop your message accordingly. For example, if you know your listener is people-oriented and want to draw her into a conversation, use stories and illustrations that contain human interest value, or use emotional examples and appeals. If your listener is action-oriented, limit your main points to three or less, and make your presentation short and to the point. If your listener is content-oriented, provide hard data when available, and use two-sided arguments whenever possible. Finally, if your listener is time-oriented and you want to capture his attention, stick to time limits and keep the details to a minimum.

Other Variables That Influence Listening Effectiveness

Each of us has a unique personality that affects our listening preferences and style. Sometimes we react emotionally to a message, and the situation becomes more complex. Becoming aware of other variables that influence listening situations will help you develop strategies to organize and present messages appropriately. As an illustration, consider the impact of message sensitivity, power differential, relationship type, and inherent risk on listening outcomes (Fielden and Dulek, 1990).

Message Sensitivity.   All messages are not created equal. Briefings, sales presentations, or even ordinary conversations can contain messages that people find sensitive and that evoke a variety of unexpected responses from them as listeners. For example, as a volunteer, Danielle worked for months on a public relations campaign for a local charity. She was proud of her work and all of the time she had invested in the project. When she presented the campaign to the board of directors, one board member (Chalessa) adamantly questioned the feasibility of the project and suggested that the board never should have assigned a volunteer to spearhead such an important task. In response to Chalessa's comment, Danielle rushed out of the room in tears, much to Chalessa's surprise. What was meant to be honest feedback about the campaign was interpreted by Danielle as negative criticism of her as a person.

How could Chalessa have rephrased her message in such a way that Danielle would have perceived it as constructive criticism rather than a personal attack? What could she have done to be more sensitive to Danielle as a listener? First, Chalessa should have avoided openly questioning the appropriateness of allowing a volunteer to direct the project, at least in Danielle's presence. Second, she could have asked relevant questions to illustrate any concerns she had about the campaign. Doing so would have given Danielle a chance to respond and to justify the reasoning behind her decision making. Third, Chalessa could have balanced negative comments with positive feedback about Danielle's presentation. In that way, a more constructive discussion might have ensued. Additionally, the board could have solved potential problems about the campaign without alienating Danielle in the process.

Power Differential.   Senders and listeners are not always created equal. Differences in perceived or actual power can cause sensitive messages to acquire a special significance and importance. For instance, criticism from a supervisor of a subordinate is perceived differently than criticism of a superior by a subordinate. In short, power has the potential to change the nature, meaning, and tone of a message.

Relationship Type.   Relationships between senders and listeners also differ. The levels of intimacy, trust, respect, shared values, shared experiences, and friendship existing between two people greatly affect the way messages are organized and phrased. Relationships can range from warm and friendly to cold and hostile. So, too, are messages created and perceived in these ways.

Inherent Risk.   Inherent risk in a message also affects listening outcomes. Risk ranges from high to low, depending on the type of message and the listener's power over, and relationship with, the sender. For example, an important message from a vice president to a subordinate may be listened to more intently than a similar message from a subordinate to a vice president. This is due to the fact that the vice president has firing power and, therefore, his or her messages carry more weight.

Improving Your Listening Skills

Now that you know more about yourself as a listener, including your primary listening preference, how can you begin the process of improving your listening skills? In the following pages, we will introduce you to three ways to approach the process: tuning into your listening behavior on a constant basis, learning all you can about effective listening, and practicing behaviors (the top ten list of listening tips) of competent listeners. Let's begin with the importance of self-awareness.

Tuning into Your Listening Behavior

Your beliefs, attitudes, and values play a significant role in how well you listen. So, too, do sensitivity and knowledge about your listening behavior. Do you constantly interrupt others while they are talking, or do you listen quietly and wait your turn? Do you ask questions to make sure you understand what others have said, or do you listen halfheartedly while they talk? Constantly observing your own and others' listening behaviors will help you grow into the kind of listener you want to be. (In addition, listening to and practicing the positive attributes of speakers you admire can help you become a better speaker as well.) In your professional and personal life, begin by watching yourself as you communicate with others during interpersonal and group interactions.

Increasing Your Awareness in Interpersonal Interactions.   Listening during a conversation requires attention, concentration, and a willingness to listen (Wolvin and Coakley, 1992, p. 401). Sometimes we get distracted by our own internal messages and forget to pay attention to the person who is talking. To illustrate, let's listen in on a conversation between Craig and David. Craig is making plans for a business trip to San Diego.

Craig: "I'm going to San Diego to meet with Sam Wainwright next week."

David: "You know, my wife and I went to San Diego last year and had a great time. We spent a lot of time sailing and eating Mexican food. The sailing is fabulous and the cuisine is out of this world!"

Craig: "Do you know anything about how Wainwright views the last building project we completed for their company?"

David: "You have got to go to SeaWorld if you have never been. Watching Shamu perform will make you feel like a kid again!"

Craig wants David to carry on a conversation with him about the Wainwright account. David is so taken up with recalling his last trip to San Diego that he does not hear a word Craig is saying. Sometimes, during the most inconvenient times, we tend to get preoccupied with our own thoughts about a subject and fail to concentrate on what the other person is saying. Let's try this conversation again, with David playing the role of a more attentive listener.

Craig: "I'm going to San Diego to meet with Sam Wainwright next week."

David: "Oh really? Why are you meeting with Sam?"

Craig: "We have an opportunity to work with him on an airport expansion project. Do you know anything about how Wainwright views the last building project we completed for their company?"

David: "I don't know, but I can give him a call. He and I are old golf buddies, and he'll give me his honest opinion. When are you leaving?"

Craig: "I'm leaving at noon tomorrow. Do you think you can talk with him sometime today?"

David: "No problem. I'll e-mail him right now. Maybe the two of you can get together for lunch and discuss the new project over Mexican food. If you have any extra time on your hands, try and get to SeaWorld. Watching Shamu perform will make you feel like a kid again."

In the second conversation, David was in tune with Craig. He actively listened to what Craig was saying and directly responded to his questions. Craig felt that David truly listened to him and was pleased that David was able to use his connections with Wainwright to help him achieve his goals.

How do you respond to others in one-on-one conversations? Have you ever been guilty of contributing to conversations like the one David had with Craig in scenario #1? If you are unsure of the answer to this question, actively monitoring your listening behavior in interpersonal interactions is a good place to begin.

Increasing Your Awareness in Small-Group Situations.   In addition to conversations with others, you also spend time in meetings, seminars, and classes. How would you classify your listening behavior in these situations? Do you listen attentively as each person talks, or do you doodle and listen only to people you like? Do you constantly attempt to dominate the interaction, or do you concentrate carefully on everything that is being said? Listening in a group can be difficult because it requires more effective verbal and nonverbal communication. You must concentrate on what each person is saying before you speak.

Learn to listen. Opportunity sometimes knocks very softly. —*Anonymous*

In group interactions, we always encounter people whose opinions differ from our own. How can you listen more effectively if someone openly disagrees with your position? If you are in a business meeting, try not to get emotionally involved. Listen carefully to what the person is verbally and nonverbally saying before you respond. Then repeat back to the person what you believe she has said to ensure that you both understand her position. Once you have done so, then proceed with your thoughts. You may find that the other person has made a valid point and that some combination of both of your thoughts offers the best solution. The key is to avoid ego involvement whenever possible.

Developing your relational life in the workplace means becoming a more effective listener in every situation. Doing so takes both awareness and knowledge about yourself and about the process of listening.

Learning All You Can About Effective Listening

Listening has been deemed the "forgotten communication skill" and the "orphan of education" by many communication practitioners. To illustrate the point, how many courses have you taken in listening? In contrast, how many courses have you completed in reading, writing, and speaking?

In the public school system, the average person spends approximately 10 to 12 years in formal writing training, six to eight years learning how to read, and one to two years in public speaking instruction. Yet, the average business person spends approximately 40 to 60 percent of each day listening, depending on his or her type of job.

In survey after survey, researchers have documented listening as the most critical managerial competency, the communication activity most important to job success, and the most important skill in the organization. As John L. DiGaetani (1980) has noted, "The effects of really good listening can be dramatic. These effects include the satisfied customer who will come back, the contented employee who will stay with the company, the manager who has the trust of his staff, and the salesman who tops his quota. Good listeners are valued highly by the people they work with" (p. 42).

What can you do to learn more about listening, given the paucity of formal courses in the area? First, check with the communication department of the college or university in which you are enrolled. Some of the larger communication programs offer one- to three-hour courses in listening. If a course is not available, at least one communication faculty member may conduct listening training outside the university. He or she may be able to direct you to a course or seminar he or she is teaching.

Second, check with your local library or favorite bookstore about current trade books in the area of listening. To give you a place to start, a number of these books are listed in the references to this chapter. Many of the authors offer useful tips and techniques for improving your listening effectiveness.

Third, practice these tips and techniques as well as those we present in the following section. Ultimately, the only way to be a better listener is to be a better listener. Begin now to hone your listening skills and you will reap the benefits: better relationships, greater job productivity, and higher esteem in your own eyes as well as the eyes of your superiors and colleagues.

Perrigo and Gaut's Top Ten List of Listening Tips

Mastering the art of listening takes time and a great deal of patience. However, you can begin today to change your old listening habits and adopt new and better listening behaviors into your lifestyle. Take a few minutes and review the following list of listening "do's." Practicing each of these suggestions can help you become a more effective listener.

1. *Limit your own talking.* It is virtually impossible to talk and listen at the same time. As a speaker, give your listener time to talk by pausing intermittently in the course of the conversation. Additionally, work to balance the amount of time you spend talking and listening.

2. *Ask questions and clarify.* If you feel that you have misunderstood a speaker, ask questions about what you have heard. Then restate or clarify the message in your own words.

3. *Paraphrase a complex or emotion-laden message back to the speaker before responding.* Sometimes speakers create complex or emotionally charged messages that are difficult to understand, or to which we may want to respond out of anger or hurt feelings. At other times, we may be only partially listening because we are tired, busy, or distracted. In each of these instances, paraphrasing what we *think* we heard before we react allows us to respond more appropriately to the message.

4. *Avoid interrupting at all costs.* Let the speaker finish his or her turn completely before you begin to talk.

5. *Concentrate intently on what the speaker is saying.* Block out any distractions you may be experiencing. Good listeners are "other-oriented." They focus on the speaker and what that person is saying.

6. *Make positive comments.* Let the person know you are listening with comments such as, "I see," "I understand," or "Please go on."

7. *Listen for the feelings behind the facts.* Often nonverbal cues will identify the true meaning behind the words.

8. *Maintain control over your emotions.* If you disagree with a statement, hold your thoughts until the person is finished speaking.

9. *Always make an effort to listen!* If the subject matter is too difficult, make a real effort to understand, and try to relate the message to your own past experiences. If the subject matter is boring, look for new points of view or new information.

10. *Develop a Listening Challenge Plan.* To firmly place your feet on the path, we have developed a Listening Challenge Plan that is designed to help you gauge your immediate progress (see Box 2.2). Identify a person to whom you have a difficult time listening, and monitor your listening behavior for one week. After a week, both you and the person to whom you are listening should notice a considerable difference in your listening behavior.

Now that you are aware of several ways to improve your own listening skills, you may be interested in knowing something about how to get people to listen to you. The last section of this chapter will address this important aspect of listening effectiveness. What you say and how you say it can make a world of difference.

How To Talk So Others Will Listen

You already know that listening habits are difficult to change, but they can be modified over time. As we mentioned earlier in the chapter, how well we listen depends on the specific situation and the credibility of the speaker. For example, you may experience difficulty getting people to listen to you, especially in meetings or in situations where everyone wants to talk simultaneously, and no one is listening. How do you gain the respect of your colleagues and business professionals so that they will listen to your point of view? While there are no foolproof answers to this question, consider the following. Whether you are meeting one-on-one or in a group setting, practical application of these concepts can help you achieve your speaking goals.

BOX 2.2

ToolBox — *A Listening Challenge Plan*

1. The name of the person to whom I need to listen more effectively is: _____.

2. The reasons I have a difficult time listening to this person are:

   a. _____

   b. _____

   c. _____

3. Specific steps I plan to take to improve my listening behavior when I am around this person are:

   a. _____

   b. _____

   c. _____

4. I will know I have achieved my goals when:

   a. _____

   b. _____

   c. _____

---

1. *Limit the number of distractions.* If you are in a position to do so, control the meeting by holding all telephone calls and faxes, turning off pagers, and letting an office professional control other interruptions that might occur. Let everyone in the office know you don't want to be disturbed, and give the person with whom you are meeting an approximate time when you will finish.

2. *Create an optimal physical environment in which to meet.* Make sure the temperature of the room is comfortable. Arrange the chairs in the meeting room so you can view the other person(s) easily. Optimize direct eye contact when you want to make a point.

3. *Time of day.* All of us have peak times when we perform our best work, and you are probably aware of your productivity levels in the morning, afternoon, and evening. When possible, choose the best time of day for you and the other party, and make the time you have set aside for the conversation work for you.

4. *Attitude checks.* Some subjects are difficult to address. A person may have had a negative experience in the past that resulted in the creation of a "sore subject." When discussed at a later date, that subject may still have negative connotations and bring back old feelings. Whatever the case may be, a person's attitude directly affects the outcome of a conversation. Whenever possible, conduct an "attitude check" regarding the subject prior to your meeting. Don't forget to check your own attitude as well.

5. *Voice projection.* Everyone's voice is unique. No two people possess the same vocal patterns. Your voice can carry a message of authority or servility, depending on your self-confidence (or lack thereof). In order to make a positive impression, articulate your words carefully. Use good intonation and speak loudly enough so that everyone can hear. A squeaky voice commands little attention and generates a negative response from your listeners.

Perhaps you can think of other appropriate behaviors that will gain the attention of your listeners.

Now that we have given you some ideas about how to talk so others will listen, experiment with some of our suggestions in conversations or group meetings. Then, attempt to actively gauge whether or not your listeners are paying more attention. You may be surprised at the outcome and how successfully you can mold the interaction.

Case Study

Listening in a Chemical Plant: Career Management in the New Team Environment

Patrice M. Johnson, M. S., Director, SPECTRA, Inc.

Like most large U.S. organizations in the late 1980s, a Fortune 500 international chemical company headquartered in the Midwest initiated a radical culture change. The company began to move away from the traditional top-down authoritative structure toward empowered teams. By the early 1990s, management at one of the company's most profitable chemical plants, located in the Southeast, realized that such a culture change was not easy. Employees at all levels, from the plant manager to hourly operators and mechanics, persisted in habitual behaviors, particularly communication behaviors that were inappropriate in the new environment.

To support adaptation to the team-based culture, the plant manager and his staff brought in a communication skills consultant to coach individual employees. The managers' objective was to ensure that employees at all levels who demonstrated expert technical skills also possessed the communication skills to contribute fully to the plant's business operations and profitability. In some cases, managers identified subordinates they felt needed coaching and called in the consultant. In other cases, individual employees who felt they could use outside support in the new environment called the consultant themselves. In the majority of contacts by managers to the consultant, employees needing coaching were described as "not listening."

In 1995, the consultant received a call from an environmental engineer who felt that his career was not progressing as he would like. His peers were moving ahead much more rapidly than he was; his performance evaluations, though solid overall, were problematic in some areas. He knew he was well-respected for his technical skills, but often his recommendations were ignored, and his projects received little management support.

By this time, the consultant had worked with the plant for several years. She had developed an understanding of plant culture and problems. One of the most significant problems was that plant employees at all levels—especially at the management level—had a great deal of difficulty dealing with conflict. Those who disagreed with current practices or raised unpopular issues were described as "not listening." And indeed they were "not listening." However, their listening weakness had little to do with disagreeing per se. It had to do with not knowing how to show respect for others' opinions while appropriately expressing their own, and the consultant knew that the most effective way of showing respect was to listen actively and to respond in a way that clearly demonstrated they had listened.

Typically, the consultant met with plant clients for six or seven one- to two-hour sessions over a period of about two months. At the first session, she asked clients to describe their problem as they saw it and helped them articulate their behavioral change objectives. Frequently clients described their problem as "not being understood" and their key objective as "being better understood."

At subsequent sessions, the consultant helped the clients identify specific behavior changes that would help them be "better understood," discussed specific work situations in which they were to practice the new behavior, and role-played the new behavior with them in preparation for the real work situation. Sometimes the consultant videotaped client meetings so clients could view and analyze nonverbal behaviors that might interfere with "being understood." Each session began with debriefings about what had happened at work since the last session and how the assigned, on-the-job practice had fared.

At the first meeting with the environmental engineer, the consultant was surprised and bemused to find herself being closely and rather suspiciously interviewed. The engineer questioned her closely about her background, her qualifications, her work at the plant, and her methodology. A nice-looking man in his late thirties, he sat somewhat hunched in his chair close to the consultant—actually invading her space—and though he questioned her aggressively, he avoided eye contact. His dress was typical of plan engineers—neatly pressed coveralls, with the plant insignia, and work boots, with a hard hat and safety glasses left on a nearby table—but his hair was somewhat longer than the plant norm for his position.

At last, the engineer was satisfied that the consultant was credible and trustworthy. The consultant was then able to direct the conversation toward the engineer's situation. The engineer described his responsibility for environmental safety and reported that his peers and superiors thought of him as negative, argumentative, and a non–team player when he pointed out environmental concerns and obstacles to their operating plans and procedures. He gave several specific examples of meetings in which he had been either completely ignored or angrily criticized for suggesting that projects simply could not go forward because the environmental hazards were too great. He said that several times in such meetings his coworkers accused him of "not listening" when, in his opinion, he was just doing his job as environmental engineer.

Questions

1. Why does plant management describe those who disagree with current practices or raise unpopular issues as "not listening?" What is the relationship between agreeing/disagreeing and listening/not listening?

2. Which components of Watson's listening model should the engineer consider in working to improve his listening skills?

3. How would you assess the engineer's listening preferences?

4. Which of the top ten listening tips would you advise the engineer to practice?

5. How would you coach the engineer to help him "be better understood"?

Summary

Building effective listening skills is a necessity if you want to achieve success. Mastering the art of effective listening takes time and practice; however, the benefits are well worth the costs.

Knowing the difference between hearing and listening is essential in understanding the listening process. Hearing is passive, while listening is active. Watson's listening model identifies the five components that are necessary for you to consider in improving your listening skills.

Gaining knowledge about listening is the first step toward achieving your listening goals. So, too, is sensitivity. However, to become an effective listener you must become more aware of your listening behavior, understand your habits and preferences, and know as much as you can about your own listening profile.

Once you understand your strengths and weaknesses as a listener, you can better practice effective listening. To do so, constantly monitor your listening behavior in conversations and group interactions. Learn as much as you can about the listening process, and actively practice good listening skills every day. Getting people to listen to you can be a challenge, depending on the other person, the subject being discussed, and the situation. Limiting distractions, creating an optimal listening environment, and choosing the best time of day for meeting can work in your favor. Checking attitudes at the door and using your voice effectively also can work to your advantage.

Knowledge Check

Key Concepts and Terms

hearing	interpretation	pseudolistening
cochlea	assessing	people-oriented listeners
listening	responding	action-oriented listeners
attending	thinking-speaking time	content-oriented listeners
perceiving	differential	time-oriented listeners

Putting It All Together

1. How does hearing differ from listening?
2. What are the five stages of listening and their distinguishing characteristics?
3. Describe some typical verbal and nonverbal characteristics of poor listeners.
4. Identify and briefly discuss the four major listening preferences that people exhibit. How can you vary your speaking style to best adapt to each listening preference?
5. List and discuss at least five ways you can become a more effective listener.
6. What are some strategies you can use to talk so that other people will listen to you?

References

Adams, J. (1987). Hearing is a sense, listening is an art. *Supervision, 49*(3), 9–11.

Borisoff, D., & Purdy, M. (1992). Gender issues and listening. In *Listening in Everyday Life: A Personal and Professional Approach,* pp. 59–86. Lanham, MD: University Press of America.

Bostrom, R. (1990). *Listening behavior: Measurement and application.* New York: Guilford Press.

Brownell, J. (1986). *Building active listening skills.* Englewood Cliffs, NJ: Prentice-Hall.

Day, C. (1980, April 28). How do you rate as a listener? *Industry Week, 205* (2), 30–35.

DiGaetani, J. L. (1980). The business of listening. *Business Horizons, 23,* 42.

Fielden, J. S., & Dulek, R. E. (1990, October). Matching messages to listening styles. *Business,* 55–57.

Golen, S. (1990). A factor analysis of barriers to effective listening. *Journal of Business Communication 27*(1), 25–35.

Gutner, T. (1993, March 1). Meeting the boss. *Forbes,* 126.

Nixon, J. C., & West, J. F. (1989). Listening: Vital to communication. *The Bulletin of the Association for Business Communication, 52,* 15–16.

Peters, T. (1988). *Thriving on chaos.* New York: Knopf.

Rasberry, R. W. (1980). Are your students listening? A method for putting listening instruction into the business communication course. *Proceedings of the Southwest American Business Communication Association,* 215.

Sayre, J. M. (1987). *How to listen: Your guide to success.* Danville, IL: The Interstate Printers and Publishers.

Steil, L. K., Barker, L. L., & Watson, K. W. (1983). *Effective listening: Key to your success.* Reading, MA: Addison-Wesley.

Sypher, B. D., Bostrom, R. N., & Seibert, J. H. (1989). Listening, communication abilities and success at work. *The Journal of Business Communication, 26*(4), 293–303.

Tannen, D. (1990). *You just don't understand: Women and men in conversation.* New York: William Morrow & Company.

Watson, K. W. (1993). Listening and feedback. In L. L. Barker & D. A. Barker, *Communication,* 6th ed., pp. 49–77. Englewood Cliffs, NJ: Prentice-Hall.

Watson, K. W., & Barker, L. L. (1992). *Personal listening preference profile.* New Orleans: Spectra, Inc.

Wolvin, A. D., & Coakley, C. G. (1991). A survey of the status of listening training in some Fortune 500 corporations. *Communication Education, 40,* 152–164.

Wolvin, A. D., & Coakley, C. G. (1992). *Listening* 4th ed. Dubuque, IA: Wm. C. Brown.

3

The Care and Feeding of an Interpersonal Network

After studying this chapter, you will be able to

- Understand the differences between formal and informal communication.

- Recognize the variables that affect communication climate in an organization.

- Be knowledgeable about "office politics" and its effect on your relational life.

- Realize the positive effects of humor in the workplace.

- Understand the pros and cons of romantic relationships in the workplace.

- Identify sexual harassment terminology and learn prevention techniques.

- Build your relational skills through networking and mentoring.

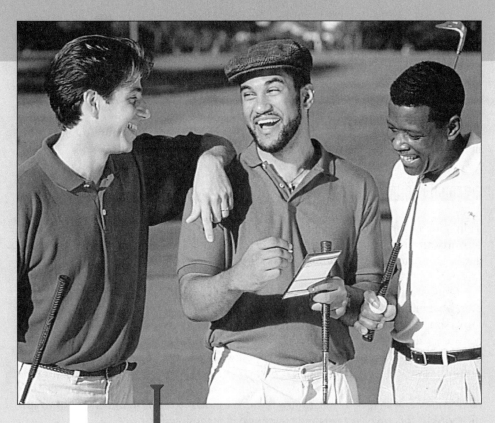

I t's no wonder Hallmark Card employees "care enough to send the very best." Since the company's founding in 1910, each one of the approximately 13,000 employees has been part of a family atmosphere where "friendships happen quite easily" (Levering & Moskowitz, 1994, p. 164). To inspire the creative staff, Hallmark brings in visiting artists and writers such as actress Betty White, sociologist and author Betty Friedan, and *New Yorker* cartoonist Gahan Wilson. There is so much interactive learning going on that you can't help but establish friendships in Hallmark's corporate culture. To further promote the friendly atmosphere and to assist in improving two-way communication between management and employees, Hallmark established "morning forums," which are periodic breakfasts with a dozen employees and the · CEO. These "morning forums" have been quite popular with Hallmark employees, who feel management listens to their ideas and values their input and opinions about the mission of the organization.

Giving employees access to information from management is essential in today's market. Employees engaging in conversation with high-level managers is one method of establishing better interpersonal communication within the organization. Because developing relationships with supervisors, subordinates, and coworkers is critical to your job success, the focus of this chapter is the care and feeding of your interpersonal network.

Defining Interpersonal Communication

Think, for a moment, about your closest friend or colleague on campus, in a community organization, or in a company in which you work. Is this person a personal friend, a colleague, a teacher or mentor, a superior or a subordinate? Why do you feel close to this person?

Only you and this other person know what makes your relationship special. However, what brought the relationship into being and what currently sustains it is your **interpersonal communication,** or the sum total of every spoken and unspoken word, gesture, or deed the two of you have shared.

Most of us don't think about everything we say or do when we enter into a relationship with someone. However, W. Barnett Pearce (1994) argues that every time we utter a word, we are entering into "a game-like pattern of social interaction" that directly molds and shapes the relationship which follows" (p. 31). To underscore the ramifications of this surprising statement, consider the following:

> As a sequence of acts, each of which evokes and responds to the acts of the other person, a conversation is not just a string of unrelated things but an interaction of interdependent events.... [As a result, there] is a sense of back-and-forth in which what I say at each moment is "because of" what you just said and "in order that" you will say something else (Pearce, 1994, p. 31).

Conversations are a series of dramatic interplays from which neither party can ever turn back. The result is the many and varied relationships in which we find ourselves in an organization, whether they are "professional," "cordial," "embittered," or "just friendly." In short, every time we communicate, either verbally or nonverbally, we mold, create, and sustain the nature of relational life that follows.

What does all of this have to do with the care and feeding of interpersonal networks in the workplace? **Interpersonal networks** are comprised of individual relationships you consciously or unconsciously develop and nurture. Relationships you cultivate within your organization are crucial to your personal and professional success. If you want to create and sustain a rich and rewarding interpersonal network on the job, you must optimize interpersonal communication. Specifically, you must:

■ be more conscious of the profound impact that every conversation you share has on your relationships,

■ maximize the primary forms of communication that prevail in your workplace (i.e., formal versus informal),

■ be able to identify and work well with differing communication styles, and

■ understand and optimize the nature of the communication climate in which you are functioning.

Because of the significant contribution of these four variables to the well-being of your social life at work, we begin this chapter with a brief discussion of each.

The Impact of Conversations on Relationships

Everything you say in conversations has a direct impact on how you are perceived within the organization. According to Pearce (1994), whenever we take part in a conversation, we initiate a series of acts, each of which simultaneously evokes a response from the other person and serves as our response to him or her. Individual conversations do not stand in isolation. Rather, as Pearce argued,

> They are a part of "clusters" of conversations, some of which are alike and some different; they are a moment in a historical process in which what comes before and after affects what happens in the moving moment of "now." (p. 33)

In short, patterns emerge in how we talk to people around us, which in turn ultimately impacts the relationships we have with others.

For example, how many times could the following simple two-turn conversation occur between two office-mates without having a deleterious effect on the relationship?

Sandy: Would you like to go to lunch?

Mark: No, thank you.

How much more positive Mark's response would have been, had he simply replied, "Not today, thanks. I have to get this report to Churchill by three o'clock this afternoon. Can I take a rain check and go with you another time?" By rephrasing his response in this manner, Mark would have shown more kindness and courtesy to Sandy. The key is to work toward coordinating your conversations in such a way that you develop and nurture positive relationships. Box 3.1 on page 62 provides some specific tips on how to make your conversations more meaningful.

Now that you are aware of the profound impact that every conversation you share has on your personal and professional relationships, we turn to a second important variable that is pertinent to your relational life at work: the patterns of formal and informal communication that define your workplace.

Formal and Informal Communication

What forms do messages take among managers and employees in a given organization? What primary means do people use to share information, accomplish tasks, and achieve common goals? The answers to these questions vary dramatically from organization to organization depending on the emphasis on formal versus informal communication.

BOX 3.1

ToolBox   *Meaningful Conversation Tips*

The following are a few basic tips for developing meaningful conversations in the workplace that are characterized by mutual respect and shared understanding.

Tip #1   When listening to others, pay close attention to what's NOT being said.

Tip #2   Realize that intent is not always spoken.

Tip #3   Work toward creating shared definitions of a situation. Do so by asking yourself two main questions: "What is my working definition of the situation in which we find ourselves?" and "How should I act so that my actions will coordinate with those of the other person?" (Pearce, p. 27)

Tip #4   Keep in mind that everything you say can and will impact your relationships and invariably will link the past to the future.

Tip #5   Conduct a periodic check on all of your relationships by asking yourself these three questions: "What kind of relational life do I want with this person? What kind of relational life am I actually creating and sustaining? How can I go about developing contact with this person that will maximize a mutual sense of dignity, respect, and joy?

Formal Communication

Formal communication is generally associated with the flow of information across an organization's chain of command. Influenced heavily by the company's organizational chart, information moves in one of three directions: downward, upward, or horizontal.

Downward communication is information that flows from supervisor to subordinate. Some examples of downward communication are when your boss gives you job instructions, outlines company policies and procedures, discusses your job performance, or motivates you to do a better job. To illustrate the nature of downward communication, let's eavesdrop on a conversation between Alessio, a supervisor at a small manufacturing plant, and Steve, her subordinate.

Alessio: "I know this is your first day on the job. You have a lot of people to meet and quite a bit of reading material to get you started. I want to go over the policies and procedures of our department with you first."

Steve: "That would be a good first step since I have a lot of questions. Will I be able to take some of the reading material home with me to better acquaint myself with the rules and regulations of the company?"

Alessio: "Yes, of course. I'm glad to see you are so willing to study outside of regular work hours. You are getting a good start in this company with a positive attitude."

Upward communication is information that flows from subordinate to supervisor. When you request additional information from your boss for a proposal you have been asked to write, or suggest ideas to improve the department or company, you are engaging in upward communication. To illustrate the concept further, let's listen to a dialogue between Susan, a computer operator, and her supervisor, Cedric.

Susan: "I would like to talk to you about a suggestion I have that will save our department time and money. When will you have time to schedule an appointment with me?"

Cedric: "Well, it sounds like we need to talk as soon as possible. Can you come by my office around two o'clock today? If you have a proposal to save the company time and money, I'm available to listen."

Susan: "Thanks, Cedric. See you at two in your office."

Horizontal communication is information that flows laterally between people of the same rank or status. Examples of horizontal communication are when people of equal rank meet to solve problems together, or give advice to each other based on past experience. In your company, a colleague may want to meet with you to share information for an idea, or support a decision you have made. To illustrate, consider the following example.

Sharon and Doug are both managers in a retail store. Sharon is experiencing problems with delays in merchandise being shipped out on time. Sharon asks Doug's advice on how to deal with the problem.

Sharon: "Doug, I'm having a problem getting this new line of silk blouses shipped in from New York. Have you ever had problems getting any of your merchandise in when promised?"

Doug: "As a matter of fact I have. What line of clothing are you dealing with? Maybe I can give you some suggestions on what has worked for me in the past."

Sharon: "Thanks, Doug. I knew you could help."

Informal Communication

When colleagues share information through the grapevine, they are engaging in **informal communication.** Interestingly enough, the grapevine is typically fast and reliable. Studies indicate that 80 percent of information traveling through the grapevine is accurate. In fact, informal messages tend to be more accurate than formal ones because status, power, and rank are disregarded temporarily when communicating.

To test this hypothesis, one of your authors' colleagues circulated a false rumor about a policy change that was going to take place within the organization. He wanted to determine how long it would take until the rumor got back to him and the degree of accuracy with which the rumor would be passed. It may alarm you to know that it took approximately 10 minutes for the information to get back to him with—100 percent accuracy! This simple test, even though it is an informal, isolated incident, supports our point about the power of informal communication.

The type of information that passes through the grapevine is both business- and gossip-oriented. When employees cannot get the information they need through formal communication channels, they invariably resort to informal channels.

Land's End is one company that knows the value of informal, face-to-face communication. To illustrate, consider the type of communication that characterizes the

Information voids will be filled by rumors and speculation unless they are preempted by open, credible and trustworthy communication. Pull no punches. When you know an answer, give it. When you don't, say so. When you're guessing, admit it. But don't stop communication.

—*Jean B. Keffeler*

corporate culture at Lands End, a well-known U.S. company that sells high-quality clothing, sheets, towels, and soft luggage through mail order catalogs. With 2,400 plus employees in the United States, few people stand on titles; they actually talk to each other. Richard Anderson, chief executive officer (CEO), makes it a habit to meet regularly with seven different employees every other week for lunch. These individuals are neither bosses nor supervisors, but people on the line such as inseamers, monogrammers, salespeople, and service people. The goal is to establish an ongoing dialogue so that people in the company feel free to talk about what's going on as well as to share what is bothering them (Levering & Moskowitz, 1994, p. 233).

Not every company is like Lands End when it comes to valuing informal communication. Other companies reflect a different emphasis on the value of formal and informal messages. Although formal communication has its place in every organization, companies that demand formality in all interactions sometimes create individual boundaries between employees that can be detrimental to the company. For example, think about how tedious and time-consuming it would be for you to have to make an appointment with your boss two weeks in advance to discuss a problem, or to write a formal proposal every time you wanted to share an idea.

Vertical versus Horizontal Organizations

Traditionally, organizations have adopted a **vertical approach** to management. This hierarchical approach creates invisible departmental boundaries, with employees and supervisors reporting to a higher level of management. Typically, resolving a problem at a lower level of the organization requires communication with upper management. Usually, when the problem has been resolved, the decision is passed down to individuals in departments or units in which the problem originated. The benefits of the vertical approach to organizational management are clearly delineated lines of communication and a formal chain of command. One disadvantage is that it may discourage employees from talking to one another.

Figure 3.1 depicts the traditional approach to organizational management as a collection of vertical departments.

Currently there is a trend toward more horizontal communication in organizations. The purely **horizontal organization** consists of two core groups: senior managers who are responsible for strategic decisions and policies, and employees who work together in different teams (Chung, 1994, p. 21). The benefits of horizontal management include increased empowerment of employees and more efficient and effective communication. With the increased use of E-mail and shared databases, companies are opening up more horizontal lines of communication among employees, managers, customers, and suppliers. Figure 3.2 represents the horizontal approach to organizational management.

The term **virtual company** describes the new corporate entity that evolves when a company relies on the power of people and technology to effectively address the needs of the global marketplace. Further, the virtual company shares customer databases and also links planning and financial systems in an extended horizontal channel of communication.

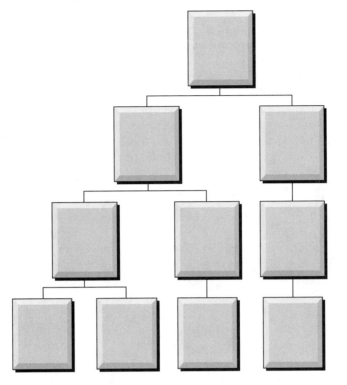

Figure 3.1

The Traditional
Vertical Approach
to Organizational
Management

As communication technology continues to expand, people are communicating more effectively across all levels of the organization and at multiple sites around the world, regardless of job status or title. Consider the new forms of communication that the information superhighway has built in the 1990s alone. We now have more channels of communication than ever before. For example, with a computer and a modem, you can E-mail the president of your company, whether he or she is at the office or on the other side of the world. You can even E-mail the president of the United States (http://www.whitehouse.gov/wh/mail/html/mail_president.html) or send faxes directly to the presidents of companies or to members of Congress. As a member of a virtual company, you can be an active participant in a videoconference or complete a college course via satellite in the comfort of your own home. These and other communication

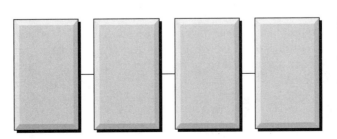

Figure 3.2

The Horizontal
Approach to
Organizational
Management

channels have changed the way we do business and have allowed us to form relationships with people whom we could never have reached before now. Communication technology will continue to shape our relational lives in the organizational setting; you will learn more about its impact in Chapter 12.

What does all of this have to do with interpersonal communication in the workplace? Relationships with your coworkers and friends will change as a result of new technology. For example, say you want to congratulate a colleague in another city because of a recent promotion. You could E-mail him immediately instead of sending him a written note that may take days to get there. However, keep in mind that E-mail is more impersonal than a handwritten letter or card. More about business etiquette will be revealed in Chapter 9.

Communication Styles

Consider the following scenario. You have been experiencing an achy shoulder for three or four months and finally make an appointment with a physician. Upon greeting her, you tell the doctor about your problem. You expect to be told what is causing the pain and given some form of treatment. Instead you are surprised by her brusk manner and a virtual barrage of medical jargon that you don't understand. After you are given a stack of prescriptions and a patronizing pat on the shoulder, you are ushered quickly out the door. You walk away feeling confused, frustrated, and angry.

Doctors are not the only professionals who are guilty of ineffective communication. Every day, around the globe, people in organizations pay little attention to the needs of their colleagues and overlook the subtle differences in the way they communicate. Just as successful physicians adapt to the communication styles of their patients, effective employees, supervisors, and managers adapt to the needs and styles of their colleagues.

What Is Communication Style?

Understanding the characteristics of different communication styles will assist you in developing your interpersonal skills in the workplace. **Communication style** is defined as the manner in which you disclose information to your coworkers, supervisor(s) and subordinates. Merrill and Reid (1980) developed a SOCIAL STYLE℠ Profile based on scientific observations of human behavior and its effects on business and personal relationships. Their profile identifies four types of communicators, based on degree of assertiveness and responsiveness: driving, expressive, amiable, and analytical (see Figure 3.3).*

Driving individuals tend to be more assertive and less responsive than other SOCIAL STYLES. They know what they want, where they are going, and how they plan to get there. Driving types want to make their own decisions; they seek power and dislike being told what to do or not to do. They base their decisions on facts and tend to take risks. Driving individuals also are action-oriented; determination and objectiveness are their

---

*Copyright The TRACOM Corporation, Denver, CO. Used with permission. All rights reserved.

Less Responsiveness

Analytical Behavior	Driving Behavior
Amiable Behavior	Expressive Behavior

Less Assertiveness

More Assertiveness

More Responsiveness

Figure 3.3

The Social Style Model™
Source: D. W. Merrill and R. H. Reid (1980). Personal Styles and Effective Performance (Radnor, PA: Chilton Book Co.) p. 53 and the TRACOM Corporation, Denver, CO. Used with permission of the TRACOM Corporation. All rights reserved.

strengths. A primary weakness of the driving individual is that they become domineering and unfeeling if they are overextended or pushed too far. Other characteristics include independence, candor, decisiveness, pragmatism, and efficiency (Bolton & Bolton, 1984, p. 65). An excellent example of a driving SOCIAL STYLE is Barbara Walters.

Individuals with an **expressive STYLE** are described as higher in both assertiveness and responsiveness than other SOCIAL STYLES. They usually abound with energy, speak rapidly, take risks, express strong opinions, and initiate projects. Expressive individuals tend to be imaginative, and they make decisions based on intuition. However, like the driving types, they, too, can be overextended; their response is to become overbearing and unrealistic. Other typical characteristics of this SOCIAL STYLE are enthusiasm, persuasive ability, an outgoing personality, and spontaneity. Rush Limbaugh definitely exhibits characteristics of an expressive communicator type.

Those with an **amiable STYLE** tend to be lower in assertiveness and higher in responsiveness than other SOCIAL STYLES. As a result, they are quiet, friendly, and relaxed. Overall, amiable individuals prefer one-on-one interactions and are relationship-oriented. Their strengths are supportiveness and an easygoing style, but when overextended they can become conforming and permissive. Other typical characteristics of this type are cooperativeness, diplomacy, loyalty, and patience. Recording artist Kenny G provides an excellent example of an amiable communicator.

Individuals with an **analytical STYLE** tend to be lower in both assertiveness and responsiveness than other SOCIAL STYLES. As a result, they usually talk less frequently and speak with a quiet tone of voice. Although they are intellectually inclined, they express ideas more tentatively and make decisions slowly. Analytical people are also serious, thorough, logical, and systematic. Their strengths include precision and systematic thinking, but when overextended they can become nitpicky and inflexible. A good example of an analytical communicator is Colin Powell.

According to Bolton and Bolton (1984), there is no one "best" communicator style; each has its own strengths and weaknesses. In fact, at different times you will exhibit characteristics of all four types. However, your dominant communicator style will influence the way you work with others.

General Colin Powell exhibits an analytical style. Not only is he thorough and logical, his strengths also include precise and systematic thinking.

Communication styles that differ from your own can cause stress and tension at work. By learning characteristics of each style and adapting your behavior accordingly, you can learn to manage your interpersonal relationships in a positive manner.

Communication Climate

What is "communication climate?" How can you effectively gauge the temperature associated with the communication climate in an organization? Unfortunately, we don't have a thermometer that can determine the temperature in a company or business. However, we have all probably experienced days on the job when we felt bright and sunny, cold and wintry, or cloudy and stormy.

Communication climate describes the way we feel about a group or organization with which we work, the extent to which we value and feel valued by others, and the overall working environment. How people communicate with each other, to whom they communicate, and how often they interact all influence our job satisfaction and productivity. When we feel that our opinion doesn't count or we feel unappreciated, our productivity and satisfaction suffer.

For example, Valerie has been an office manager for 15 years and recently received her bachelor's degree in management. She now expects to be treated like a professional. She has gained extensive knowledge of current management techniques and continually offers recommendations for improvements in her department. However, Valerie's supervisor, who has been with the company for 25 years, continues to treat her like a secretary who is responsible for mundane clerical tasks. To what extent do you think Valerie feels valued by her boss and company overall?

Let's explore two additional variables that affect the communication climate in an organization: open versus closed communication and patterns of defensive versus supportive communication.

> You'll be bothered from time to time by storms, fog, snow. When you are, think of those who went through it before you, and say to yourself, "What they could do, I can do."
>
> —Antoine De Saint-Exupery

Open versus Closed Communication

Open communication is defined as communication through which people feel free to share information and opinions. As such, open communication requires an environment steeped in trust and friendship. To illustrate, let's listen to a conversation that might take place between you and an "open" supervisor.

You: "I'm trying to meet a 3:00 deadline today with the proposal you asked me to submit. Can my budget report wait until after I complete the proposal?"

Boss: "Okay, the budget can wait until tomorrow. Be sure to call the accounting department and let them know your budget will be late."

In contrast, **closed communication** involves little sharing of information; people feel little freedom to voice their opinions. In an office setting, closed communication is often encouraged by strict adherence to deadlines, lack of flexibility, low trust, and an absence of general friendliness and empathy. An example of a typical reaction from a closed supervisor might be:

You: "I'm trying to meet a 3:00 deadline today with the proposal you asked me to submit. Can my budget report wait until after I complete the proposal?"

Boss: "You knew the budget had to be in today. Why couldn't you schedule your workload to accommodate both projects? You must complete your proposal and the budget before you leave the office today."

As you can see, open communication fosters a healthier communication climate as well as job productivity and satisfaction. Additionally, openness encourages more effective interpersonal relationships, which are important to sustaining a satisfying relational life.

Defensive versus Supportive Communication

A second factor that directly affects the communication climate of an organization is the pattern of defensive versus supportive communication that occurs in the workplace. **Defensive communication** results when people lack openness and honesty with one another. **Supportive communication** is based on openness and honesty. While defensive communication tends to impede communication effectiveness, supportive communication enhances job productivity and satisfaction.

In his now-classic eight-year study of small groups, Jack Gibb (1961) identified six defensive and six supportive communication behaviors. Table 3.1 on page 70 provides an overview of characteristics associated with both.

Evaluation versus Description. The use of evaluative versus descriptive language is Gibb's first distinction between defensive and supportive communication. **Evaluation** is associated with "you" language and directed toward another person's worth or ideas. **Description** involves "I" language, which describes a speaker's thoughts about the person or idea. For example, if someone on your team suggests a solution to a problem, which you think is ridiculous, you can respond in one of two ways. You can say, "I think this is the most ridiculous solution I have ever heard. It will never work," or you can say, "The solution you have proposed seems like it may have some problems. Have I

Table 3.1	Gibb's Defensive and Supportive Behaviors	
DEFENSIVE BEHAVIORS	**SUPPORTIVE BEHAVIORS**	
Evaluation	Description	
Control	Problem Orientation	
Strategy	Spontaneity	
Neutrality	Empathy	
Superiority	Equality	
Certainty	Provisionalism	

Adapted from J. Gibb (1961). "Defensive Communication," *Journal of Communication, 11*(3), pp. 141–148. Adapted with permission of Publisher.

missed something?" According to Gibb, the use of descriptive language leads to greater trust and cohesiveness, whereas evaluative language directly provokes defensiveness.

Control versus Problem Orientation.   When people attempt to **control** others, the latter often get defensive. For example, if a colleague badgers you into answering questions about a problem you are having on a project, then intentionally tries to manipulate you into solving the problem her way, you immediately become defensive. Using a **problem orientation** is a more effective approach. If that same colleague had attempted to understand your concerns and then helped you brainstorm several possible solutions to the problem, chances are she would have been more effective. If you offer solutions that are good for the group or organization as a whole, rather than attempting to manipulate people, your managers and colleagues will perceive you to be more supportive.

Strategy versus Spontaneity.   We have all met people with hidden agendas who try to convince us to think and believe their way. To persuade us to do things their way, they may use a number of strategies, including flattery, appeals to logic, or appeals to emotion. The use of such **strategies** is controlling and manipulative and often results in defensive behavior. In contrast, **spontaneity** is associated with the absence of hidden agendas and involves open, honest communication.

For example, if an automobile salesperson approaches you and tells you "how intelligent you look," or that "you look like a person who knows a good deal when you see one," he or she is strategizing, and trying to "schmooze" you and win you over. A spontaneous salesperson asks what you are looking for, and tells you that he or she is available if you have questions. The spontaneous salesperson's communication behavior represents a more supportive approach.

Neutrality versus Empathy.   People like to be acknowledged as human beings in the work setting. For example, if someone is uncaring and has an indifferent attitude toward our problems, he or she is showing evidence of **neutrality.** On the other hand, the person who is concerned and caring about our problems is demonstrating empathy.

Neutrality promotes more defensive behavior on everyone's part, while empathy encourages supportive behavior. For example, if one of your colleagues sends you an E-mail on a sensitive issue and you don't respond, your noncommunication sends a message of indifference. An empathic person responds right away to the needs and concerns of others.

Superiority versus Equality.   When people believe they are brighter, faster, or more productive than their managers or colleagues, they are demonstrating a **superior attitude,** which reflects and evokes defensive behavior. In contrast, an attitude of **equality** promotes a more supportive environment, since all perceive themselves to be on the same level.

For example, a professor who feels superior to her students will attempt to make them feel inferior, which in turn reduces their motivation, productivity, and satisfaction. In contrast, an instructor who believes in the power of equality and treats his students as equals will be more well-liked and supportive.

Certainty versus Provisionalism.   Surely you have known people who feel and act like they "know it all." This type of person is characterized by **certainty,** or is sure of himself. As a result, others constantly feel the need to prove that person wrong, which is counterproductive to the goals of an organization and defensive in nature. Provisional people accede, listen well, and adapt appropriately in the face of differing viewpoints. **Provisional behavior** is more supportive than "certain" behaviors and promotes positive relationships.

How many supportive and defensive characteristics have you observed in your own behavior, now that you are aware of Gibb's typology? Can you think of a conversation you had this week in which you exhibited defensive behavior? If so, what could you have said that would have been more supportive of your friend or colleague? As you can see, reliance on supportive communication behavior and elimination of defensive communication is the key to creating and sustaining a positive communication climate.

Aspects of the Workplace That Affect Job Productivity and Satisfaction

In the previous section, we addressed four variables that contribute to the well-being of your relational life at work. However, job productivity and satisfaction are affected by four additional aspects of the workplace: office politics, humor, romantic relationships, and sexual harassment.

The Crazy Mixed-Up World of Office Politics

Rules exist in every organization. Some rules are written; others are learned through experience. The ability to identify the unwritten rules and play the game correctly defines the world of office politics.

To give you an example of how office politics works, consider Jim, a bright, loyal sales manager who worked at a large chemical company for eight years. He received outstanding evaluations and was well liked by his coworkers and supervisor. Jim was a golfer and enjoyed playing a few rounds with his fellow co-workers and his supervisor, Ron. One day, while golfing, Ron asked Jim if he was interested in moving to another city to enhance his career. Jim was less than keen on the idea, since he was content with his present job and the friends he had made in Chicago. When Jim was offered a lateral position in another city a few months later, he refused, thinking the company had invested too much time and money in him to terminate his employment. When the company decided to "downsize," Jim was given his 90-day notice. If Jim had only known how to play "office politics" more successfully, chances are he would still be with the company.

How would you have handled this situation if you were in Jim's shoes? How could he have played office politics more effectively? First, Jim could have asked Ron why he was interested and what city he had in mind, rather than simply saying "no." By doing so, Jim would have shown Ron that he was willing to consider being wherever the company needed him. Second, Jim assumed the company would never let him go since he had longevity and a history of positive evaluations. Such assumptions are always deadly for a career. Third, Jim could have asked if Ron would give him an opportunity to think about the question. That way, he could have given Ron a more thoughtful reply.

Over the past decade, many books have been written regarding the power of office politics. Dubrin (1990) in his book, *Winning Office Politics,* makes a variety of suggestions. Included among the topics he addresses are how to: get the boss on your side, impress the higher-ups, gain the support of coworkers, outwit difficult people, and boost your career in the process. For instance, Dubrin offers the following cogent statement regarding the nature of office politics overall:

> Senior management sets the stage for the type of political game playing that takes place at lower levels in the organization. When top management manipulates people, discredits the opposition, and covers up the truth, similar machinations are found down the line. When senior management plays sensible and ethical politics, a good example is established as to what kind of behavior is acceptable and encouraged. (p. 321)

Developing a compatible relationship with your supervisor is the first step toward playing the game of office politics effectively. Establishing compatibility first requires an understanding of what makes him or her tick. To begin the process, you might ask yourself the following questions:

- ■ What are my boss's professional objectives and how can I help him/her achieve them?
- ■ What channels of communication does my boss prefer to use?
- ■ What is my boss's preferred style of working? Does he or she thrive on conflict or try to minimize it?

By answering these questions and adapting your behavior accordingly, you will be well on your way to understanding your boss's behavior and management style. How-

Many business decisions are made outside of the office. Knowing how to play office politics may mean developing your game both on and off the course.

ever, understanding your supervisor is only half of the battle. The other half is understanding your own needs, strengths, weaknesses, and personal style. In most cases, it is difficult to change your personality—and nearly impossible to change your boss's personality. Nevertheless, you can become more aware of variables that impede working well with your boss and take action that will make the relationship more productive.

In coping with the many faces of change in Workplace 2010, we must continually learn to understand and manage the fine art of office politics, which, in turn, assists you in developing business savvy. Those who adapt well are those who succeed in establishing a power base that allows them to function well within the organization. You, too, can establish a power base by creating liaisons with mentors who have access to pertinent information that will help you achieve your objectives and perform your tasks more efficiently. You can also join professional and social groups outside the work environment, which will help maximize your credibility within the organization.

Humor in the Workplace

Companies in corporate America are finding that employees who laugh together stay together, produce more, invent more, and work more cohesively as a team (Swift & Swift, 1994). Examples of companies promoting the use of humor in the workplace include

Having a sense of humor in the workplace promotes health, reduces stress, increases motivtion, and improves morale. Being able to laugh at yourself is imperative to enjoying your day-to-day work environment.

AT&T, Dupont, Kodak, IBM, Ben & Jerry's Homemade, Mobil, and the American Institute of Banking, to name a few.

One compelling example of a company that encourages humor in the workplace is Kodak, which has created a humor room at its corporate location in Rochester, New York (Caudron, 1992). The thousand-square-foot room houses four areas: 1) a resource library that stocks joke books and videotapes of various comedians, 2) a group meeting area that allows up to 20 people to meet comfortably in creative brainstorming sessions, 3) a toy store that stocks items such as rubber eyeballs and punching bags, and 4) a high-tech area that houses personal computers, called "humor processors," that are loaded with creative software to help employees generate new ideas. The humor room is used by a cross section of Kodak's 20,000 employees at different times during the day, which gives them a new perspective on work.

Another example of a company that has invited humor into the workplace is Ben & Jerry's Homemade, based in Waterbury, Vermont. Under former president Jerry Greenfield's direction, the company created a "Joy Gang" that is charged with disseminating joy grants to work units that come up with creative ideas for bringing long-term joy to the workplace. The grants, worth up to $5,000 each, have been used in a variety of ways, from the purchase of a hot chocolate machine to company roller skates for employees.

What are some of the benefits of humor? Humor promotes health, reduces stress, increases employee motivation, improves employee morale, and heightens learning and retention, to name a few. As you can see, your overall health and well-being can be improved by laughter. It takes 43 muscles to frown, but only 17 to smile (DeBats, 1990).

The health benefits of laughing also are numerous. Laughing speeds up heart rate, raises blood pressure, accelerates breathing, and increases oxygen consumption. As laughter subsides, respiration and heart rate slow, often to below-normal levels. Blood pressure drops and muscles relax. Whether it's the arousal, the relaxation, or both, enough laughter may reduce the risk of heart disease, depression, and other stress-related conditions (Long, 1987).

By taking humor breaks, your spirits are uplifted, which increases your motivation to face the tasks ahead of you. For example, one way that companies are supporting humor breaks is by encouraging employees to keep a book of cartoons or jokes in their offices and to let their colleagues know where they keep it. (You, too, might consider keeping a cartoon or joke book nearby. We guarantee that your morale and the morale of your colleagues will be improved after reading a few humorous cartoons or stories.)

Many studies indicate that humor also heightens our learning and retention. Think about how you react in a classroom situation when your professor stops and tells a really great joke. Chances are that you will remember the point he or she made simply because of the joke.

Finally, according to a survey conducted by Wilde (1988), those who view their work as fun are more productive and get along better with their coworkers. Additionally, employees who are allowed and encouraged to have fun at work usually score higher marks in job satisfaction, productivity, creativity, and morale. (Caudron, 1992) In short, humor simply relaxes people and eases stressful situations.

The results of sharing humor in the workplace are immediate and long-lasting. Humor is memorable. Humor is appreciated by people at all levels of the organization. Everyone knows how good it feels to laugh just a little.

One simple way to create humor is to clip your favorite comic strips and tape them to your office door for your colleagues to enjoy at their leisure. Another way is to wear a humorous lapel pin on your suit with a trendy saying or quotation that will make people laugh when they see it. Think about how much time you spend with your colleagues every day in the same work environment. A little laughter lightens the workload and stimulates creativity.

Some people argue that humor in the workplace has its drawbacks, that people may not be taken seriously if they are always laughing and telling jokes. Some of these barriers may be real, and some may be perceived. To help you develop a positive sense of humor in the workplace without the aforementioned drawbacks, we offer the following guidelines.

Refrain from using sarcastic humor, which can hurt another person's feelings. Mocking or contemptuously ironic remarks have no place in the workplace. In short, watch what you say and how you say it.

Avoid telling racist, sexist, or offensive jokes. Such behavior may lead to charges of harassment and can have legal implications. Learn to laugh at yourself and make yourself the brunt of the joke—not someone else.

Resist joking about your supervisor, coworkers, or subordinates; what you say may get back to them. How would you feel if you learned that you were the object of the latest office joke? Although jokes about other people may be funny to you, how would you feel if the tables were turned? This type of humor is potentially dangerous to all parties involved. For that reason, such jokes should be avoided.

> A sense of humor is what makes you laugh at something which would make you mad if it happened to you.
>
> —*Anonymous*

Avoid joking about sensitive subjects such as politics and religion. Your coworkers and associates may be involved with a particular political party or religious organization. You don't want to risk offending people because of their political or religious beliefs.

No doubt, you have heard the basic tenet of workplace humor, "take your job seriously and yourself lightly." When we take ourselves "lightly," invariably others around us begin to feel more comfortable. Self-effacing humor is acceptable in business, but keep your humor relevant to the message at hand and watch for nonverbal cues from your colleagues. Knowing when to add humor in a conversation and when to stay serious takes time and practice. Timing is crucial to the humorous message. Use humor to make a point, and then move on to your next point.

Above all, learn to laugh at yourself, especially when you make mistakes. By learning to take your job seriously but yourself lightly, you will reduce stress and form a more collegial workplace.

Romantic Relationships

Because we are together with people in the same work environment day after day, it is no wonder that we form close personal relationships over time. We work together, laugh together, and socialize with others both inside and outside the organization. We experience trials and tribulations as well as joy and happiness while working on various projects with colleagues. Whether we approve or disapprove, perceptions of impropriety and office romances may result. And the consequences can run the gamut from nasty rumors and charges of sexual harassment to joyous celebrations of marriage.

To help you better understand the implications of office romances, let's take a look at some of the benefits and costs of entering into a dating relationship with an office colleague. Once we have addressed the pros and cons of such romantic involvements, we will provide some guidelines for managing these relationships.

Benefits and Costs of an Office Romance.   When two people are attracted to each other, they tend to feel happy and positive about themselves. Since this feeling of overall happiness is contagious, it creates improved morale in the office. A romantic relationship can be energizing and can stimulate increased productivity, as long as the couple keeps their personal and professional lives separate at the office. Lisa Mainiero (1989), psychologist and author of *Office Romance: Love, Power, and Sex in the Workplace,* says that a creative synergy emerges between two people who are attracted to each other. That synergy can lead to innovation, brainstorming, and the courage to apply new, risky approaches to old problems.

A romantic relationship can also improve teamwork, communication, and cooperation between departments. If the two people who are dating work in different units, their personal relationship can serve as a channel for communication. For example, Peter works in the accounting department of a medium-size corporation. Luna, one of his peers, works in the sales office at the same company. Communication between the two departments was strained before Peter and Luna started dating. Because of their emerging personal relationship, however, Peter and Luna are now able to communicate the concerns of their respective departments, thereby enhancing teamwork and cooperation.

On the other hand, office romances can be emotionally costly for everyone involved. For example, they have the potential to create a fury of controversy, interfere with everyday professional relationships between coworkers, and terminate in negative behavior. In some cases, reputations are tarnished, credibility is lost, and career advancements are aborted or deferred.

If you find yourself getting romantically involved with someone at the office, understand that others will pick up on what is happening. Think about how this relationship will affect not only the two of you, but coworkers as well. Then, ask yourself the following questions before going further:

- Will our credibility and reputation within the organization be altered?
- Will our respective relationships with coworkers, supervisors, and subordinates change or become strained in any way?
- How will our relationship be viewed by our respective supervisors when it's time for annual evaluation?
- Will our new relationship help or hinder our advancement opportunities?

These are questions you need to think about before plunging into an office romance. If you have addressed these questions and elect to proceed, find out about any dating policies that exist in your company. Human resources departments in most businesses have a policy about dating in the workplace, since charges of sexual harassment can emerge. Results of a 1991 survey administered by the Society for Human Resources Management revealed that almost half (47 percent) of the respondents believed that dating can lead to sexual harassment. However, their results also indicated that 70 percent considered office dating acceptable. Generally, human resource professionals agree: Employer interference in personal relationships in the office is inappropriate, unless employee behavior adversely affects office productivity and performance.

If you have conducted this analysis and you still elect to proceed, it's smart to be prepared for what will follow. Harriet Braiker (1988), a clinical psychologist, offers the following suggestions. First and foremost, keep your job performance high. You don't want to give your supervisor any hint that your performance will slack off. Second, be discreet. You want to maintain the respect of your coworkers. Third, establish periodic emotional checkpoints to evaluate your feelings and reactions. It's a good idea to monitor each other's progress in this sensitive temperamental area. Fourth, keep personal matters out of the office. If you have a disagreement, discuss the nature of the problem before or after work hours. Finally, don't feel that you must continue the relationship simply because you have initiated it. If you find that the quality or quantity of your work is declining, be assertive and discuss the problem with your partner.

Sexual Harassment

Tailhook. Clarence Thomas/Anita Hill. Senator Bob Packwood. Bill Clinton/Paula Jones. All of these names share one common element for which they were highlighted in the media: allegations of sexual harassment. Unfortunately, stories of this caliber share the national media spotlight again and again. Yet, many more of these stories are never told.

Sexual harassment isn't about sex at all; it's about power—the abuse of power. In 1994, research by Freada Klein Associates, a workplace-diversity consulting firm in Cambridge, Massachusetts, revealed that 90 percent of Fortune 500 companies have dealt with sexual harassment complaints. More than a third have been sued at least once, and approximately one fourth have been sued multiple times.

Employers spend an average of $200,000 on each valid complaint that is investigated inhouse, whether or not a case ever goes to court. In comparison, by the year 2000, sexual harassment could be the next "asbestos" problem, costing American businesses more than $1 billion in damages (Fisher, 1993).

We would all be happier if everyone in the workplace could live and work harmoniously and share mutual respect for each other. Unfortunately, the world of work is anything but idyllic. With the influx of women in the workplace, sexual harassment on the job is real and increasing. Harassment is a serious matter, not to be taken lightly.

In the workplace, rules about behavior between the sexes have changed dramatically in the last decade. One of the turning points in the battle was the Clarence Thomas/ Anita Hill case. Anita Hill's allegations of sexual harassment by Clarence Thomas, her former employer, focused national attention on the issue. It became extremely clear to American businesses that sexual harassment is an important business issue.

In her book, *Talking From 9 to 5,* Deborah Tannen (1994) points out that "our utterances are exuberant in the sense that others always take away meanings we did not intend or suspect, because they have associations with words and expressions that we do not have" (p. 27). In other words, what you say in a conversation to a person of the opposite sex may be perfectly harmless in your opinion. However, the other person may consider your comments to be a form of sexual harassment. To many, the fear of sexual harassment has placed a damper on working with other people, since conversations may be misunderstood, or words may be taken out of context.

As we approach the 21st century, we must become more sensitive to how others respond to our behavior in the office. The definitions and examples in Box 3.2 provide you with important terminology regarding sexual harassment.

When we think about sexual harassment, we tend to think about men harassing women, but a growing number of cases involve women harassing men. As with males, female supervisors generally harass their male subordinates as a form of power. Such a situation was dramatized in Michael Crichton's best-selling novel, *Disclosure.* In the book, Meredith Johnson, the vice president of a major corporation, summons her male subordinate, Tom Sanders (a former boyfriend) into her office for a strategic planning session. (Not coincidentally, Meredith had been promoted to the position that Tom expected to have.) Meredith proceeds to seduce Tom in her office and then denies the seduction ever happened. Tom feels trapped between the truth and what his coworkers perceive actually happened.

Even though *Disclosure* tells the story of a "fictitious" sexual harassment case, the novel actually was based on a true story. However, the majority of sexual harassment cases continue to be pursued by women against men. Keep in mind that allegations of sexual harassment in the workplace involve substantial risk for the individual as well as the corporation.

BOX 3.2

ToolBox   *Sexual Harassment Definitions*

Sexual harassment: any unwelcome behavior of a sexual nature.

Example: a man whistles at a woman as she walks by, or a woman looks a man up and down as he walks toward her.

Sexual discrimination: when employment decisions are based on an employee's sex, or when an employee is treated differently because of his or her sex.

Example: a female supervisor always asks her male employees to move boxes of computer paper, or a male supervisor always asks his female employees to make coffee and plan office parties.

Subtle sexual harassment: unwelcome behavior of a sexual nature that, if allowed to continue, could create a quid pro quo or hostile work environment for the recipient.

Example: someone in the workplace who is constantly telling sexual jokes or making sexual comments or innuendoes that are unwelcome.

Quid pro quo harassment: when employment decisions regarding an employee are based on that employee's acceptance or rejection of unwelcome sexual behavior.

Example: a supervisor fires an employee because that employee will not go out with him or her.

Hostile work environment: an environment created by unwelcome sexual behavior or behavior directed at an employee because of that person's sex. The behavior in question is seen as offensive, hostile, or intimidating, and adversely affects that employee's ability to do his or her job.

Example: pervasive unwelcome sexual comments or jokes that continue even though the recipient has indicated that those behaviors are unwelcome.

Adapted with permission from S. Anderson (1988). *Intent vs. Impact* [Videotape]. (Available from BNA Communications, Subsidiary of the Bureau of National Affairs, Inc., Rockville, MD.)

Preventing Sexual Harassment.   Sexual harassment negatively affects people in the business world, which, in turn, affects the company bottom line. Educating both men and women is crucial in order to prevent sexual harassment from occurring. Most organizations offer sexual harassment training programs for managers as well as employees.

What should you do if you are suddenly accused of sexual harassment, or if you are sexually harassed? It would be wise to check into policies and procedures that govern the handling of such claims within your company. Most organizations have clear procedures for handling sexual harassment complaints. Some organizations have employee assistance programs coordinated through their human resources departments. Employees can be referred to an external consultant on a confidential basis through the employee assistance program. If someone's behavior is unwelcome, you have told the person repeatedly to stop, and the negative behavior continues, you need to take some form of action based on appropriate counsel.

Perhaps the best way to prevent sexual harassment in the workplace is to establish an atmosphere of mutual respect. Take the time to discover how people like to be treated, and treat them in a respectful manner. Eliminate any behavior that may be perceived as offensive, and you will earn respect and appreciation from your coworkers.

Building Interpersonal Skills in the Workplace

Building strong interpersonal relationships in the workplace is critical to your professional success. Effectively managing your work relationships, both within and outside the organization, optimizes the chance that you will do your job well and also benefits your organization overall.

Three ways that you can build your interpersonal communication skills and develop a strong interpersonal network in the process are networking, mentoring, and increasing your "friendliness" quotient.

The Value of Networking

The old saying, "It's not what you know, but who you know," is even more salient as businesses approach the 21st century. **Networking** is the art of developing and maintaining contacts to assist you in obtaining desired information, support, and advice on a variety of topics. As such, networking has become a staple in American business and industry.

What are the benefits of networking? First, people who network form a solid foundation of relationships on which they can rely when the need arises. For instance, one of the most common benefits of networking is to assist you in a job search. The average person changes jobs six to eight times over the course of his or her lifetime, so maintaining potential job contacts is essential.

Another advantage of networking is building long-term relationships. Networking is a two-way process. For example, if someone helps you with a job contact, perhaps you can return the favor at a later date. Effective networking means mutual assistance and shared respect.

A third advantage of networking is an increased ability to exchange valuable information, knowledge, and resources. For example, you may need information or advice regarding a project on which you currently are working. You know a valuable contact in another department who can help you, so you call that person for information.

As an example of the networking process in action, consider the following scenario. Chalessa, a broadcast journalism major, interned with a local ABC affiliate. Her goal was to work as an assistant producer at CNN in Atlanta. Before she graduated, Chalessa made a list of her former classmates in broadcast journalism. She then contacted the alumni office, and learned that one of her classmates was currently working at CNN. When Chalessa contacted Jim by phone, she found out about an entry-level position available in the production department. Chalessa sent her resume and sample videotaped clips to Jim, who sent them to the person who was involved in the hiring process. As a result of Jim's efforts, Chalessa was selected for an interview and offered the job a week later.

Without networking, Chalessa probably would never have gotten her foot in the door at CNN. She took advantage of the opportunity to network and was successful. Because she feels a great deal of gratitude toward Jim, she will be happy to return the favor in the future.

How do you go about developing networking opportunities? Dee Helfgott (1994), author of several books and articles on the topic, suggests the following six-step process.

Step 1. Begin by developing a strategic marketing plan. Think of the plan as your road map—where you are going and how you are going to get there.

Step 2. Determine "who's who" in your network. You will be surprised at the number of people you already can include. Consider the following: relatives, friends, neighbors, current and former instructors, classmates, former coworkers, alumni, and members of on-campus and off-campus organizations, to name a few.

Step 3. Everywhere you go, carry your #1 networking tool, business cards. When you meet someone and hand her your business card, you are leaving her with permanent information: your name, mailing address and phone number. Even if you are a student, it's a good idea to get business cards made.

Step 4. Practice self-introductions. Before you meet someone you hope to impress, prepare and practice your introduction. Make a list of general topics to discuss before you attend a social or civic event where you know you will meet new people.

Step 5. Network everywhere. Expand your network by meeting as many people as possible. A few places where you can meet people are at the bank, the grocery store, your dentist's office, your church or temple, and meetings of special interest groups in which you are a member.

Step 6. Follow up! Keep in touch with your contacts by sending them written notes, corresponding via Internet and fax, or calling them on the telephone. Send them greeting cards, congratulatory cards, and articles of interest, or just call occasionally to say, "Hello."

In addition to developing interpersonal relationships through networking, you also may do so by cultivating one or more "mentoring relationships" with people who can give you guidance throughout your career.

Mentoring

A **mentor** is a person who is mature, experienced, and successful, and who can provide guidance and support to mentees (or proteges) in the decision-making process. The mentor acts as a role model and gives advice to (usually) younger employees.

The benefits of having mentors are many. First and foremost, the mentor serves as a role model and friend. A mentor can give you public recognition. A mentor also can help you get promoted, change jobs, or gain access to more challenging work assignments.

A mentor can serve as a role model and friend, and can challenge you to do your best work

How do you go about finding a mentor? First, you must keep in mind that, like networking, mentoring relationships represent a two-way street. Both persons must agree on their roles and responsibilities and understand the reasons why they are working together.

Some ways you can go about finding a mentor are:

1. Ask the human resources department if they have a formal mentoring program.
2. Identify people in the organization who share your interests. Conduct an information-gathering interview with them, and let them know you are interested in a mentoring relationship.
3. If you have an interest in asking someone to be your mentor, explain any benefits to him or her that you feel will accrue from the relationship. Additionally, tell him or her why you have made the choice you have made. In most cases, you will be selecting mentors because they have a good track record and success in their jobs, and are easily accessible.
4. Let your potential mentor know you are interested in learning as much as you can about the organization.
5. Remember: You can have more than one mentor at a given time, and you can change mentors throughout your career development. In turn, you may become a mentor yourself someday, which is extremely rewarding.

And Then, There's Old-Fashioned Friendliness. . . .

There is one important element in the workplace over which you have complete control, and which carries a lot of weight with coworkers, supervisors, and subordinates. It is something you can do without even thinking, but which everyone in the office appreciates. We call this behavior old-fashioned friendliness.

In this hectic, turn-of-the-century world filled with thousands of possibilities that technology has to offer, we sometimes forget that business and personal relationships go hand in hand. "Friendliness" in the workplace doesn't mean being others' best friend, lending them money, or letting them do whatever they want to do. Friendliness

---

BOX 3.3

How Do You Measure Up? | *Your Friendliness Quotient*

Directions: To gauge your current "friendliness quotient," on a scale of 1 to 10 (1=low, 10=high), how would you rate the extent to which you are consistent in doing the following:

_____ Greeting your colleagues with "good morning" or "good afternoon"?

_____ Saying please and thank you?

_____ Making sure you are on time for every appointment?

_____ Answering telephone and E-mail messages promptly?

_____ Apologizing when you are late or have to interrupt a meeting?

_____ Not interrupting people when they are speaking?

_____ Smiling and exhibiting pleasant facial expressions?

---

is doing and saying considerate things, being polite and courteous toward others, and showing respect for everyone with whom you work. How friendly are you with other people in your workplace? Box 3.3 can help you gauge your friendliness quotient.

By exhibiting these simple communication behaviors, you show people that you care about and respect them. Friendly people are nice to be around, they smile a lot, they are easy to talk to, and they are polite and thoughtful of others. All of us like to be around friendly people. By learning to maintain more friendly relationships with your coworkers, you will develop and sustain more lasting and satisfying relationships in the workplace.

Case Study

Coaching and Counseling Employees at Marriott International

Steven Siler, Assistant Human Resources Director

As a manager for Marriott International at corporate headquarters, Donna supervises a staff that includes two males and five females. The majority of her staff represents countries located in Latin America and Europe. The primary responsibility of Donna's work group is to assist clients in completing a federal tax credit program. These clients consist of internal and external businesses. The majority of the interaction between her clients is via telephone and, thus, requires strong interpersonal and phone skills.

Donna's work group, when combined with another work group, comprises a department within Marriott managed by Walter Price. Walter has been with the company for fourteen years and has worked his way up the corporate ladder—first as a temporary worker, then as an administrative assistant, a manager, and a director. Throughout his time with Marriott, Walter has worked with several executives, including Mr. Marriott, and has seen the company grow from a small company to an organization with revenues exceeding four billion dollars. In the short time that Donna has worked with Walter, she has identified his "hot buttons," such as arriving late to work, creating conflicts with coworkers, and wasting work time. One of the things Donna has greatly enjoyed is the complete support Walter has given her.

During the eighteen months before Donna's arrival at Marriott, her work group had two supervisors. One of the supervisors, Paul, managed the group since its inception and was promoted within the company. Mary, the manager who replaced Paul, worked her way through the work group and was managing for the first time. It wasn't long before Mary accepted a job outside of Marriott and left. During this transition, Walter discovered some serious operational problems: Program objectives had not been met, bad work habits had ensued, and morale was low in the group. Donna's first day at Marriott was two weeks after Mary's departure.

The positions within Donna's work group are entry level, with a high turnover rate. Two members of the staff have worked in the group for more than four years, three for approximately one year, and the remaining two for the four to twelve weeks prior to Donna's hiring.

After completing her training and a brief indoctrination period, Donna began making changes in the operations performed by the work group. The changes were met with resistance but, in time, productivity and morale improved. The changes she made ranged from very minor in nature (new scheduling procedures) to major (revamping job duties for staff members). In essence, Donna reorganized the work group, created new positions, and added responsibilities for all staff members.

Recently, during a one-week period, Donna was approached by three staff members: Marie, Jose, and Anna. On each occasion, she was presented with a variety of complaints. Marie was concerned because, when she was hired, promises were made and have yet to be met. (She is currently working in an administrative capacity, coordinating communications between Donna's work group and end users. This is a paper-intensive task that requires strong organizational skills.) Marie indicated that, during her interview, she was promised that she would train and manage end users. After speaking with Walter, Donna learned that these responsibilities were discussed as possibilities in the future. Walter also assured Donna that Marie had been told that all of her job responsibilities would be reviewed once the new manager (Donna) was hired.

Jose and Anna's job responsibilities focus on interaction with customers and completing the necessary paperwork and documentation for the tax credit. This is a tedious and repetitive job that requires strong communication skills. Jose's concerns dealt with all of the changes that Donna has implemented and Donna's expectations for the work group. He feels her expectations are unrealistic. For the last several years, there have been no written or stated expectations for the work group, and Jose feels that everything works—so why make changes now? Anna voiced many of the same concerns as Jose, but presents more of a challenge because she is not meeting expectations for the work group. She is disruptive, arrives late to work, takes extended breaks, and flagrantly misuses time. Additionally, her productivity has diminished below acceptable levels.

Questions

1. What should Donna do with her work group to help address the concerns that are being brought to her?
2. From what you have read, what might you have done differently as a manager of this work group?
3. How would you take care of the individual problems presented by Marie, Jose, and Anna?

Summary

Building quality interpersonal relationships with coworkers, supervisors, and subordinates is extremely important to your relational life. To do so requires understanding the differences between formal and informal communication, and the various patterns of communication that can result. Additionally, communication with our coworkers can be more efficient and effective if we know what style of communication they prefer. Each style has its own strengths and weaknesses depending on the situation. Our communication climate and the care and feeding of our interpersonal networks have a profound impression on our relational lives.

Being keenly aware of office politics and how to play the game is of utmost importance for survival in the 21st century workplace. Taking time to weave humor into your daily activities relieves stress and adds to your overall job satisfaction. Romantic relationships and sexual harassment matters are serious issues not to be taken lightly. Make sure you know the do's and taboos of dating relationships and the policies and procedures regarding sexual harassment that govern your organization.

Building social skills through networking, mentoring, and old-fashioned friendliness can only assist you in your career development. Carefully monitoring yourself on how well you are doing in these three departments is also critical if you want to optimize your relational life and nurture positive interpersonal relationships with others.

The person who will succeed in the 21st century workforce will be adaptable and flexible to the changing needs of the organization. By incorporating some of the interpersonal communication skills you learned in this chapter, you will be well on your way to establishing successful working relationships within your workplace.

Knowledge Check

Key Concepts and Terms

interpersonal communication

interpersonal networks

formal communication

downward communication

upward communication

horizontal communication

informal communication

vertical approach

horizontal organization

virtual company
communication style
driving style
expressive style
amiable style
analytical style
communication climate
open communication
closed communication
defensive communication

supportive communication
evaluation
description
control
problem orientation
strategies
spontaneity
neutrality
empathy
superior attitude

equality
certainty
provisional behavior
sexual harassment
sexual discrimination
subtle sexual harassment
quid pro quo harassment
hostile work environment
networking
mentor

Putting It All Together

1. Describe three different types of formal communication.

2. What is the difference between the traditional vertical hierarchy and the horizontal approach?

3. What are the advantages and disadvantages of the driving, expressive, amiable, and analytical communication styles?

4. How does the communication climate affect your relationships in the office?

5. Distinguish between Gibb's defensive and supportive behaviors.

6. How can learning about office politics assist you in your job?

7. What are the pros and cons of romantic relationships in the workplace?

8. Briefly describe the concepts of networking and mentoring.

9. Why should you be knowledgeable about sexual harassment?

References

Anderson, S. (1988). *Intent vs. Impact* [Videotape]. Rockville, MD: BNA Communications (Subsidiary of the Bureau of National Affairs, Inc.) [Producer and Distributor].

Bolton, R., and Bolton, D. G. (1984). *Social Style/Management Style: Developing Productive Work Relationships.* New York: Amacom.

Braiker, H. (1988, November). The etiquette of love. *Working Woman, 13*(11), 148–151.

Caudron, S. (1992, June). Humor is healthy in the workplace. *Personnel Journal, 71*(6), 63–68.

Crichton, M. (1994). *Disclosure.* New York: Knopf.

Chung, R. K. (1994, May). The horizontal organization: Breaking down functional silos. *Business Credit,* 21–24.

Coates, J. F., and Jarratt, J. (1994, Spring). Workplace creativity. *Employment Relations Today,* 11–22.

DeBats, D. (1990). The life regard index: Reliability and validity. *Psychological Reports, 67*(1), 27–34.

Dubrin, A. (1990). *Winning office politics.* Englewood Cliffs, NJ: Prentice-Hall.

Fisher, A. (1993, August). Sexual harassment: What to do. *Fortune, 128*(4), 84–88.

Gibb, J. R. (1961, September). Defensive communication. *Journal of Communication, 11*(3), 141.

Hamilton, C., & Parker, C. (1993). *Communicating for results* (4th ed.). Belmont, CA: Wadsworth.

Helfgott, D. (1994). Take 6 steps to networking success. In *Planning job choices: 1994* (pp. 61–64). Bethlehem, PA: College Placement Council.

Levering, R., & Moskowitz, M. (1994). *The 100 best companies to work for in America.* New York: Plume.

Long, P. (1987). Laugh and be well? *Psychology Today, 21*(10), 28–29.

Mainiero, L. (1989). *Office romance: Love, power, and sex in the workplace.* New York: Rawson Associates.

Merrill, D. W. and Reid, R. H. (1980). *Personal styles and effective performance.* Radnor, PA: Chilton Book Co.

Pearce, W. B. (1994). *Interpersonal communication: Making social worlds.* New York: HarperCollins.

Schein, E. (1985). *Organizational culture and leadership.* San Francisco: Jossey-Bass.

Swift, W. B., and Swift, A. T. (1994, March). Humor experts jazz up the workplace. *HR Magazine, 39*(3), 72–75.

Tannen, D. (1994). *Talking from 9 to 5.* New York: William Morrow & Co.

Wilde, L. (1988). Beat stress: Stress humor. *Association Management, 40*(7), 130.

4

Successful Communication in Groups and Teams

After studying this chapter, you should be able to

- Identify and distinguish among various types of small groups and teams.

- Develop a better understanding of formal and informal groups.

- Create an awareness of the "contingency model" of small group communication.

- Discover problem-solving techniques and recognize appropriate situations in which to use them.

- Understand how to work effectively in teams both as an individual and as a group member.

- Manage and learn how to make effective contributions in meetings.

Through its drive for perfection, Motorola has become the ultimate team company. As one of the world's leading makers of electronic equipment such as pagers, cellular telephones, and semiconductors, Motorola's teams reduced product defects from 6,000 per million in 1987 to 20 per million in 1994. Their fundamental objective as a company is "total customer satisfaction" (Weiland, 1994, p. 48).

To meet the company's objective, Motorola holds Total Customer Satisfaction (TCS) team competitions in order to solve problems company-wide. Teams meet regularly during the week, and often at nights and on weekends. The competition "fortifies the participants with the realization that they are a part of something bigger than their team" (Weiland, 1994, p. 55). It also affords team members a chance to grow both personally and professionally and to be recognized by the highest level of management at Motorola. Employees attend training sessions on team building, leadership, and handling difficult people. Such training equips them with the tools they need to take action. The entire team-building process (i.e., goal-setting, skills training, encouragement from teammates, empowerment, group effort, and coaching/advice from peers and supervisors) produces confident, motivated employees.

Teamwork is a concept that is familiar to everyone. You learned about its value and importance when you were a kid. What you may not be aware of, however, is the increasing role that employee involvement and teamwork play in companies of all shapes and sizes. Teams are only one example of the many small groups you will experience in your relational life. However, in order to understand how teams function effectively, a working knowledge of small group communication is useful.

In this chapter, we will explore the many types of small groups, including teams, that are necessary for organizations to conduct business effectively. You also will learn more about problem-solving techniques used in organizations and discover how to conduct effective meetings.

Using groups of people to become better, faster, and smarter than the competition has become the goal of organizations on the move. The goal of this chapter is to help you become a more competent small group communicator, whether you are striving to be a more effective employee or an organizational leader of tomorrow.

The Elements of Successful Group Communication

Working in a group can be rewarding, exciting, and mutually beneficial to everyone. Or it can be a painful and demanding experience, depending on the relationships among the people in the group. Ideally, group life should provide a positive experience for all concerned.

A Definition of "Small Group"

Let's begin by defining a small group. A **small group** is a collection of three or more individuals who interact with one another to achieve a common task or goal. As such, groups come in many different forms: automobile racing teams, arts committees, and political task forces, to name just a few. No matter how they are constituted, no matter how long they exist, the common denominator is a shared purpose or goal.

There are many advantages and disadvantages of working in small groups. For example, consider the pros and cons of working with a group of volunteers to plan an annual benefit for troubled kids in an inner-city neighborhood. Let's begin with the advantages of small group communication in such a scenario.

Advantages of Groups

Opportunity for Affiliation with Others. Being a member of a group can be satisfying and rewarding, and can provide a sense of camaraderie between you and your peers. Consider, for example, the satisfaction our group of volunteers would experience

If two heads are better than one, then think about how much a small group can achieve together.

if they were planning and executing a celebrity beach volleyball tournament to benefit inner-city kids on the streets of Los Angeles. In order to choose a location for the tournament (e.g., Venice Beach, California) and to develop the list of celebrities to be invited, everyone might meet for dinner at Peter's house. To get a jump on planning the benefit, each person might be responsible for contacting at least three talent agencies prior to the meeting. As they share information over dinner, the group might learn they have ten major talent agencies interested in supporting the project. What enthusiasm and excitement would result!

The feelings of warmth, comradery, and affiliation that might follow such a meeting also emerge every day for small groups in the organizational setting. To illustrate, say you are one of 16 writers working for an advertising firm in Boston. The president of the firm decides to initiate a little friendly, in-house competition by establishing four teams to compete for "Advertising Slogan of the Year." After much hard work, your group is declared the winner and gets treated to lunch on the company. You have a feeling of accomplishment, satisfaction, and closeness with your colleagues by participating actively in your group. As a side benefit, your group gains recognition in the eyes of the entire company for creating the winning slogan.

Better Understanding of Self.   Other people see you differently than you see yourself. As a functioning member of any group, you can make each interaction a personal learning experience by constantly monitoring feedback from other group members. For example, say you were a member of our fictional volunteer group that helped raise money for disadvantaged kids in Los Angeles. Through active participation in the group, you might (1) gauge your effectiveness as a group member, (2) understand parts of your hidden self that you didn't know existed, and (3) learn more about your leadership ability. On the flip side, you might determine that you need to change your behavior in some way in order to participate more effectively in group interactions. For instance, you might note that you have a bad habit of interrupting others. Through greater self-understanding, you can correct this and other undesirable group behavior on your part.

> It is amazing how much people can get done if they do not worry about who gets the credit.
>
> —*Sandra Swinney*

Greater Problem-Solving Ability.   You have heard the old adage, "Two heads are better than one." Nowhere is this more true than in group problem solving. Individual group members have different contributions to make, based on differences in background and experience. Not only do groups generate more viable solutions during brainstorming sessions, but the quality of those solutions is generally higher. Additionally, groups are better able to analyze a problem at the outset, due to an increase in collective intelligence and the breadth of information that is available about the problem or situation.

Disadvantages of Groups

Within every group, potential problems exist. Identifying the obstacles associated with group communication can help you understand and better cope with them. Consider the following problems.

Group Activities May Encourage "Social Loafing."   Surely you have been part of a group in which one or two members decide to take a "free ride" and let all the other group members do the work. This well-known small group phenomenon has been labeled by Mosley Pietri, & Megginson (1996) as **social loafing.** A danger of being part of any group is knowing that other group members will contribute good ideas and believing that we can get by without doing our part. Or other times, we may feel that our opinion doesn't count, or that we simply don't have any good ideas to contribute. Feelings such as these form the basis for social loafing and should be avoided at all costs. To illustrate, what would have happened at our volunteer's dinner to plan the volleyball tournament if only half of the people had made phone calls to talent agencies in advance? The entire outcome of the dinner would have been altered.

One means of overcoming social loafing is to encourage each member to become part of the solution and help them realize that everyone's input is needed. Another is to assign each group member specific responsibilities and to encourage every member of the group to attend all meetings.

One Person May Dominate the Discussion.   We have all been in groups in which one person attempts to dominate the discussion—you know, the "floor hogger" who never allows other group members to get a word in edgewise. The outcome of this particular problem is less effective group communication and reduced problem-solving ability. An incessant talker deters others from making effective contributions toward the group's goal.

To overcome this problem, try using the dominant person's enthusiasm for the group's advantage. For example, assign the talkative member a special research project. If this solution doesn't work, one or two members of the group might quietly confront the person during a break. If all else fails, the official group leader (or a respected group member) may need to confront the individual openly during the meeting. In the latter two instances, confrontation should be approached with care and diplomacy, but with firmness. Remember: The goal is not to alienate any group member, but to optimize his or her best input.

"I'd Rather Do It Myself" Syndrome.   Let's face it. At times, groups do take more time than individuals working alone to define, analyze, and solve a problem. Simply finding a place and time for all group members to meet sometimes presents a major problem in itself. For our volunteer group, letting Michael, a talent agent himself, make all the calls would have been a viable alternative. However, doing so would have taken all of the fun out of the project and possibly would have limited the outcome in scope.

One way to overcome the time problem and eliminate "I'd rather do it myself" syndrome is to delegate specific tasks to individual group members to be completed by an assigned date, which gives each group member some autonomy. This way, individuals can work on their own and report back to the group collectively. More tasks are accomplished, and in-group work time is optimized.

Pressure from Other Group Members to Conform.   Most people do not enjoy conflict; in fact, they generally try to avoid it. In groups, conflict avoidance may lead to **groupthink,** a term coined by social psychologist Irving Janis (1982). Groupthink is " . . . a mode of thinking that people engage in when they are deeply involved in a cohesive in-group, when members' strivings for unanimity override their motivation to realistically appraise alternative courses of action" (Janis, 1982, p. 9).

How can you determine if your group is suffering from groupthink? Box 4.1 on page 94 provides a comprehensive list of symptoms developed by Dalmar Fisher (1993) in a synthesis of Irving Janis's work.

Say you are in our volunteer group in Los Angeles, hear too much agreement too quickly, and observe that Jane and Pam are a little too quiet. Janis (1982) offered the following four suggestions for overcoming these symptoms of groupthink. First, have each member of the group act as a "critical evaluator," and ask constructive questions of all other members throughout the decision-making process. For instance, Toni might ask Jane, "How do you feel about holding the volleyball tournament in Venice Beach? You were telling us earlier about how wonderful Laguna Beach is." In short, each group member should take the opportunity to ask questions of other group members.

Second, invite interested third parties who may differ in opinion to participate in the group's interactions. For example, our volunteer group might ask board members from three different charities that will benefit from the fund-raiser to attend a meeting and voice their opinions. Sometimes group members are too close to a situation to effectively analyze the real problem. An outside objective opinion may lend a new perspective.

Third, the group leader should attempt to keep personal opinions to herself to avoid unduly influencing other group members. Sometimes the group leader can impose her opinions on other group members simply because of the leadership role she assumes.

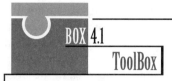

BOX 4.1

ToolBox   *Symptoms of Groupthink*

Whenever you take part in group decision making, be on the lookout for symptoms of groupthink. If one or more of the following symptoms appear, practice the suggestions we discuss.

Illusion of Invulnerability	Members feel they are beyond criticism and incapable of making mistakes.
Tendency to Rationalize	Members ignore contradictory data and warnings. Alternatives are not considered thoroughly.
Sense of Morality	Members feel their actions are inherently right from an ethical standpoint.
Stereotyping	Members view outsiders unrealistically, typically seeing them as inept or evil.
Pressure toward Conformity	The group exerts pressure [on] any member who argues against its viewpoints or decisions.
Self-censorship	Members do not express their questions and reservations to the group.
Illusion of Unanimity	Members accept decisions prematurely, assuming that silence implies consent.
Mindguarding	Members buffer the group from exposure to information that might disagree with the group's beliefs and positions.

Source: D. Fisher. (1993). *Communication in Organizations,* 2nd ed. (Minneapolis: West Publishing Company), p. 339.

Fourth, before a final solution is implemented, ask group members to discuss, one last time, any doubts they may have about the solution. This discussion will give each person time to make additional comments or suggestions before implementing an irreversible decision.

Types of Small Groups Operating in an Organization

Small groups come in a variety of shapes and sizes, depending on the organization. However, they generally may be placed into one of two major categories: formal and informal groups. **Formal groups** are those that are established by someone within the managerial ranks of a company. They usually are formed to accomplish either short-term or long-term objectives. **Informal groups** emerge as a result of social interaction, or as a spin-off from the formal group. Informal group members have common interests, but the group itself is more social in nature. For example, certain people who work together may want to socialize after work at someone's home or at a local restaurant. Another group of individuals may decide to form a volleyball team or join a bowling league as an extension of their work-related friendship. Since both types of groups are integral to the success of any organization, let's take a closer look at each.

Formal Groups

Perhaps, the most common formal group that exists in a company or business is a **department,** or a group of individuals who are bound together by a common goal or purpose (e.g., accounting, sales, or production). Figure 4.1 provides an organizational chart of the formal departmental groups that might comprise the fictional Debleen Company.

Committees are another type of formal group, and are comprised of people who meet on a regular basis to compile information and make reports to an individual (e.g., vice president) or larger group (e.g., the board of directors). Perhaps, you serve on one or more committees in your college or community.

Another formal group in which you may participate is a **task force,** or a group that is designed to bring people together to work on a common problem. To achieve its goal, a task force investigates the nature of the problem or issue, gathers pertinent information, and reports back to a committee or department head. Task forces usually meet a number of times until the issue in question is resolved. Consider the following example.

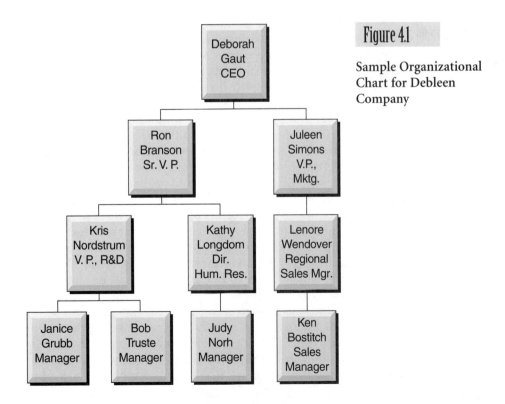

Figure 4.1

Sample Organizational Chart for Debleen Company

A newspaper was faced with an interesting dilemma: negative reaction by employees and advertisers to the name of one of the newspaper's departments. While conducting one of their annual communication audits, the company's marketing department discovered that the name, "Department of Accounting," was somewhat intimidating to people who think of accounting types as "bean counters" or "watchdogs." To address this concern, the publisher formed a task force to change the name of the department to a more approachable and appealing title. After meeting a couple of times, the task force reached a consensus: Change the name of the unit from "Department of Accounting" to "Business Department." This term was considered to be more "user-friendly" and accurate when it came to the nature of the department's work. It satisfied the employees within the organization as well as advertisers and clients. In this case, the task force met only twice to resolve the issue before reporting back to the publisher with the results. Sometimes task forces meet for weeks or months to address an issue or solve a problem.

Teams constitute a fourth type of formal group that operates within the organizational setting. Generally, teams take one of four forms, depending on the level of employee involvement: intrafunctional, problem-solving, cross-functional, and self-directed teams (Zenger, Musselwhite, Hurson, & Perrin, 1994).

Intrafunctional teams are comprised of employees within a department or unit, all of whom assume added responsibility to solve problems and make improvements in the unit overall. For example, the vice president of an international association works with his new education and marketing directors on the development of a new "hot topics" seminar series. In turn, the education and marketing directors involve their respective units in brainstorming and problem solving about the new program. As soon as the latter two intrafunctional teams are able to assume complete responsibility for the series, the vice president is freed up to complete his own duties and functions, and the two units play the primary role in day-to-day decisions about the program.

> The nice thing about teamwork is that you always have others on your side.
>
> —*Margaret Carty*

Problem-solving teams also play a vital role in companies and businesses. Generally appointed on an ad hoc basis, these temporary teams are created to address specific problems or possible opportunities. For example, the president of a small independent bank learns that an adjacent lot is for sale. Because the bank's customer base is growing at an astronomical rate, she appoints a team of employees to complete a feasibility study regarding possible expansion, and to work with the bank's original architect to develop a set of new plans.

Cross-functional teams are generally permanent in nature and are established "to monitor, standardize, and improve work processes that cut across different parts of [an] organization" (Zenger, Musselwhite, Hurson, & Perrin, 1994, p. 12). Cross-functional teams generally represent different departments or units and meet regularly to address shared problems. Consider, for example, Ben & Jerry's "Green Team," an ongoing, cross-functional team in operation at the innovative ice cream company's plant in Vermont. To ensure that the company meets its own high environmental standards, the team meets twice a month and sponsors such activities as a Green Flea Market (profits from which are contributed to the Environmental Federation), Merry Mulching (a Christmas tree recycling project), reforestation projects, and a column entitled "The

Daily Planet," which appears in the company's monthly newsletter (Levering & Moskowitz, 1994, p. 48).

The fourth basic form is **self-directed teams.** Self-directed teams are generally intact work groups that handle most of their daily operational issues with minimal supervision. To give you an example of a self-directed team in operation, let's look at Corning, Inc. In 1989, Corning reopened a plant in Blacksburg, Virginia, with an emphasis on hiring people for multiskilled, team-based production. The workforce has been trained extensively and formed into teams that work three or four 12-hour shifts per week. The teams make decisions, discipline fellow workers, rotate jobs, conduct quality reviews, and implement productivity improvements. In essence, they manage themselves and work as though the company were their own (Smith & Green, 1993).

Informal Groups

Informal groups grow out of our human needs for social interaction, friendship, and a sense of belonging. Most informal groups are loosely structured because members choose to become part of the group, rather than being appointed by management. Informal groups usually have common interests such as volleyball, softball, aerobics, or socializing outside the business environment.

Both outside and inside the workplace, informal groups play a valuable role in meeting the social needs of group members. Since informal groups are made up of voluntary members who share something in common, they get to know each other in a more casual environment, which promotes cohesiveness in the formal work environment.

Informal groups also create excellent networking opportunities. For example, many members of corporate America play golf as a favorite pastime. Others get together for a brown-bag lunch on a weekly basis. While playing golf or lunching, they may discuss business, politics, upcoming weekends, vacations, families, or whatever else they share in common. When they are back in the office and a problem or issue arises, members of these informal groups may turn to each other for advice or information. Informal groups are subject to change in membership from time to time. However, such change promotes interesting conversation and adds a new dimension to the group's life.

Demographic Variables That Affect Group Life

A number of variables affect group productivity and satisfaction, which in turn impact attitudes toward "group life." Among the demographic variables most often identified are: educational background, past work experience, expectations, time constraints, gender, age, task- versus people-orientation, and culture. As we briefly discuss the impact of each of these variables, conduct a self-analysis to discover which components most often affect your personal satisfaction and productivity in groups.

Each group member brings with him or her a specific educational background. In fact, one of the first questions we often ask of someone who is new in a group is, "Where did you go to school?" Two of the primary reasons we are attracted to others who share our educational experience are reduced interpersonal uncertainty and greater ease of communication. Business majors tend to associate with other business majors because they can "talk the same talk." Social science majors tend to group with members of similar education because they share common concerns.

Employment background is another important factor in determining group productivity and satisfaction. Additionally, this variable often determines the "pecking order" of members within a given group. Because we rightly or wrongly associate an individual's group communication skills with the "status" of his or her profession, we tend to elevate members of "high status" (or white-collar) occupations to leadership roles. Mixed occupational groups (i.e., groups comprised of both white-collar and blue-collar workers) may experience a more complex decision-making process, depending on the range of occupational status represented by group members.

Each group member has a certain set of expectations for himself or herself as a member and for the group overall. For example, if you are assigned a group project in a college course, one person may want to get an "A" out of the group project, while another is happy to just get by with a "C." Thus, the overall motivation level of the group, as well as the commitment of each group member, will be affected by individual members' expectations.

In this day and age of continuous activity and involvement with so many groups (i.e., work, family, social, school, and religious), finding the time to commit to any one group is difficult. Because we tend to prioritize activities based on their personal value to us, our priorities may be inconsistent with those of other group members.

On the other hand, we may want to devote more time than will other members to see a project through. Discussing the amount of time that each person wants to spend on accomplishing group goals is advisable early in the formation stage of the group. Doing so will save time, energy, and possibly hurt feelings as the group progresses.

Does it matter if a group's composition is of the same sex or mixed sex? The results of studies conducted on gender behavior in small groups say, "Yes!" When women and men work together in groups, men are more instrumental and tend to talk more than women, while women are more expressive in what they say (Pearson, Turner, & Todd-Mancillas, 1991). In general, men tend to be dominant, goal-oriented, competitive, and aggressive. Women tend to be submissive, less inclined to make risky decisions, more cooperative, and more concerned with including all group members (Pearson, et al., p. 222). Research indicates that both men and women are competent and effective in small-group settings. Think about the make up of groups in which you are a member. Does it matter if the group includes males, females, or both? Does it make a difference in the outcomes associated with your groups' goals? You will learn more about these and other gender issues in Chapter 5.

Members from groups representing a variety of ages tend to identify with people of their own age. Depending on the nature of the group, older people are viewed as more knowledgeable than younger people. Younger group members sometimes need nurturing and recognition for their contributions to the group, thereby acting out a parent/child relationship. In this type of environment, it is difficult for individuals to maintain equality among group members.

In some cases, younger people may feel intimidated by older people, due to the increase in years of experience. Groups that include a mixed age range of members may find it more difficult to have satisfying social conversations that encourage group cohesiveness.

Does a group function more effectively if all of its members are task-oriented? The answer to this question lies in the nature of the task and the goals of group members. If one purpose of the group is to provide a sense of belonging or encourage expressions of emotion, then people-oriented personalities would function better. For example, if you were part of a support group for an alcohol and drug abuse recovery program, a people-orientation would be needed.

If a group has a deadline for accomplishing a task, the more task-oriented persons in the group, the better (Napier & Gershenfeld, 1993, p. 202). In either event, the task- versus people-orientation of group members plays a significant role in group cohesion—again, depending on the needs and goals of the group.

Like individuals having similar educational experiences, people from similar ethnic backgrounds tend to identify more closely with one another. As a result, working in a mixed ethnic group may be difficult if group members take little time to get to know one another, or to understand one another's beliefs, attitudes, and values. The keys to successful cross-cultural communication in groups are getting to know one another better and treating each other equally. Individuals who have the ability to work effectively in ethnically or culturally diverse groups not only experience a sense of accomplishment, but also are vital to the success of any organization.

The Group Decision-Making Process

Whether you are a member of Pennzoil's famous racing team, a cross-functional team at Dow Chemical, or a group that is canvassing votes in the next presidential election, effective decision making is the name of the game. Small-group experts Marshall Scott Poole, David Seibold, and Robert McPhee argue that how a group operates depends on a number of contingencies, including the group's "objective task characteristics," "group-task characteristics," and "group structural characteristics." Additionally, they believe these characteristics lead to different types of "talk" among group members, thereby leading groups along different decision-making paths (Poole, 1983; Poole, Seibold, & McPhee, 1985). After reviewing various studies by Poole and his associates, Littlejohn (1992) synthesized Poole's "contingency theory" in the following way.

The **objective task characteristics** of a group include the nature of the problem to be solved; the kind of expertise that is required to solve the problem; the extent to which solutions to the problem are predetermined; the possible impacts of the problem; and whether the ultimate solution is a "one-shot response" or has broader policy implications.

Group task characteristics include the extent to which a group has prior experience with the problem, the urgency of the problem, and whether innovation and creativity, rather than a standard course of action, are required to solve the problem. **Group structural characteristics** include the cohesiveness, distribution of power, history, and size of the group.

Depending on a group's characteristics, or "contingencies," certain types of talk will ensue. In turn, through talk, one of three major decision-making paths will emerge. A **standard unitary** decision-making path involves the analysis and definition of a problem, followed by the generation of possible solutions. In contrast, the **complex cyclic** path is one in which a group goes back and forth several times between defining the problem and generating solutions. Third, a group may go straight to the generation of solutions, with little or no analysis of the problem. Poole and Roth (1989) labeled this type of decision making **solution-oriented.**

No matter what decision-making path is followed (i.e, standard unitary, complex cyclic, or solution-oriented), a group will move along three interwoven tracks, each of which is comprised of various activities. **Task-process activities** include introducing subjects, analyzing problems, designing and evaluating solutions, and going off on tangents. **Relational activities** are actions that affect interpersonal relationships in the group, such as socializing, managing conflict, and creating harmony within the group. **Topic-focus activities** involve talk about substantive issues and concerns of the group over time.

According to Fisher and Ellis (1990), these three tracks, or group activities, " . . . can change at different rates and at different times" (p. 165). The point in the flow of communication when one track ends and another begins is called a **breakpoint.** Examples of breakpoints include " . . . delays, disruptions, adjournments, topic shifts, and planning periods" (p. 165).

By interweaving various group characteristics and activities, different decision-making paths will result. For example, in a weekly staff meeting of a small manufacturing firm, Amy brings up a problem that she has encountered with an outside vendor. As the group discusses the problem (task-process activity), Amy begins to show signs of frustration. Her supervisor, Brad, senses how upset Amy is, and tells her not to worry; the group will find a solution to the problem (relational activity). From there, the group begins to discuss other issues and concerns about the project (topic-focus activity). Brad makes a list of all the problems on a flip chart, and addresses each problem one by one (task-process activity). At first glance, the interwoven nature of these three group activities appears to be leading the group down the complex cyclic decision-making path. Had the group stayed with a discussion of Amy's original problem, then followed with a discussion of possible solutions, their talk would have constituted the standard unitary decision-making path . . . and so on.

As we discussed in our model of communication presented in Chapter 1, talk (i.e., communication) indeed creates shared meaning. In the group scenario we just described, talk created the type of decision-making path that the group ultimately followed.

> [Group] members' strategic choices, mediated by and realized in group interaction, give the group direction and lead to whatever decision results.
>
> —*Poole & Roth (1989, p. 588)*

Tools for Effective Problem Solving

Every formal group has a purpose, establishes goals, and works within a time frame. Likewise, they all encounter conflicts and have problems to solve. The decision-making process presented in the previous section describes three typical paths that groups take to solve problems. However, a number of specific problem-solving tools have been developed by researchers to assist groups in staying on track. Two of the most effective problem-solving tools are the single-question procedure and the reflective thinking process.

The Single-Question Procedure

The **single-question procedure** is appropriate if your group is small, the task is simple, the group is meeting only once, or a temporary decision is needed. Using the technique is a simple process that involves answering one primary question: "What is the single question to which the answer accomplishes the group's purpose?"

Small-group researcher Carl Larson (1969) suggests answering four related questions in order to completely implement the single-question procedure:

1. What subquestions must be answered before we can answer the single question we have formulated?
2. Do we have sufficient information to answer confidently the subquestions? If yes, then answer them. If no, continue below.
3. What are the most reasonable answers to the subquestions?
4. Assuming that our answers to the subquestions are correct, what is the best solution to the problem?

To illustrate how the single-question procedure works, let's take a problem you might be assigned to solve in your company. On Monday, you and four other employees, representing five different departments, are asked by your manager to plan a get-together after work on Friday. He wants everyone to meet socially before the group begins work on a major project. Your group meets one time and asks each other the "single question," "At what location can we meet without requiring anyone to drive, and what time should the get-together begin?" You choose everyone's favorite "watering hole" located three blocks from the office, set the time at 5:30 P.M. (30 minutes after everyone gets off work), and ask Rick to make reservations for a private meeting room. This was a simple task that could be accomplished easily in a single meeting. As such, there was little reason to proceed through the six steps associated with the reflective thinking process, discussed in the following section.

The Reflective Thinking Process

First developed by John Dewey in 1933 and presented in his classic book, *How We Think,* **reflective thinking** is a clear, concise, step-by-step, problem-solving procedure that is easy to follow. Although a number of respected writers have attempted to expand and improve Dewey's original process, common to all are the following six basic problem-solving steps.

Define the Problem. Establishing agreement on the general nature of the problem is the first step in the reflective thinking process. Each person in the group should clarify the problem as he or she understands it, and then the group as a whole should establish some form of initial agreement. By having individuals and the group overall identify the problem, the group will gain cohesiveness and understanding at the beginning of the discussion. Sometimes stating the problem in terms of a question will assist group members in more clearly establishing its parameters.

Research and Analyze the Problem. During the second phase of reflective thinking, the group attempts to gather specific information regarding the nature and scope of

By understanding the nature and scope of a problem, a group member can better contribute to the problem-solving process. Conducting research on the Internet is an excellent way to access information globally.

the problem. Information can be obtained from the library, personal interviews, the organization's records, or any other related source. By conducting a thorough analysis of the problem and collecting factual information, group members are better able to discuss the problem in an intelligent manner.

Establish Criteria for Evaluating Alternatives.   Once the nature and scope of the problem have been established, the group should identify and agree on the criteria by which solutions will be evaluated. Establishing criteria for evaluating solutions at the outset provides a framework for later decision making. Additionally, doing so maximizes objectivity and makes decision making easier. To identify the criteria by which solutions will be evaluated, the group should create a checklist of items against which all alternatives will be measured. For example, if you and your teammates were attempting to agree on a place to meet for a working lunch, you might informally come up with the following criteria:

■ must be inexpensive (Amy has $10 to her name);

■ must be close to the office (Donna has to get back by 1:00); and,

■ absolutely must serve something other than junk food (David's been living on hamburgers and fish 'n' chips since the team first began work on the project).

Depending on the nature of the problem, your criteria may take the form of a short list or a more extensive list.

List Possible Alternatives.   Brainstorming solutions is the next step in the reflective thinking process. **Brainstorming** consists of jotting down creative ideas and solutions without judging them positively or negatively in any way. The goal is to develop a comprehensive list of suggested alternatives, so quantity, not quality, is the name of the game. No one is allowed to offer an opinion, positive or negative, about any other person's suggestions. Outrageous ideas not only should be condoned, they should be encouraged. An unusual or bizarre idea may trigger another spontaneous and novel idea from a group member.

Evaluate Each Alternative.   Evaluating the solutions your group generates is a simple process, if you have carefully followed the first four steps. This stage of reflective thinking involves holding each solution up against the measuring stick that your criteria provide. For example, let's say that our fictional team planning the working lunch works in the Lincoln Park area of Chicago. They have brainstormed five possible restaurants to which they can go: The Cheesecake Factory, The Chart House, Mastrioni's, Boston Market, and Johnny Rockets. Because the first three restaurants have long waiting lines and are fairly expensive, they are ruled out immediately. Because Johnny Rockets serves mainly hamburgers and other great junk food, Boston Market is the clear winner. This small but incredibly wonderful restaurant is inexpensive (Amy can eat for $9), close to the office (within 2 miles so Donna can get back to the office quickly), and David couldn't order a hamburger if he wanted one.

Narrowing down a list of alternatives can be time consuming, depending on the number of criteria and solutions your group has generated. However, doing so gives each person a fair opportunity to voice an opinion and minimizes the chances for hurt feelings and possible conflict.

Select the Best Alternative and Discuss Implementation.   Does more than one solution fulfill the criteria you outlined in step #2? If so, three methods exist by which your group can reach a final decision. The first method is **consensus.** When a group reaches consensus, all members decide to go along with a particular solution, even though some group members may not particularly agree on that choice. The key to consensus is that everyone understands why a choice is being made and agrees that the process overall was fair. Note: At this point during the process, the group should be on guard for signs of groupthink.

The second method by which a best solution may be determined is **compromise.** In a compromise, one or more group members give something up in order to ensure the progress of the group. Hence, compromise often is perceived as a win/lose proposition. A compromise can be win/win, however, depending on how group members handle the situation. Let's say that everyone in our fictional team decides they would like to go to Chart House, a wonderful, moderately expensive seafood restaurant. Because Amy has only $10, everyone may decide to chip in the extra money so Amy can eat. (She has done the same for her teammates on several previous occasions.) What could have been a win/lose situation (everyone but Amy goes to Chart House, and Amy stays at the office) actually produces a win/win scenario. Everyone gets to eat something good, and nobody is left out in the process.

The third method by which a group may choose a best solution is **voting,** a practice that should be used only as a last resort. When a group takes a vote, clear winners and losers emerge, thereby creating internal turmoil. If the group continues to meet for other reasons, the members who lose may hold a grudge. As a result, they may decide to withhold information, double-cross the "winners," or manifest other negative group behavior in the future.

Performing Effectively in Teams

Problem-solving teams. Intrafunctional teams. Cross-functional teams. Self-directed teams. The creation and maintenance of such "high-performance" groups as these constitute the latest trend in companies around the world. For this reason, a more comprehensive discussion of teams is warranted.

Teamwork has become an integral part of managing complexity and change and is a building block whereby any progressive organization will compete in the 21st century. Teams are the key to improving performance in companies and organizations. In fact, teamwork is becoming an integral part of almost every company in operation today (Turner, 1989).

Why has "teamwork" become the buzzword of the nineties? According to Katzenbach and Smith (1993), teams outperform individuals acting alone or in larger organizational groups, especially when performance requires multiple skills, judgments, and experiences. Managers in organizations around the world are becoming more aware of the capabilities of teams as well as the relationship between total team output and goal achievement in the organization.

In their book, *The Wisdom of Teams,* Katzenbach and Smith (1993) define **team** as "a small number of people with complementary skills who are committed to a common purpose, performance goals, and approach for which they hold themselves mutually accountable" (p. 45). The key to understanding the power of this definition is its emphasis on accountability. Now, let's take a look at its five components.

1. Generally, the key to team success is to keep the group *small in number,* although larger groups can be successful.

2. *Complementary skills* fall into three categories: technical or functional expertise, problem-solving and decision-making skills, and interpersonal skills. The challenge for any team is the right mix of these skills to balance what team members need in order to fulfill their purpose.

3. The team must be *committed to a common purpose and performance goals.* These two elements must go hand-in-hand in order to maximize the efficiency and effectiveness of a team. If your team has one without the other, team members become confused and revert to mediocre performance.

4. The team must be *committed to a common approach.* In other words, each individual must share the same perspective about how they will work together to achieve the team's purpose: economically, administratively, and socially.

5. The team must have *mutual accountability.* They must hold themselves accountable for their actions, which means commitment and trust in each other.

To give you an idea of what is required for successful teamwork, let's eavesdrop on a conversation between an associate of Zenger-Miller, an international consulting firm, and Sharon Faltemier, operations manager of Raychem Corporation.

Zenger-Miller: "In building a team environment, where do you start? How do you get people motivated?"

Sharon Faltemier: "To begin with, people need to understand the need for change— why it's important and how it'll improve things. If they start to understand this and if they can see how it fits with their own needs, it's much easier to effect a change in their behavior."

Zenger-Miller: "How do you determine who should make decisions here?"

Sharon Faltemier: "First, you have to identify the decisions and then decide who the most appropriate people are to make those decisions. If you're looking at manufacturing flow, you want the manufacturing work teams to make most of the day-to-day decisions. If you're looking at the needs of the outside customer, then maybe it should be a cross-functional business team centered around the customer. All the teams need to be focused around a process that they own."

Zenger-Miller: "What level of independence do you give to people?"

Sharon Faltemier: "Our people have a lot of independence in how they manage their businesses. . . . They clearly understand the areas in which they can go off and make decisions."

Zenger-Miller: "Are there special things you've done to get people to work as a team?"

Sharon Faltemier: "There's a lot of training—team building, problem-solving skills, interpersonal skills."

Zenger-Miller: "So you coach on interpersonal skills."

Sharon Faltemier: "That's right. I just don't let them hang. But I wouldn't come up with the solution or the answer or fix it for them. It's the same with team issues. If there's a rework issue between one team and that other team, the people from those teams need to get together and discuss it, try to work it out, before I get involved."*

From this conversation, we hope you realize the value of teamwork. Everything you are studying about teams and other small groups either directly or indirectly affects your relational life in an organization.

Qualities of an Effective Team Member

You often hear about the importance of being a good team player, but have you ever thought about the qualities that are required by the job description? How many times have others told you, "I want you on my team because you will be committed and work to accomplish our objectives," only to turn around and not follow through on their end of the bargain? You have probably experienced this dilemma in the classroom situation,

---

*Source: J. H. Zenger, E. Musselwhite, K. Hurson, & C. Perrin (1994). *Leading Teams: Mastering the New Role* (Homewood, IL: Business One Irwin), pp. 255–260. Adapted with permission of the publisher.

and wished that a certain team member would share equally in the work. Unfortunately, this type of negative behavior takes place in the boardroom as well. As a result, conscientious team members are highly sought after in companies around the world.

How can you be the person who is the prized member of a team? The answer lies in the characteristics you would look for in choosing a team member. Think about the type of person with whom you like to work in a team setting. The following list outlines qualities that are significant in developing and maintaining high-performance teams.

The Willingness to Contribute Your Best as a Team Member.   Willingness to contribute your best translates directly to follow-through on assignments. Chances are good that the reason you have been selected to serve on a team is the special expertise you offer the group. People want team members who show initiative and follow-through, no matter if the team is work- or socially related.

A Spirit of Compromise.   In any group, teams make decisions by compromise. Each person in the group speaks his or her mind and then a decision is made. Even though you may disagree with an overall decision, you have an obligation to publicly support the conclusion. The ability to agree or disagree is your right. However, supporting your group's decision in a spirit of compromise adds to the esprit de corps among group members.

A Willingness to Have an Open Mind.   Effective team members look for new ways of doing things and innovative solutions to old problems. To unlock new doors of opportunity, you must go the extra mile and stretch your imagination beyond its present limits. The best team members are open-minded.

The Ability to Think Clearly.   In any group that is assembled to solve problems, the first item on the agenda is to accurately define the problem. In other words, you must determine your group's primary purpose for meeting. To do so requires an ability to think clearly about the problem and to analyze all variables related to that problem. If you (1) cultivate an ability to objectively approach any problem, (2) listen carefully to all input from team members, (3) establish appropriate criteria for evaluating solutions, and (4) brainstorm solutions, no matter how crazy they sound, you will be well on your way to becoming an effective team member.

Let the Team Leader Lead the Meeting.   In some cases, the team leader will be appointed by upper management. This is usually the case if a person has proven leadership ability and has demonstrated leadership skills. No matter how you feel about this person, let the team leader "lead" the meeting, at least until you can gauge how successfully the team is performing. If all is going well, you can relax and make effective contributions. If the team seems to be straying from the goals of the group, you can do one of several things to get the group back on task: (1) talk privately with the leader about your concerns; (2) gently emerge as a leader by using your expertise in such a way that it complements that of the designated leader; or, (3) find ways to help keep the group on track when they seem to be straying. You can read more about the topic of leadership in Chapter 7.

Managing Meeting Mania

How do you transform a stuffy meeting into a dynamic and meaningful interaction? A lot depends on the personalities of the group members and their job status. If all members demonstrate mutual trust and respect, conducting business and making sound business decisions will be less cumbersome and more pleasurable. Blessed with this luxury or not, the keys to managing meeting mania are as follows:

1. Establish shared agreement on the necessity of the meeting;
2. Circulate an agenda prior to the meeting;
3. Arrive early to ensure that all details of the meeting have been addressed;
4. Arrange the room and furniture to make the best use of the physical environment; and
5. Follow the "six golden rules of meeting management."

Let's take a closer look at each.

Establish Shared Agreement

You may find yourself in a position to organize and conduct a business meeting. The first question you need to ask yourself is, "Is this meeting necessary?" Although an answer in the affirmative may seem intuitively obvious, the key is to establish shared agreement among group members regarding the importance of the meeting. This is especially true since time is money, and meeting time is time away from other important duties and responsibilities.

Circulate an Agenda in Advance

The second key to success is circulating an agenda prior to the meeting so that participants will be prepared to discuss important issues. Doing so will establish the importance of the meeting; it also will give participants time to think about the issues to be addressed and to prepare any information they may need or want to provide. To give you some ideas about how to create one, a sample agenda for a regular monthly meeting is provided in Figure 4.2 on page 108.

In addition to leading regular monthly meetings, you may be asked by your boss to set up a workshop or conference about some special topic. Organizing a workshop or conference takes a lot of time and cooperation. Getting speakers to commit time, writing letters, setting up break times, developing luncheon menus, and arranging for rooms and audiovisual needs are only a few of the many tasks you will have to accomplish. You also must consider the number of people attending and set appropriate workshop fees. To give you an idea of what to expect and the kind of agenda you

Figure 4.2

Sample Monthly Meeting Agenda

> I. Opening remarks from the chair
> II. Minutes of previous meeting
> III. Treasurer's report
> IV. Standing committee reports
> V. Previous business
>   A. Revisions made to Hot Topics Seminar proposal (Deb)
> VI. New business
>   A. State Department of Transportation Census (Connie)
>   B. Presentation of preliminary marketing plan (Ron)
>   C. New budget (Art)
> VII. Announcements
> VIII. Next meeting date, time, and place
> IX. Adjournment

will need to develop, Figure 4.3 offers you a sample agenda for a hypothetical leadership workshop.

Arrive Early

After you plan the time, date, and place of a meeting and send out an agenda, you need to arrive at the meeting room in plenty of time before the meeting takes place. Make sure the necessary audio and visual equipment is available, along with other supplies participants may need. When everyone arrives and is seated, you can begin the meeting. Remember to follow the agenda that you distributed.

Always visit a meeting room before you speak in order to make the best use of the room arrangement.

Leadership Workshop
April 23, 2000
The Westin Hotel
Atlanta, Georgia

8:00–8:30 A.M.	Coffee and Registration
8:30–8:45 A.M.	Welcome, Introductions Carol McElroy, Workshop Coordinator
8:45–9:30 A.M.	Leadership Roles within the Community Blake Edwards, First National Bank Mary Ann Good, Monsanto Corporation
9:30–10:15 A.M.	Sources of Professional Development Christine Knasel, Disney, Inc.
10:15–10:30 A.M.	Break
10:30–12:00 P.M.	Pursuing Leadership Positions (Panel discussion among five selected leaders in major corporations.)
12:00–1:00 P.M.	Lunch
1:00–1:45 P.M.	Positioning Yourself Professionally for Leadership Opportunities Stacey Siler, Dow Chemical Co.
1:45–2:30 P.M.	What Do You Do Once You Get Where You Want to Go? Scott Smith, Toys R Us
2:30–2:45 P.M.	Break
2:45–3:15 P.M.	The Responsibilities of Leadership Jane Faircloth, Texas Instruments
3:15–4:00 P.M.	How to Function Effectively in Leadership Positions Stephan Est, Delta Air Lines
4:00–4:30 P.M.	Closing Remarks Carol McElroy, Workshop Coordinator

Figure 4.3

Sample Leadership
Workshop Agenda

Layout and Design of Meeting Rooms

The layout and design of a meeting room, including the furniture, should be comfortable for the people who are planning to attend. Visiting the room prior to the meeting is useful, so you can determine how to best use the space provided. There are many different designs you may use to physically set up a room. Let's take a look at some of them. (See Figure 4.4 for an illustration of each meeting room setup.)

Circular.   This set-up is considered to be more informal than a rectangular set-up and encourages an equal sharing of information. Generally, this layout implies that leadership will be shared and that no single individual will run the meeting.

Rectangular.   This set-up is often used by Boards of Directors, with the chairperson sitting at the head of the table, farthest from the door. A rectangular room set-up is most often used for formal meetings and works well for many business meetings.

U-shaped.   The U-shaped set-up encourages frequent group interaction since each attendee can see all other meeting participants. This setting can be formal or informal, depending on how the meeting is conducted.

Satellite.   This meeting room set-up requires several tables, each surrounded by equally spaced chairs. The satellite set-up allows the leader to move freely around the room and to work with subgroups of people who are implementing different tasks or projects. This type of set-up works well for training situations or informal group meetings.

Classroom.   You obviously are familiar with this meeting room set-up. A designated person leads the meeting, but also encourages interaction from group members.

If we could underscore any one tip regarding meeting room set-up, that tip would be to make this decision *consciously.* Never walk into a meeting room cold and feel that

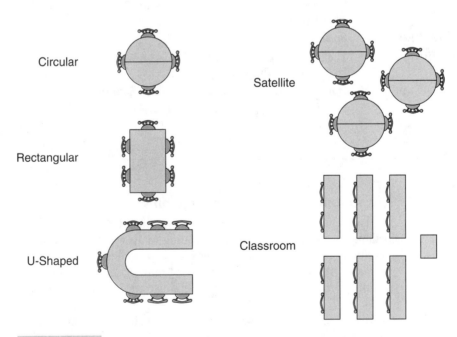

Circular

Satellite

Rectangular

U-Shaped

Classroom

Figure 4.4   **Five Types of Meeting Room Set-ups**

you must "buy the arrangement" automatically. Make the room yours before the meeting begins. Research in the area of nonverbal communication is conclusive about this single point: The way that a meeting room is arranged can and does significantly affect meeting outcomes.

Six Golden Rules for Meeting Management

As you can see, suggestions for conducting effective meetings are many and varied. Six "golden rules" for meeting management that we have found to be helpful are presented in Box 4.2.

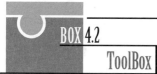

BOX 4.2

ToolBox *Six Golden Rules for Meeting Management*

1. Always start the meeting on time. If you begin on time, committee members who show up late will realize the value of time. Beginning on time reflects skill as an effective time manager and sets a precedent for others to follow.

2. Assign a note-taker or arrange to have the meeting audiotaped. You may need to refer back to an issue that was discussed during the meeting at a later date. Good record-keeping is a sign of a good meeting manager as well.

3. Learn to listen. So many times we think about what we are going to say and, in the process, block out valid points that other group members may be contributing. Additionally, we often hear only what we want to hear, rather than really listening to other people. As we suggested in Chapter 2, effective listening is a skill that must be developed. Meetings that are characterized by effective listening are successful meetings. We suggest reviewing the topics we covered in Chapter 2 in order to improve your listening skills during meetings as well.

4. Keep the discussion on track. Many times important issues can get sidetracked in a meeting, especially when everyone has a different opinion about the topic. If you anticipate a conflict prior to the meeting, discuss the issue with participants in advance. If an unanticipated conflict develops once the meeting is in progress, either (1) appoint a subcommittee to look into the problem, or (2) ask participants involved in the conflict to meet with you after the meeting. Doing so will help keep the discussion on track and minimize the chances of wasting participants' valuable time.

5. Give everyone an opportunity to be heard. Some people tend to monopolize meetings, whereas others wait to be asked their opinions. As the leader of the meeting, you need to keep an open mind and make sure everyone feels welcome to contribute and express ideas without criticism.

6. End on time. If you said the meeting would last no longer than one hour, make sure the meeting lasts for only an hour. Meeting participants tend to plan the rest of their day around the time allotted for the meeting. Running late with a meeting makes members tardy for other appointments, increases the chances that members will mentally leave the meeting, and reduces your credibility as an effective meeting manager.

How to Stand Out at Someone Else's Meeting

Even though you may not be running the show, you can still stand out in a meeting. The following are a few tips from Julie Bailey (1987) to make you a sought-after meeting participant.

■ Do your homework before the fact. When an agenda hits your desk a few days before a meeting, read it. Make notes about relevant points to discuss next to each entry. If you have questions, ask them sooner rather than later. The more information you have compiled before entering the boardroom, the better.

■ There are no small parts, only small actors. This holds true in the workplace as much as it does on stage. There's no need to hog the limelight or threaten the chairperson's authority by attempting to gain control. Instead hold your thoughts until the time is perfect. Then let them wow your coworkers.

■ One great idea is better than a handful of so-sos. Limit idea-making to one or two issues where you can back up your proposals with statistics, experience, or new research. Try to test the reaction to these issues before the meeting if you can. Talk to your coworkers, even your superiors. It's better to rework your proposal beforehand than risk the prospect of a no-go vote in front of peers.

■ When you're the new kid on the block it's important to follow someone else's lead. Stand back and let people assume their regular seats before you take one. Observe a meeting's dynamics before jumping into the action.

■ All ears? Three cheers. Listening attentively—with your eyes and your body as well as your ears—can win points, not to mention the same consideration when you've got the floor. If you're whispering to your neighbor, you'll never know when important information is flying past.

■ Link your ideas to a promise of action and the prospect of immediate benefits.

■ Carry through with your ideas. If you've been asked by the chair to investigate an idea or develop a proposal, do so. Send a memo or E-mail summarizing your findings within several days.*

These tips can help polish your business savvy at meetings and also assist in boosting your career. Everyone wants a person who will pay attention to detail and follow through with suggestions and recommendations.

---

*First appeared in WORKING WOMAN in August 1987. Written by Julie Bailey. Reprinted with permission of WORKING WOMAN Magazine. Copyright © 1987 by WORKING WOMAN Magazine.

Case Study

Teambuilding in Turbulent Times

Debra Jacobs, President, Jacobs Consulting Group, Inc.

In August of 1994, employee dissatisfaction was more intense and troubling than any seen in the history of a large utility company headquartered in the Southwest. Historically, the company was known as a tight-knit, insular, "family-feel" utility. The company had, until recently, been led by a highly homogeneous, paternalistic, and benevolent succession of leaders. The numbers showed that the company performed very well overall, and this performance had lulled the leaders into believing more of the same leadership behavior was called for.

Similarly, employees believed that as long as they were polite, caring, good-humored, and easy to get along with, they would have jobs for life. Work hours were short, the pace was leisurely, customers came second to family or work group needs, and pay was above average. Communication was indirect, somewhat superficial, and laden with euphemisms or sarcasm when someone did have a concern. Supervisors made all the business decisions, and employees were delighted to be free of all responsibility except the execution of a carefully defined set of tasks. It was seldom that work needed to be performed with an innovative eye. The emphasis was on conformity and predictability. Employees who deviated from the norm were gently persuaded to step back in line. Products and services were grossly outdated, but no one paid much attention to that, unless a customer complained. When customers were unhappy, someone tried to smooth things over, but improvements were seldom made in response to the original complaint.

However, all of this changed in 1993 when an "outsider" was named CEO and with him came new organizational leaders, structures, expectations about more creative and lower-cost ways of meeting internal and external customer expectations, and more rigorously measured individual and departmental performance results. Some of the human resource practices that had been taken for granted were questioned or abandoned. Free meals, plush recreation facilities, thirty-two-hour workweeks, large and subjective spot bonuses, numerous "free days"—these and other practices were replaced with more performance-based systems.

It soon became apparent that everyone would be held accountable for contributions centered around customer "value-add," and that some people would have to work differently from what they had come to expect in the past. The gravest concerns emerged when a significant part of the business was sold to help create greater strategic and operational focus around the core competencies of the organization. The sale paved the way for the acquisition of a small but important utility company located in the Northwest.

As rumors abounded, the chief information officer became aware of specific changes in employee behavior within the Information Systems and Client Services Groups. These included lowered employee participation and involvement, withdrawal, absenteeism, deep drops in performance, cover-ups of problems, blame-laying, and slowed decision making.

Several mid-level managers told the CIO that they needed help in overcoming the extreme sentiments of distrust and lowered motivation that seemed to permeate every interaction. "We used to be the good guys," one manager said with exasperation. "Now, my employees won't even talk to me and they avoid talking with anyone else they think had a hand in changing the company."

Another leader, a project manager, reported, "I don't feel very hopeful about things getting any better. We don't know where we are headed, what we are supposed to do, what methods to use to get there, or how to communicate with those making all the decisions. All we know is that we feel betrayed."

To make things more complicated, the CIO confided to a peer that "these people are shell-shocked. The world as they know it has been turned upside down and they expect me to fix it. I don't know what is coming down the pike most days any more than they do!"

Questions

1. How would you describe the culture clash between the old business and the new?

2. What are the basic fears that are getting in the way of people embracing the new workplace expectations?

3. What working structure does the new business need to meet the needs of its customers while people grow in their sense of power and influence? Describe how supervisors should lead, members of a work group should interact with each other, and top leaders should behave.

4. If the structure were the right one, what would the communication look like within work groups? How would people feel about being members of these groups?

5. What information do people need to know to best respond to the new business requirements?

Summary

The group process plays a significant role in the business world. The goal of this chapter has been to introduce the tools you need to be successful in many different types of groups.

In summary, you learned a definition of groups as well as their advantages and disadvantages. You discovered the meaning of groupthink and learned methods with which to overcome this difficult communication problem.

Knowing the differences between formal and informal groups will assist you in determining how to approach group interactions. Individual characteristics of group members also make a difference in the dynamics of the group. It is important to know the process that groups go through in order to make decisions. In case you experience difficulty in a group, you now understand the contingencies that affect group decision making, the paths that groups may follow as a function of "talk," and the types of communication activities associated with every decision-making path.

Group decision making may be enhanced through the use of two major problem-solving tools. The single-question method is useful in instances where time is of the essence, the task is simple, and the number of group members is small. The reflective thinking process can assist you in taking a step-by-step approach to problem solving.

Teamwork and effective team membership are extremely valuable within an organization. Successful teams share five major characteristics: a small size, complementary skills, a common purpose and performance goals, a common approach, and mutual accountability. Additionally, a number of qualities are required for high-performance teams. These include a willingness to contribute best efforts, a spirit of compromise, an open mind, the ability to think clearly, and a commitment to let the team leader lead the meeting.

Knowing how to conduct meetings is advantageous to your career development. Following the guidelines presented in this chapter can help you more effectively manage meeting mania.

Knowledge Check

Key Concepts and Terms

small group	cross-functional teams	relational activities
social loafing	self-directed teams	topic-focus activities
groupthink	informal groups	breakpoint
formal groups	objective task characteristics	single-question
informal groups	group task characteristics	procedure
department	group structural	reflective thinking
committees	characteristics	brainstorming
task force	standard unitary path	consensus
teams	complex cyclic path	compromise
intrafunctional teams	solution-oriented path	voting
problem-solving teams	task-process activities	team

Putting It All Together

1. What are the advantages and disadvantages of small group communication?
2. How do formal and informal groups differ?
3. Distinguish among intrafunctional, problem-solving, cross-functional, and self-directed teams.

4. Discuss "contingency theory" as it relates to small groups.

5. What are the six steps associated with the reflective thinking process? When would you use this approach instead of the single-question procedure?

6. Name the six golden rules for conducting an effective meeting.

7. Identify and sketch out five different arrangements you can use to layout a meeting room.

8. Briefly discuss at least five ways you can stand out at someone else's meeting.

References

Armstrong, T. (1996). Team development and empowerment strategies. In D. Mosley, P. Pietri, & L. Megginson. *Management leadership in action* (5th ed.). New York: Harper Collins.

Bailey, J. (1987, August). The fine art of leading a meeting. *Working Woman, 12*(4), 68–71.

Beebe, S. A., & Masterson, J. T. (1994). *Communicating in small groups: Principles and practices* (4th ed.). New York: HarperCollins.

Dewey, J. (1933). *How we think.* (Boston: Heath).

Fisher, B. A., & Ellis, D. G. (1990). *Small group decision making: Communication and the group process* (3rd ed.). New York: McGraw-Hill.

Fisher, D. (1993). *Communication in organizations* (2nd ed.). Minneapolis: West Publishing Company.

Gray, G. (1993, Spring). Quality circles: An update. *SAM Advanced Management Journal, 582,* 41–47.

Green, F. (1994). College grads on the factory floor: A case study of high commitment work teams. *Production & Inventory Management Journal, 35*(1), 8–12.

Janis, I. L. (1982). *Victims of groupthink: A psychological study of foreign policy decisions and fiascos* (2nd ed.). Boston: Houghton-Mifflin.

Katzenbach, J. R., and Smith, D. K. (1993). *The wisdom of teams.* Boston: Harvard Business School Press.

Larson, C. E. (1969). Forms of analysis and small group problem-solving. *Speech Monographs, 36,* 452–455.

Levering, R., & Moskowitz, M. (1994). *The 100 best companies to work for in America.* New York: Plume.

Littlejohn, S. W. (1992). *Theories of human communication* (4th ed.). Belmont, CA: Wadsworth Publishing Co.

Mueller, F. (1994). Teams between hierarchy and commitment: Change strategies and the 'internal environment.' *Journal of Management Studies, 31*(3), 383–403.

Napier, R., & Gershenfeld, M. (1993). *Groups: Theory and experience* (5th ed.). Boston: Houghton-Mifflin.

Pearson, J., Turner, L., & Todd-Mancillas, W. (1991). *Gender and Communication.* New York: Wm. C. Brown.

Poole, M. S. (1983). Decision development in small groups, III: A multiple sequence model of group decision development, *Communication Monographs, 50,* 321–342.

Poole, M. S., and Roth, J. (1989, Summer). Decision development in small groups V: Test of a contingency model. *Human Communication Research, 15*(4), 549–589.

Poole, M. S., Seibold, D. R., & McPhee, R. D. (1985). Group decision-making as a structurational process. *Quarterly Journal of Speech, 71,* 74.

Smith, A. C., and Green, F. B. (1993, Summer). Managing employees as if they were volunteers. *SAM Advanced Management Journal, 58*(3), 42–46.

Summers, L., and Rosen, B. (1994, May). Mavericks ride again. *Training & Development, 48*(5), 119–124.

Turner, L. (1989). Three plants; three futures. *Technology Review, 92*(1), 38–45.

Weiland, R. (1994, June). Esprit de corps. *Successful Meetings, 43*(7), 48–55.

Wellins, R. S. (1992, December). Building a self-directed work team. *Training & Development,* 24–28.

Zenger, J. H., Musselwhite, E., Hurson, K., & Perrin, C. (1994). *Leading teams: Mastering the new role.* Homewood, Il: Business One Irwin.

Managing Workplace Diversity

5

After studying this chapter, you should be able to

■ Identify gender differences in communication.

■ Use the three gender-related language styles appropriately.

■ Understand ways to create a harmonious work relationship between men and women.

■ Build relationships with people from diverse backgrounds.

■ Relate to coworkers with physical disabilities.

On the chalkboard:
Aristotle's parts
of dramatic action
1. Character
2. Music
3. Spectacle
4. Dialogue
5. Idea
  Structure

David Kosel, an executive at Eastman Kodak Company, says, "It just doesn't make business sense to alienate employees and customers" (Gala-gen, 1993, p. 32). In fact, Kodak executives like Kosel feel so strongly about diversity concerns in the workplace that they developed a "Diversity Framework" that supports and enhances diversity programs for employees.

Kodak's Diversity Framework is divided into six categories: external relations, communication, improving representation, career development, education, and work-force-support systems. Within this framework, issues such as dependent care, alternative work schedules, and family leave policies are addressed.

For example, when Kodak decided to revise its family benefits program, it made sure to address the needs of all of its employees, including those with al-ternative lifestyles. For example, to identify the needs of their gay and lesbian employees, a gay/lesbian network was established. The network focuses on sensitive issues such as being passed over for promotions, receiving poor performance reviews, and having fewer benefits for their significant others due to their sexual preference. When Kodak officially endorsed the network, gays and lesbians gained privileges such as access to company facilities for network meetings and a forum for management to listen to their concerns. In this case, management wanted to help gay and lesbian employees overcome their fears about other employees' reactions to them. By allowing this specialized group to initiate a network, the message from management was clear: Kodak will not discriminate against any employee due to race, religion, or sexual preference.

Kodak's support of employees with alternative lifestyles is just one example of the many changes taking place in the workplace with regard to the advancement of diversity issues. What has contributed to these and other changes in the 20th century workplace? How will you respond to others in the diverse 21st century company for which you will work?

The world of business has changed dramatically over the last 20 years, with the influx of women and a more culturally diverse workforce. What was once a male-dominated workplace has evolved into a highly diverse population that includes women, people from various ethnic and cultural backgrounds, and the physically challenged. Learning how to work effectively with the idiosyncrasies and diversity of today's eclectic workforce is a challenge you will be facing in the 21st century.

In this chapter you will learn about another piece of the puzzle that affects your relational life at work: issues associated with gender, multicultural diversity, and physically challenged colleagues in the workplace.

Children learn gender roles at an early age by observing male and female behavior, conversing with parents and older siblings, and playing gender-related games.

Gender Issues in the Workplace

We are living in an exciting, changing business world where men and women work side by side, sharing ideas and strategies on a daily basis. As a result of the influx of women in the workforce at levels equal to or exceeding those of men, the roles of both men and women have changed. Every single medium—books, magazines, newspapers, film, television, video, radio, and the Internet—carries stories about the changing roles of men and women.

As guidelines for acceptable human behavior, gender roles tell us how to act with each other. **Gender roles** are defined as the learned behavior associated with being male or female. As such, they structure our everyday meetings with one another in any given interpersonal or social interaction. To understand the differences between masculine and feminine communication styles that result from our assigned gender roles, think back for just a moment to your childhood.

> ... As the male baby is barely entering the outside world, he starts to become indoctrinated into the ways of guyness, because of the way he will be treated by his parents, particularly his father. Some fathers will attempt to teach their sons to play catch right there in the delivery room. ("No, son! Always catch the ball AWAY from your umbilical cord!")
>
> —*Humorist,*
> *Dave Barry*

The Development of Gender Differences in Communication

The conversations you shared with your parents and others important in your life during your early childhood shaped your feminine or masculine identity. According to Deborah Tannen (1990), noted gender researcher and sociolinguist, "Even if you [grow] up in the same neighborhood, on the same block or in the same house, girls and boys grow up in different worlds of words" (p. 27). Children learn how to talk from their parents and peers. Although some of the activities that boys and girls pursue are similar in nature, their favorite games are different, and their ways of using language in their games are separated by a world of difference.

For example, boy's games usually involve sports activities in fairly large groups, such as football, baseball, or soccer. Most boys' games are competitive, driven by clear goals, and organized according to strict rules. There are winners and losers, leaders and followers. In boys' games, an individual's status depends on standing out, being better, and often dominating other players (Wood, 1994, p. 139).

From their games, boys cultivate a number of communication rules such as:

- ▪ I should use communication to assert myself and my ideas.
- ▪ I should use communication to attract and maintain an audience.
- ▪ I should use communication to compete with others.

Notice that an emphasis is placed on individuality and competition.

On the other hand, girls tend to play in pairs or very small groups, in which everyone has equal status. Generally, the center of a girl's social life is her best friend, and intimacy is of utmost importance in their relationship. Girls' games are often unstructured (e.g., playing house, playing with dolls, or jumping rope). Typically, girls generate their own game rules. Girls rarely give orders, and they express their preferences as suggestions. As a result, their suggestions are likely to be accepted. For their games to work, girls must communicate ideas effectively and cooperate with one another. From these kinds of play, girls learn a whole different set of communication rules, such as:

- In order to create and maintain relationships, my talk should be collaborative and cooperative.
- I should avoid criticizing, outdoing, or putting others down through communication.
- I should pay attention to others and to relationships.

Note that, for girls, an emphasis is placed on cooperation, collaboration, and sensitivity to others' feelings.

Report Talk versus Rapport Talk

The lessons that we learn about communication, as well as about masculinity and femininity, during our childhood carry over into adulthood. In fact, the basic rules of communication between men and women are only refined and elaborated versions of the games we play as children. As a result, men tend to lean more toward "report talk," while women rely more heavily on "rapport talk" (Tannen, 1990). **Report talk** is communication that is designed to elicit information and facts about a certain subject. **Rapport talk** is communication that usually centers on relationships.

As a rule, women derive more pleasure from emotional conversation (rapport talk), which involves an expressive awareness of feelings. In this type of talk, emotion is at the forefront of the conversation. Conversely, men shun emotionally charged interactions. Their preferred mode of communication is intellectual (report talk)—that is, focused on what they are thinking rather than on what they are feeling. The major focus of men's conversation is presenting factual information.

Additionally, Tannen (1990) argues that men feel more comfortable talking in the public sphere, or in front of large groups, whereas women are more comfortable speaking privately with one or two individuals (p. 77). The reason for the latter is that most women like to establish commonalities, relationships, and connectedness with other people through communication. In short, women focus on discovering similar areas of interest and matching past or present experiences.

In contrast, men like to talk as a "means to preserve independence and negotiate and maintain status in a hierarchical social order" (Tannen, 1990, p. 77). Men prefer to talk in order to hold center stage with a large audience and impart factual information, in contrast to women who like to build relationships with one or two people. To illustrate this point, consider the following conversation between Martha and Joe.

Martha: Who did you see at your Sertoma Club meeting this morning?

Joe: Oh, the usual people.

Martha: Specifically, who did you see, Joe? Was Coreen or Melissa there?

Joe: Yeah, both of them were there.

Martha: Well, what did they have to say? How did they look? Is Coreen happy with her new marriage? What's going on with Melissa's new job?

Joe: I don't know. I just told you I saw them. I don't know any of the details.

If Martha had attended the meeting, she would have discovered all the details about Coreen and Melissa, because she is interested in conversations about people and relationships. Conversely, Joe was interested in attending the meeting and listening to the guest speaker. It didn't matter to him who else was attending the meeting. The conversation between Joe and Martha illustrates the fact that, stereotypically, men tend to look for the big picture rather than the details. If Martha had attended the meeting, you can bet she would have come home and told Joe every detail about Coreen's and Melissa's lives.

One additional observation that gender researchers have made about male/female communication is: In the workplace, men speak differently to other men than they do with women, and women speak differently to other women than they do with men. For example, have you ever witnessed the following scenario? During a normal business day, two or three men are talking and laughing in the hallway and a woman approaches the group. Invariably, what happens? More than likely, the topic of conversation will change. Likewise, if two or three women are talking together and a man enters the group, the conversation also may change to a different subject. Typically, men enjoy discussing certain topics with other men, just as women prefer talking about specific topics with other women.

The Emergence of Three Language Styles in the Workplace

Indeed, both feminine and masculine language styles reflect specific stereotypical tendencies inherently tied to male and female gender roles. For example, the content of feminine talk emphasizes feelings and relationships; phrases such as, "I feel that . . . " or "How do you feel about . . . " are common. In contrast, the content of masculine talk emphasizes tasks and competitive achievements. For instance, men will say, "I want this project completed by . . . ," or "Give me a ballpark figure by tomorrow." Their focus is on goals, plans, and accomplishments, not necessarily the relationship or feelings of the person with whom they are speaking.

A third language style, which is referred to as nonsexist or inclusive language, has become more acceptable for the 21st century workplace. **Nonsexist** or **inclusive language** is a combination of interpersonal and task-oriented communication. To illustrate, an employee who uses nonsexist language might say, "In order for the report to be completed on time, department heads from all three units will have to work together cohesively." The employee may go on to say, "The information that emerges from the report will be discussed over lunch at The Cheesecake Factory at the company's expense." This illustration demonstrates that task and interpersonal content are given equal weight when the speaker uses nonsexist language.

How often do YOU think about your language style? Are you already attempting to use nonsexist language in your everyday life? Just for fun, take a moment and complete Box 5.1 on page 124. See how many of the sentences you can convert to nonsexist language.

BOX 5.1
How Do You Measure Up?
Using Nonsexist Language

Directions: For each of the statements listed below, change the sentence to reflect nonsexist or inclusive language without changing the context of the sentence.

1. Humpty Dumpty sat on a wall,

   _____

   Humpty Dumpty had a great fall,

   _____

   All the king's horses and all the king's men

   _____

   Couldn't put Humpty together again.

   _____

2. The fireman and the salesman asked the waitress for a piece of peanut butter pie.

   _____

   _____

3. Little girls must not take the same risks as little boys, or else they might get hurt.

   _____

   _____

4. The businessman invited his colleague, a career girl, out for lunch.

   _____

   _____

5. The cleaning lady and busboy arrived at the party two hours early.

   _____

   _____

Benefits of Using Nonsexist Language in the Workplace

A number of noted gender researchers believe that people benefit from the use of nonsexist language in the workplace. For instance, Daily and Finch (1993) argued that "the elimination of sexist language can improve the quality of work life and heighten employee satisfaction within the workplace" (p. 30). Additionally, they believe a better working relationship with the opposite sex will result.

With a little effort and some creativity, words such as position titles that are biased and exclusive can become neutral and inclusive. For example, using words such as "salesperson" instead of "salesman," "worker" instead of "workman," and "chairperson" instead of "chairman" demonstrates the use of inclusive language. Try using nonsexist language in a conversation with your friends, and see if they notice a difference. Doing so will help you prepare for gender-neutral communication.

There are many advantages of using nonsexist or inclusive language in your daily work environment. For example:

- Nonsexist language puts the emphasis on job roles and the work produced, not on gender.
- Nonsexist language helps employees reach their full potential.
- Nonsexist language helps create a supportive work climate.
- Nonsexist language unifies the workforce instead of dividing it (Daily & Finch, 1993, p. 32).

Table 5.1 on page 126 provides a brief comparison of the characteristics of the three gender-related language styles.

Interruptions

Do men interrupt women more than women interrupt men? Is interrupting an issue of intrusion or a person's attempt to dominate a conversation? Interruptions carry many **metamessages,** or nonverbal cues other than the actual content of a message. For example, interruptions may indicate that a person doesn't care, doesn't listen, or isn't interested in what the other person has to say. Research suggests that, in the past, men interrupted women more often than women interrupted men. However, with the increasing number of women in the workplace, women have learned to counter interruptions and claim air time, and many men have learned to share it (Rudman, 1996, p. 14).

Additionally, men and women tend to interrupt people for different reasons. In general, men tend to interrupt to take control of a conversation, or to dominate or change the subject. On the other hand, "women tend to interrupt to agree with, support, and elaborate on what the other person is saying" (Rudman, 1996, p. 20).

While men tend to interrupt to dominate a conversation or to change the subject, women tend to interrupt to agree with or to support what another person is saying.

Table 5.1   Three Gender-Related Language Styles

INDICATORS OF FEMININE LANGUAGE

1. Content emphasizes feelings and relationships: one's own emotions, the listener's reactions, the feelings of other people. Focus is on identity and relating more often than it is on the physical or technical features of task achievement.
2. Uses indirect rather than direct assertions; uses questions rather than statements, or "tag" questions that combine elements of both. Uses indirect verb forms such as "might" or "would" more often than direct forms such as "can" and "will."
3. Shows respect for or deference to the listener; allows options for the other person through the use of questions or references to the other's goals or preferences.
4. Uses adjective and adverb qualifiers within statements (e.g., very, kind of, possibly, really).
5. Uses standard speech; rarely uses nonstandard or taboo words.

INDICATORS OF MASCULINE LANGUAGE

1. Content deals primarily with tasks, especially jobs done outside the home, and with competitive achievements. Time and space elements of action are stressed, and objects are treated as parts of systems.
2. Uses direct assertions far more often than questions; uses present and future verbs such as "can" or "will" rather than indirect forms.
3. Refers to self more than to the listener. May focus on goals, plans, or accomplishments; rarely mentions anxiety, doubts, or personal limitations, except as followed by a "We should do this" statement.
4. Uses unqualified nouns and verbs; rarely uses qualifiers.
5. Uses the language of sports and the military, and expects partners in conversation to do the same.
6. Uses nonstandard speech for emphasis to produce identification in the listener, or to show a bond between self and others.
7. Shows willingness to confront a listener or other person, if necessary.

INDICATORS OF NONSEXIST OR INCLUSIVE LANGUAGE

1. Emphasizes both task and interpersonal content of talk.
2. Uses "I" rather than "you" at the beginning of statements to convey individual opinions or feelings directly instead of through labeling or attacking the listener.
3. Refers to the listener as a peer, not as a superior or subordinate.
4. Gives evidence in support of own claims, whether about task or interpersonal issues.

Adapted from B. Bate (1992). *Communication and the Sexes* (Prospect Heights, IL: Waveland Press), p. 95.

How do you deal with people who constantly interrupt you? Carol Rudman (1996), in her book *Frames of Reference: How Men and Women Can Overcome Communication Barriers—and Increase Their Effectiveness at Work,* makes several excellent suggestions:

■ Straighten your posture, look the interrupter directly in the eyes, and calmly say, "Please don't interrupt." Then raise your voice slightly and keep on talking. The more you practice, the easier it gets to make your point.

■ "Level" repeated interruptions. **Leveling** means bringing something out into the open, and stating a problem directly so you can deal with it directly. For example, you might say, "I have been interrupted five times in the last ten minutes. I would like to finish what I have to say and then you can respond."

■ Designate a conversational ally. If you are going to be discussing a touchy subject or talking to a tough audience, enlist the support of a coworker before the meeting. Brief him or her on what you are going to say, and then ask for help in turning the subject back to you, if necessary (pp. 20–21).

Think of a time when you walked away from a conversation totally annoyed at yourself for allowing the other person to interrupt you. Now that you are aware of some ways that you can manage interrupters, you can more effectively communicate with a rude person the next time you are interrupted.

Differences between Male and Female Managers

Corporate life used to be so predictable. In the past, a male employee would begin work at a company with a group of peers his same age. He would move up the ranks until he reached a management position. Then, he would supervise a number of younger workers, one of whom would eventually take his place as a manager.

Corporate restructuring and downsizing have changed the face of corporate life. For example, a 55-year-old male worker may report to a 26-year-old female supervisor. A seasoned female sales director may find herself teamed up with a young, male whiz kid right out of college.

Do men and women differ in management styles? The jury is still out on this question. Several studies have determined that women and men are not significantly different as managers, while other studies have reported significant differences (Pearson, West, & Turner, 1995, p. 219). For example, some studies indicate that men tend to be more assertive or aggressive than females in their interactions with others. In contrast, studies about female managers indicate that women reveal more information about their feelings, beliefs, and concerns. Both men and women have the capability of assuming managerial roles. For example, female managers can be highly cooperative and supportive. So, too, can male managers even if they are more competitive and dominant in their managerial roles. Regardless of gender, an effective manager will be flexible and adaptable in carrying out the mission of an organization.

Anne Statham (1987) conducted another study among male and female managers that provides insight into gender differences in managerial styles. In her study, respondents perceived that female managers were both task- and people-oriented, and that male managers were more concerned with image and autonomy (p. 409). Women were seen as "focusing more on the task to be done and the people working for and with them, . . . interacting with others a great deal, [and] encouraging individual career growth. . . ." In contrast, men were seen as "focusing on themselves and the need to 'back away' from those who work for them, emphasizing the power they have" (p. 425). Perhaps the point to be made is this: Male and female managers have different communication styles, and these differences can cause misunderstandings in the workplace. Understanding both the male and female managerial viewpoints allows you to sort out the differences and minimize misunderstandings between men and women.

How to Create Harmonious Relationships in the Workplace

What are the ingredients for a harmonious work relationship between men and women? Can men and women find a middle ground on which to meet and communicate effectively? In a study conducted by Bunker (1990), several groups of men and women were asked to contribute to the development of a model of the ideal working relationship between men and women (p. 147). Four characteristics emerged in both men's and women's descriptions of their best working relationship with a person of the opposite sex.

First, meaningful friendships were described as those in which the relationship enlivened the work, and the work enlivened the relationship. For example, Desmond and Amy, coworkers for a major airline company, shared a mutual interest and love of theater. Amy recently won two tickets to *Sunset Boulevard* and asked Desmond to be her guest. As a result of sharing their outside theater interests, the friendship between Amy and Desmond grew stronger which, in turn, enhanced their work relationship.

The second characteristic of an excellent working relationship that emerged was a sense of shared history over time. To illustrate, Art and Debbie worked together for more than three years to develop a viable strategic and operating plan for a small nonprofit association. During that time they shared good times and bad times—victories and defeats. These ups and downs contributed not only to the development of their professional relationship, but to their sense of a shared history over time. When Art unexpectedly resigned, Debbie never quite recovered from the loss. Their sense of shared history was gone, and all of the fun went out of Debbie's work. Two months later, she also resigned.

The third attribute associated with an excellent working relationship was that it was collaborative rather than competitive. Each partner had certain strengths and weaknesses, which positively contributed to their working relationship. To illustrate, Marcio and Jane collaborated on a special project for the CEO of an organization. Marcio was the "creative" component of the duo, and Jane was the "planning and implementing" element. Each person brought his or her respective strengths to the project, which resulted in recognition and monetary rewards for both coworkers.

Finally, a strong sense of valuing and mutual affirmation was important for Bunker's participants. This affective bond served as a source of energy in the relationship (p. 148). Think about the last time you worked closely with a colleague or friend on a project that was important to both of you. Chances are good that the positive reinforcement and energy you shared not only made the work more exciting, but also drew you much closer together.

Women and men need to recognize the differences between male and female communication styles in the workplace to avoid costly communication problems. In order for more effective communication to take place between the sexes, individuals must be able to understand and appreciate each other's differences. To do so effectively requires a change in people's attitudes and values as well as their behavior.

What Men and Women Want from Each Other in the Workplace.   So what DO men and women want from each other in work relationships? With over 40 years of combined work experience in a variety of small, medium, and large businesses in education, nonprofit organizations and corporations, your authors have developed some recommendations on how to create a harmonious work environment for both sexes. Feel free to add your own suggestions.

- **Mutual respect.** By having mutual respect for each other you create a symmetry with your coworkers.
- **Honesty and truthfulness.** These are essential in any work environment. Always telling the truth and being honest will add to your personal credibility.
- **Equality.** Treat your coworkers as you want to be treated. Fairness and equality go hand in hand in the workplace.
- **Friendliness.** Being friendly to each other creates a bond among colleagues. A simple, "Good morning" or "Have a good weekend" promotes a caring attitude about your coworkers. Expressing interest in your colleagues' families and outside interests lets them know you are interested in them.
- **Information sharing.** Share information or provide opinions or advice when asked.
- **Compliments.** Compliment your coworkers for their awards, accomplishments, or a job well done. Let them know that you support them in all of their endeavors.
- Add your own suggestions to the list:

_____

_____

Communication between men and women is not the only issue facing today's workforce. Because of the make-up of the 21st century workplace, you will be working with people who represent a broad spectrum of diversity. How can you interact effectively with people whose age, race, religion, or cultural backgrounds are different from yours? In the next section, we will closely examine the concept of diversity in the workplace and provide you with some possible answers to this important question.

Other Forms of Diversity in the Workplace

If you were to take a tour of the headquarters of a large multinational corporation, you would gain firsthand knowledge of the scope of diversity in the workplace. For example, you would find differences in such demographic variables as race, sex, age, religion, marital status, number of children, and differing physical and cognitive abilities. In addition, you would discover other social variables that influence workstyles and communication such as ethnic and cultural identity, gender orientation, social class, and occupation. As Ingram (1993) noted, workforce diversity "can also apply to differences in aptitudes, outlooks, backgrounds, and learning styles" (p. 15).

An example of one global company that has recognized the value of a diverse workforce for over half a century is International Business Machines. IBM's global workforce diversity plan helps the company focus on increasing opportunities for all of its employees. In fact, the company motto consists of ten powerful words: "None of us is as strong as all of us." IBM's board of directors, senior management, employees, and the human resources network champion workforce diversity at all levels of this thriving multinational company. Together, IBM employees strive for a work and life balance plan through a common theme of access to the workplace. Their goal is to demonstrate to IBM employees and customers that the "ties that bind us are stronger than the issues that divide us" (Hilliard-Jones, 1996). By being sensitive to and balancing diversity issues, IBM continues to develop a winning, progressive team.

Is your classroom environment, like IBM, highly diverse and rich in differences among people? More than likely, if you attend a large college or university, the make-up of students in your classroom reflects the broad spectrum of diversity you will find in the workplace today. Diversity brings a rich element of culture into any group and adds flavor and fresh ideas to topics of discussion.

> Human beings are more alike than unalike, and what is true anywhere is true everywhere.... It is necessary, especially for Americans, to see other lands and experience other cultures. The American, living in this vast country and able to traverse 3,000 miles east to west using the same language, needs to hear languages as they collide in Europe, Africa, and Asia.
>
> —*Maya Angelou*

Implications of a Diverse Workforce

Why should you be interested in the concept of diversity in the workplace? What are the implications of a highly diverse workforce in the 21st century? According to The Society for Human Resource Management and The Commerce Clearing House, **diversity** is best described as the "management of an organization's systems and cultures to ensure that all people are given the opportunity to contribute" (Freeman-Evans, 1994, p. 52). Note that the Society's definition of diversity includes everyone: all ages, all races, both sexes, all sexual orientations, all people. You should be concerned about diversity because diversity includes YOU. Effectively managing diversity in the workplace enables an organization to get the most from its employees and gives employees the greatest opportunities to succeed. "The diversity management process recognizes and values the differences of all individuals in the workplace, then creates an environment that allows everyone to work together, [with] each person reaching his or her highest potential" (Freeman-Evans, 1994, p. 53).

To illustrate the positive outcomes that accrue when diversity is valued, consider Marshall Field's, Inc., a highly successful retail company. Marshall Field's is committed to optimizing diversity among its employees and customers, and everyone who shops there knows it. In fact, management feels so strongly about diversity that on the side of every Marshall Field's shopping bag is the following credo:

> We respect the individuality of all customers and employees—a fact that guides the way we do business every day. We strive to create a comfortable, welcoming atmosphere for all of our customers, complete with a wide array of quality merchandise and excellent personal service. All of our employees and their individual viewpoints, beliefs, experiences and backgrounds are highly valued, and we are dedicated to making the most of each person's abilities.

When you read this statement, what kind of feeling do you get about Marshall Field's? You probably feel that Field's is genuinely concerned and committed to the differences among people. Diversity management requires a long-term commitment that changes an organization's value system and corporate culture.

Different cultures and backgrounds bring new perspectives to the workplace. You should be concerned about diversity because diversity includes YOU!

Barriers to Valuing Diversity

Unfortunately, not everyone embraces differences among people and, hence, the concept of diversity. Some of the barriers may be easy to overcome; others may take more time. Clearly, a workplace supportive of all people simply makes good business sense.

Barriers to valuing diversity come in all shapes and sizes. The following are just a few that your authors have noted:

1. *Lack of knowledge and communication about differences.* Some people are simply unaware that differences exist. For example, did you know that people from many Native American, European and Asian cultures are taught to avoid direct eye contact with other people? For these cultures, direct eye contact is considered rude and intrusive, except in specific situations. Yet, people who have been raised in other cultures, where direct eye contact is perceived to be a sign of honesty and sincerity, may believe that you are trying to hide something if you do not share direct eye contact. Knowledge of, and communication about, such differences is necessary if you hope to communicate effectively.

2. *Stereotypes and their associated assumptions.* Do your assumptions and biases get in the way of your ability to appreciate others' differences? Regardless of how hard you try to be objective, you may be influenced by certain biases as a result of early childhood socialization.

3. *Not enough flexibility in the organizational structure.* An organization's policies, procedures, and practices may not support cultural differences. For example, is there reference to valuing diversity in the company's mission statement? Support for diversity must begin with and be communicated by the CEO and other administrators within an organization.

4. *Difficulty in talking about differences.* Your past experiences have influenced your beliefs and feelings about others who are "different" from you. These experiences may include real-life encounters, or simply things you have "learned" from movies, television, and the nightly news. As a result, you may be fearful of talking about your perceived differences with other people with whom you work. For example, when you were growing up, you may have been conditioned to view people of different races in a negative way. By learning to question your perceptions and feelings,

and to begin talking about your differences without fear, you can destroy old stereotypes and perceive others who are different in a more positive manner.

5. *Expectation of overnight results.* It's unreasonable to expect everyone to instantly accept diversity. Every person in an organization has a unique background that contributes to varying levels of acceptance of diverse cultures.

Perhaps you can think of additional barriers to accepting diversity in the workplace.

Overcoming Barriers to Valuing Diversity

Once you have identified your own personal barriers to valuing diversity, you can focus on redirecting your behavior to overcome those barriers. Let's look at some ways you can begin to value differences among people.

1. Make a commitment now to communicate openly with others about diversity issues. Open, honest, and sensitive communication with people about your differences demonstrates respect and an attempt on your part to understand other people.

2. Recognize your assumptions and stereotypes and how resulting actions can affect communication outcomes. Set aside your past biases and assumptions, and take the time to understand people as they are. By analyzing how you have been influenced in the past, and by whom, you will be able to adjust your behavior for a more positive outcome.

3. The development of diversity policies and procedures are essential in order for people to work effectively in an organization. Ask management whether diversity policies have been incorporated into the structure of the company, and learn those policies if they have been implemented.

4. Create an environment in which you will be able to discuss differences openly. Adapt your communication style to the situation. For example, if you have a Japanese colleague with whom you work on a daily basis, make an effort to learn a few key Japanese words and phrases. You will be surprised how impressed and responsive your colleague will be if you use these phrases appropriately. Additionally, you will be creating a more harmonious environment in which both of you can work.

5. Learning how to value differences takes time. Creating an awareness of the sensitivities and differences of others also is an ongoing process. Look for common ground that builds a bridge to establishing better relationships. In most large companies, diversity training is available to help you communicate more effectively with people from different backgrounds.

Implementing Diversity Programs in the Workplace

What are some examples of diversity programs that currently exist in the workplace? When you enter the workforce, you may discover that "diversity programs" have existed in many companies for years, without your even knowing they were diversity programs. For example, subsidized day care is an integral part of many organizations today. Some companies actually have a day care facility on site to assist parents with the care of their children. One such example is Chase Manhattan Bank, which has a full-time child care center at its corporate headquarters. Another program at Chase provides two months of free on-site day care for children of parents returning to work after the birth or adoption of a child (Hilliard-Jones, 1996). These programs illustrate that Chase Manhattan cares about its employees and wants to help them balance their personal and professional lives. Many other companies, both for profit and nonprofit, have similar day care programs.

An example of two diversity programs that are becoming more common is flex-time and job-sharing. **Flextime** involves the ability to schedule your work hours around your own personal and family lifestyle (e.g., 5:30 A.M. to 1:30 P.M. rather than the standard 9:00 A.M. to 5:00 P.M.) **Job-sharing** is the sharing of similar job duties and responsibilities between two people on a given day or over a stated period.

To illustrate the concept of job-sharing, consider Evangelina and Marcia, who work full-time in the marketing department of a large Fortune 500 company. Evangelina and Marcia were pregnant at the same time, and they both wanted to work part-time after they had their babies. Because of a generous job-sharing program recently initiated at the company, Evangelina and Marcia were able to work half-days at both the office and home, which allowed them the opportunity to continue working "full-time." (Evangelina came into the office from 8:00 A.M. to noon, and Marcia worked in the office from 1:00 P.M. to 5:00 P.M.) As a result, Evangelina and Marcia became even more productive employees because they were comfortable in their adjustable work environments. Due to the hectic pace of employees who are attempting to balance work and family life, both flextime and job-sharing have gained momentum in the corporate world.

Another company that believes in creating an environment where people can meet their full potential is Rockwell International Corporation, a high-technology company. Rockwell employees organized a diversity initiative called "A Celebration of People," a week-long festival held at the company's southern California headquarters. The event celebrated the many backgrounds and cultures of Rockwell employees. (Rockwell employs over 80,000 people in more than 35 countries around the world!) The celebration was an enlightening experience and underscored the true diversity of Rockwell's labor force. Special events such as the "Celebration of People" promote a caring attitude within a company, and make employees feel appreciated and, therefore, more productive (Hilliard-Jones, 1996).

Both companies and individuals benefit from differences when the former develop effective diversity programs. Advantages of implementing quality diversity programs include greater employee retention, increased productivity, lower absenteeism, higher morale, and an expanded marketplace. In short, when employees are satisfied with their work environment, both the employee and the company benefit.

Developing Your Own Diversity-Management Profile

Managing diversity at the personal level "means respecting cultural, age, gender, and lifestyle differences in the workplace" (Jorgensen, 1993, p. 70). Personal management of diversity also means creating a work environment in which everyone can achieve his or her potential. How well do you personally manage diversity? If you are interested in assessing your diversity-management skills, take a moment and complete your own Diversity-Management Profile in Box 5.2 on page 134.

How to Work with People from Different Backgrounds

Now that you have a better understanding of your own diversity profile, how can you build better relationships with people from different backgrounds? It is impossible for you to identify and totally understand the background of every single person whom

BOX 5.2

How Do You Measure Up?   *Your Diversity Management Profile*

Directions: Read each of the following questions. Then circle the number in the right column that best corresponds with your current behavior. (Note: 1=low and 5=high)

	Low				High
1. To what extent do you have a difficult time accepting people with alternative lifestyles?	1	2	3	4	5
2. To what degree do you experience difficulty accepting viewpoints of people representing different cultural backgrounds?	1	2	3	4	5
3. How would you rate your tendency to stereotype people who are older or younger than you?	1	2	3	4	5
4. How uninformed are you about the nonverbal behaviors of people from different cultures?	1	2	3	4	5
5. To what extent do your biases about people with different backgrounds inhibit your communication with them?	1	2	3	4	5

Total Your Score Here: _____

Scoring:

9 and below	Congratulations! You have succeeded in learning how to manage diversity at the personal level.
10–14	You're getting there. Maybe a little more practice in opening your mind is in order.
15–19	You're on the edge. You may need to contact your company's "diversity hotline" for more information.
20–25	Help! Call your nearest "diversity hotline" now!

you meet in the workplace. However, if you want to build relationships, increase cooperation and participation, and facilitate open, respectful communication, we recommend the following guidelines:

■ *Actively listen to others.* As you communicate with people from different origins and backgrounds, make sure you listen carefully to both the verbal and nonverbal messages they are sending.

■ *Continually ask for feedback.* By doing so, you will be able to monitor your behavior as well as your listener's behavior.

■ *Use appropriate language.* Appropriate language is the language that best serves the needs of your listener. For example, if English is your primary language, but it is not the first language of your listener, then you both may need to check for understanding. Try asking the listener to paraphrase what you just said, and do the same for him or her. Doing so with sensitivity and concern will let the person know you are listening and care about understanding what is being said.

■ *Be aware of differences in nonverbal behavior.* Every culture has its own idiosyncrasies; hence, the nonverbal behavior of someone from another culture may seem foreign to you. For example, the Japanese often bow as a sign of respect when they are meeting and greeting superiors and visitors from other countries. Therefore, when you are greeting Japanese visitors, returning a bow is appropriate and will be appreciated. Take the time to study and learn about such nonverbal differences of people from other cultures. The more you are aware of cultural differences, the more sensitive, credible, and savvy you will be perceived to be.

■ *Check your assumptions and biases.* Do you have assumptions or biases that seem to contribute to misunderstandings with people who have different backgrounds than you? If so, try to determine the origins of your behavior; then, valiantly attempt to change your behavior appropriately.

Coworkers with Disabilities

Do you know someone who has a physical or cognitive disability? Perhaps you have a friend, a neighbor, or a family member who has experienced such a challenge. If so, then you know that he or she has probably adapted well to the work environment— with support and coaching from supervisors and other caring employees. For example, you may remember the television program "Life Goes On," which featured a character named "Corky," played by Chris Burke. Burke had the same real-life cognitive disability as Corky, and became a productive, well-loved member of the cast. By starring in the show, Burke sent a strong message to viewers that, despite their physical or cognitive challenges, persons with disabilities can succeed in whatever they do.

"One out of every 10 American families has a member with a disability" (Aaron, 1994, p. 46). Like Corky's character in the television series, when a physically or mentally disabled individual is viewed by society as a productive, contributing member, opportunities are opened up for other persons with disabilities. Fortunately, there has been an increased public acceptance of individuals who are fighting some of life's biggest battles, such as Alzheimer's, Down syndrome, lung disease, or cancer, to name just a few.

Employers today make accessibility accommodations for workers with physical disabilities. For example, you may have noticed ramps in front of building entrances or raised desks to make space for wheelchairs. These accommodations are necessary in order for employees with disabilities to function in organizations. Since the Americans with Disabilities Act (ADA) of 1993 was passed, more physically disabled individuals than ever before have been able to enter the workplace. The ADA is a "civil rights statute that prohibits the discrimination of disabled citizens in employment, public services, transportation, public accommodations, and telecommunications" in businesses with 15 or more employees (The Florida Governor's Alliance for Employment of Disabled Citizens, Inc., 1993, p. 9). The ADA protects approximately 43 million U.S. citizens who have physical or mental disabilities that significantly limit activities in the workplace. It should be noted

Being sensitive to individuals with physical disabilities means "doing unto others as you would have them do unto you."

that, even though the ADA has been enforced since the beginning of the 1990s, many employees still have concerns about interacting with physically disabled individuals.

Communicating with Physically Disabled Individuals

How would you change your work habits if you worked side by side with a person who uses a wheelchair or who is hearing-impaired? Perhaps the best answer lies in the often quoted dictum, "Do unto others as you would have them do unto you." Depending on each individual situation, some reasonable changes in the way you communicate will be appreciated. For example, persons who use wheelchairs see their wheelchairs as extensions of their personal space. Improperly touching or even leaning on a wheelchair, as you might with other pieces of furniture, is inappropriate unless you have a close or intimate interpersonal relationship with the person.

Kaye McDevitt, director of vocational programs in the long-term disability division of UNUM Life Insurance Company of America, offers some tips for interacting with physically disabled persons in four different situations:

1. *Introducing yourself to individuals who use wheelchairs.* The best way you can introduce yourself to someone who uses a wheelchair is to bend over slightly to be closer to eye level. If the person is able to extend his or her hand for a handshake, offer your hand. For lengthy conversations, it is more comfortable for the person using a wheelchair if you sit down so you are both eye to eye.
2. **Offering assistance.** If someone with a disability looks as if he or she needs assistance, it's proper to offer help. However, instead of assuming the person wants or needs help, ask. Offer assistance in the same way you would approach someone carrying several packages.

3. **Speaking to hearing-impaired people.** People with hearing impairments most often have some ability to hear, but will often combine their residual hearing ability with lip reading. Make sure you face the person to whom you are speaking and speak more slowly than usual. Avoid speaking louder than normal when interacting with persons who are hearing impaired. Doing so only embarrasses you and the person with whom you are speaking and does little to increase communication fidelity.
4. **Making presentations.** When making speeches or presentations to a group, consider the needs of visually impaired or hearing-impaired individuals. For example, hearing-impaired workers might find a copy of overhead transparencies useful. For visually impaired workers, an audiotape of the presentation might be helpful for future reference (Flynn, 1995, p. 19).

When working with persons with disabilities, treat them as you would any other employee—as a significant contributor in the workplace. In turn, they will treat you with the same level of courtesy and respect.

The Language of Sensitivity

According to Petrini (1993), "Language that respects diversity begins with an understanding that people are people first" (p. 35). In other words, the language we use should respect men and women of all races, ethnic backgrounds, sexual orientations, and physical and mental characteristics. For example, instead of saying a person is "handicapped," the more appropriate term is "physically disabled." People respond to what they want to be called. To illustrate, many people who have AIDS or have tested positive for the HIV virus indicate that they are offended by the term "AIDS victims." A more appropriate and acceptable alternative is "people with AIDS," which is more accurate and more easily understood (p. 36). Being sensitive to the needs and feelings of others will assist you in using the appropriate terminology for each individual.

Choosing appropriate words makes a difference. "In a culture where language is considered a primary indicator of intelligence, many people have preconceived ideas about disabilities" (Aaron, 1996, p. 44). It is important for you to be able to communicate with coworkers who have specific disabilities. For example, Bob, an accountant who is hearing impaired, uses E-mail to communicate with coworkers and his supervisor. However, Bob enjoys using American Sign Language (ASL), but very few employees are familiar with how to use ASL. You may want to tell Bob you are willing to take time to learn sign language from him during your lunch hour or after work. Another way to let Bob know you are interested in communicating through sign language is to enroll in a course in ASL at a local community or school program. By demonstrating interest in learning sign language, you show that you are a team player who is willing to promote social inclusion in the workplace.

The Future of Workplace Diversity

By the year 2000, only 15 percent of the net increase in the U.S. workforce will be white males; the remaining percentage will be represented by women, minorities, and immigrants. Additionally, as the Americans with Disabilities Act gains a greater foothold, the percentage of people with disabilities in the workforce will increase. Finally, the average age of the work population is rising (Ingram, 1993).

To maintain a viable work culture, companies not only must be attuned to the changing nature of society, but must reflect the very fabric of society that they represent. For many organizations, doing so will involve changes in their approaches to accomplishing work. Life/work planning, increased educational opportunities, and unique work arrangements such as flextime, job-sharing, and permanent part-time employment are only a few alternatives that are being implemented in response to the changing nature of the workforce (Naisbitt and Aburdene, 1985).

Case Study

Managing Diversity

Sheila K. Reed, Public Service Director, Pensacola News Journal

Gannett Company, Inc., is recognized as a leader in corporate America and the newspaper industry in its hiring, promotion, and development of women and minorities. Diversity is important to the company, both internally and externally. Through its affiliate newspapers, as well as radio and television stations, Gannett prides itself on being a "world of different voices," one that mirrors those of our global community.

In late spring 1995, the *Pensacola News Journal,* a Gannett newspaper, initiated diversity-training sessions for all employees. The training material, developed at the corporate level and titled, "A Matter of Trust," was supplemented with materials and activities by a professional trainer hired to facilitate the sessions. The supplemental activities and materials personalized the program for the Pensacola plant and geographic region to enhance the core corporate program.

The *News Journal*'s public service director, chair of diversity efforts, scheduled a diversity-training session with department heads and key managers. The materials and information were presented on two fronts: (a) to leaders as individuals, and (b) to individuals as leaders, showcasing material being presented to their staff.

The trick was making the session meaningful and applicable to the leadership of the newspaper, a diverse group that, overall, relates well to one another. However, diversity is a broad topic involving more than predictable issues such as race and gender. Recognizing the diversity among their different departments, including their styles of management, was a focus in personalizing their session. The challenge for the diversity committee chair during this group's session was to help the leaders relate to one another's style.

Questions

1. Do you think that it is important to include a discussion of diversity across departments in company-wide diversity training? Why or why not?

2. What kinds of issues, problems, or challenges can be addressed if such a discussion is included?

3. What major activity or exercise would you plan that would serve as a compelling and novel way to emphasize the point regarding the importance of understanding interdepartmental diversity?

Summary

In a present and future world full of diversity, learning how to navigate differences in all facets of your relational life will assist you in developing positive relationships in the workplace. In this chapter you learned how gender differences developed in early childhood. Even though these differences were learned at a young age, male and female communication patterns transfer to the world of work. Understanding the three types of language styles, masculine, feminine, and nonsexist (or inclusive), will help you accept gender communication differences.

Creating a harmonious work relationship between men and women involves mutual respect, honesty and truthfulness, equality, friendliness, information-sharing, and complimenting one another. Following these guidelines will establish mutually beneficial cooperation among employees.

Being able to function in a diverse organization is a valuable asset to every professional. Benefits include employee retention, increased productivity, less absenteeism, better morale, and an expanded marketplace.

Five ways to build relationships with people from diverse backgrounds include actively listening, using appropriate language, continually asking for feedback, being aware of differences in nonverbal behavior, and checking your biases and assumptions. Taking a genuine interest in your coworkers' cultural backgrounds is a positive step toward valuing diversity.

Interacting with physically or cognitively disabled coworkers involves being sensitive to their needs, offering assistance when asked, and treating them with courtesy and respect, just as you would every employee with whom you work. Demonstrating interest and learning a special skill in order to communicate more effectively with a hearing-impaired coworker, for example, will benefit you, your coworker, and the organization.

In order to be successful in the 21st century workplace, you must be able to weave yourself into the fabric of our multicultural society. Possessing adaptability and flexibility in the ever-changing work environment is a definite asset in any company.

Knowledge Check

Key Concepts and Terms

gender roles	inclusive language	flextime
report talk	metamessages	job-sharing
rapport talk	leveling	
nonsexist language	diversity	

Putting It All Together

1. How do differences in gender communication develop?
2. What is diversity and why should you be concerned about it?
3. Why should you use nonsexist language in your daily work environment?
4. Describe the three types of language styles and provide examples of language associated with each.
5. How can you create a more harmonious work environment when it comes to communication between the sexes?
6. What are some ways that you can build relationships with coworkers from different countries?

References

Aaron, C. (1994, November). Hiring the inspirational employee. *Credit Union Management, 17*(11), 43–46.

Bate, B. (1992). *Communication and the sexes.* Prospect Heights, IL: Waveland Press.

Bunker, B. A. (1990). Appreciating diversity and modifying organizational cultures: Men and women at work. In S. Srivastva, ed., *Appreciative management and leadership: The power of positive thought and action in organizations* (pp. 126–149). San Francisco: Jossey-Bass, Inc.

Daily, B., & Finch, M. (1993, March/April). Benefiting from nonsexist language in the workplace. *Business Horizons, 36*(2), 30–34.

Filipczak, B. (1994, February). Is it getting chilly in here? Men and women at work. *Training, 31*(2), 25–30.

The Florida Governor's Alliance for Employment of Disabled Citizens, Inc. (1993). *Americans with Disabilities Act: A resource guide to Title I in Florida* (HRS Publication, pp. 1–10). Tallahassee, FL: Author.

Flynn, G. (1995). Five tips for interacting with physically challenged co-workers. *Personnel Journal, 74*(12), 19.

Freeman-Evans, T. (1994, February). Benefiting from multiculturalism. *Association Management, 46*(2), 52–56.

Galagen, P. A. (1993). Navigating the differences. *Training & Development, 47*(4), 29–33.

Hilliard-Jones, A. (1996, April 15). Diversity: A global success strategy, a special report. *Fortune,* special supplement.

Ingram, R. (1993). Training in the kaleidoscope. *Training & Development, 47*(4), 15–22.

Jorgensen, B. (1993, September). Diversity: Managing a multicultural work force. *Electronic Business Buyer,* 70–76.

Naisbitt, J., & Aburdene, P. (1985). *Re-inventing the corporation.* New York: Time Warner Books.

Pearson, J. C., West, R. L., & Turner, L. H. (1995). *Gender and Communication* (3rd ed.). Dubuque, IA: Wm. C. Brown.

Petrini, C. (1993). The language of diversity. *Training & Development, 47*(4), 35–37.

Rudman, C. (1996). *Frames of reference: How men and women can overcome communication barriers—and increase their effectiveness at work.* Princeton, NJ: Peterson's/Pacesetter Books.

Statham, A. (1987). The gender model revisited: Differences in the management styles of men and women. *Sex Roles, 16*(7/8), 409–429.

Tannen, D. (1990). *You just don't understand: Women and men in conversation.* New York: Ballantine Books.

Tannen, D. (1994). *Talking From 9 to 5.* New York: William Morrow & Co.

Wood, J. T. (1994). *Gendered lives: Communication, gender and culture.* Belmont, CA: Wadsworth Publishing.

Work life is the second puzzle piece of organizational life you are expected to master in the business and professional world. Included in this area of mastery are your interview skills, leadership skills, stress and conflict management skills, and business etiquette and protocol.

We open the unit with tips and techniques for writing resumes and job interviewing. To give you a picture of what it's like during the employment interview, we discuss the process from both the interviewER's and interviewEE's perspectives. In addition, in Chapter 6, we present information about five additional types of interviews that you will encounter in your work life: group interviews, informational interviews, performance appraisal reviews, coaching and counseling interviews, and exit interviews.

In Chapter 7, we present an update on leadership and power in organizations. In the process, we help you identify your own personal leadership style, provide you with tips on how to relate to the leadership styles of others (especially your boss), and work with you to develop your hidden leadership potential.

Chapter 8 deals with stress and conflict management, two increasingly important skills for employees at all levels in the corporate world. In this chapter, you will learn about the causes of stress, as well as our positive and negative responses. Tips and techniques about how to handle stress in the workplace will be provided. We will also discuss the types of conflict that exist in an organizational setting, as well as five primary methods that you can use to better manage conflict.

Business etiquette and protocol, an extremely important aspect of your work life, is the subject of Chapter 9. In this chapter, we will discuss how to make a positive first impression and how to use body language that communicates your desired message. In addition, we will walk you through business etiquette in all four stages of your relational, work, public, and techno-life.

As you can see, "work life" takes many forms and affects employees' daily lives. Our goals for this unit are to raise your awareness about the significant communication issues related to work life, to provide you with information on how to successfully address those issues, and to increase your understanding regarding what it will take to maximize competence in these areas. Hopefully, upon completing this unit, you will have increased knowledge and skills, and will be able to better manage your "work life" in the future. ■

unit
3

Managing

Work Life in

the Workplace

6

Interviews You Will Encounter in Your Worklife

After studying this chapter, you should be able to

- Prepare a resume and cover letter for the employment interview.

- Discuss the different types of interviews commonly encountered in your work life.

- Develop employment interview strategies from both the interviewER and the interviewEE perspective.

- Explain how to survive the group employment interview.

- Describe the techniques of the informational interview.

- Understand the purpose of the performance appraisal interview.

- Realize the importance of the coaching or counseling interview.

- Recognize the purpose and expectations of the exit interview.

If you are interested in being hired by Southwest Airlines, you need to be "the kind of person who can relate to everybody and everything" says Rita Bailey, manager, corporate employment. As an interviewer seeking a marketing representative who could attract more businesswomen, elderly travelers, and young people, Bailey was looking for a "self-starter who has a willingness to pitch in on any job, even blowing up balloons for festive events" (Zellner, 1995, p. 69).

Bailey's interview technique consists of an informal group session with applicants chatting about everything from their experiences in their childhood years to how they handled tough problems they have faced on the job. Evidently her interviewing technique works. The airline has discovered that an informal group approach yields more information about potential employees than a structured, one-on-one meeting. Between 1991 and 1995, the staff at Southwest Airlines increased by 97 percent which translates to an additional 17,000 employees (Zellner, 1995, p. 69). The group interview is one way that rapidly growing companies such as Southwest hire new employees.

The informal group interview approach is just one of many interviewing techniques in today's fast-paced job market. **Interviewing** is a "communication process in which two or more people interact within a relational context by asking and answering questions designed to achieve a purpose" (Wilson and Goodall, 1991, p. 11). In addition to the group interview, as a part of your work life, you will experience many different types—such as the informational interview, the employment interview, the performance appraisal interview, the "coaching and counseling" interview, and the exit interview, to name a few. Once you learn the "how-to's" of the process, you will be prepared for a lifetime of interviews.

In this chapter, we will discuss these six types of interviews. How prepared you are and how you act in these interview situations disclose information about how well you will perform on the job.

Prior to the employment interview, you will need to know how to construct a resume. This chapter will outline the topics to include, provide you with a structure, and discuss the various types and styles of resume formats. How to write a persuasive cover letter will also be addressed.

Since we all have different educational and employment backgrounds, no two resumes are alike. The following section will provide an overview of structure and formats.

Introduction to Resumes

In 1996, the editors of *Job Choices*, a publication produced for college students by the National Association of Colleges and Employers (NACE), talked to six employer recruiters and asked them what they wanted to see on a college graduate's resume. The answers were varied, but the recruiters agreed that no one resume is going to please every type of interviewer. They also concurred that what they really look for in a resume is "scannability," or the efficient and accessible presentation of critical information. Finally, the recruiters said they look for a brief, well-organized resume, good grammar and spelling, a clear objective, and bulleted information rather than paragraphs for ease of reading ("Write the Resume Employers Want to See," pp. 33–38).

Your resume is the single most important tool you will use to get a job interview. A **resume** is a document that records your education, work experience, military experience, honors, awards, activities, interests, and other job-related information. In short, a resume provides a prospective employer with an overview of your job qualifications. We will discuss each of these categories in detail and present three types of resume formats in the following section.

Topics to Be Included on Your Resume

Before you begin writing your resume, you must target your objective and take an inventory of your background. "Targeting your objective" means determining the specific job you want to pursue (e.g., special events coordinator, account executive, or sales representative), and directing the focus of your resume in such a way that it highlights your qualifications for that specific job. "Taking an inventory of your background" means determining the specific attributes you possess that match those desired by the prospective employer.

We strongly recommend that you develop several resumes and customize each one to fit the different positions for which you may be applying. As we approach the 21st century, the ease with which you can change your resume electronically makes it practical to custom-tailor this important document. For example, if you are applying for a position in international public relations, target your resume to highlight any special qualifications, such as that internship you completed in a European PR firm. If you speak any foreign languages, be sure to include them on your resume. Perhaps you took an International Public Relations course and had an opportunity to work with an individual from another country on a team project. By taking time to think through how your background applies to the specific needs of an employer, you increase your chances of being contacted for an interview.

Identifying Information. Your "identifying information" includes your name (preferably in boldface type), present address (including zip/postal code), and telephone number (with area, city or country code), as well as a permanent address and telephone number where you can be reached. A permanent address is especially important if you will be moving from your present address within a short period of time. If you have a fax number or an E-mail address, it is appropriate to list both of these under your telephone number.

Employment Objective. If you decide to include an employment objective on your resume, you should briefly state the type of position you are seeking. For example, if you are a public relations graduate, your employment objective might read:

> Seeking an entry-level public relations technician position within a small public relations agency.

You should indicate how your qualifications relate to your objective. If you decide not to include an employment objective on your resume, be sure to write a specific job objective in the first paragraph of your cover letter. (Additional information about cover letters is provided later in this chapter.)

Educational Background. An interviewer will want to know the highest degree you have completed, so we suggest you begin by listing your most recent college degree first and work backwards. For example, you may have completed a general associate of arts degree (A.A.) followed by a bachelor of arts degree (B.A.) in management. List the B.A. degree first, followed by your A.A. degree. Be sure to include your college major and minor, the name of the college or university you attended, the city and state in which the institution is located, and the date of your graduation. You usually include your grade point average (GPA) if it is 3.0 or higher on a 4.0 scale. You also may want to insert, in this section, relevant course work in your major area of study.

Employment Experience. Prospective employers also are interested in your work record, beginning with your most recent experience. As with your educational background, we recommend that you list jobs you have held in reverse chronological order. In addition to full-time work experience, you also may want to include in this section any internships, cooperative education experiences, volunteer work, summer work, or part-time employment that you have completed.

Military Service.   If you have served in the military, identify your branch of service (e.g., army, navy, etc.) and the span of time you spent in the service. Give a *brief* synopsis of your assignment(s), even though you may have served for more than four years. You may want to break down your experience into skill categories. You will learn more about skill categories in the functional resume section of this chapter.

Honors and Awards.   This section of your resume should include scholarships and academic honors and awards you have received. Be sure to mention the type of award, the name of the agency bestowing the honor, and the date you received it. For example, if you have been on the dean's list or president's list at least one time (hey, that's quite an accomplishment!), be sure to include dean's list, name of your college or university, and the semester during which you received the honor.

Interests/Activities.   Interviewers want to know your organizational involvement both on and off campus. In this section, identify the organizations to which you belong and the role you play in each. For instance, if you hold an office in an organization, indicate the title of the office and then list the name of the organization. Perhaps you are the treasurer of the Student Government Association or you serve as a volunteer in the community for Habitat for Humanity. Highlight any activities that demonstrate your current or past involvement in such organizations.

References.   Employment professionals' opinions differ regarding whether or not you should list references on your resume. Some employment specialists suggest writing a statement such as "References available upon request" at the bottom of your resume. Still others recommend listing specific names, addresses, and phone numbers of references on your resume. Should you choose to include such references, limit the number to three, and list the names of faculty members or former employers who can recommend you based on your qualifications and past job experiences. Another option is to include a separate reference page, listing your name, address, and phone number at the top of the page before identifying your references. Whatever format you choose, make sure you ask your references for permission to use their names.

Topics to Be Excluded from Your Resume

Personal data such as height, weight, religious or political affiliation, and marital status are discriminatory and should be avoided when writing a resume. However, there are some exceptions. For example, if you are applying for a staff position with the Republican or Democratic party, then your political affiliation should be documented on your resume. Another exception might be if you are applying for the position of talk show host (and who hasn't these days?), your appearance would be an important factor in the hiring process. In this case, a photograph may be enclosed with your resume.

Now that you have an idea about what to include and exclude, we will discuss how to create an appealing, attention-getting resume.

Resume Structure

How do you structure the document so it will grab the attention of the people who will hire you? The following list includes suggestions and recommendations for creating a top-notch resume.

- Length. For the inexperienced college graduate, a one- page resume is usually sufficient. If you are an experienced graduate, you should limit the length of your resume to two pages.

- Appearance. Resumes are similar to interviews, in that first impressions count. To illustrate, if your resume is graphically pleasing to the eye, neat, and free from typographical errors and smudges, it tells the reader you care about your appearance. On the other hand, if your resume is hurriedly written, has misspelled words, and is cluttered, the reader may get an entirely different impression.

- Grammar and Spelling. Make sure everything on your resume is spelled correctly and is grammatically correct.

- Paper. The content of your resume is more important than the color or kind of paper on which it is written. However, we recommend that you use a minimum of 20 lb. weight, quality bond paper. Interviewers tend to prefer white, cream-, or ivory-colored paper for ease of reading.

- Relevant Information. Make sure you highlight your achievements, using powerful action verbs to reflect your duties and responsibilities. Additionally, use strong verb phrases instead of complete sentences to minimize wordiness. Box 6.1 provides a list of powerful action verbs that you might use to construct your resume.

BOX 6.1

ToolBox   *Powerful Action Verbs*

achieve	build	condense	decide
act	calculate	conduct	decrease
administer	carry out	consolidate	delegate
advise	clarify	construct	deliver
allocate	classify	consult	demonstrate
analyze	coach	contact	design
approve	collaborate	contract	designate
assess	collect	contribute	determine
assign	communicate	cooperate	develop
attain	compile	coordinate	devise
audit	compose	correlate	direct
authorize	compute	correspond	display
balance	conceive	create	distribute
budget	conceptualize	customize	*(continued)*

BOX 6.1

ToolBox

Powerful Action Verbs (continued)

document	integrate	produce	set up
draft	justify	program	shift
earn	keep	project	ship
eliminate	launch	promote	simplify
employ	lead	propose	solve
enable	locate	prove	sort
enact	log	provide	staff
enhance	maintain	purchase	start
ensure	manage	raise	stimulate
establish	market	realize	streamline
evaluate	master	receive	strengthen
examine	merge	recognize	structure
execute	minimize	recommend	succeed
expand	moderate	reconcile	summarize
expedite	monitor	record	supervise
facilitate	motivate	recruit	supply
file	negotiate	redesign	support
finalize	observe	reduce	surpass
finance	obtain	reevaluate	survey
forecast	offer	refer	tabulate
form	open	regulate	test
formulate	operate	relate	trace
gain	order	reorganize	train
gather	organize	research	transact
generate	originate	resolve	transfer
handle	overcome	restore	transform
head	oversee	retrieve	treat
hire	participate	reverse	troubleshoot
identify	perfect	review	unify
illustrate	perform	revise	update
implement	place	save	upgrade
improve	plan	schedule	utilize
increase	predict	secure	validate
initiate	prepare	select	verify
inspect	present	sell	win
install	prevent	separate	work
institute	process	serve	write
instruct			

Source: R. Sorensom, G. Kennedy, and I. Ramirez (1997). *Business and Management Communication: A Guide Book,* (Upper Saddle River, NJ: Prentice-Hall) p. 125.

Electronic Resumes

You will want to consider writing a "hard copy" or paper resume as well as an electronic resume. As the term suggests, an **electronic resume** is written for companies that are seeking job applicants on-line. The primary difference between electronic and hard copy resumes is that, when you list your work experience, the "key words" in electronic resumes are usually nouns, while hard copy resumes stress action verbs. Box 6.2 provides some computer-friendly resume tips to assist you in developing an on-line resume.

Resume Formats

There are three basic resume formats from which to choose: chronological, functional, and targeted. Whatever format you select, take the time to prepare your resume properly. Choose the format that will highlight your best qualities, and allow your resume to be visually appealing and reader-friendly.

Chronological. The chronological format continues to be popular, especially for candidates seeking positions that are closely related to their education and experience. In the **chronological (paper) resume,** biographical information is presented in reverse chronological order by date, with your most recent experience listed first under each heading.

A chronological resume requires selective wording in order to minimize the amount of interpretation required by a prospective employer. For example, use action verbs to

BOX 6.2

ToolBox *Computer-Friendly Resume Tips*

By following these simple suggestions, you can create a computer-friendly resume.

- Focus on nouns, not verbs. Recruiters search for "key words" that have been programmed for a particular job search. For example, key words in a job search for an accountant might include: B. S. accounting, accounts payable, accounts receivable, and CPA. If your electronic resume fails to include these key words, you may be overlooked by a recruiter, even though you possess the necessary job qualifications.
- Your name should be in boldface type and grab the attention of the person scanning your re-

sume. Make sure you place your name at the top of each page of your resume for continuity.

- Keep graphics simple. For example, use non-decorative typefaces and a font size of 10 to 14 points for ease of reading.
- Try to minimize the use of italic text, script, and underlined passages. Capitalized words and boldface are much more easily scanned and pleasing to the reader.

Adapted from Joyce Lain Kennedy (1996). *Computer-Friendly Resume Tips* (National Association of Colleges and Employers), p. 35.

When you are composing an electronic resume, keep in mind key words that potential employers may use to search for prospective new hires.

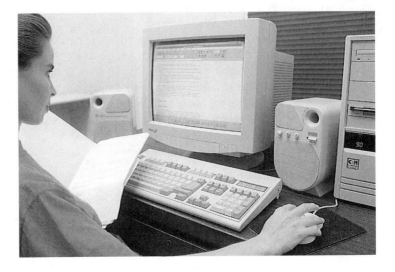

describe your experiences and to highlight transferable skills. Figure 6.1 provides an example of a chronological format.

Functional.   Using a functional resume enables you to focus on skills, aptitudes, and qualities that can be applied to a number of situations. Additionally, the **functional resume** "focuses on accomplishments and results on the job rather than on a linear job description" (Sorenson, Kennedy, & Ramirez, 1997, pp. 126, 129). Skills are organized into categories of related work. For example, your background may include skills in management, finance, human relations, and communication. By listing your proficiencies separately under a "skills" category, you can highlight those commensurate with your background.

The functional resume is especially valuable for candidates who (1) lack direct job-related experience, (2) have worked for one employer for a long period of time, (3) want to work in fields not related to their academic background, or (4) have breaks or gaps in time in their employment history. Figure 6.2 on page 152 provides an example of a functional resume.

Targeted.   With the **targeted resume,** your capabilities and accomplishments are presented in a format that "targets" a specific position or field. Targeted resumes differ from chronological and functional resumes in that the former is used to focus on a specific job objective and tailors your information accordingly. You may include a summary of your qualifications at the beginning, which briefly outlines your skills for the reader.

Cover Letters

Whenever you send a resume, you should include a cover letter. A **cover letter,** also known as a letter of application, provides the interviewer with an overview of your qualifications. Your strategy should be to demonstrate that your qualifications fit the requirements of

---

Jeremy Thomas
1234 Times Square
New York, New York 54321
Ph: (123) 456–7890
FAX: (123) 789–4565
E-mail: jthomas@nyc.edu

EDUCATION
University of New York City. Bachelor of Arts, Communication Arts.
Concentration: Public Relations. GPA 3.5/4.0.
Graduation: April 1998.

EXPERIENCE

8/97 to present	**Free-lance writer, Catholic Hospital,** NYC. Write press releases and develop monthly calendar for Catholic Hospital.
5/97 to 8/97	**Public relations intern, Catholic Hospital.** Wrote and distributed press releases. Developed monthly calendar of events. Assisted with media relations including coordination of the videotaping of a **Rescue 911** segment and arrangement of a press conference with the Governor of New York. Wrote profiles of employees of the month.
Summer 1996	**Courier, First City Bank,** NYC. Delivered postal and interoffice mail between five offices. Made daily runs to airport with bank documents. Sorted and ran postage for daily mail.

HONORS AND AWARDS
Phi Eta Sigma Honor Society
New York Undergraduate Scholarship recipient
John C. Pace Scholarship recipient

ORGANIZATIONS
Captain, UNYC Sailing Club
Member, NY Public Relations Society
Editor, Communication Arts newsletter

COMPUTER SKILLS
WordPerfect 6.0, 7.0; PageMaker 6.5

REFERENCES
References and portfolio provided upon request.

Figure 6.1   **Sample Chronological Resume**

the position you are seeking. Study the position description carefully and decide how you can match your background and qualifications to the position (Banis, 1994, p. 46).

Mechanics of the Cover Letter

One persuasive marketing principle you may use to write a cover letter is the **AIDA principle.** As an acronym, AIDA stands for attention, interest, desire, and action. By structuring your letter of application with these four words, you will be able to gain the

Alexander Brilliant
1000 Brookstone Rd.
Tampa, FL 88889
Ph: 305–999–9999

Summary of Experience
- 10 years writing
- 10 years customer relations
- 8 years cost analysis
- 6 years public speaking

Skills

Writing
  Wrote articles for military newspaper. Developed military base recycling guidelines. Created first military base housing cleaning contract. Edited Hazardous Waste Management Plan.

Customer Relations
  Fielded calls and ensured guest satisfaction in condominium setting. Managed service contracts in excess of $1 million and ensured customer satisfaction. Coordinated Hazardous Waste project.

Cost Analysis
  Prepared detailed cost estimates. Supervised proper payment distribution and justified nonpayment actions. Assisted Environmental Chief with appropriation of $7.3 million for environmental projects and studies.

Public Speaking
  Prepared and conducted briefings for senior personnel. Developed and conducted training courses for base personnel. Coordinated environmental seminars.

Experience
  1994–96   Environmental Management Technician
              52 Civil Engineering Squadron, Spangdahlem Air Base, Germany

  1991–94   Technical Assistant
              Robins Air Force Base, Warner Robins, GA

Education
  University of Tampa, Tampa, FL, Bachelor of Arts in English. GPA 3.67/4.0.
  Graduated with honors, May 1998.

Awards
  Dean's List, University of Tampa
  Air Force 1995 Employee of the Year

                    References available upon request.

Figure 6.2   **Sample Functional Resume**

reader's attention, interest, desire and, hopefully, action to contact you for an interview. We will take you through the step-by-step process of using the AIDA principle.

The first paragraph of your cover letter should gain the *attention* of the reader. This paragraph should reveal your purpose for writing and your interest in the position. If someone has referred you for the job opening, mention his or her name in the first paragraph. Doing so will provide the reader with a frame of reference.

The second paragraph of your letter should create *interest.* Outline your strongest qualifications in such a way that they match the position requirements. As much as possible, provide evidence of your related experiences and accomplishments, and make sure you refer to your enclosed resume.

In the third paragraph, convince the employer that you have the *desire,* personal qualities, and motivation to perform well in the position. Be persuasive and sell your qualifications to the employer.

The fourth paragraph should create an *action* plan. Be assertive and request an interview. Indicate that you will call during a specific time period to discuss interview possibilities. Close your letter by showing appreciation to the reader for his or her time and consideration.

Remember, the interviewer will read your cover letter first before reviewing your resume. Make sure your letter is convincing and persuasive.

The Employment Interview

The employment interview is the single most important determinant of whether or not you get hired. Your resume opens the door by briefly outlining your background and experience, but an interview is the deciding factor between you getting the job or the job going to someone else. You want your first few minutes in the interview to make a statement about YOU. Your appearance, communication skills (verbal, non-verbal and listening), knowledge of the company, and background experience all reflect your personality and affect how well you come across to the person you are meeting.

> You never get a second chance to make a good first impression.
>
> —*Anonymous*

InterviewER Preparation

For an applicant, the interviewer's task seems easy. The interviewer asks most of the questions and then determines the best candidate for the job through a process of elimination. On the surface, most applicants would rather trade places with the interviewer, whose primary objective is to make a decision about the most qualified applicant. However, interviewing a candidate is not as simple as it looks. For instance, consider the preparation phase from an interviewer's perspective. Reviewing the process can help you better prepare for a job interview. (Additionally, you may find yourself in the position of interviewer in the not-so-distant future.)

Preparation actually begins with determining the type of job opening available within the company. For example, in large companies, the human resource director usually confers with the head of the department in which the position is open. Together,

Your first few minutes in an interview set the stage for the entire interview process.

they (1) discuss the job qualifications and the criteria for the "ideal" candidate, and (2) make sure the job description accurately reflects the current job opening.

Employment Application.   The employment application should ask pertinent, legal questions that are nondiscriminatory. Questions about marital status, age, religion, sex, and physical characteristics are illegal and, therefore, should not be asked unless the job requires it. (For example, if the job demands heavy lifting, repetitious motion, and so forth, questions about specific physical traits would be appropriate.) The job application should be preapproved by the human resources department or your company's legal counsel. You want to make sure that your application adheres to federal government regulations so as not to discriminate among any group of people for any reason.

Advertising the Job Opening.   The basic rule of thumb is to advertise in publications where qualified applicants tend to look for jobs. Most job-seekers read local, regional and national newspapers, trade publications, journals, and occupational magazines. The Internet also provides a variety of web sites on which you can announce job openings. Currently, one of the best web sites on which to advertise jobs that are available for college graduates is JobWeb, which is owned and operated by the National Association of Colleges and Employers (NACE). Their web address is http://www.jobweb.org

Reviewing Legal Guidelines for Questioning.   Every person in the United States has an equal opportunity to apply for employment. Federal legislation has created several agencies and organizations to enforce federal laws that have been passed over the years. As the interviewer, you should be briefed on these guidelines in order to adhere to federal laws. If you have questions about legal interpretation of the law, ask the human resources director or legal counsel in your company for the most current information available. Likewise, make sure the questions you ask applicants are relevant to the job qualifications. Familiarizing yourself with the federal laws, as both an interviewer and interviewee, will assist you in the interview process.

Organization of the Interview.   In an ideal situation, an interviewer should explain the various topics that will be discussed at the beginning of the interview. If you tell the applicant what will be discussed and the order in which you will discuss it, and provide an approximate time frame for the interview, the candidate will feel more relaxed and less anxious (Gorman, 1989, p. 40). It is important to make a candidate feel comfortable, and as the interviewer, you set the tone and establish the comfort level of the interview at the outset.

In an ever increasingly competitive marketplace, interviewers sometimes deliberately set up "stress interviews" to determine how well you can handle hypothetical situations. A stress interview is particularly appropriate for high-stress jobs like sales. For example, an account executive in a computer firm will have constant stress on the job as a result of new technologies and competition in the job market. If you are interviewing candidates for that position, you might present one or more hypothetical situations and ask candidates how they would respond in order to see how effectively they would handle the problems.

During the employment interview, a good interviewer will ask one question at a time and allow enough time for the interviewee to respond. One of the most important components of the interview is the ability of both parties to listen attentively. (See Chapter 2 for more information on listening.) Keep in mind that you must concentrate on what the interviewee is saying instead of thinking about the next question that you will ask. In successful employment interviews, interviewers talk about 25 to 30 percent of the time to allow interviewees time to answer the barrage of questions. After all, it is your job as an interviewer to find out as much about the applicant's background as possible in a short period of time.

Questions should focus on educational background, employment history, and work-related activities. Strengths and weaknesses of the applicant should be discussed, along with the expectations of the job. Provide the candidate with enough time to ask questions toward the end of the interview. Finally, be sure to let the interviewee know when you will be making a decision about the position.

Physical Setting.   The best setting for an interview is one that eliminates distractions. Keep in mind that the interview is a stressful situation for both interviewees and nervous interviewers.

Ideally, the interview room should be in a relatively quiet setting that is conducive to easy conversation. Everyone within the interviewing area should be made aware that an interview is in progress in order to alleviate any possible disturbances. Comfortable chairs and a table or desk for writing are common in the interview room. The interviewee should take the lead from the interviewer, and the interviewer should maintain control and direct the interview.

However, in a stress interview, for example, the interview may take place in a room with a single table and no chairs. At the outset, the absence of chairs in the room makes the interview stressful. Another example of a stressful situation might be the interview that is set up to have constant interruptions. For example, the telephone may constantly ring, a fax may come in, the supervisor may interrupt and request a report that was due an hour earlier, and the office assistant may call in sick. Conducting an interview under these circumstances is difficult for both you and the interviewee, but will allow you to observe how he or she will react in a stressful situation.

Topics to Be Discussed.   Whether or not the selection interview will be formal or informal is determined by the type of job opening you are trying to fill. Most professional-level jobs employ a more formal, structured interview. Following are topics most often discussed during a formal job interview:

- ■ *Job expectations*—What the company expects from the candidate. What the candidate expects from the company.
- ■ *Academic background/scholastic record*—College GPA and relevant coursework in the candidate's major field of study. Minor coursework. Favorite and least favorite courses or professors. Reasons why.
- ■ *Past employment experience*—Employment record on a consistent basis. Relevant work experience in candidate's major field of study. Internships or cooperative education experiences.
- ■ *Knowledge about the organization*—Candidate's knowledge about company products or services. Knowledge about the competition. Location of corporate offices. Other geographic locations.
- ■ *Short-term/long-term career goals*—What the candidate expects to be doing three years from now, five years from now, and ten years from now.
- ■ *Interests/activities*—What the candidate does in spare time. Involvement in campus or community organizations.
- ■ *Strengths/weaknesses*—Skills candidate has to offer. Perceived areas of needed improvement.

Framing specific questions to reflect these topics can be a difficult task. We recommend that you cover the topics by structuring the interview according to content areas. Box 6.3 provides you with a list of frequently asked interview questions. How many of these questions could you answer easily if you had an employment interview this afternoon?

Now that we have discussed the employment interview from the interviewER's perspective, we now turn to a discussion of the employment interview from the viewpoint of the interviewEE.

InterviewEE Preparation

No matter where you are in your college career, now is the time to begin preparing for the job interview. Unfortunately, some people wait to plan until the day or evening prior to the interview. You can begin to prepare now by conducting a self-assessment and taking an inventory of the skills you have to offer a prospective employer.

The employment interview is a two-way street. It is an opportunity for two people to provide and evaluate information that will hopefully lead to a mutually satisfying conclusion. Think of the interview as a "conversation with a purpose." Your role in this

BOX 6.3

How Do You Measure Up?

Frequently Asked Employment Interview Questions

Education

1. Why did you select your major area of study?
2. Why did you select your college/university?
3. What subjects were most interesting? Useful? Why?
4. What classes did you do well in? Why?
5. What classes were difficult for you? Why?
6. What is the most important thing you learned from your college experience?
7. What does it mean to you to have a college degree?
8. How did you finance your college education?

Experience

9. Describe each of your work experiences.
10. Describe the type of employee with whom you most enjoy working.
11. Describe the type of employee with whom you least like working.
12. Describe your ideal supervisor.
13. What are some of the pressures you have encountered in your work experience?
14. What frustrations have you encountered in your work experience? How have you handled these frustrations?
15. What aspects of your last job were difficult for you?
16. In what areas has your boss suggested you improve? What did you do to improve?

Position and Company

17. Why did you select this company?
18. Why did you decide to apply for this particular position?
19. What about this position is especially attractive to you?
20. Why should I hire you?
21. What do you know about our company?
22. Are you willing to relocate?

Self-Evaluation

23. Describe yourself.
24. If you could relive your life, what might you do differently?
25. What do you see as your strengths? Give examples of each.
26. What do you see as your weak points? What have you done to improve these?
27. Describe a specific work problem you had. How did you solve this problem?
28. What do you consider to be your greatest work achievement? Why?
29. What factors in a work situation provide motivation for you?

Goals

30. Where do you see yourself in your profession in five years? In ten years? What do you need to do to achieve these goals?
31. What are your salary expectations for this position?
32. What or who has influenced you most to choose your career goal?

Adapted from G. L. Wilson and H. L. Goodall, Jr. (1991). *Interviewing in Context* (New York: McGraw-Hill), pp. 122–123.

conversation is to provide adequate and accurate information that will assist the interviewer in evaluating your skills, experiences, goals, objectives, and personal traits as they relate to the job opening. Additionally, your other role is to listen and obtain information from the interviewer that will assist you in determining whether or not you want to continue pursuing this job opportunity.

Planning. Consider what the interviewer will be attempting to learn about you during the interview. In sum, the interviewer will be trying to answer three questions: (1) Can you do the job? (2) Will you do the job? and (3) Are you the right "fit" for the job and the company? Now that you are aware of the importance of these three questions for the interviewer, you can begin to prepare your answers.

> A ccomplishment will prove to be a journey, not a destination.
>
> —*Dwight D. Eisenhower*

Preparation. As we said earlier, the preparation phase of the interview from the interviewEE's perspective involves a self-assessment, research about the company, and attention to the following details:

- Yourself: Your career interests; any special abilities and skills that might make you stand out from the other applicants; your educational background and work experience; your values, strengths, and weaknesses.

- The company: Their products and services; their competition; location of corporate offices. (Note: answers to these questions may be found in the library, in the career placement office of your college or university, or on the Internet.)

- Appearance: You MUST present a professional image when interviewing. Dark business suits are preferred for both women and men. However, an alternative for women is a jacket over a dress or skirt; for men, a sports coat over slacks is acceptable. Remember that the interviewer is looking for people who match the "company's image."

- Punctuality: Plan to arrive at the interview at least 10 to 15 minutes in advance to have time to collect your thoughts and relax. Allow enough travel time. Try to avoid scheduling interviews at peak traffic times in the morning, at lunch, and in the evening.

- Key Information: Know details about the meeting. Know the name of the person who is interviewing you, as well as the time and exact location of the interview.

- Rehearsal: Practice interviewing with someone else prior to the appointment. Practicing will assist you in hearing your responses to potential questions so you can reframe your answers ahead of time.

The Actual Interview. During the interview, be prepared for a variety of open-ended questions. Potential questions were outlined in Box 6.3. If you are well prepared to answer these questions, you will improve your chances of getting a job offer. Additionally, Box 6.4 describes typical stages and topics to be addressed, as well as what interviewers are looking for in your answers.

Typical Job Applicant Questions. Toward the end of the job interview, the interviewer will ask if you have any questions. Always be prepared to ask a minimum of two or three relevant questions. Doing so shows you are interested in the company and that you have taken the time prior to the interview, to think about the questions you want answered. The following is a list of ten appropriate questions to ask during an employment

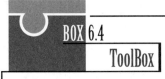

BOX 6.4

ToolBox

*The Whens, Whats, and Whys
of an Initial Employment Interview*

Stages	Interviewer Topics	Interviewer Looks For
First impressions	Introduction and greeting (Interviewer engages in conversation about news, traffic, weather, etc.)	Firm handshake. Eye contact. Businesslike appearance. Ease in social situations.
Your record	**EDUCATION** Reasons for choice of school and major. Grades and courses enjoyed most and least. Reaction to teachers.	Intellectual ability. Value placed on achievement. Reaction to authority.
	WORK EXPERIENCE Level of responsibility. Duties liked most, least. Supervisory experience. Relations w/others.	Responsibility. Ability to follow directions. Leadership ability. Ability to motivate and get along w/others.
	ACTIVITIES & INTERESTS Role in extracurricular activities. Personal interests.	Diversity of interests. Awareness of world outside academia.
Your career goals	Type of work desired. Immediate objectives. Long-term objectives. Desire for further education. Geographic preferences. Attitude toward relocation.	Preparation for employment. Career-orientation. Knowledge of company. Company's chance to get and keep you.
Presentation of information about the company	Company opportunities. Where you might fit. Current & future projects. Training programs and other benefits.	Informed & relevant questions. Indications of interest in company.
Conclusion	Further steps you should take (application form, transcripts, references). Further steps company will take (which department is interested, notification of decision).	Candidate's attention to detail.

interview. Of course, your questions will vary, depending on the type of job for which you are applying and if the questions have not already been clarified.

1. What type of training program do you provide for new employees? How long is the training program? Where is it located?
2. What are the company's future growth plans? What specific areas of the company are expanding?
3. What is the frequency of travel for this job?
4. How often are employees expected to relocate?
5. What are my opportunities for advancement within the company?
6. When will you be making a decision about this job?
7. What would you say is the number-one priority for the person who accepts this job?
8. Will I have an opportunity to meet the people who would be my coworkers?
9. How would you describe a typical day on the job?
10. What traits or characteristics would the ideal candidate have who takes this job?

Thus far, we have given you the tools to survive the initial employment interview from both the interviewer's and interviewee's perspectives. After you have interviewed, remember to send a follow-up letter thanking the interviewer. Be sure to mention the date, time, and place of the interview, and any other information you feel might make a difference in the selection process (e.g., important information you forgot to tell the interviewer, reiterations of important points discussed, etc.). Sending a follow-up thank-you letter could make the difference between you getting the job offer and the job being offered to someone else.

Now let's turn to a discussion of another employment interview you may encounter: the group interview.

Surviving the Group Employment Interview

When interviewing for an entry-level position, more than likely your first interview will be with one interviewer; however, in some cases you may experience a group interview. The reasons companies conduct group interviews vary, but before we tell you how to survive a group interview, let's listen to a conversation between Jill and Nikolas as they discuss a recent employment group interview that Jill experienced.

Jill: "I wish someone had told me about the possibility of a group interview before applying for my first job. I was not prepared for the barrage of questions that were fired at me by five different interviewers."

Nikolas: "Five different interviewers! Weren't you intimidated by all of those people asking you questions?"

Jill: "Yes, it was the most awkward experience I ever had. Sometimes two people would ask me a question at the same time and I wouldn't know who to answer first. It was like they were all competing for my attention."

Nikolas: "So what happened? Did you get the job?"

Jill: "No, probably because I never saw that kind of interview coming. The next time you have an interview, be sure to ask questions before it takes place so you know how many people will be interviewing you. Be prepared and expect the unexpected. I will ALWAYS ask questions beforehand from now on. I don't want to be caught in that situation again!"

Nikolas: "Thanks for the warning, Jill. I have an interview next week and I'm going to call them right now to find out how many people are interviewing me so I can be prepared."

Lucky for Nikolas that he and Jill had this conversation before his group interview with an advertising agency. Otherwise, Nikolas might not have landed his job as an account executive.

Group interviews occur at all job levels, ranging from the entry-level employee to the CEO. The reasons companies have group hiring interviews vary. One reason is to save valuable management time. For example, a group interview will solve the problem of each person interviewing candidates one on one. By holding group interviews, managers can discuss among themselves the applicant who is best qualified for the job. Another reason for having group interviews is for managers to see how you handle yourself in a stressful situation. They are looking for your ability to hold up well under pressure as well as to observe if you appear to be "in control."

How can you prepare yourself for a first-rate group interview? The following are some suggestions based on your authors' first-hand personal experiences.

First, expect the unexpected. The interviewing team will probably interrupt one another, and the conversation will jump from topic to topic. Expect to have less time to think about your responses. For example, while some interviewers are asking questions and listening, others are already formulating the next question. In this type of chaotic environment, you have to be able to field several different questions at one time. Again,

Sometimes group interviews can take place over an informal lunch.

the interviewers may be testing you to see if you can handle the pressure. Likewise, the interview may be a clear indication that your job will be as turbulent as the interview.

Next, before going into the interview, find out as much as you can about the interviewers, especially their respective backgrounds, their job titles, and where they fit into the organization. This information will also help you discover common interests between you and the interviewers. By asking the right questions beforehand, you will be able to acquire the information you need. Remember, an interview is a two-way street. You are interviewing representatives from the company to see if the company is right for you at the same time they are interviewing you for that perfect job match.

Third, when one interviewer asks you a question, give primary eye contact to the person who asked you the question but continue to glance at the other group members. Try to establish a good rapport with everyone, and be careful not to alienate anyone. The quiet person who is not asking many questions just might be the primary decision maker.

Fourth, keep your answers brief and to the point. At times you may feel you haven't been able to appropriately respond to one question before another one is asked of you. Don't let this feeling shake you. Just do the best that you can.

Fifth, try to appear "in control." Be as assertive as possible, and show strength and credibility in your responses. You will be outnumbered in a group interview, so if you can stand up to the pressure, your "prize" may be a job offer.

And last but not least, be honest. Employers want to know they are hiring someone who has integrity and can be trusted to carry out company policies and procedures (Bamford, 1986, p. 191).

Thus far, we have given you many tools to prepare for employment interviews. Over a lifetime, you will probably use this information to assist you with many job and career changes. Another type of interview that will be prevalent in your work life is the informational interview.

The Informational Interview

The goal of the **informational interview** is basically for an individual to acquire information about a person, subject, or process. When conducted properly, an informational interview has the smooth flow of informal, intelligent conversation. Newspaper and television reporters, talk show hosts, radio personalities, writers, organizational consultants and trainers, and advertising and marketing specialists are only a few of the people who use the informational interview in their daily lives.

Informational interviews also are used to seek out information about specific career or job opportunities. For example, if you are trying to decide between a career in marketing or accounting, we recommend that you identify a person with whom to talk from each of these fields and set up an informational interview with each of them. If you don't know anyone employed in your fields of interest, ask family members, friends, or professors if they know of anyone. Before you talk with them, think about what you would like to know about each profession (e.g., type of positions available, typical job duties and responsibilities, future employment possibilities, opportunities for upward mobility, and salary expectations, to name a few).

Informational interviews also are a valuable communication tool between managers and employees. For example, the manager who needs to communicate information to employees about a policy change, might want to conduct informational interviews with the department heads to determine how the policy change would affect the productivity of the employees. Results of such an informational interview would be beneficial to the manager and department heads alike in implementing the policy change.

The Performance Appraisal Interview

A performance appraisal interview is conducted by your supervisor in order to evaluate your job performance. If you are in an entry-level position, a performance evaluation may take place after the first six months of employment. However, most employees are evaluated on an annual basis after the first year in the position.

The **performance appraisal interview** is an exchange of information between the supervisor and the employee about the employee's on-the-job performance for a given period of time. The primary purpose of the appraisal interview is to improve individual performance by (1) clarifying job requirements and standards, (2) providing feedback to the employee about his or her progress, and (3) guiding future performance by preparing an action plan (Brownell, 1994, p. 11). Feedback from your supervisor is essential to inform you about the areas in which you excel on the job as well as areas in which you need improvement. In most cases, your supervisor is also the person who guides and directs your future performance within the department or organization.

Conducting a performance appraisal review is an arduous task for the supervisor because he or she must act as both judge and jury. An ideal session consists of feedback about the employee's performance of job duties and responsibilities, including positive comments, constructive criticism, and future goals. The performance appraisal interview should provide a balance of praise and constructive comments for the employee's improvement.

During the review process, a written evaluation is presented to, and generally signed by, the employee. In some organizations, employees complete self-evaluations and present them to the supervisor prior to the appraisal meeting. The supervisor then reviews the document to determine if the employee's annual objectives were met. After the face-to-face interview, a copy of the signed appraisal form is given to the employee, and the original is usually placed in the human resources file for future reference.

To give you an idea of what to expect in the performance appraisal interview, the following are some typical questions that may be asked:

1. Did you meet your planned goals and objectives for this year? What are your specific accomplishments?
2. What are your goals and objectives for next year? What do you need to do in order to achieve them?
3. In what areas do you feel your strengths lie? What about your weaknesses?
4. Do you feel you need further education in order to do your job more effectively? to become more promotable? If so, in what training areas?
5. Do you feel you are ready for a promotion?

BOX 6.5

ToolBox   *Performance Appraisal Review Suggestions*

1. Answer all questions as completely as possible.

2. Offer explanations, but do not make excuses or place blame.

3. Ask for clarification when appropriate.

4. Ask for specific suggestions for improvement.

5. Ask how much time is available to solve a particular performance problem.

6. Set priorities; avoid trying to improve everything at once.

7. Avoid getting angry or overreacting.

8. Reiterate the problem or solution for clarification and understanding by both parties.

9. Maintain a positive relationship with the interviewer.

10. Close the interview on a positive note and with an open mind.

Adapted from R. Berko, A. Wolvin, and R. Ray (1997). *Business Communication in a Changing World* (New York: St. Martin's Press), pp. 221–222.

A good appraisal interview will be conversational in nature, and should allow time for the employee to ask questions. Employees who want to advance in the company usually want to know what they can do to improve their job performance, and how they can contribute to the progress of the department and the overall mission of the organization.

Whether you are the interviewer or interviewee, remember to keep an open mind and approach the performance appraisal interview with a positive attitude. Because your performance will be reviewed no matter what position you are in, we offer some suggestions for successfully navigating the performance appraisal review in Box 6.5.

The Coaching or Counseling Interview

Roberto is a star forward on his soccer team. His coach knows that, in order for the team to win, he must work closely with Roberto to improve his offensive skills. Just as the soccer coach assists Roberto through guidance and training to improve his playing ability, so too does your supervisor provide "coaching" and counseling for you to enhance your skills on the job.

The **coaching or counseling interview** provides a method for managing employees and helping them understand the culture of a work group. For example, a seasoned employee can assist a new employee by helping him or her "make sense of the mass of information acquired in the first few weeks on the job" (Colby, 1989/90, p. 296). A coaching interview can also assist new managers by giving them an opportunity to gain perspective on what they will be experiencing prior to entering their new job.

Another purpose of the coaching or counseling interview is help an employee solve a job-related problem. For example, as a new employee in a high-tech firm, Adrianna is learning a new software program to sell to her clients. However, Adrianna is experiencing some problems with interpreting the user's manual, so she approaches her supervisor for help with the problem. After some coaching from her supervisor, Adrianna learns that she has misinterpreted some of the wording in the user's manual. Together, Adrianna and her supervisor solve the problem.

The Exit Interview

For one reason or another, you will probably terminate employment many times within the course of your professional career. Some reasons for leaving the company include: (1) you have accepted a position with another company, (2) you are being transferred to a different company location, (3) you are retiring, (4) the company is reorganizing and your job was eliminated, or (5) your spouse was transferred and you are going to be leaving the area. Whether you discontinue your job to accept a new one, or whether you have been caught in a company reorganization and your job was eliminated, it is to your and the company's benefit to conduct an exit interview. Hopefully, you will have had a good experience with the company and will leave on a positive note. You never know when you may want to work for the organization in the future, so the old adage, "Never burn interviewing bridges behind you," is especially true in the case of the exit interview.

An **exit interview** is a tool for management to "help identify ways to improve the organization." The exit interview can also "help uncover possible reasons for an employee's departure" (Brotherton, 1996, p. 45). The purpose of the exit interview is to provide an opportunity for the person leaving the company to say good-bye and gain closure with the company. It also creates goodwill for the organization.

Who usually conducts the exit interview and what can you expect? Many times it is conducted by a member of the human resources department. Sometimes, a supervisor or manager leads the exit interview. No matter who conducts the interview, it is best to let the interviewer lead the discussion by allowing him or her to ask specific questions for you to answer. In some situations, the person leaving will be asked to complete a written form instead of going through a formal exit interview. In either case, typical questions asked during an exit interview are provided in Box 6.6. on page 166.

Depending on the reason for leaving, the employee may be suspicious about the intent of the interview and, therefore, may be reluctant to give pertinent information. For example, John was dissatisfied with his salary. Although he had been employed with his company for five years, he had received only two salary increases. During his exit interview, one of the questions John was asked was, "Why are you leaving the company?" At first, John was reluctant to tell the interviewer the real reason for his departure, but since he had already turned in his resignation, John felt he had nothing to lose. When John left the interview, he felt good about being honest in his reason for leaving.

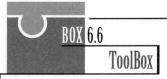

BOX 6.6

ToolBox   *Typical Exit Interview Questions*

1. When you were initially hired with this company, why did you want to work here?

2. What kind of assignments did you enjoy most during your tenure with our company?

3. Was the training you received while you were here adequate?

4. Can you tell me why you want to leave the company?

5. What could we have done differently to keep you here?

6. What did you like most about working here?

7. What did you like least about working here?

8. What are some of the strengths of our organization?

9. What are some of the weaknesses of our organization?

10. Is there any other information you would like to add before you leave?

If you are the person leaving, you should ask several questions, particularly ones dealing with ongoing benefits such as insurance plans, pension programs, stock options, and references. Depending on your reason for leaving (e.g., you are the victim of corporate downsizing), you may want to discuss the possibility of using outplacement services. Remember, the exit interview is designed to provide closure for both you and the organization.

Case Study

Tackling Corporate America as a Recent College Graduate

Melissa Crooke, Administrative Assistant, Sony Music Entertainment, Inc.

Sometimes, to achieve your goals in life, you have to take risks. As a person who grew up in a small town, my dream was to relocate to New York City to work in the music industry. The problem facing me was, "How can I compete with everyone else in the United States who also shares a similar dream?"

One way to get my foot in the door in the music industry was to intern. In order to intern, I had to submit a resume to companies in which I was interested in New York City. I knew my resume had to stand out from all the rest in order to get noticed. If I sent my resume through the mail, I was afraid it might get lost or surely be thrown into a pile, never to be reviewed by the people who might be interested in my credentials.

In my opinion, the ONLY way to accomplish this overwhelming task was to travel to New York City, knock on doors with my resume in hand, and hope that someone would grant me an interview. First of all, getting around in New York City was a feat in itself. After locating the companies that I was interested in, I took a deep breath and realized that the only person who could make this happen was me. I mustered up enough self-confidence to convince myself that I flew all this way and was not going to return to my hometown without at least one interview. As luck would have it, I interviewed with two major record companies in a two-day period. Although the interviewers asked me some tough questions, I was able to pass the interviews with flying colors. Luckily, the intern coordinator at Sony offered me an internship in the Epic Records division.

Questions

1. If you were I, what would you have done to get your resume noticed?

2. How would you prepare for a prospective impromptu employment interview with a large corporation?

3. Upon completion of an internship, what could you do to convince an employer to hire you?

Summary

Being knowledgeable about how to write an attention-getting resume and cover letter is the beginning of your job search. Topics included on your resume and the resume format you choose provide an outline of your background for a prospective employer. The three types of resume formats from which to choose include chronological, functional, and targeted. You should select the format that matches your background and the type of employment you are seeking.

This chapter also covered six different types of interviews you will encounter in your work life: the employment interview, group interview, informational interview, performance appraisal interview, coaching and counseling interview, and exit interview.

Approaching employment interviews from both the interviewER's and interviewEE's perspectives hopefully will provide you with keen insight for future job searches. Various stages of the employment interview were discussed, including preparation and planning, interview organization, and specific questions to ask during the interview.

Knowing what to expect and how to prepare for a group interview is key to your employment interviewing success. Recommendations about how to approach a successful group interview were provided.

Informational interviews have a variety of uses in your work life. In addition to conducting research on the job, they are valuable communication tools between managers and employees.

The performance appraisal interview can be an intimidating experience unless you know what to expect. An effective performance appraisal should provide a balance of praise and constructive comments for on-the-job improvement.

At some point, you may need to ask for guidance or advice from your supervisor, especially about a tough problem-solving situation. A coaching or counseling interview will assist you in determining solutions to problems you may encounter in the workplace.

Knowing what to expect during the exit interview and specific questions to ask as you leave a company are also part of your work life. Whatever the reason you are leaving the company, remember to exit on a positive note. Doing so creates goodwill for both you and the organization.

Knowledge Check

Key Concepts and Terms

interviewing	functional resume	informational interview
resume	targeted resume	performance appraisal interview
electronic resume	cover letter	coaching or counseling interview
chronological (paper) resume	AIDA principle	exit interview

Putting It All Together

1. Describe the similarities and differences among the three types of resume formats.

2. Using the AIDA principle, write a cover letter using your background for a job you plan to seek after graduation.

3. Brainstorm situations in which you can use the informational interview in a business environment.

4. How would you prepare for an employment interview from the interviewER's perspective? from the interviewEE's perspective?

5. What is the purpose of a coaching or counseling interview?

6. How should you approach the performance appraisal interview as a supervisor? as an employee?

7. What kind of questions can you expect in an exit interview? What kind of questions should you ask?

References

Bamford, J. (1986, March). Surviving the group interview. *Forbes,* 190.

Banis, W. J. (1994). The art of writing job-search letters, *Planning: Job choices 1994,* Bethlehem, PA: College Placement Council, Inc. 44–51.

Barrier, M. (1996, June). Hiring the right people. *Nation's Business 84*(6), 18–27.

Berko, R., Wolvin, A., and Ray, R. (1997). *Business communication in a changing world.* New York: St. Martin's Press.

Brotherton, P. (1996, August). Exit interviews can provide a reality check. *HR Magazine 41*(8), 45–50.

Brownell, J. (1994, June). The performance appraisal interview: A multi-purpose communication assignment. *The Bulletin,* 11–21.

Colby, L. (1989/90, Winter). Laying the groundwork for successful job transitions. *Employment Relations Today,* 289–297.

Gorman, B. (1989, January/February). Becoming a better interviewer. *Journal of Property Management,* 40–43.

Kennedy, J. L. (1996). Computer-friendly resume tips. *Planning: Job choices 1996.* Bethlehem, PA:

National Association of Colleges and Employers, 35.

Sorenson, R., Kennedy, G., and Ramirez, I. (1997). *Business and management communication: A guide book,* 3rd ed. Upper Saddle River, NJ: Prentice-Hall.

Wilson, G. L., and Goodall, Jr., H. L. (1991). *Interviewing in context.* New York: McGraw-Hill.

Write the resume employers want to see. (1996). *Planning: Job choices 1996.* Bethlehem, PA: National Association of Colleges and Employers), 33–38.

Zellner, W. (1995, February). Southwest. *Business Week,* 68–69.

7

Leadership

After studying this chapter, you should be able to

- Understand the differences between leadership and management.

- Differentiate among autocratic, democratic, and laissez-faire leadership styles and know the value of matching the appropriate style with the situation.

- Recognize the role that birth order and gender play in your leadership style.

- Identify and understand five different types of power.

- Understand when to use power and empowerment appropriately.

- Develop leadership competencies for the 21st century.

Fred Smith was unaware of the impact he would have on the world when he gave birth, in 1971, to an overnight parcel delivery service called Federal Express. Smith's idea was simple. Couriers would pick up packages from individuals and businesses, deliver them to the airport, and then fly them to a central hub. From there, a team of employees would work together to ensure that packages arrived at their destinations in a timely fashion. To consistently make good on such a risky guarantee, Smith had to build a highly committed and motivated team. In turn, to create such a team required leadership and commitment to employee satisfaction. As chief executive officer of the Federal Express (FedEx) team, Smith succeeded in creating not only a dedicated group of employees, but also the number-one overnight parcel delivery service in America.

Over the years, FedEx hasn't been content with building a company based solely on the team concept. In addition, FedEx has nurtured the leadership potential of its employees. For example, employees interested in management positions go through the Leadership Evaluation and Awareness Process (LEAP) at the corporate headquarters in Memphis. There, first-line supervisors learn leadership skills as well as the corporate philosophy of P-S-P, or "People, Service, Profit." FedEx believes that if you take care of employees first, they will deliver the service demanded by customers. In turn, excellent service will create profitability for the future of the company (Levering & Moskowitz, 1994, p. 122).

Another reason FedEx is still number one in overnight delivery service is that the company's leaders are visionaries. For instance, the primary goal of the company is to bring superior service to their customers. To do so, FedEx has fostered a sense of esprit de corps among employees within the organization. To illustrate, CEO Fred Smith relates the following typical story about a company employee who went above and beyond the call of duty:

> As the building rumbled and shook at the whim of the October 1989 San Francisco earthquake, Federal Express courier Maurice Jane't continued to scan each package he was picking up at Hitachi Data Systems. He then struggled to get them down nine flights of rubble-filled stairs to his waiting van and on to the airport just in time for the plane . . . . (Lee, 1991, p. 32)

FedEx leaders recognize their employees who do a good job by rewarding achievement with bonuses based on individual and company performance. They also publicize their heroes, like Mr. Jane't, which makes employees feel that company loyalty is rewarded.

What about you? How can you develop your own leadership potential? What skills must YOU cultivate to become "one of the best in the business?"

> Example is not the main thing in influencing others. It is the only thing.
>
> —*Albert Schweitzer*

Think back for a moment to when you were a child playing with friends in a group activity. Someone was always the "leader" of the group— you know, a "take charge" kind of kid with great ideas. Someone in your neighborhood, maybe *YOU*, assumed the leadership role by organizing a game of softball or rounding up two teams of kids to go play football. Or maybe that person just wanted to hang out at the mall and took the initiative to call a few friends to organize a place and time to meet.

In this chapter, we are going to help you cultivate these and other important leadership skills. To do so, we will begin by discussing leadership as a concept, the differences between a manager and a leader, and the characteristics of effective leaders. From there we will identify three leadership styles (and help you identify yours), two variables that influence each of those styles, and the best way to relate to people with differing styles. We will conclude with a discussion of power and empowerment and provide specific suggestions for developing your leadership potential.

What Is Leadership?

In the most simple terms, **leadership** is the art of getting someone else to do something we want them to do. As such, " . . . leadership revolves around vision, ideas, direction, and inspiring people as to direction and goals. . . ." (Bennis, 1989, p. 139). As Bennis and Nanus (1985) note, leadership is " . . . what gives an organization its vision and its ability to translate that vision into reality" (p. 20).

Effective leaders do not necessarily have all the answers, but they know how to ask thought-provoking questions and listen carefully to the responses. A good leader takes risks by carefully considering the information available and then acting on it decisively. In short, effective leadership relies on effective communication, and knowing the difference between being a leader and a manager.

Leadership versus Management

Every organization needs effective leaders and managers to accomplish its mission and goals. Some people use the terms "leader" and "manager" interchangeably without stopping to think about the differences. Organizations that succeed employ both.

As Manske (1987) notes, "Leaders light the way for the future and inspire people to achieve excellence" (p. 7). They have vision, and they guide, direct, and influence the course of action the company takes. In contrast, managers " . . . ensure that day-to-day operations run smoothly and that the assets of the corporation, both human and physical, are cared for and protected" (p. 7). Managers bring about the course of action and are responsible for carrying out the direction of the leader.

Bennis (1989) further distinguishes between leaders and managers by arguing that, "Leaders are people who do the right thing; managers are people who do things right" (p. 36). Both roles are crucial in order for a company to be successful in the business world. Furthermore, in his best- selling book *On Becoming a Leader,* Bennis (1994) indicates that leaders are "those who master the context . . . [while managers are] those who surrender to it" (p. 44). Table 7.1 on page 174 summarizes additional differences between these two important organizational roles. As Kouzes and Posner (1987) note, "If there is a clear distinction between the process of managing and the process of leading, it is in the distinction between getting others to do and getting others to want to do" (p. 27).

Both leadership and management are important to an organization and, of course, these roles may not be mutually exclusive. For example, in many offices the office manager also may act as a leader due to the primary responsibilities within his or her department. To illustrate, Jane, an office manager with a small computer software firm, is aware of departmental goals and has a long-range view of what needs to be accomplished in order for the department to succeed. She has been the office manager for over ten years, which gives her credibility. The people with whom she works know that she will take care of their professional needs and prioritize the most important projects first. Jane is her own person and, in most cases, will not hesitate to provide an innovative idea to streamline policies and procedures within the department. As a leader,

Table 7.1	Differences between a Manager and a Leader	

MANAGER	LEADER
Administers	Innovates
Is a copy	Is an original
Maintains	Develops
Focuses on systems and structure	Focuses on people
Relies on control	Inspires trust
Has a short-range view	Has a long-range view
Asks how and when	Asks what and why
Has eye on bottom line	Has eye on horizon
Accepts status quo	Challenges status quo
Classic good soldier	Is own person
Does things right	Does the right thing

Adapted from M. Z. Hackman & C. E. Johnson (1991). *Leadership: A Communication Perspective* (Prospect Heights, IL: Waveland Press).

Jane moves the organization in a new direction by taking risks and making changes. As a manager, she keeps a sharp eye on the bottom line and effectively oversees departmental systems.

Effective Leadership Characteristics

Think of two or three people you know who are successful leaders. They may be your friends, people in the community, political or religious figures, or famous people throughout history. What leadership characteristics do these individuals embody? Do you think they were born with a predisposition toward leadership, or did they learn how to lead sometime during their lives?

Researchers have studied these questions for decades and have uncovered a variety of leadership characteristics. As you read through the following qualifications, think of the leaders whom you admire. Which of these qualities do they exhibit?

■ *Has a strong, internal drive to achieve and succeed.* Kotter (1990) says that "it takes a sustained effort for years . . . to accomplish the kinds of changes associated with leadership. It is difficult to imagine people with less than a high level of internal drive handling the hours and the problems over such a long period of time" (p. 106).

■ *Is mentally and emotionally stable.* Mental and emotional stability allow you to view the world without creating complex personal problems. Leaders must pos-

Leaders challenge the status quo and have a strong internal drive to achieve.

sess a strong emotional balance to overcome the myriad of obstacles in the daily work environment.

- *Possesses integrity.* Successful leaders value other people and care about their well-being. Integrity is a core ingredient for leaders if people are to follow their direction.

- *Is trustworthy.* Trust is vital. "People trust you when you don't play games with them, when you put everything on the table and speak honestly to them" (Bennis, 1994, p. 169).

- *Is willing to empower people.* Competent leaders empower others to make decisions on their own and give them freedom to accomplish tasks without looking over their shoulders. Afterward, successful leaders give credit to their employees for a job well done.

- *Has vision for the direction of the organization.* In order to move a department or organization forward, leaders must have vision. They must have an image of the future and how they are going to get there.

- *Is decisive.* Being able to make decisions quickly and accurately is a quality of effective leaders. Have you ever known a successful leader who is not a good decision maker?

- *Has proven communication skills.* Successful leaders must have proven communication skills in order to communicate the goals and direction of the department and organization to employees.

As you were thinking about people you know who are successful leaders, how many of these leadership characteristics did they possess? You were probably able to identify many of the attributes commonly associated with effective leaders from the list above. Even though most leaders possess a majority of these characteristics, they may exhibit a number of different leadership styles.

Leadership Styles

You probably have heard the terms "autocratic," "democratic" and "laissez-faire" in reference to leadership styles. These well-known styles of leadership were identified by Lewin, Lippitt, and White in 1939. Each of these styles reflects certain patterns of communication behavior.

When a leader sees himself as a central authority figure and retains a high degree of control and power over his followers, he is exhibiting an **autocratic leadership style** (Barge, 1994, p. 38). For instance, the autocratic leader tends to give direct orders and rarely involves others in the decision-making process. He or she feels that followers need specific direction and, if left on their own, will be unproductive. Autocratic leaders also create distance between themselves and their followers as a means of clearly defining role expectations. For example, a navy officer usually does not associate with enlisted personnel on a regular, social basis. Since the military structure is hierarchical and officers oversee enlisted personnel, fraternization between the two is discouraged.

A **democratic leadership style** is used when leaders and followers make decisions together and jointly determine courses of action (Barge, 1994, p. 38). In contrast to the autocratic leader, the democratic leader tends to involve everyone in the decision-making process and works toward group consensus. The democratic leader encourages team cooperation and believes that each member has something of value to contribute. Democratic leaders are generally fair and do not intimidate others.

To illustrate, Tatsuya was recently promoted to general manager of a bank. Several of her employees suggested that every Friday be designated as "casual day," when bank employees could "dress down" by wearing nice shirts and slacks instead of suits. Before Tatsuya made her decision, she asked all of her employees for their opinions on the subject. The employees overwhelmingly agreed that Fridays should be designated as "casual days." As a bonus, the company provided golf shirts with the bank logo on the pockets to promote a sense of teamwork and cooperation among bank employees. From this illustration, can you think of other examples of democratic leadership behaviors?

Laissez-faire, a French word meaning "leave them alone," refers to the type of leader who allows a group to make decisions on their own. The laissez-faire leader does not directly participate in the decision-making process unless requested to do so by team members. For example, Margaret is chairperson of the Communication Department at a major university in the southeast. She has hired faculty who teach courses in such subjects as public relations, advertising, broadcast journalism, print journalism, and communication theory. Margaret believes that each faculty member is autonomous and can make effective decisions regarding courses. She allows them freedom to offer as many courses as possible in their respective areas of expertise. Her laissez-faire leadership style is appealing to her faculty. Perhaps you can think of some other examples of laissez-faire leaders.

Based on the definitions we have provided thus far, what is your style of leadership? How can you determine the leadership style of others? To help you decide, we have developed Box 7.1 for you to use based on extensive research by Hackman and Johnson (1991). Before checking any of the boxes that describe yourself, read through all of the choices. Doing so will give you a greater understanding of yourself as well as the leadership styles of others.

You will note that you may have checked some boxes associated with each leadership style. If so, do not be alarmed. At times you identify with characteristics from each style. Additionally, as Fisher and Ellis (1990) have noted, effective leaders move from

---

BOX 7.1

How Do You Measure Up? | *What's Your Leadership Style?*

Directions: For each of the three leadership styles listed below, read across and check the box which you prefer. After you have completed the exercise, add up each column. The column with the most checks reflects your preferred style, the second number reveals your secondary style and the third column indicates the style you identify with the least.

Autocratic	Democratic	Laissez-Faire
1. ☐ Sets individual goals	☐ Involves followers in goal setting	☐ Allows free rein to set their own goals
2. ☐ Controls discussion with followers	☐ Facilitates discussion with followers	☐ Avoids discussion with followers
3. ☐ Sets policy and procedures unilaterally	☐ Solicits input re: the determination of policy and procedures	☐ Allows followers to set policy and procedures
4. ☐ Dominates interaction	☐ Focuses interaction	☐ Avoids interaction
5. ☐ Personally directs the completion of tasks	☐ Provides suggestions & alternatives for completion of tasks	☐ Provides suggestions, alternatives for completion of tasks only when asked to do so
6. ☐ Provides infrequent positive feedback	☐ Provides frequent positive feedback	☐ Provides infrequent feedback of any kind
7. ☐ Exhibits poor listening skills	☐ Exhibits effective listening skills	☐ May exhibit either poor or ineffective listening skills
8. ☐ Uses conflict for personal gain	☐ Mediates conflict for group gain	☐ Avoids conflict

Adapted from M. Z. Hackman & C. E. Johnson (1991). *Leadership: A communication perspective.* Prospect Heights, IL: Waveland Press.

No matter if your leadership style is autocratic, democratic, or laissez-faire, make sure you are able to relate to the leadership styles of others.

one style to another, even though they are aware of their preferred style. Leaders must be able to adapt to both the situation and the people involved.

Relating to the Leadership Style of Others

As we said earlier, in any work environment you will find leaders who are able to exhibit all three leadership styles: autocratic, democratic, and laissez-faire. The problem is that we generally tend to use (and prefer a boss who exhibits) one style more than another. For example, if you enjoy participative decision making and group activities, you probably are more comfortable with a democratic leadership style. On the other hand, if you like to "call the shots" and are comfortable giving and receiving direct orders, you may lean more toward an autocratic style of leadership. If you want to lead by giving little direction and by letting employees have autonomy, and are more comfortable with a boss who does the same, then you may prefer the laissez-faire leadership style. So how can you best relate to someone else's leadership style if his or her style differs from your own? To create harmony in the workplace, it is best to "let the leader lead" in the style to which he or she is accustomed. If you are the subordinate, you must adjust to the leader's style, even though it may not be your preference.

In Chapter 1, we discussed the value of achieving the best "organizational fit" possible between you and the company in which you work. The style of leadership that exists in your company and the "organizational fit" between you and its leaders are crucial to your effectiveness and job satisfaction. One way to get along better with people who prefer alternative styles to yours is to understand the advantages and disadvantages of each style. To illustrate, let's look closer at the three.

If you work for an autocratic leader, you can expect your supervisor to maintain control over policies and procedures in the organization. Autocratic leaders tend to dominate discussions and assign all tasks to be completed. This style of leadership is appropriate for routine or highly structured tasks. Autocratic leadership also works well when a leader is much more knowledgeable than his or her followers, or when there is insufficient time to engage in democratic decision making. For example, when a surgeon performs an emergency operation, he or she is responsible for directing a team of qualified individuals to save someone's life. The surgeon must take charge and dominate the situation to get the best possible results from the team in the operating room. You, too, may find yourself in a task-oriented organization where autocratic leadership is the preferred style.

A democratic leadership style generally fosters increased productivity, satisfaction, and commitment because everyone is asked for input in the decision-making process. If you like to voice your opinion and contribute your ideas to the organization, you may find that working for a democratic leader suits you. In most situations, democratic leaders provide frequent feedback to keep you up to date on the status of projects and assignments. One disadvantage of this style is that collecting opinions is time consuming and may delay the intended outcome of the situation. The credo of the democratic leader is "two heads are better than one." To illustrate, imagine you are a pharmaceutical sales rep for a new drug that has been approved for over-the-counter sale. Your district manager asks for your input about how to display the new product in your stores. By involving you in the process and requesting your feedback, your district manager is exhibiting characteristics of a democratic leader.

A leader who possesses a laissez-faire leadership style allows you to set your own agenda. If you like to work alone with little direction, working for a laissez-faire leader is for you. Laissez-faire leaders rarely provide feedback, except when asked. They also tend to avoid conflict. As a result, they are most effective with groups comprised of motivated and knowledgeable experts, since these groups generally require little direct guidance and produce better results when left alone (Hackman & Johnson, 1991, p. 27). For example, a graphic arts designer must be able to work independently to create new images for product development. A laissez-faire leader will allow the designer to work at his or her own pace and provide suggestions, if asked.

> The only safe ship in a storm is leadership.
>
> —*Faye Wattleton*

Adjusting to these three different leadership styles takes time because (1) leaders are different in every work environment that we encounter, and (2) leaders can move from style to style depending on the situation. However, once you identify a persons's primary leadership style and know what to expect, you can adapt more quickly to that leader's behavior.

Two Variables That Influence Leadership Style

There are many factors that influence leadership style. Two important variables that have an impact on leadership are birth order and gender. As we explore the reasons why these factors affect leadership style, take a look at yourself to determine what influence they have on you.

Leadership Style and Birth Order. Are you the oldest, youngest, or middle child in your family? Did you know that birth order and leadership style may be related? According to noted psychologist Kevin Leman (1989), "Firstborns are most generally the leaders, the ones who see what needs to be done and who plunge ahead and do it." Since "taking the initiative is a natural tendency of firstborns, . . . [this] often leads them into positions of leadership" (p. 34).

Birth order and leadership style may be related. Are you a firstborn, middle child, youngest, or only child?

People have a tendency to look for guidance and direction from firstborns. For example, as children growing up, " . . . younger siblings tend to look to [older brothers or sisters] to be their leaders" (p. 261). It's not easy for the person who has assumed such a leadership role in early life to go back.

What are the qualities of firstborns that contribute to their leadership abilities? Why do firstborns often seem to be natural-born leaders?

One exemplary quality of firstborns is their tendency to be self-starters. They have the ability to look ahead and see what needs to be done, similar to people who are visionaries. They are self-reliant and self-motivated, and have a tendency to push themselves to the limit. However, firstborns must remember that they cannot do it all. They must know their limits and learn when to say no.

Second, firstborns tend to think problems through before acting on them. They look at all sides of a problem before recommending the best possible solution. Additionally, firstborns are ambitious as a rule. They place themselves under great pressure to accomplish multiple tasks and have a predisposition toward perfectionist behavior.

Finally, firstborns are analyzers. They are noted for asking numerous questions and for wanting to know all the details to get a firm handle on a situation (Leman, 1989, p. 263). Thinking carefully about a situation and weighing the pros and cons are definitely two of their strengths.

Is it any wonder that firstborns are so common among the ranks of U.S. presidents and other prominent world leaders? In fact, more than half of the U.S. presidents (52 percent) have been firstborns (Leman, p. 22). Famous firstborns throughout history include such notables as Wilbur Wright, Jimmy Carter, Maya Angelou, Franklin D. Roosevelt, and Leonardo da Vinci. Although Roosevelt and da Vinci were only children, Leman (1989) indicates that only children tend to take on the characteristics of firstborns.

Middle and youngest children should not despair, because firstborns are not the only leaders. Regardless of birth order, if you display leadership qualities and truly want to be a leader, opportunities exist for you to demonstrate your leadership ability both in the workplace and as a volunteer in community organizations.

Leadership Style and Gender.   Do males or females make better leaders? Are businesses dominated by males more successful than those that are led primarily by females? According to Nelton (1991), "Smart companies are making room for [both] by drawing on the complementary leadership styles of both men and women" (p. 16). While some people still tend to believe that men make better leaders than women, there is no substantial evidence to support males' superiority as leaders (Wood, 1996, p. 258). In fact, it is helpful to realize that both masculine and feminine styles of leadership are effective in organizational settings. Even though the two styles are different, both are equally valid (p. 258).

Stereotypes and assumptions that most people hold about male versus female leaders are difficult to shatter. For example, male leaders are perceived to be more competitive, strong, tough, decisive, and in control, while female leaders are perceived to be more cooperative, emotional, supportive, and vulnerable. These two "styles" of leadership, one predominantly masculine and the other predominantly feminine, are also perceived to have emerged from two different types of life experiences: men's in the military and on the playing field, and women's in managing the home and nurturing husbands and children (Nelton, p. 18).

Interestingly enough, both men and women have much to learn from one another regarding leadership behavior. In fact, in many organizational settings today, leadership training emphasizes this fact as well as the value of more androgynous leadership behaviors.

Androgyny is the term used to describe a combination of male and female traits. Therefore, leaders who exhibit both male and female characteristics in their leadership style are called **androgynous**. An example of how men and women could benefit from more androgynous behavior in the workplace would be for men to share more information and women to share less information—something both are reluctant to do. As Perrigo (1996) has noted, "Whether you are a male or a female, a more androgynous style of leadership can be the key to your success." For instance, both male and female leaders will be more effective if they exhibit the following androgynous behaviors:

- Be a good listener. Listening doesn't always mean agreement. It means that you are willing to hear another person's perspective or point of view.

- Be willing to express your emotions. Leaders who are emotional show their human side. Doing so conveys that you care about your employees.

- Be decisive. Time yourself so that you know when to build consensus and gather information to make a decision. Once you make a decision, stick to it.

- Be yourself. Do what you think is right and natural. Build on your strengths but know that you can learn from the experience and leadership styles of others.

One caveat that we do need to add is that it is possible to go too far when it comes to borrowing characteristics of the opposite sex. According to Deborah Tannen (1994), a noted researcher in gender issues, both women and men pay a price if they do not behave in ways expected of their gender in leadership positions (p. 40). For example, male leaders who are unaggressive may be perceived as "wimps," while female leaders who are unaggressive may be seen as too "feminine."

Leadership and Power

Think for a moment about the person who holds the highest political office in America. The president of the United States is a leader who has "legitimate power," both nationally and globally, because of the office he holds. As such, the power and leadership he exhibits are interdependent. Leaders have the ability to influence others by exerting authority and power. In turn, how they use their power and authority defines them as leaders.

Sources of Power

Theorists John French and Bertram Raven (1959) isolated five major sources of power: coercive, reward, legitimate, expert, and referent power. **Coercive power** arises from the ability to administer punishment or give negative reinforcement. Coercive power is used to force others to comply with the rules or else they will have to accept the consequences. For example, the professor who lowers student's grades if they miss more than three classes is coercing students to attend class on a regular basis.

Reward power is the ability to deliver something of value to another person. For example, when you work extra hours on a special project, your supervisor may reward you with a monetary bonus. In this instance, your supervisor has "reward power" to compensate you for all of your hard work, and uses that power to positively reinforce desired behavior.

Legitimate power arises from the position in which one serves, rather than from his or her characteristics as a person. For example, if you are driving 85 mph in a 55 mph zone, a police officer may decide to pull you over and issue you a speeding ticket. In this example, the police officer possesses legitimate power because he or she has been given authority to enforce the speed limit.

Expert power arises from characteristics or traits of a person rather than the position in which he or she serves. For example, if you require surgery on your knee due to an unfortunate accident, you would more than likely prefer an orthopedic surgeon rather than a general practitioner to oversee the course of your treatment. In this instance, the surgeon possesses greater expert power than the general physician because of her medical specialization.

Referent power is role model power, or the power to lead others because of the roles we play in a company, community, or other highly visible arena. For example, Michael Jordan and Magic Johnson are role models for children and adults alike because they are great basketball players. As a rule, professional athletes and other media celebrities have referent power because of their visibility, extraordinary abilities, and popularity with the general public. So "powerful" are these people that companies like Nike, Reebok, Pepsico, and Coca-Cola bank on them constantly to sell their products and services.

Effective leaders need access to all five types of power, and often must use more than one type of power to achieve their goals. For example, a person who is the president of an organization can benefit by using legitimate, expert, and referent power. To

> **P**ower is strength and the ability to see yourself through your own eyes and not through the eyes of another. It is being able to place a circle of power at your own feet and not take power from someone else's circle.
>
> —*Lynn V. Andrews*

illustrate, Denise is president of a group of newspapers in the Midwest. She automatically possesses legitimate power because she holds the highest-ranking office in the company. Denise also has expert power because she has more than 20 years of experience in the newspaper business. She has referent power because she serves as a role model to others, especially to women within the organization.

Power and Empowerment

During the past decade, the concept of "empowered organizations" has come into vogue. **Empowered organizations** are those in which leadership is shared throughout the organization, often in the form of self-managed teams. In empowered organizations, people at all levels are actively engaged in managing themselves. "Empowered organizations value autonomy as an end in itself—an end that contributes to personal fulfillment and advances democratic ideas in organizations" (Carr, 1994, p. 39).

Herman Miller, Inc., a commercial furniture manufacturer in Zeeland, Michigan, is an excellent example of an empowered organization. At the core of the Herman Miller corporation is the belief that power should be shared. For example, CEO J. Kermit Campbell gives people at all levels more freedom to take ownership in the company by giving them flexibility in the decision-making process. One specific way Campbell accomplished this goal was to restructure the company, eliminate several layers of management, and give employees freedom to make decisions at every level of the organization. To provide employees with the parameters they needed for making effective decisions—Campbell knew that freedom with no boundaries is always a curse—he carefully articulated the goals and values of the company. Today, Herman Miller, Inc., is consistently listed in *The 100 Best Companies to Work for in America* and, in 1988, was selected as one of America's "ten most admired companies" (Levering and Moskowitz, 1994, p. 292). Both leaders and subordinates gain power when the former empower the latter. **Empowerment** is defined as the delegation of responsibility, power, or authority to employees, thereby allowing them to take independent actions as well as responsibility for the outcome of those actions. Employees feel more powerful when they are given the opportunity to make decisions on their own, as long as they have clear parameters and guidelines within which to operate. When you are **empowered,** you are given the opportunity to assume responsibility for managing yourself within an organization.

Empowered leaders not only need to communicate well with others, but also need to facilitate communication among their employees. In empowered organizations, employees themselves decide what information they need, and they access knowledge through every available medium and technological innovation that is available (Carr, 1994, p. 42). The primary role of the empowering leader is that of facilitator. As leaders empower others to act, the entire organization benefits because employees have had a voice in making business decisions.

What are the benefits of empowerment to employees? According to Bennis (1991, p. 15), four primary benefits accrue:

■ *People feel significant.* Everyone feels that he or she makes a difference to the success of the organization. When this happens, people feel that what they do has meaning and significance.

- *Learning and competence matter.* Empowering leaders value learning and mastery, and so do people who work for these leaders. For example, empowering leaders allow employees to make mistakes, but then give them feedback on how to fix the problem.

- *People become part of a community.* Where there is empowering leadership, there is a team environment. Employees know that their colleagues care about them and their well-being on both on a personal and professional level.

- *Work is exciting.* Where there are empowered employees, work is stimulating, challenging, and fun.

Empowered leaders make employees feel significant and successful as the latter make contributions to the organization. To show you how effective empowerment can be, let's take a look at a first-hand experience of one empowering leader with whom you are becoming more familiar.

One of your authors was the chairperson for a national annual Arts Festival during the time she was writing the text. Since the committee was comprised solely of volunteers who worked full-time at other jobs, she knew she had to empower her members and give them responsibility outside of the monthly committee meetings. For example, the Concessions Committee chair was given his own budget and assigned to work closely with the food vendors. The Concessions Committee also had to work with the city, the health department, the fire marshal, and other city and county agencies to acquire permits, overcome potential health hazards, and deal with other possible environmental concerns. These time-consuming tasks provide just a few examples of the many concerns for which your author was ultimately responsible. Obviously, the only way to approach this and other considerable tasks was to empower the chairpersons of each of the nine committees, and allow them to manage their own subcommittees outside of the regular meetings. As a result of empowering each of her committee chairs, the three-day festival was a grand success—the outcome of a truly empowered team.

Developing Your Leadership Competencies

Among the hundreds of studies that have been conducted on leadership, there is no perfect predictor of leadership success. We do know that it is possible for ordinary human beings to learn to lead. Ordinary people can become extraordinary leaders, sometimes as a result of unpredictable circumstances.

For example, prior to her son's fatal automobile accident, Candy did not see herself as a leader. But due to the way in which she lost her son, she became passionate about helping others who had lost loved ones due to drivers under the influence of alcohol. Candy Lightner founded MADD (Mothers Against Drunk Driving) in 1980. MADD's mission is to provide support for those who have experienced the tragedy of a drunk driving accident and to advocate against the act of operating a vehicle under the influence of drugs or alcohol. Today MADD has established more than 400 chapters across the United States. The leadership that Candy initiated continues to aid many families who have experienced unfortunate tragedies as a result of drunk drivers. Candy is a typical example of an ordinary person who became an extraordinary leader because of her passion to help others in similar circumstances.

How about you? Do you feel you have natural leadership tendencies? Indeed, you may possess leadership potential without being aware of the skills you already have. On the other hand, if you feel you do not have a predisposition toward leading, take comfort. Leadership competencies can be cultivated.

Profiling Your Current Leadership Traits

To commence the process of developing your leadership competencies, let's begin by identifying some of your own unique leadership qualities through the Personal Attributes Inventory presented in Box 7.2. Take a few minutes to complete the inventory.

BOX 7.2

How Do You Measure Up? | *Personal Attributes Inventory*

Circle the number that best fits how you presently see yourself (1 = low and 5 = high).

1. I enjoy the role of a leader.	1	2	3	4	5
2. I have a firm sense of purpose.	1	2	3	4	5
3. I am a self-confident person.	1	2	3	4	5
4. I am self-motivated.	1	2	3	4	5
5. I have a strong drive to achieve.	1	2	3	4	5
6. I am a person of integrity.	1	2	3	4	5
7. I have a clear set of values.	1	2	3	4	5
8. I am willing to speak my mind.	1	2	3	4	5
9. I am a decisive person.	1	2	3	4	5
10. I am continually learning.	1	2	3	4	5

Total Score _____

45–50	Excellent. You're in the top 10%.
40–44	Good. You definitely have leadership potential.
20–39	Average. A little polish and you'll be on your way.
15–19	Fair. You've lots of room to improve. Just get out there and do it!
10–14	Whoa! You're really the shy and retiring type. Go for it. We promise it won't hurt a bit.

Adapted from W. D. Hitt (1988). The *Leader-Manager: Guidelines for Action* (Columbus, OH: Battelle Press), p. 221.

Now let's take a closer look at each of these personal attributes and determine if you "have what it takes" to become a leader.

The Role of a Leader and a Sense of Purpose.

To become a leader, you must be able to establish goals and objectives and articulate them effectively to others. Additionally, you must have a strong sense of purpose for yourself, your department, and the organization overall. For example, every organization should have a mission statement, purpose, values, and goals that employees strive to implement or achieve. If you have the vision to imagine how each of them may be implemented and the ability to communicate that vision to others, you definitely have the potential to become a leader.

Self-Confidence, Self-Motivation, and the Desire to Achieve.   Most leaders have a high degree of self-confidence. They must have confidence in themselves in order to work well with others. High expectations that leaders have of themselves translate to high expectations of others. A confident leader will "walk the talk" and lead by modeling his or her expectations for company employees. Self-confident leaders expect others to follow in their footsteps and achieve the highest standards possible for the company.

In order to motivate others, leaders must have an established track record of demonstrated achievements and successes for others to emulate. Additionally, the standards and performance levels that a leader sets affect his or her followers' motivation levels and desire to achieve.

If you are self-confident, self-motivated, and achievement-oriented, you have already won half the battle. If you currently feel deficient in any of these areas, start believing in yourself, take (calculated) risks, and try new things. Challenge yourself to become the best you can be—an expert at something like running, cooking, horseback riding, weight training, or biking. Additionally, if you have the time and money to invest in yourself, you might try a "supervised adventure." Companies like Outward Bound provide just such adventures, which are designed to build self-confidence and self-esteem.

Personal Integrity.   One of the reasons people follow a leader is because they respect, admire, and trust that person. A leader who is trustworthy cultivates loyalty among followers. If you possess personal integrity, people will trust you to guide them in the right direction.

A Clear Set of Values.   As a leader, you must have a fundamental set of values and beliefs on which to base all your decisions. Clarifying these values and beliefs is a highly personal matter that only you can achieve. Your beliefs must be congruent with your personal and professional actions. It is good business practice to review your values and beliefs periodically to determine if they mesh with your present goals and behavior.

Decisiveness and the Ability to Speak Your Mind.   What would have happened had General H. Norman Schwarzkopf not been decisive about the plan of action for U.S.

troops when he led them to victory in the Persian Gulf War? From his many years of leadership experience, Schwarzkopf commented on the importance of decisiveness in *Inc. Magazine* (1992):

> When in charge, take command. Leaders are often called on to make decisions without adequate information. As a result, they may put off deciding to do anything at all. That's a big mistake. Decisions themselves elicit new information. The best policy is to decide, monitor the results, and change course if necessary. (Gendron, 1992, p. 62)

Commitment to Continuous Learning. Successful leaders know that developing leadership skills is a lifetime learning process. If you want to reach your highest potential as a leader, you will need to continually update your knowledge and skills. Invest the time and energy to learn all you can about how to be an effective leader. Commit to a continuous program of self-improvement and leadership enhancement. Read materials that broaden your leadership knowledge and sharpen your leadership skills. Leadership seminars and courses are also available at colleges and universities to strengthen your leadership competencies.

Developing Your Leadership Skills

How can you further develop your leadership skills? As we stated earlier, most college campuses offer leadership training through courses and seminars. Additionally, you can visit your on-campus student activities or student affairs office and explore other avenues that are available to you.

You can also get involved in campus organizations and committees, such as student government organizations, environmental groups, political groups, team sports, and, of course, sororities and fraternities. You also may want to get involved with off-campus associations in the community, such as the American Heart Association, American Cancer Society, March of Dimes, a local hospital, or various cultural groups. Opportunities abound to demonstrate your leadership potential. Campus and community leaders are ready and willing to give you advice and get you involved in any organization of your choice. So what are you waiting for? Take time now to let someone know you are interested in becoming a leader. Get involved. Who knows, you may be the next president of your campus or community organization!

Just as leadership training and experience are important while you are in college, so too are opportunities to cultivate your leadership skills in the organization for which you ultimately work. Fortunately, many companies around the globe realize the need to cultivate future leaders within their organizations. As a result, companies like Goodyear Tire and Rubber, General Motors, Delta Air Lines, and Weyerhaeuser have developed in-house leadership development training programs. These and other companies are doing more than identifying future leaders. They are training "up and coming" managers to lead their respective organizations by encouraging them to participate in "in-house" leadership training, or sending them to internationally recognized leadership seminars. President and CEO of Corporate Performance Center, Barry Sheehy (1993/94) sums up years of leadership research: "Leaders are not extraordinary people as much as they are ordinary people who have been given an extraordinary opportunity" (p. 5).

At this point, you may be thinking, "Why is this information important for me? I'm just trying to finish college and find my dream job!" No matter what size of company or organization constitutes your desired career, its interviewers are looking for leadership potential in new hires. Corporate executives and small business owners " . . . realize that they can no longer wait for a talented junior executive, an energetic research analyst, or an enthusiastic sales representative to emerge from the pack. They are aggressively searching college campuses for graduates who show vital signs of leadership potential, qualities required at all levels if their companies are to be successful in the twenty-first century" (Green & Seymour, 1991, p. 160).

Today, while interviewing for a professional-level job, you may be asked some particularly challenging questions in order for companies to identify your potential leadership skills. For example, corporate reengineering expert Don Blohowiak (1995, pp. 181–184), author of *How's All the Work Going to Get Done?* recommends that companies ask questions such as those outlined in Box 7.3

Across the board, interviewers are searching for potential leaders who can move their respective companies forward. If you have been involved with campus or community organizations and have demonstrated your leadership potential, you will have a better opportunity to land the job you want.

For example, Adriana and Steve were both applying for a position as a trainer with a Fortune 100 company. They both maintained excellent grades in college, they were both involved in student organizations, and they both knew the dynamics of the in-

---

BOX 7.3

ToolBox   *Interview Questions Designed to Identify Your Leadership Potential*

1. Tell me about the best boss you ever had. Why do you favor that person? And how did that affect your work?

2. Tell me about the worst boss you ever had. And how did that affect your work?

3. How do you know when you deliver quality?

4. What have you done when people around you fail to deliver quality?

5. What charitable or volunteer work do you do?

6. Tell me about the person you admire the most.

7. Are you better at starting, changing, or finishing something?

8. If given a preference, would you rather fly solo or in a group?

9. Describe a work experience where things went terribly wrong. What did you do?

10. What have you done to improve your skills in the last year?

Adapted from D. Blohowiak (1995). *How's All the Work Going to Get Done?* (Franklin Lakes, NJ: Career Press), pp. 181–184.

terviewing process and prepared well for the interview. The difference was that Adriana was the president of her student government association on campus. Since the position of SGA president required her to train volunteers and pull together the entire community in an annual fund-raising effort, Adriana was better able to develop her leadership skills. Because she had demonstrated such leadership ability in college, Adriana was offered the position of trainer over Steve. Like Adriana, you too can land the job of your dreams. When you do secure such a position and decide you want to further advance your leadership capabilities, where can you go from there?

Once you determine that you *want* to lead at a higher level of an organization, and feel you have the capability and confidence to lead, the next step is to determine *how* to lead. To begin, you need to ask yourself some important questions. For example, how much do you understand about what is going on in your unit? your department? your organization? In what direction do you think your organization is headed? How strong is your relationship with your peers, subordinates, and administrators? These are some of the many questions you need to answer before taking the next step: letting management know you are interested in increasing your leadership responsibilities.

Cultivating Your Visionary Proficiency

One skill that you can cultivate to prepare for a greater leadership role is your visionary proficiency. By **vision,** we mean your innate ability to anticipate and plan a successful future for your department, unit, and organization. You can begin by identifying people who hold leadership roles in your company and asking them questions about how you and your department or unit fit into the "big picture," or the future direction of the organization. Then you can take your own steps toward establishing individual and departmental goals that support the company's vision.

Why should you be concerned with cultivating visionary proficiency? A company's vision is inextricably linked with its success. Many leaders seem confused about the role of vision in leadership. A clear vision aids in planning, organizing, staffing, developing, directing, evaluating, and controlling a unit, department, and organization. Having a clear vision helps the leader focus on essentials. Foremost on every leader's mind should be this question: Are our current decisions and results moving us *toward* or *away* from the vision of our organization? (Hitt, 1988, p. 53)

One company that has captured a visionary spirit and achieved continuous excellent performance is Neiman-Marcus. CEO Stanley Marcus communicated his vision for providing superior service to customers by demanding that Neiman-Marcus employees "offer only the finest merchandise and service to customers seeking original and unusual items" (Alexander, 1989, p. 59). By openly sharing his expectations with employees, his ideas were transformed and implemented company-wide. As a result, employees of Neiman-Marcus enjoy customer acceptance, community support, and an enhanced reputation.

Without a clear vision, a leader is like Alice in Wonderland when she asks the Cheshire Cat, "Which way should I go?" Of course, the Cheshire Cat responds by asking, "That depends on where you are headed." Alice responds, "I don't know." Then the Cheshire Cat, with a cantankerous grin on his face, says, "Then it doesn't matter which way you go." Indeed, there is an important lesson to be learned about vision from this children's story.

The 21st Century Leader

As we move toward the 21st century, what will be expected of our future leaders? What additional skills will be necessary in order to function in our global environment?

Leadership at the turn of the 21st century faces a difficult challenge. To succeed, the leader must master a plethora of issues, concerns, and dilemmas facing the business or corporation. The business environment today is challenging and changing so rapidly that effective leadership is no longer optional for survival and growth of a company.

What are some of the major forces of change that will affect future leaders? McFarland and Senn (1993) interviewed 100 U.S. leaders representing a cross section of business, education, government, health, environment, and service sectors about changes in 21st century leadership. Their research uncovered three major driving forces of change:

1. globalization and its consequence of increased competition,
2. the acceleration and complexity of change, and
3. the decrease of hierarchies and "position power" (p. 3).

Not surprisingly, these findings have implications for you as a future leader.

First, a well-educated workforce is necessary in order for people and companies to compete on a global basis. Leaders today have the responsibility to educate and train the next generation of leaders. As future leaders, you have an opportunity to learn about global competition from leaders on your campus, in your community, your country, and the world. Second, you have heard the old saying, "the only thing that remains the same is change." Nowhere is this expression more appropriate than in the dynamics of leadership. As future leaders, you must be adaptable and flexible in today's quickly changing job market. Third, with fewer hierarchical levels in organizations today, leaders are empowering employees to do their jobs rather than attempting to control them. Future leaders must know how to empower others to move the organization forward and to implement the organization's mission.

As we said earlier, the business environment today is changing so rapidly that competent leadership is no longer optional. Emerging leaders will be responsible for the future direction of the workforce which, in turn, will impact the global marketplace. Effective leadership is imperative to move companies forward in our increasingly competitive, complex, changing society. Perhaps the following quotation from McConnell (1994) sums up the essence of 21st century leadership:

> True leadership is of the spirit as much as of the mind. It is about vision, inspiration, courage, human relationships and profound knowledge. A true leader develops other leaders, in the sincere hope that one day the student will surpass the teacher. (p. 26)

Case Study

Leadership and the Management of Strategic Change at Shell Internationale Petroleum Maatschappij B.V. (Holland)

John R. Lickvar, Director of Purchasing

Since the mid-1980s, companies in the oil and gas industry have faced extreme competitive pressures as a result of numerous factors, most notably:

- an increase in worldwide demand for hydrocarbon products;
- a declining price for crude oil and refined products; and
- increasing costs associated with exploration, production and environmental legislation.

To meet these pressures, companies have concentrated on lowering their costs, often by selling off noncore businesses and marginal assets, reducing workforces, and completing mergers or joint ventures with other companies.

In an effort to improve its cost structure and overall performance, Shell Oil International investigated the value of implementing a new worldwide purchasing strategy. Results of the study by Shell revealed several opportunities for improvement:

- the annual corporate spending on goods and services was nearly four times larger than annual employee costs;
- the autonomous operating companies around the world seldom worked together on purchasing matters;
- similar strategies had proved to be successful in other industries; and,
- the strategy had the potential to be applied across the corporation.

The New Purchasing Strategy and the Company's Commitment to Change

The new strategy was developed by the central office's Purchasing function, and was endorsed by senior management. Additionally, the following steps were taken to create awareness of and commitment to the new strategy:

- the strategy was documented in a professional, attractive brochure and was widely distributed;
- purchasing managers visited major operating companies to explain and "market" the strategy;
- the strategy was featured prominently in conferences, workshops, and training courses; and,
- guidelines, tools, and techniques regarding the new strategy were developed and disseminated to operating companies to facilitate its implementation.

Barriers to Strategic Change

During the two years that followed, business performance improved. However, within the purchasing function, the feeling existed that those improvements were only the "tip of the iceberg." To document their belief, purchasing conducted an assessment of "barriers to further progress." Results of the study revealed two important barriers (1) Shell's corporate culture and (2) less-than-optimal attention being paid by management to the purchasing function. Specifically, purchasing found that:

■ because of the details involved in the purchasing function, the new strategy remained outside of the company management limelight. In turn, the lack of attention by management fostered a perception that "everything is fine if no one is complaining";

■ personnel outside of purchasing considered the strategy a "purchasing strategy"; therefore, it wasn't their responsibility to support the strategy. Stimulating people to become "process oriented" and to work across function and department borders was also difficult.

■ Purchasing personnel were often regarded as managers of inventory, not purveyors of corporate strategy. As a result, the responsibility of sponsoring the strategy and demonstrating its benefits was often passed to the purchasing manager or supervisor, who were untrained and had little time for such a role.

■ rather than working together to optimize corporate buying power, operating companies often focused on why they were different and defended their current purchasing practices.

Questions

1. What efforts could senior management and the purchasing function have made to better support implementation of the new purchasing strategy?

2. What means, other than the four mentioned above to create awareness, could have been used by company leaders to create "ownership" for the strategy across the business?

3. What risks might be associated with empowering others to take a leadership role in an organization such as this?

4. What costs accrue if leadership isn't shared?

Summary

As an organizational variable, leadership is highly complex. As a result, it is difficult to determine a universal definition or specific qualities that are similar in all leaders. In this chapter, you learned the differences between leadership and management. While leaders focus on people, managers focus on systems and structure. Leaders have a long-range view; managers have a short-range view. Leaders ask what and why; managers ask how and when. Both leaders and managers are essential to the internal and external functions of the organization.

Understanding the three types of leadership styles and being able to relate to autocratic, democratic, and laissez-faire leaders will assist you in your professional development within a company. Knowing how to adapt to each leadership style will greatly enhance your business savvy.

Two variables that play a significant role in leadership style are birth order and gender. In many cases, firstborns tend to be leaders because they are self-starters. Early in life, others look to them for guidance and counseling. Gender is another variable that affects leadership style. Both masculine and feminine styles of leadership are effective in organizational settings.

Five sources of power have been identified by researchers: coercive, reward, legitimate, expert, and referent power. Effective leaders know when to use each source of power and when to empower people to accomplish organizational goals. Empowerment is defined as the delegation of responsibility, power, or authority to employees and allows them to take action in an organization.

Identifying your personal leadership attributes is the first step in developing your leadership competencies. If you enjoy the role of a leader, are a self-motivator, have a strong drive to achieve, and like to learn continuously, you definitely have leadership potential. If you want to further develop your leadership potential, leadership training may be your next logical step.

Cultivating visionary proficiency is important if you aspire to become a leader in the next century. Developing leadership competencies should be your primary goal if you are pursuing promotional opportunities within any organization.

Knowledge Check

Key Concepts and Terms

leadership	androgynous	referent power
autocratic leadership style	coercive power	empowered organization
democratic leadership style	reward power	empowerment
laissez-faire leadership style	legitimate power	empowered
androgyny	expert power	vision

Putting It All Together

1. What are the differences between a leader and a manager? Is it possible to effectively achieve both roles? If yes, how?

2. What are five qualities of an effective leader?

3. Distinguish among the three types of leadership style.

4. Does gender make a difference in leadership? Provide some persuasive arguments for your response.

5. List the five sources of power and give an example of each.

6. What are the benefits to employees of having leaders who empower them? What are the benefits to employers?

7. How do you know if you have leadership potential? What does ethics have to do with leadership?

References

Alexander, J. W. (1989, May/June). Sharing the vision. *Business Horizons, 32*(3), 56–59.

Barge, J. K. (1994). *Leadership: Communication skills for organizations and groups.* New York: St. Martin's Press.

Bennis, W. (1989). Why leaders can't lead. *Training & Development Journal, 43*(4) 35–39.

Bennis, W. (1991, Winter). Learning some basic truisms about leadership. *Phi Kappa Phi Journal,* 12–15.

Bennis, W. (1994). *On becoming a leader.* Reading, MA: Addison-Wesley Publishing Co.

Bennis, W., & Nanus, B. (1985). *Leaders: The strategies for taking charge.* New York: Harper-Collins Pub., Inc.

Blohowiak, D. (1995). *How's all the work going to get done?* Franklin Lakes, NJ: Career Press.

Carr, C. (1994, March). Empowering organizations, empowering leaders. *Training & Development, 48*(3) 39–44.

Fisher, B. A., & Ellis, D. G. (1990). *Small group decision making,* 3rd ed. New York: McGraw-Hill.

French, J. R. P., & Raven, B. (1959). *The bases of social power.* Ann Arbor, MI: Univ. of Michigan Institute for Social Research.

Gendron, G. (1992, January). Schwarzkopf on leadership. *Inc. Magazine, 14*(1), 11.

Green, K. D., & Seymour, D. T. (1991). *Who's going to run General Motors?* Princeton, NJ: Peterson's Guides.

Hackman, M. Z., & Johnson, C. E. (1991). *Leadership: A communication perspective.* Prospect Heights, IL: Waveland Press.

Helgesen, S. (1990). *The female advantage: Women's ways of leadership.* New York: Doubleday.

Hitt, W. D. (1988). *The leader-manager: Guidelines for action.* Columbus, OH: Battelle Press.

Kotter, J. P. (1990). *A force for change.* New York: The Free Press.

Kouzes, J. M., & Posner, B. Z. (1987). *The leadership challenge: How to get extraordinary things done in organizations.* San Francisco: Jossey-Bass.

Lee, C. (1991). Followership: The essence of leadership. *Training, 28*(2), 27–35.

Leman, K. (1989). *Growing up firstborn: The pressure and privilege of being number one.* New York: Delacorte Press.

Levering, R., & Moskowitz, M. (1994). *The 100 best companies to work for in America.* New York: The Penguin Group.

Lewin, K., Lippitt, R., & White, R. K. (1939). Patterns of aggressive behavior in experimentally created "social climates." *Journal of Social Psychology, 10,* 271-299.

Manske, F. A., Jr. (1987). *Secrets of effective leadership.* Memphis, TN: Leadership Education and Development, Inc.

McConnell, J. (1994, March). On lemmings, managers and leaders. *Journal for Quality and Participation, 17*(2), 26–28.

McFarland, L., & Senn, L. (1993, April). 21st century leadership. *Executive Excellence, 10*(4), 3–4.

Nelton, S. (1991). Men, women and leadership. *Nation's Business,* 16–22.

Perrigo, E. (1996, March). Gender and androgyny. Lecture presented at The University of West Florida, Pensacola, FL.

Sheehy, B. (1993/94, Winter). Quality leadership—What does it look like? *National Productivity Review, 13*(1), 1–5.

Schuster, J. P. (1994). Transforming your leadership style. *Leadership, 46*(1), 39–42.

Tannen, D. (1994). *Talking from 9 to 5.* New York: Wm. Morrow & Co.

Wood, J. T. (1996) *Gendered relationships.* Mountain View, CA: Mayfield Publishing Co.

Managing Stress and Conflict

8

**After studying this chapter,
you should be able to**

- Identify the physical and psychological causes of stress.

- Distinguish between negative and positive responses to stress.

- Recognize your own unique symptoms of stress.

- Manage your stress more effectively through a number of stress management tips and techniques.

- Understand the nature and causes of conflict in your work life.

- Identify symptoms of, and tactics associated with, workplace conflict.

- Recognize and use five different conflict management styles.

- Implement several different conflict management strategies in your personal and professional life.

Sun Tzu, author of *The Art of War*, gave us some sound advice when it comes to managing conflict with people: "[Always] . . . build your opponent a golden bridge to retreat across" (1988). That way, you will rarely make an enemy and everyone can win. To provide you with an example of Sun Tzu's "philosophy on conflict," consider the following contemporary event that took place in the early years of film-maker Steven Spielberg's life:

"When I was about thirteen, one local bully gave me nothing but grief all year long. He would knock me down on the grass, or hold my head in the drinking fountain, or push my face in the dirt and give me bloody noses when we had to play football in phys. ed. . . . This was somebody I feared. He was my nemesis. . . . Then, I figured, if you can't beat him, try to get him to join you. So I said to him, 'I'm trying to make a movie about fighting the Nazis, and I want you to play this war hero.' At first, he laughed in my face, but later he said, yes. He was this big fourteen-year-old who looked like

John Wayne. I made him the squad leader in the film, with helmet, fatigues, and backpack. After that, he became my best friend." (Spielberg, 1985; as cited in Ury, 1993)

What do you think happened in this scenario? We believe that the creative Spielberg recognized the need to make this bully feel important. To do so, he created an alternative method of recognizing his adversary. By asking his tormentor to play a role in his film production, Spielberg intuitively built a "golden bridge" for him to cross and, in the process, made him a friend (Ury, 1993).

When you were young, you also may have had a bully in your life. That person may have been the terror of the neighborhood, an older kid with too much free time, or your own older brother or sister. The problem is that bullies grow up and often find their way into the workplace. As a result of their antics, we often feel so frustrated that we wish we could stay home in bed. We know what is waiting for us at the office: backstabbing and confrontation. Or worse yet, we will experience that terrible unspoken tension that always seems to fill the air.

Every day, millions of people work in similar situations. While some respond by experiencing stress, others react with open conflict. After completing this chapter, you will be able to (1) identify the primary causes of stress and conflict, (2) describe positive and negative responses to both, and (3) more effectively use stress and conflict management strategies. You should find these tools to be helpful both in the workplace and in your everyday personal life.

Stress in the Workplace

Have you ever had a knot in your stomach, sweaty palms, or a headache that appears just before you go in for a "chat" with a professor or boss? Do you experience similar physiological responses before a first date or meeting with someone whom you really admire? According to Seyle (1974, p. 64), **stress** is " . . . the common denominator of all adaptive reactions in the body." More specifically, stress is a person's mental, emotional, and physical responses to overwhelming situations in life. As you will see in the following section, a job promotion, a wedding, physical illness, and the death of someone close all have stress-producing results, whether the stressor is positive or negative.

Causes of Stress

Stress can be categorized into one of two major types: physical and psychological stress. **Physical stress** is caused by physical demands on your body, such as exercise, illness, a work-related accident, a demanding work schedule, or prolonged psychological stress. **Psychological stress** results from mental and emotional demands on your body from yourself and your family, colleagues, work, or friends. Psychological stress also results when you find yourself in unfamiliar or uncomfortable situations.

For example, Tia has been asked to organize a work team to create a new ad campaign for a client. She likes her work as an artist, but she hates the idea of working in groups. Your boss has asked you to work with Tia on the project. Since you are new, you know that your job depends on the success of the campaign. The problem is that no one wants to be part of Tia's team. In fact, talk around the copy machine is that Tia always ends up completing team projects alone and at the last minute. Over the next few weeks, your colleagues keep dodging meetings, and Tia is now sending angry memos to everyone involved. You have been the only person who shows up consistently, and all Tia does is complain about the lack of assistance from her team. What are some of the causes of stress in your personal and professional life? Take just a moment and think about this question before you continue with your reading.

Positive and Negative Responses to Stress

Generally, people respond to stress in one of two primary ways: "fight" or "flight." For instance, some people believe that stress is exactly what they need to help them perform at their best. An experienced actor or musician who channels his excitement into a stellar performance provides an excellent example of a positive response. So, too, does the consultant who uses her excitement to make a powerful, dynamic presentation to a prospective client.

On the other hand, stress can produce negative results, ranging from a constant, nagging feeling of anxiety, to a belief that you are coming down with the flu, to a full blown panic attack. Rather than stay and fight, people who experience these and other negative effects often want to flee because their fear, pressure, or frustration is overwhelming.

Individuals who thrive on stress and, consciously or unconsciously, set up situations to meet their need for pressure have been labeled "urgency addicts" by Covey, Merrill, and Merrill (1994). Urgency addicts wait until the last minute to begin or complete a task. They believe that the rush of adrenalin and pressure helps them produce their best work. At the other end of the spectrum, people who consistently respond in a negative way to stress tend to become "absentee workers." Their reactions to stress are maladaptive and literally make them physically ill.

According to Peurifoy (1995), negative stress can be short term (e.g., the fear that is produced when an oncoming car swerves into your lane) or long term (e.g., the stress you may feel in a high-pressure job). As Peurifoy notes, "Too much stress, especially over a long period of time, can drain energy, cause undue wear and tear on the body, and make you vulnerable to illness and premature aging" (p. 38). Pictures of Presidents Bill Clinton and Jimmy Carter before and after four years in the White House provide an excellent example of this fact.

Gaining energy from stressful situations is not necessarily negative. However, what happens when this type of person works in a group or team setting? The group tries to function effectively, while the urgency addict stalls progress until his or her best work level has been met. Conflict ensues, stress levels rise, more conflict follows, and the process becomes cyclical. Eventually confrontation results, or one individual completes the entire project alone.

> A certain amount of stress is not always bad. It varies from person to person how much stress one can handle easily. Sometimes, stress can push us on to greater achievement. But excessive stress can be self-defeating.
>
> —*H. Winter Griffith, M. D. (1985)*
> Complete Guide to Symptoms, Illness & Surgery

Depending on the situation, stress may produce a positive or negative response.

What about the people who consistently exhibit the flight response? How often have you been in a class when an assignment is due, and one of your group members is nowhere to be found? How many times have you been asked to make a group decision and find yourself working with people who will say nothing, and remove themselves—not physically, but mentally—from the discussion? These individuals feel they cannot handle the situation and, again, have maladaptive responses to stress. Again the cycle of conflict, stress, conflict, and stress repeats itself. The result is similar to the experience of the urgency addict's group.

When your primary response is negative, job stress can sabotage your success in a company, as well as the productivity of the company overall (Hales and Hales, 1996). In fact, stress is one of the most often cited reasons for people not coming to work. The problem is that a passive or negative response to stress is rarely successful. In fact, this type of response results in even more stress as a function of missed deadlines, resentment from coworkers, and eventually the loss of a job.

We often are hampered from dealing well with stress because we may have learned ineffective coping strategies in our childhood. In turn, less-than-desirable coping strategies may have traveled with us into adulthood.

As an illustration, think back to a time when you were playing with neighborhood kids. If you were lucky, one of the children suggested a game to play, and everybody went along with the idea. However, if your neighborhood was like many, two kids were constantly angry because both of them wanted to be the boss. When one failed to get his way (that would be Bob), he would take the ball—depending on the season and the sport—and go home, leaving the rest of the kids to play kick the can. After a big emotional blow-up, his face turned red and purple; unusual words came out of his mouth; and he left, physically shaken by the encounters. As he grew up, he exhibited similar "leaving behaviors" on the playground, later in school elections, and finally in his first marriage. Dealing with stressful situations wasn't Bob's strong suit. Unfortunately, he never figured out that his behaviors were a part of the problem.

If you are aware of the positive and negative stressors in your life, and how you react in stressful situations, then you are well on your way toward developing a successful stress management program. However, additional information that is exceptionally useful involves the symptoms associated with stress.

Symptoms of Stress.   One of the first steps you can take to more effectively manage stress is to identify the symptoms you experience during times of extreme duress. One excellent way you can accomplish this task is through the process of introspection. **Introspection** is the examination of your physical, mental, emotional, spiritual, and relational states at a given point in time. By using this self-reflection technique to identify your symptoms now, you can implement coping strategies more quickly and effectively in the future, before your stress level becomes unmanageable.

To help you recognize your body's own unique symptoms of stress, take a few minutes and complete the "Stress Symptom Inventory" presented in Box 8.1 on page 202.

Once you have identified your body's early warning signals, you are ready to determine what people, events, or situations create stressful situations for you. Like the previous exercise, the following activity will allow you to realize that you are experiencing stress and do something about the situation immediately.

Begin by identifying a specific event in your past that generated tension. It may have been a group presentation, a confrontation with a friend or colleague, or a public speech you gave in front of a class. Second, identify how you reacted physically and emotionally in this situation. Were you able to function effectively? Did you find yourself excited and able to respond in a successful manner? (If you need a memory jog for any negative symptoms, return to the "Stress Symptom Inventory" in Box 8.1.)

Third, mentally note the exact moment when you stopped feeling stressed. Was it the minute the event concluded, or were you able to call on past successful stress management skills to achieve your goals? Fourth, honestly evaluate how well you handled the situation. Did you successfully manage or lessen your stress level in any way? What could you have done to manage your symptoms more appropriately? Do you feel more prepared to meet this type of challenge in the future?

As time allows, consider starting a journal and noting other events, people, or situations that cause you to experience symptoms of stress. Learning to recognize your body's early warning signals, as well as your stressors, will help you progress toward more successful stress management.

BOX 8.1

How Do You Measure Up? | *Stress Symptom Inventory*

Directions: Think of several times when you have experienced excessive stress, and check any of the symptoms you experienced during those times.

Physical Symptoms

[　] Appetite change
[　] Colds/flu
[　] Digestive upsets
[　] Fatigue
[　] Finger drumming, foot-tapping, etc.
[　] Frequent sighing or yawning
[　] Headaches
[　] Increase of accidents
[　] Increased alcohol, drug, tobacco use
[　] Insomnia
[　] Irregular breathing or hyperventilation
[　] Muscle aches
[　] Pounding heart
[　] Rash
[　] Restlessness
[　] Teeth grinding
[　] Tension
[　] Weight change
[　] Others

_____
_____
_____

Mental Symptoms

[　] Boredom
[　] Confusion
[　] Difficulty thinking clearly
[　] Dull senses
[　] Forgetfulness
[　] Lethargy
[　] Low productivity

[　] Negative attitude
[　] Poor memory
[　] Reduced ability to concentrate
[　] "Weird" or morbid thoughts
[　] Whirling mind
[　] Others

_____
_____

Emotional Symptoms

[　] Anxiety
[　] Bad dreams or nightmares
[　] Crying spells
[　] Depression
[　] Discouragement
[　] Frustration
[　] Increased use of profanity, put-downs, or sarcasm
[　] Increased emotionalism
[　] Irritability
[　] Little joy
[　] Mood swings
[　] Nervous laughter
[　] Short temper
[　] The "blues
[　] Others

_____
_____
_____

Spiritual Symptoms

[　] Apathy
[　] Cynicism

[　] Doubt
[　] Emptiness
[　] Inability to forgive
[　] Loss of direction
[　] Loss of faith
[　] Loss of meaning
[　] Need to "prove" self
[　] "No one cares" attitude
[　] Pessimism
[　] Sense of helplessness
[　] Sense of hopelessness
[　] Others

_____
_____

Relational Symptoms

[　] Avoidance of people
[　] Blaming
[　] Distrust
[　] Fewer contacts w/friends
[　] Increased arguing/disagreements
[　] Intolerance
[　] Lack of intimacy
[　] Lashing out
[　] Less loving and trusting
[　] Lowered sex drive
[　] Nagging
[　] Resentment
[　] Others

_____
_____
_____
_____

Reprinted by permission of Warner Books, Inc. New York, New York, U.S.A. From *ANXIETY, PHOBIAS, & PANIC* by Reneau Z. Peurifoy, Copyright © 1995. All rights reserved.

Values, Expectations, and Hot Spots. In his best-selling book, *The 7 Habits of Highly Effective People,* Stephen Covey (1989) identified yet another set of questions to address if you want to effectively manage stress in the workplace. In leadership workshops around the world, Covey argues that effective stress management means being proactive rather than reactive. However, to become more proactive, you must be aware of your values, expectations, and emotional triggers. By identifying these influential variables in your life, you can gain greater control over your reactions to people and situations. The questions Covey poses regarding these variables are presented in Box 8.2.

BOX 8.2

How Do You Measure Up? *Values, Expectations, and Hot Spots*

Directions: When you have a quiet moment, complete the following questionnaire as thoughtfully as you can.

1. What is the most important goal in your life?

   _____

   _____

2. What do you see yourself doing in five years?

   _____

   _____

3. What do you value the most about yourself?

   _____

   _____

4. What is the most important value you look for in others? _____

   _____

   _____

5. On a scale of 1 to 5 (1=Low; 5=High), how important is honesty to you? _____

   Why? _____

   _____

   _____

6. On a scale of 1 to 5 (1=Low; 5=High), how important is trust to you? _____

   Why? _____

   _____

   _____

7. How do you feel when you think someone is not being fair to you? to others? _____

   _____

   _____

8. What are your roles in life? at work? at home?

   _____

   _____

9. Can you subordinate your moods to your will? Do you? _____

   _____

10. Who are the people whom you admire most? Why? _____

    _____

    _____

As we said earlier, Covey argues that greater self-control emerges through identification of your values, expectations, and "hot spots." In doing so, you can (1) become more proactive than reactive, (2) begin to take greater responsibility for your own actions, and (3) reduce your stress level in the process.

At this point, you may be thinking, "So *I'm* in control. What about the other people who are bouncing off the walls?" Perhaps the best response to this question is that you can choose to play their game or not. Some organizations have certain rituals or "hoops" through which you are expected to jump. You still may have to complete formidable tasks or work with people whom you dislike, but the amount of stress you associate with these tasks and people is now under your control.

Some people thrive in a stressful environment. However, it is not necessary for you to become an "urgency addict" to be successful in the workplace. A person who avoids stressing out over every single task may be a welcome change to a company or business. You may even become the proverbial hand that calms the stormy seas.

Stress Management Tips and Techniques

Now that we have introduced you to the causes, symptoms, and contributors to stress, what are some tips that you can use to better manage stressors in your life? Peurifoy (1995) made some excellent recommendations, which are summarized below:

- Accept your body as a machine with a limited supply of energy that varies from day to day. Once your energy supply is used up, you must take time to rest and nourish yourself. Otherwise, your body will begin to break down.

- Build your tolerance for stress with a balanced diet and exercise. A strong and healthy body handles stress more effectively than an unhealthy one.

- During periods of extreme stress, set priorities and reduce your overall activity. Avoid major decisions; wait until you are less stressed. If you must make a major decision, slow down the decision-making process and consult with trusted friends or colleagues who can be more objective.

- If you know that a stressful event or situation is coming up, plan ahead, make decisions, and take action in advance while your stress level is still low.

- Develop a lifestyle that is based on stress management principles. That means taking time daily to relax, play, or decompress with a good book, movie, hobby, or friend. It also means to avoid taking yourself so seriously, to inject humor in your life, and to find a person with whom you can share emotional support.

- Leave time for your spiritual self, or time for something in your life that helps you make sense out of the world around you. Meditation, inspirational books, or a quiet walk in the woods are only a few of the ways you can see events in a larger context and feed your inner self.

- Finally, take time to develop traditions and routines that are regular, fun, and rejuvenating. Try planning dinner once a week with a partner or significant other, a movie night with a friend once a month, or a special time daily for each of your children. Traditions and routines give you something special to which you can look forward, and help provide structure to what can be an otherwise chaotic world (pp. 64–71).

Stress can never be eliminated completely, especially if you desire a natural, normal life. Rather, the ultimate aim is to channel your energy in such a way that you minimize the negative effects of stress. Problems, deadlines, rocky relationships, and crises are bound to happen. However, your ability to respond in a calm and less stressful manner will aid you both personally and professionally.

Conflict in the Workplace

What is conflict and how does it begin? Although a number of definitions abound in the literature, a particularly useful one that highlights the nature of conflict in the workplace was developed by organizational communication experts, Linda Putnam and Michael Poole. Putnam and Poole (1987) defined **conflict** as "the interaction of interdependent people who perceive opposition of goals, aims and values, and who see the other party as potentially interfering with the realizations of these goals" (p. 552). As Putnam and Poole note in this succinct definition, three variables are necessary and sufficient for conflict to develop: (1) incompatibility of goals, aims, and values; (2) interdependence of activities or behaviors among the individuals involved; and, (3) the actual expression of incompatibility through interaction (i.e., communication). To illustrate the efficacy of Putnam and Poole's definition and how easily conflict can arise, consider the following illustration.

Saeed was a sales representative with an international pharmaceutical company. Because his job required substantial travel, and Saeed was one of the company's best reps, he was given permission to work at home whenever he was in town. He also was asked to visit the office once a month for the company's monthly sales meetings.

When Saeed worked at home, he took breaks whenever he needed them. In fact, as far as Saeed was concerned, his salary and the flexibility of hours were two of the greatest perks of his job.

One day, Saeed's manager asked him to come in and supervise the office for a week while she was on vacation. His travel schedule was open, so Saeed told her that he would be happy to step in. When Saeed arrived at the office, his colleagues greeted him warmly. However, during the course of the day, they became dismayed. Saeed took breaks whenever he wanted, visited cordially with other workers, and didn't seem to respect the general work ethic at the office. How could Saeed take breaks any time he wanted, when everybody else was allowed only 15 minutes in the morning and 15 minutes in the afternoon? Their breaks were closely monitored, and his coworkers resented the fact that Saeed worked differently. Obviously Saeed had little discipline, and probably got even less accomplished when he worked at home. By Wednesday, the air was filled with tension, and Saeed couldn't figure out why his colleagues seemed angry.

Return for a moment to Putnam and Poole's definition of conflict, and the three variables they believe are necessary and sufficient for conflict to arise. In the illustration above, incompatibility over "organizational procedures" served as the basis for conflict. Specifically, Saeed and his colleagues clashed over beliefs about how time should be managed. Interestingly enough, Saeed's colleagues had incredible respect for him prior to his supervision of their work, and always talked and joked with him when he came in for meetings. However, once they were required to work interdependently, a perceived "incompatibility" regarding time surfaced. As his colleagues talked among themselves about Saeed's "irresponsible behavior," the perceived conflict became his colleagues' "reality." However, it wasn't until his boss returned and told Saeed about the "problem" that Saeed even had a clue about what he had "done wrong."

As you can see, Putnam and Poole's definition of conflict provides an excellent starting point for identifying and analyzing the nature of conflict. However, to bring you closer to an understanding of conflict in the workplace, a few more facts and details are in order. Specifically, we will identify (1) two additional causes of organizational conflict, (2) the symptoms and resulting tactics often associated with it, (3) strategies for more effectively managing conflict, and (4) the benefits of organizational conflict.

Causes of Conflict in the Workplace

We all have goals and expectations about what our jobs or careers will be like, how we should treat others, and how others should treat us. The distance between what we believe should happen and what actually occurs is a major source of conflict in the workplace. According to Handy (1993), conflict can be further classified as resulting from two fundamental issues: (1) differing ideologies, which are reflected in Putnam and Poole's definition, and (2) territoriality.

Conflict can emerge from an unknown, external source and can produce devastating outcomes.

Ideology may be defined as a set of political or cultural beliefs about how we should behave, and about the goals, standards, and values that we should hold. Ideological differences emerge in an organization when:

- formal goals and objectives diverge,

- definitions of roles differ,

- perceptions of allegiances and relationships collide, or

- objectives become unclear or concealed (Handy, 1993, pp. 301–303).

To illustrate how differences in ideology can cause conflict in the workplace, consider the effects of a "simple" change in personnel.

Robin served as manager for 17 years with a national chain of electronics stores. She was bright, loyal, organized, and known for her outstanding sales record. As a result, Robin's former district manager, Tony, allowed her to make decisions about her store and implement them whenever she wanted. Robin gave Tony updates regarding her decisions at their regular monthly meetings.

Later, Robin began working with a new district manager, Miriam, who was transferred into the district from Chicago. The new manager wanted to have final approval before Robin, or any other store manager, implemented changes. Robin and Miriam experienced conflict as a function of their differing expectations. Robin thought her role, responsibilities, and freedom to make decisions would continue as they had in the past. Miriam's demands made Robin wonder, "Doesn't Miriam think I can do a good job? Did I do something wrong?"

Chances are that the new district manager was just continuing her work as she did in Chicago, and her management approach with Robin had nothing to do with Robin's past performance. Now, unless Robin can find a way to bridge the distance between her and Miriam's disparate ideologies, she may find herself looking for a new job. Or, even worse, she will stay in her job, grow to resent her district manager, and make a substantial investment in her favorite antacid.

Differences in ideologies represent only one source of conflict in our work lives. Territoriality also plays a vital role. In his book, *The Territorial Imperative,* nonverbal expert Robert Ardrey (1966) defined **territory** as "an area of space, whether of water or earth or air [that is defended or delineated] . . . as an exclusive preserve" (p. 3). Cats rub against their owners to claim their territory, and dogs chase off other animals who get too close. Similarly human beings erect fences, call the police to arrest invaders, and declare war if another country enters their airspace.

In the organizational setting, territoriality is generally viewed as psychological rather than physical—as a sphere of influence rather than a particular space. As Handy (1993) noted, the implications of the metaphor are fascinating as they relate to our work life:

- Territory is prized and not willingly relinquished or allowed to get overcrowded;

- Some territories are prized more than others;

> **M**an...is as much a territorial animal as is a mockingbird singing in the clear California night...if we defend that title to our land or the sovereignty of our country, we do it for reasons no different, no less innate, no less ineradicable, than do lower animals.
>
> —*Robert Ardrey (1966)*
> The Territorial
> Imperative

■ Trespassing is viewed as a violation; you enter by invitation only;

■ People seek to increase or improve their territory even to the detriment of the organization as a whole; and so on (Handy 1993, pp. 303–4).

Transferring these "imperatives" to human work space, indeed, creates some fascinating results.

If someone enters our office and takes a file without our knowledge, then we perceive our territory or space to be violated. When a group of six people are working on a project and a new outside team leader is appointed, the group may feel overcrowded and become territorial. Should a committee head override a decision or recommendations of a subcommittee, then the subcommittee may view the chairperson's act as a violation of territory. If one group of people is given a brand new work space, then other groups may become jealous and covet that territory.

These are only a few examples of how territoriality can create organizational conflict. Take just a moment and think of the last time you felt your "territory" was violated, or felt jealous because you were left out of the loop on an important decision. How did you respond? Positively or negatively? Were you able to manage conflict in a constructive way?

More often than not, we respond to conflict in a negative way, as you will see in the following discussions of symptoms and tactics. However, conflict can lead to new and different ways of looking at the world, if we learn how to manage it effectively. Conflict also can serve as a source of innovation and positive change.

Symptoms of and Tactics Associated with Workplace Conflict

How do you know when conflict is brewing in the workplace? Generally, you know when you first feel tension in the air. However, six additional symptoms or warning signs of conflict are:

■ Poor communications laterally and vertically;

■ Intergroup hostility and jealousy;

■ Interpersonal friction, icy formality and arguments;

■ Increased use of arbitration by management to settle intergroup conflicts;

■ Increased emphasis on who is and isn't following the rules, regulations, and norms; and

■ Low morale expressed in the form of frustration about inefficiency (e.g., "We just can't seem to get anything done these days," or "No matter what you do, the pay's the same. Just get the job done and move on to something else.") (Handy, 1993, p. 299).

When these symptoms of conflict emerge, people generally respond with a number of tactics: (1) deliberately controlling information; (2) distorting information to one's advantage; (3) creating new rules and regulations to deal with similar conflicts in the future; (4) using informal networks to bypass formal procedures; (5) refusing to give well-earned promotions; (6) rejecting recommendations by a warring party;

and, (7) pointing out the flaws in an opposing group or its efforts. As you can see, tactics such as these can be disastrous and ultimately escalate the conflict (Handy, 1993).

Conflict Management Strategies

Self-reflection. Just as with stress, knowing your own values, expectations, and "hot spots" can help you when conflict arises. Additionally, you will experience heightened awareness and avoid allowing yourself to respond automatically if you know what creates conflict for you.

As Covey (1991) and Wisinski (1993) point out, our personal values and belief systems are often at the root of conflict. Much of the literature on organizational conflict supports their argument, and reveals that conflict can usually be traced to communication problems and personal value systems. It is important for you to begin now to identify what is important to you. On what issues are you willing to bend? What are you NOT willing to compromise?

Know thyself.

*—Inscription at
the Delphic
Oracle
from Plutarch,
Morals*

Are we saying that you need to sit down and make a list of everything that is important to you? According to the newest conflict literature, the answer is, "Yes!" In fact, more and more management seminars are addressing the issue of personal value systems and their impact on the workplace (Covey, Merrill, & Merrill, 1994). If you take the time for self-reflection, will you still encounter conflict? Definitely, but you will be more prepared than the average person. Knowing who you are, what makes you tick, and where your boundaries are makes you a stronger and more reliable employee and a more dependable boss.

Once you have identified what is important to you, you will recognize that your values will differ from those of others. Whether you are working in a large or small office or even in your own home, you will need to be ready to deal with other perspectives.

Understanding of Conflict Styles.   According to Kenneth Thomas (1976), each of us has a style, or set of strategies, that we use when we find ourselves in a conflict situation. The five primary styles that Thomas identified are competition, accommodation, avoidance, compromise, and collaboration. As you will see in the following paragraphs, each style has its own particular strengths and appropriate times for implementation, identified by Wisinski (1993).*

Competition is a Win-Lose strategy and involves approaching conflict with a dominance mind set. This is a "winner takes all" approach with a focus on success at all costs. Generally, your concerns are placed above the other party's interests, even at the expense of the relationship. Competition is appropriate when:

1. other approaches have failed,
2. unpopular issues or changes need to be implemented, or
3. a necessary and quick decision is imperative (Wisinski, pp. 17–18).

---

*Excerpted by permission of the publisher, from RESOLVING CONFLICTS ON THE JOB by Jerry Wisinski. ©1993 AMACOM, a division of American Management Association. All rights reserved.

In contrast, **accommodation** is a Lose-Win style and involves approaching conflict management with a more yielding mind set. In other words, you are willing to allow the other person's interests to be placed above yours. Accommodation is appropriate when:

1. protecting a relationship with the other party is more important than the outcome,
2. the issue is paramount to the other person and not as important to you, or
3. involving others in the discussion is important (Wisinski, p. 18).

Avoidance is the third style that Thomas identified and represents a Lose-Lose approach to conflict management. Avoidance involves not talking about the issue in question or avoiding the other party altogether. As you might gather, when used alone, this strategy is rarely effective in dealing with conflict. However, many of us use this style or strategy far too often because (a) we think the problem is trivial, or (b) we simply don't know how to approach the conflict in question. The problem is that, if neglected too long, conflict can stifle productive work and ultimately harm relationships. Perhaps the only time that avoidance is an appropriate strategy to use is when tempers flare and both parties agree to a "cooling off" period. That way the two people or groups can analyze the situation more carefully and approach the problem more constructively at a later time.

With **compromise,** both parties are willing to give and take (i.e., Win/Lose-Win/Lose) in order to manage the conflict effectively. This approach is appropriate to use:

1. when you want to find common ground and power is not an issue,
2. to reach a solution in a difficult situation that must have a conclusion, or
3. the personal relationship needs to be maintained (Wisinski, p. 20).

Collaboration is considered to be a Win-Win conflict management style. Through collaboration, both parties work toward understanding the position of the other and, hence, mutual agreement. For collaboration to work, trust between parties must be high. Collaboration is most appropriate to use:

1. when both parties are willing to creatively solve a problem,
2. when trust levels are high and all hidden agendas are out in the open, and
3. to get at previously unresolved issues that may have hindered progress (Wisinski, p. 21).

How can you use this information to better manage conflict in the workplace? First, realize that each of these styles presents you with a number of strategies from which you can choose to deal with a specific problem. Rather than relying on one particular style, which we often do, you can consider the parties involved, the political implications, and the impact of resolving (or not resolving) the conflict. Then you can select the best conflict management strategy for the given situation.

Second, if one style or set of strategies fails to work, you can choose another strategy or tactic through which to approach the conflict. Sometimes knowing that you have a number of strategies at your command allows you to keep the situation in perspective and empowers you with the knowledge that a number of options are available.

A point to remember is, once you have identified and implemented a strategy, to evaluate how well you actually use it. If one strategy fails to resolve or address the issues, try another. Having multiple strategies upon which to draw will ultimately serve you well.

Through collaboration, people work toward mutual understanding.

Problem Solving.   Depending on the nature of the conflict, the people involved, and the leadership style of management, a simple problem-solving technique may be all that is required to manage a conflict successfully. As Blanchard and Peale (1988) noted, "Every problem can be solved if you take some quiet time to reflect, seek guidance, and put things into perspective" (p. 77). Once you have completed this initial introspective process, you are ready to begin a dialogue with the other people involved in the conflict.

One six-step problem-solving technique you can use to resolve conflict is presented as follows. Initially, each individual works through the steps on his or her own, and then everyone who is involved comes together for discussion. The goals of the process are greater understanding and the ultimate resolution of the conflict.

- Step One: *Define the conflict.* In this step, define what YOU think the problem may be. Then speculate about how the other party or parties may define the conflict.

- Step Two: *Analyze the situation.* Begin by asking the following questions:

  1. **Who** is involved? Identify all affected parties.
  2. **What** is the problem? What is its nature and scope?
  3. **When** did the problem occur? How much has the problem escalated? Does the problem involve an isolated event, or is it a lingering problem?
  4. **Where** did the conflict occur? In what context, situation, or place did the problem surface?
  5. **Why?** Can you identify why the problem happened? Could conflict have been avoided?
  6. **How?** What occurred that precipitated the conflict? Was someone not paying attention? Does anyone have a hidden agenda? Once you have sufficiently answered these questions, you are ready to move to Step Three.

- Step Three: *Generate alternative solutions.* Here you can use different brainstorming techniques to generate possible solutions. Remember that, when brainstorming, no idea is too wild or crazy.

- Step Four: *Project the possible outcomes of implementing each alternative solution.* Follow each idea to its completion in order to see where it can lead.

211

■ Step Five: *Select and agree on a plan.* The important issue here is to AGREE on a plan. To agree, you must discuss each solution and come to consensus on the best one for all parties involved.

■ Step Six: *Implement the plan and evaluate.* Not only should you act immediately on the plan that has been selected, but you should follow up with an honest evaluation of your success. If the plan fails to work, then everyone should review the alternative plans or, if necessary, reevaluate the group's definition of the conflict.

The AEIOU Model.   Wisinski (1993) offered us yet another approach to conflict management called the AEIOU Model. Note that assertive individuals may be more comfortable with this technique.

A *Assume* that the other person means well. Try to find positive elements in the other person's position.

E *Express* your feelings and expectations regarding positive intentions on his or her part. Then, affirm what you believe the other position is and state your own specific concerns.

I *Identify* your desired goal. Using positive language and nondefensive behavior, propose changes you would like to see implemented. Be aware of language choices. It is better to say, "I would like to see . . . ," or "I think . . . ," than "I want . . . ," or "You should. . . ."

O *Outcome* should be defined as expected. Discuss both the possible positive and negative outcomes of your idea. Honestly assess the merits of your plan before you present it.

U *Understanding* should occur on a mutual level. Determine whether the person understands your position, and attempt to gain agreement to try out your plan. At this point, you must be flexible and willing to listen to any of the other person's concerns (pp. 28–29).

The AEIOU Model can be more complex than the six-step problem-solving technique we presented earlier. The AEIOU Model involves no joint identification of the conflict, nor any discussion regarding alternative solutions. As such, the most appropriate times to use this technique are situations in which (1) the conflict involves little emotional identification, and (2) the relationship is not in jeopardy. However, like all conflict management techniques, dialogue is paramount. Without open and honest communication, the model will fail.

Covey's Conflict Resolution Technique.   Finally, a fifth technique that is being used in organizations around the world was suggested by Covey (1989). This best-selling author recommends that you complete the following four-step process:

1. First, see the problem from the other person's point of view. Take the time to really address the concerns and needs of the other party.
2. Second, identify the key issues and concerns (not positions) involved. Here you separate the person from the issues.
3. Determine what results would mean a completely acceptable solution—not to one, but to all parties.
4. Identify any possible new options available to achieve those results.

Covey suggests that this approach, when used with care, will produce a Win/Win scenario for all affected parties. With this technique, the emphasis is placed on listening to, and gaining an understanding about, the concerns of the other people, groups, or companies involved.

The Beneficial Results of Conflict

Is conflict always negative? Can conflict be positive? Although we answered these questions earlier in the chapter, you may be surprised by the benefits that can accrue as a result of conflict. For example, Kreps and Thornton (1984) argued that six different benefits can result. We encourage you to remember the following merits before you define any situation as hopeless:

- Conflict can be a warning signal for larger problems.
- Conflict can act as a "safety valve" and a chance to release pent-up frustration.
- Conflict can be used as an opportunity to engage in communication and dialogue.
- Fresh approaches and creative solutions can result when old approaches to conflict are ineffective.
- Problem solving may be facilitated.
- Conflict provides an opportunity to "share" information across boundaries. In short, conflict can increase the quality and quantity of communication, and ultimately improve ideas.

Since stress and conflict play intricate and complex roles in our lives, having a variety of tools and techniques at your disposal will ultimately serve you well. Additionally, knowing your reactions, values, expectations, and personal resources will better prepare you for the 21st century workplace.

Case Study

How to Reduce Stress in a New Job

Jim Knasel, Account Executive, AT&T

After graduation from college, Theressa was fortunate to land a job as an account executive with AT&T. She knew that her first professional job was critical to her career success. She realized the first impression she gave to her business colleagues would be a lasting one, so she wanted to make sure she was perceived in a positive manner. Among other things, Theressa knew she would be judged by her managers and peers on such factors as job performance, communication skills, relationship with others, appearance, and how she handled projects and deadlines. In order to manage what Theressa hoped would be the beginning of her career with AT&T, she had to learn how to manage her time appropriately to reduce potential stress and conflict in her new job.

Questions

1. How could Theressa win the respect of her new peers and managers from a professional standpoint?

2. Within the first two months of her employment, Theressa faced the following situation: She had a project due for her supervisor in one week, two important customers wanted sales proposals immediately, and her branch manager wanted to send her to a two-week product training seminar in New Orleans, which began the next day. How could she handle this situation to reduce stress and potential conflict?

3. The vice president of marketing was so impressed with Theressa's on-the-job performance that he asked her to give a presentation to all of the sales support managers about a new product line. Theressa was flattered by his request, but she was not yet familiar with the new product line; however, she knew this was a high-profile opportunity that could either make or break her career. How should she handle this stressful situation?

Summary

Stress and conflict play a significant role in our work lives as we approach the 21st century. Physical stress is caused by physical demands on the body, while psychological stress results from mental and emotional demands on the body. Generally we respond to stress in one of two ways: fight or flight. Given the many physical, mental, emotional, spiritual, and relational symptoms of stress, the two extremes (i.e., urgency addiction and absenteeism) can cause major problems in the workplace.

Values, expectations, and emotional hot spots are contributors to both stress and conflict. Stress can never be completely eliminated if we want a normal life; however, we presented at least seven ways that you can reduce stress more successfully.

Conflict has three major components: incompatibility of goals, interdependence among persons involved, and the expression of incompatibility through interaction. Two additional contributors are differences in ideologies, and territoriality.

In this chapter, we discussed seven symptoms or warning signs of conflict. We also presented five conflict management strategies: self-reflection, understanding conflict styles, problem solving, the AEIOU Model, and Covey's Conflict Resolution Technique. Stress and conflict can be beneficial. To manage them more successfully in your life, you must understand their nature, causes, and symptoms.

Knowledge Check

Key Concepts and Terms

stress	introspection	territory	avoidance
physical stress	conflict	competition	compromise
psychological stress	ideology	accommodation	collaboration

Putting It All Together

1. How is stress defined? What are some examples of physical and psychological stressors?

2. In what five areas of life can people experience mental and emotional symptoms of stress?

3. How do values, expectations, and emotional triggers affect each person's unique definitions of stress and conflict?

4. Name seven ways to better manage stress.

5. How is conflict defined? What roles do ideology and territoriality play in the development of conflict?

6. Distinguish among the five styles of conflict management that people often use.

7. What are the primary differences between the problem-solving and AEIOU models of conflict management?

8. Briefly discuss six benefits that can result from conflict.

References

Ardrey, R. (1966). *The territorial imperative.* New York: Dell.

Blanchard, K., & Peale, N. V. (1988). *The power of ethical management.* New York: Fawcett Crest.

Covey, S. (1991). *Principle-centered leadership.* New York: Fireside/Simon & Schuster.

Covey, S. (1989). *The 7 Habits of highly effective people: Powerful lessons in personal change.* New York: Fireside/Simon & Schuster.

Covey, S., Merrill, A. R., & Merrill, R. (1994). *First things first.* New York: Fireside/Simon & Schuster.

Griffith, H. W. (1985). *Complete guide to symptoms, illness & surgery.* Los Angeles: The Body Press.

Hales, D., & Hales, R. (1996). You can beat stress on the job. *Parade Magazine,* 24–25.

Handy, C. (1993). *Understanding organizations.* New York: Oxford University Press.

Kreps, G., & Thornton, B. (1984). *Health communication: Theory and practice.* New York: Longman.

Peurifoy, R. Z. (1995). *Anxiety, phobias, & panic: A step-by-step program for regaining control of your life.* New York: Time Warner.

Putnam, L. L., & Poole, M. S. (1987). Conflict and negotiation. In F. Jablin, L. Putnam, K. Roberts, & L. Porter, eds., *Handbook of organizational communication,* (pp. 549–599). Newbury Park, CA: Sage.

Seyle, H. (1974). *Stress without distress.* Philadelphia: Lippincott.

Spielberg, S. (1985, July 15). "I dream for a living." *Time, 126*(2), 54–63.

Thomas, K. W. (1976). Conflict and conflict management. In M. Dunnette, ed., *Handbook of industrial and organizational psychology* (pp. 889–936). Chicago: Rand McNally.

Tzu, Sun. (1988). *The art of war.* Boston: Shambhala Publications, Inc.

Ury, W. (1993). *Getting past no: Negotiating your way from confrontation to cooperation.* New York: Bantam Books.

Wisinski, J. (1993). *Resolving conflicts on the job.* New York: American Management Association.

Etiquette for the 21st Century Workplace

9

After studying this chapter, you should be able to

- Understand the importance of etiquette in business and professional communication.

- Know what it takes to make a great first impression.

- Practice the rules of effective greetings and good-byes.

- Avoid awkward moments and etiquette gaffes in the workplace.

- Extend office courtesies that will be appreciated and handle appointments effectively.

- Introduce others and yourself in a public speaking setting.

- Exercise cybersensitivity and practice etiquette for new technologies.

Etiquette isn't learned once and then mastered for a lifetime. Instead, achieving social savvy requires diligence and self-discipline. Just ask etiquette guru Letitia Baldrige (1993), author of *Letitia Baldrige's New Complete Guide to Executive Manners*. As one of America's foremost authorities on executive etiquette and protocol, and former chief of staff for Jacqueline Kennedy during the White House years, Ms. Baldrige will certainly agree with our opening statement.

For example, Baldrige once forgot to invite Chicago Mayor Richard J. Daley to a White House reception, no small problem given that John F. Kennedy felt he owed his winning bid for the presidency to Daley (McGarvey & Smith, 1993). She also tells a story about a set of picture frames that she selected as gifts for the president to take on one of his official trips to India. There was only one problem: the incredibly handsome frames were made of cowhide, and Hindus believe the cow to be sacred. Fortunately the gaffe was caught before the president arrived in India, and another set of gifts was dispatched immediately from the United States.

217

We probably would all agree that Ms. Baldridge is not the only person ever to commit an embarrassing social gaffe. How many times have you had to think twice about how to properly introduce two important people to one another? whether or not to shake hands with someone? what to do if you forget someone's name at an inopportune moment? Because good manners and social savvy are important for people to succeed in both the social and business worlds, corporate America is turning to etiquette experts for advice and training.

Making a Positive Impression in Business and Professional Communication

Why Etiquette Training?

Consider for a moment the following conversation:

Bonnie: "Why do we have to pretend be someone we're not? I just hate to wear business suits and high heels!"

Vergie: "I know! I'm glad we still have our jobs, but this merger with Bigtech has been a nightmare! And now they're changing all of the rules."

Bonnie: "Really! Can you believe they demoted Dawn from the position of supervisor for 'fraternizing' on the job? She and Doug have been dating for two years! And new management's only been here a month. Are we not supposed to even smile at each other any more?"

As we approach the 21st century, conversations like this are taking place more and more in the workplace. Although knowing how to behave in the business world has long been a universal issue for workers, increased global competition, a renewed emphasis on quality, and "the role that good manners play in the quality promise" contribute more than ever to corporate survival. As McGarvey and Smith (1993) note, rudeness costs customers! People simply won't do business with companies whose personnel are inattentive or rude.

Another reason that business etiquette has become an important issue in organizations today is "increasing evidence that recent graduates of business schools do not possess the basic etiquette skills that are necessary to succeed in today's business world" (Schaffer, Kelley, & Goette, 1993, p. 330). For instance, in a survey conducted by Disbie in 1990, 88 percent of senior managers were perceived to have impeccable manners, while only 44 percent of middle-level managers were perceived to be equally well-mannered. For recent MBA graduates, the figure fell to 12 percent.

Interestingly, according to Schaffer, Kelley, and Goette (1993), the business etiquette skills of American college graduates are perceived to have worsened over the past ten years. Furthermore, because business etiquette is considered by many colleges and universities to be a "soft" communication skill, business students are given little or no training at the college level.

Once they arrive in the business world, graduates have few on-the-job opportunities to receive etiquette training. Expected to pick up social savvy at work, new college graduates often have to learn the hard way about social gaffes and their ramifications.

> Etiquette is what you are doing when people are looking and listening. What you are thinking is your business.
>
> —*Virginia Cary Hudson*

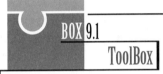

BOX 9.1

ToolBox

The Ten Most Common Etiquette Blunders

1. Inappropriate language—demeaning salutations, diminutive names, vulgar or tasteless humor, and gossip.

2. Disregarding others' time—arriving late, being unprepared for meetings or appointments, barging into someone's office, turning in an assignment late, interrupting meetings for nonemergency calls or unrelated business.

3. Inappropriate dress and poor grooming.

4. Misuse of the telephone—keeping people on "hold" too long, not returning calls, not giving messages, slamming down the phone, not identifying who is speaking, and eating while speaking.

5. Failure to greet someone appropriately—greeting people with no handshake, a limp handshake, or a death grip; making poor introductions.

6. Poor listening skills—cutting off or interrupting other people, avoiding eye contact, and asking a question without waiting for an answer.

7. Disregarding shared property and others' space—invading someone's property, misuse of the fax machine, copier, and coffee pot.

8. Embarrassing others—poorly delivered feedback, putdowns, and rudeness.

9. Poor table manners.

10. Inappropriate or inconsistent recognition of others—including paying undue attention to someone's gender (women are always asked to make the coffee and men to change the fluorescent tubes in the lights), or forgotten praise.

Adapted from B. Pachter and M. Brody (1995). *Complete Business Etiquette Handbook* (Englewood Cliffs, NJ: Prentice Hall), pp. xv–xvii.

To provide you with a glimpse of the most common business faux pas committed, consider Box 9.1.

A third reason that organizations are becoming more aware of the importance of business etiquette is increasing stress and confusion in the workplace caused by the rapidly changing roles of women and technology (McGarvey & Smith, 1993). For example, conflicts erupt between men and women at work when there is " . . . a failure to separate social and workplace behavior—a failure to understand why some actions that might be acceptable socially are repugnant and even illegal at work" (Baridon & Eyler, 1994, p. 32). Rules about the appropriateness of a pin-up calendar in someone's cubicle, touching of any sort, or rude comments about the sexuality of a colleague are only a few of the issues about which companies must institute new rules. As you will recall from Chapter 3, workplace romances also require an etiquette all their own.

Similarly, the increasing role of technology in the workplace (in the forms of fax machines, voice mail, cellular phones, E-mail, the Internet, etc.) presents entirely new challenges ("The New Workplace Requires New Etiquette, 1995, p. 22). In fact, one need look no further than the nearest business journal to find a slough of articles offering new rules for using technology in the business environment.

How confident do you feel about your business etiquette skills? Do you know how to handle yourself in most business and social occasions? According to Mausehund, Dortch, Brown, and Bridges (1995), students in American colleges of business (COBs) have a number of concerns about social etiquette. In their 1994 survey of 457 juniors, seniors, and graduate students enrolled in accredited COBs, students reported a great deal of "social discomfort" with regard to: (1) dressing for business, (2) surviving the business meal, (3) appropriate nonverbal behaviors in the workplace, (4) getting along with coworkers on the job, (5) gender issues (e.g., "Which is more proper: Mrs. or Ms.?"), (6) whether to consume alcohol at quasi-social functions such as lunches or office parties, (7) presenting a business card, (8) introducing a business associate, and (9) whether using first names in the workplace is appropriate.

You, too, may have questions about what is considered appropriate business etiquette. Just for fun, consider Box 9.2, an Etiquette IQ Test to help you gauge your present knowledge.

BOX 9.2

How Do You Measure Up? | *Etiquette IQ Test*

Directions: Determine whether the following statements are true or false. Circle T for true or F for false.

T F **1.** Always introduce a woman to a man.

T F **2.** Women should wait for a man to make the first move when shaking hands in a business setting.

T F **3.** Refer to people using Mr., Mrs., or Ms. until they give you permission to use their first names.

T F **4.** Military personnel give up the right to be addressed by their rank (e.g., Lieutenant Colonel) when they retire.

T F **5.** Always allow your guests to enter a stairwell first, then follow them to the floor of the building that is your destination.

T F **6.** If you are a little late for an appointment, avoid apologizing. Doing so will only call attention to the fact.

T F **7.** Power is an important element of corporate life. If you want to show people that you have more power than they do, it is entirely appropriate to keep them waiting for a meeting.

T F **8.** Once you greet a guest, it is customary to begin with small talk.

T F **9.** When introducing yourself prior to giving a presentation, give background information that is relevant to the subject of your speech.

T F **10.** Talk to a voice mail system like you would to a person face-to-face.

Answers: 1-F; 2-F; 3-T; 4-F; 5-F; 6-F; 7-F; 8-T; 9-F; 10-F.

So how did you do? Are you ready to take on Letitia Baldrige or Emily Post? Or does your career image still require a little polish?

In this chapter, we will address a number of questions you may have about business etiquette. Using the survey conducted by Mausehund and colleagues, and our Puzzle Model of Business and Professional Communication, we will brief you on the most crucial social skills that you must possess to survive and thrive in the 21st century workplace.

Let's begin with how you can best manage first impressions, which crosses all four areas of business and professional communication: relational, work, public, and techno-life.

Managing First Impressions

Imagine yourself in an interview for the dream job you have always wanted. You have done your homework on the company; you know what questions you want to ask; and, you are ten minutes early for the meeting. You are professionally dressed, well-groomed, and ready to face your interviewer.

At last, you are ushered into the interviewer's office. She is late, so her assistant asks you to have a seat. While you are waiting, you glance around her office. Her desk is a mess—piled a mile high in paper—and several empty soda cans are sitting by the phone. Papers are spilling off of the remaining two chairs, and two of her filing cabi-

You never get a second chance to make a good first impression.

net drawers are ajar. Ten minutes after the interview is to begin, a harried woman rushes into the office. Her arms are full of printouts, her clothes are disheveled, and she mumbles a half-baked apology before plopping down in her chair. Additionally, she doesn't respond when you extend your hand to greet her.

What kind of impression would this interviewer make on you? What would you think about her as the company's representative? about the management team who hired her? about the company overall? According to Julius Fast (1970), it takes less than 60 seconds for us to form a first impression. In turn, this impression affects every perception that follows and is very difficult to overcome.

In order to become a well-mannered professional, you must begin with the basics of making a great first impression. Of course, the place to start is by being impeccably dressed and groomed, and dressed appropriately for the audience, setting, and occasion. Although this might appear simple to do, you can easily make errors in judgment, especially if you are new to a company or job. For example, one of your authors learned the hard way to ask about appropriate attire when her job required her to travel to different types of meetings. Imagine how surprised she was to attend her first meeting of the board of directors, only to find that she was the only person "professionally dressed" for the meeting. The rest of the board was dressed appropriately for the beach, where the meeting was being held. Much to her dismay, she spent the entire meeting feeling quite out of place.

Because this chapter addresses many aspects of business etiquette, time and space do not allow for a complete discussion of professional dress. However, Sabath (1993) offers the following basic tips:

- When in doubt, ask about appropriate dress for an occasion.
- Keep your hair neat and styled in a fashion that is flattering to your face.
- Wear quality jewelry that is appropriate for the event and situation.
- Give the same attention to your shoes that you give to your hair and apparel; they should always look new.
- Men, use the one-finger test when buying a dress shirt; if you cannot comfortably place one finger between your neck and a buttoned collar, the shirt is not a good fit.
- Women, always keep an extra pair of stockings in your bottom desk drawer; runs in your hosiery make a negative impression on other people.
- Men, wear socks that cover your calves completely when you are seated (pp. 14–15, 29).
- Women, use the "Rule of Seven" with jewelry. After you are dressed, count every piece of jewelry (or accessory) that you are wearing, excluding ornate buttons on your suit, dress, or blouse. If you count more than seven pieces, decide which ones are unnecessary and remove them. Wear rings only on the third finger of each hand.

Making Your First Ten Words Count

Certainly your hair, your dress, and the ways in which you adorn yourself make powerful nonverbal impressions on other people. So, too, do the first words that you utter when you meet and greet others. One way that you can make a positive first impression with the words you choose is to prepare for conversations in advance. Pachter and Brody (1995), authors of *The Complete Business Etiquette Handbook,* recommend reading at least one newspaper a day and several magazines a month to stay abreast of current events. In fact, Terrie Williams (1994), president of one of America's premier public relations agencies and author of *The Personal Touch,* reads seven newspapers a day. When she started her own PR firm in 1988, Ms. Williams was a young social worker with no money or agency experience. Today her list of clients reads like a Who's Who celebrity list, including such notables as Eddie Murphy, Miles Davis, Janet Jackson, Dave Winfield, Jackie Joyner-Kersie, AT&T, and 20th Century Fox . . . just to name a few. Terrie Williams believes that "the key to success in today's increasingly impersonal world is personal consideration." That means knowing what's going on in the world and what's happening in the lives of people with whom you interact.

Professional journals in your area of interest and simple observations of the world around you can also provide interesting insights and conversational food for thought. For instance, if you are at a luncheon, surrounded by people with whom you aren't acquainted, you will be a conversational hit if you can talk easily about community events, cultural happenings, or even that crazy traffic jam on the way to the luncheon.

Second, as Pachter and Brody (1995) so aptly put it, make your opening line " . . . no longer than most bumper stickers" (p. 37). In the process, strive to make a connection with the person with whom you are talking. A few opening lines that accomplish these two goals might be:

"It's so good to *finally* meet you, Mr. Samms."

"What a wonderful party, Ron!

"Thank you for agreeing to have lunch with me, Ms. Finnegan."

Although simple, all three of these greetings open the door to a warm and friendly conversation.

Notice another common thread among the three opening lines: use of the person's name. We all love to hear our own names; such an acknowledgement makes us feel connected to others around us. Just make sure you use the right name! Nothing is more embarrassing than finding out after an important event that all evening you called Joanie, "Janie"—your new boss's wife.

Finally, a simple "thank-you" is a good way to start a conversation. Doing so helps get the conversation off on the right foot, no matter what the occasion is. For instance, consider the following opening lines and the various scenarios that might spawn them:

Meeting the director of human resources for high tea:

"Thank you for inviting me to tea, Mrs. Jones. My supervisor has told me so much about the new training program you have put together."

Meeting a business acquaintance for lunch:

"Thanks for suggesting that we meet here, Donna. You were right! What a delightful restaurant this is."

Managing a crisis at the office:

"Thank you for coming on such short notice, Jim. I really would like your advice."

As you can see, a simple thank-you can go a long way as an opening line. Using individuals' names makes them feel important and acknowledges their contribution to the occasion.

Using Body Language That Communicates the Desired Message

While the way you dress and the words you choose contribute substantially to first impressions, these components of meetings and greetings carry only a portion of the message that you communicate to others. The remaining part of the message is carried through body language: your posture, movements, gestures, facial expressions, and eye contact. In fact, researchers in the area of nonverbal communication have known for decades that more than 70 percent of a message is carried through these five channels.

So how can you ensure a positive first impression with the body language you use? Pachter and Brody (1995) offer a "nonverbal conversational checklist," presented in Box 9.3.

Finally, the best conversationalist is the person who listens well. He or she is the person who makes the speaker feel like the only person in the universe, or at least in the room, whether the topic is the weather or the most intimate details of one's life. Listening well means following our suggestions in Chapter 2, listening with your eyes and ears, and not interrupting others when they are talking. Listening well means pausing and thinking before you answer a question.

As you can see, making a powerful first impression isn't difficult; it just takes a little thought (and thoughtfulness) of others. If you are interested in finding out more about ways to make a positive first impression, we encourage you to complete the exercise in Box 9.4. This box presents seven ways that you can actually sabotage a first impression as well as ways that you can overcome these conversational errors.

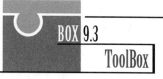

BOX 9.3

ToolBox *Nonverbal Conversational Checklist*

1. Be genuine when you smile.
2. Smile appropriately for the occasion.
3. Keep your body language open.
4. Avoid crossing your arms in a defensive stance.
5. Lean toward people rather than away from them.
6. Exude enthusiasm with your voice.
7. Sound interested in what people are saying.

8. Look at the person with whom you are conversing at least 80 percent of the time.
9. However, avoid staring or looking over someone's shoulder when you are conversing.
10. Periodically nod and signal agreement.

Source: B. Pachter and M. Brody (1995). *The Complete Business Etiquette Handbook* (Englewood Cliffs, NJ: Prentice-Hall).

BOX 9.4
How Do You Measure Up?

Seven Easy Ways to Sabotage a First Impression

Directions: None of us makes a perfect first impression every time. Even the most well-mannered person can be caught off guard. However, you can easily sabotage a first impression if you exercise any of the following habits. Take just a moment and search your memory bank. Do you ever _____? If so, check the box that applies, and refer to the corresponding column on the right for appropriate, well-mannered behaviors.

[ ] **1.** Use sloppy language (e.g., towards, anyways).

Use terms and words that are appropriate for the situation.

[ ] **2.** Use lazy words (e.g., yeah, you guys, okey dokey).

Choose words in such a way that they maximize your credibility (e.g., yes, you, I will.)

[ ] **3.** Giggle.

Laughter is appropriate for many situations. Giggling is not. Try to avoid giggling at all costs.

[ ] **4.** Initiate inappropriate touch (e.g., pats, nudges, touches on a coworker's arm).

Avoid touching coworkers; a handshake is generally the only exception to the rule.

[ ] **5.** Hide your hands in pockets.

Learn to gesture appropriately or keep your hands where they can be seen.

[ ] **6.** Chew gum.

Never chew gum in the workplace!

[ ] **7.** Constantly clear your throat during a conversation or meeting.

Try swallowing instead.

Adapted from A. M. Sabath (1993). *Business Etiquette in Brief: The Competitive Edge for Today's Professional* (Holbrook, MA: Bob Adams, Inc.), pp. 15–16.

Etiquette and Your Relational Life

Greetings and Good-Byes

One of the questions that people often ask etiquette experts is, "What is the proper way to handle greetings and good-byes, especially handshakes?" Other popular questions address the most appropriate way to make introductions, use names and titles, and handle potentially "deadly" social gaffes (e.g., dealing with sweaty hands, repeating difficult names, or forgetting names altogether). Although these four issues associated with your relational life may seem difficult to manage at first, there are a few key guidelines that you can use to increase your business savvy.

Handshakes: The Perfect Greeting and Good-Bye.   Believe it or not, etiquette guidelines about handshakes have become simpler than ever before. One reason is that men and women today prefer to be treated as equals. For example, if you are sitting in your office and someone approaches you to say hello, you should:

- rise,
- move forward,
- establish eye contact,
- smile,
- be sincere,
- speak clearly and distinctly, and
- repeat his or her name
- as you extend your hand (Phillips & Phillips, 1990, pp. 84–85).

These guidelines apply to men and women, as well as to greetings and good-byes. Even if you are sitting in an exhibit booth or other cramped space that makes it difficult to stand, Sabath (1993) recommends that you "do the bob" (i.e., at least make an effort to stand).

Another important point to remember about handshakes is that, whether you are a man or woman, you should extend a full hand and shake hands confidently and firmly. That means coming from around any barrier that may be between you and your guest (e.g., a desk) and minimizing the space between you. You also should avoid wearing an oversized ring on your right hand because doing so can make a firm handshake quite painful.

Your handshake itself should last about as long as the verbal greeting or good-bye itself (e.g., "Hello, Mr. Smith. I'm Jane Allsbrook. So nice to meet you."). Men, when you are shaking hands with a woman (and vice versa), avoid the "wet fish" handshake, or just shaking each other's fingers (Oooh, Yuk!). We have all been victims of those handshakes; for women, they are insulting and make them want to dart into the nearest powder room to rinse their hands. Now that you know more about proper handshakes, what about introductions? Rules for introductions often seem to be the most difficult to remember.

Four Rules for Making Introductions

Believe it or not, if you want to master introductions, you have to remember only four rules. First, *The Biggest Star Usually Takes Top Billing.* We define "The Biggest Star" as the person with the greatest authority or the person of most importance. Note that, in some situations, a person of importance may need to be considered The Biggest Star over a person of authority. For example, clients should take top billing if they are highly valued, or if you wish to honor them in some way. Given this brief introduction to Rule #1, let's test your understanding. See if you can identify The Biggest Star among the pairs of titles listed in Box 9.5.

Once you have determined star status, the second rule to remember is: *Say The Biggest Star's Name First!* For instance:

"*Senator Williams,* may I present the vice president of Craig and Company, Mr. Boudreaux."

BOX 9.5

How Do You Measure Up?   *I'm The Biggest Star! I Am By Far. . . .*

Directions: Circle The Biggest Star in each of the following pairs of titles. (Note: The answers are provided at the bottom of the box.)

1.	superior	new subordinate
2.	female supervisor	male client
3.	colleague	fiancé (fiancée)
4.	president of your company	visiting dignitary from a country overseas
5.	senator	Vice president of your company
6.	sales representative in your company	division head in your company
7.	male supervisor	female client
8.	colleague in your company	friend
9.	man (in a restaurant)	woman (in a restaurant)
10.	older person (status equal)	younger person (status equal)

(Answers: 1-superior; 2-male client; 3-whomever you wish to compliment the most; 4-visiting dignitary; 5-senator; 6- division head; 7-female client; 8-whomever you wish to compliment the most; 9-woman; 10-older person.)

"*Ms. Client,* I'd like you to meet my supervisor and director of marketing, Mr. Stevens."

"*Mr. Lu,* allow me to present Ms. Coyle, president of the Carrie Coyle Agency. Ms. Coyle, I'm pleased to introduce you to Mr. Lu, Director of Japan's Ministry of Tourism."

You will rarely go wrong in a business setting if you remember these two cardinal rules.

The third rule of introductions enters the picture when the picture begins to get fuzzy. What if you don't know which person is The Biggest Star, or if everyone's position is equal in status? The rule in this case is: *Appoint the Person Whom You Want to Compliment the Most as The Biggest Star.* As before, mention that person's name first in the introduction. For example,

"*Chrishulle,* I'd like you to meet my new friend, Jim. Jim, this is Chrishulle, my talented and beautiful fiancée."

If you don't know whom you want to compliment the most, Pachter and Brody (1995) recommend that you fall back on traditional rules. Treat an older person as The Biggest Star when you are introducing an older person and a younger person, for example:

"*Mr. Older Person,* I'd like for you to meet my friend, Ms. Younger Person."

Consider a woman to be The Biggest Star when you are introducing a woman and a man, for instance:

"*Patti*, this is Keith."

What about business-social situations like a dinner at your home or a cocktail party hosted by your company at a local restaurant? These ambiguous circumstances provide an opportunity for you to implement Rule #4: *Assess the SITUATION and Appoint the Person Who SHOULD BE CONSIDERED The Biggest Star.* According to Pachter and Brody (1995), the key to successfully implementing this rule lies in your knowledge of both the people and the situation. For example, if your husband, wife, or significant other has worked all day to cook a special dinner for you and your colleagues, you may want to honor this person by appointing him or her to be The Biggest Star. Generally, the same honor should be bestowed on your significant other if you run into one of your superiors at a cultural event. However, if your company is hosting a social event, your superior should probably be considered The Biggest Star. Again, say the Biggest Star's name first in each of these introductions:

(At a dinner hosted by you and your significant other)

"*Sammie*, I'd like you to meet Mr. Evans, our director of finance. Mr. Evans, this is my wife, Sammie Nichols-Bryan.

(At a cocktail party hosted by your company)

"*Mr. Evans*, I'd like you to meet my wife, Sammie Nichols-Bryan. Sam, this is Mr. Evans, our director of finance."

Names and Titles

How do you know when to call someone by first or last name? Equally important, when should you refer to people by their formal titles? In the business world, the general rule of thumb is to refer to someone using Mr., Mrs., or Ms. until you are given permission to do otherwise. This directive is especially true when it comes to addressing superiors. Usually, individuals who are comfortable having you refer to them using their first names, will say something like, "Please, call me Joe." Avoid asking a business colleague whether he or she minds if you use a first name. Doing so places both you and the other person in an awkward position if she says, "No, I'd rather you call me Ms. Jones." To avoid embarrassment, wait for others to give you permission to use their first names.

The rule is much the same when it comes to using either professional titles (e.g., doctor) or official titles (e.g, governor, ambassador, or senator). Even if a person no longer holds a position such as governor or senator, he or she retains that title for life. Similarly, retired service personnel retain their highest respective ranks (e.g., sergeant major, colonel, general, etc.). Thus, when you introduce two people who hold titles or ranks, you would say:

"Governor Smith, may I present Lieutenant Colonel Mary Jenkins."

If only one person holds a title, introduce the person with the lowest status to the higher-ranking official. Again, you would say the higher-ranking official's name first:

"Governor Smith, I'd like you to meet Mary Jenkins."

How to Avoid Awkward Moments and Etiquette Gaffes

We have all found ourselves in awkward positions at times when it comes to using appropriate business etiquette. For instance, what should you do if you have been asked to introduce someone with a difficult name? Worse yet, what should you do if you forget someone's name during the course of a conversation? The first thing to remember in such situations is that etiquette is finding ways to make other people feel more comfortable. With this simple definition of etiquette in mind, the rules become fairly self-evident.

> Good manners have much to do with the emotions. To make them ring true, one must feel them, not merely exhibit them.
>
> —*Amy Vanderbilt*

For example, the most respectful and courteous way to ensure that you pronounce someone's name correctly is to ask the person for the correct pronunciation. It is entirely appropriate for you to say, "I'm not sure how to pronounce your name correctly. Would you say it one more time for me?" Similarly, if you forget someone's name, all is not lost. Just be calm and forthright and say, "I recall our being introduced at the annual meeting, but I cannot remember your name." Of course, if you anticipate that someone has forgotten your name, simply reintroduce yourself by extending your hand and saying, "Hi. I'm Donna Lathem. We met at the St. Louis Museum of Art fundraiser."

Two other relatively awkward situations in which you may find yourself involve handshakes. For instance, if you have sweaty palms and know you will be shaking hands in the next few moments, (1) go to the restroom, wash your hands, and dry them well, or (2) gently pat your right hand against your pant leg or skirt to eliminate the moisture and then shake hands. If you are mingling with people at a social event, hold whatever you are drinking in your left hand and keep your right hand free for shaking hands. Doing so will help you avoid constantly juggling your drink, and will eliminate "cold, wet-hand syndrome."

Etiquette and Your Work Life

Getting along with other people on the job is expected of you by top management as well as by your supervisor and coworkers. To enjoy and excel in your work, while creating lasting productive work relationships, is your ultimate goal. Accomplishing this feat is difficult at times because not everyone will have your same positive approach toward work life.

Three areas of work life etiquette about which questions often arise are: appropriate entrances and exits, appreciated office courtesies, and the proper handling of appointments. In this section, we will offer etiquette tips regarding each of these potentially troublesome areas. Let's begin with a few basic rules about entrances and exits that will enhance your work relationships.

Making Appropriate Entrances and Exits

In some ways, we are at a crossroads between old rules and new standards when it comes to treatment of others in the workplace. For example, women no longer automatically expect men to open doors for them. Instead, as Pachter and Brody (1995) noted, "Courtesy has become increasingly gender-blind" (p. 67). Today, the person who arrives first generally opens the door, and holds the door for the person or persons behind them. Exceptions include people with disabilities or people whose hands are full. In these instances, it is more courteous for you to move around them and open the door.

Elevators, escalators, and stairs also raise potential questions for young professionals who are unfamiliar with the informal rules of a company. This statement is particularly true regarding organizations whose corporate headquarters occupy either an entire building or at least several floors. General guidelines you can use in these instances are presented in Table 9.1. Note the subtle differences in rules for using elevators and stairs.

Table 9.1   Guidelines for Using Elevators, Escalators, and Stairs

WHO ENTERS FIRST?	FOR WHOM SHOULD YOU YIELD?	ADDITIONAL TIPS
Elevators		
Persons of higher rank (if known)	Persons with disabilities	Hold the door or button for people who are entering or exiting.
Guest enters before host; host exits and holds door for guest	People getting off	Make room.
Person who arrives first (if others are unknown)		Briefly greet people whom you know.
		Don't gossip or speak too loudly.
		If you bump someone, say, "Excuse me."
		If you are in the back and about to reach your floor, let coworkers know.
Escalators and Stairs		
Persons of higher rank (if known)	Persons with disabilities	Avoid stairs if difficult for guests. Ask.
Host first; then guests	People in a hurry	Stay to the right.
First arrivals (if others are unknown)		Don't rush people. Excuse yourself and go around.
		Don't follow too closely.

Adapted from B. Pachter & M. Brody (1995). *The Complete Business Etiquette Handbook* (Englewood Cliffs, NJ: Prentice-Hall), pp. 67–68.

Knowing the rules of elevator etiquette contributes to your overall professional demeanor in the workplace.

Extending Office Courtesies

Sharing work space with grace and style is easy to achieve, whether you are an up-and-coming professional or an executive vice president. All that is required is respecting your colleagues and their space, remembering a few rules about office equipment etiquette, and knowing how to courteously use shared facilities (e.g., equipment, kitchens, and employee lounges).

Respecting Your Colleagues and Their Space.   This comes in a variety of forms, from helping him carry an oversized box if you see him struggling with it, to asking if she has a moment before you interrupt her work. For example, Sergio has just been hired as the new marketing director of a Fortune 500 company. Having come from a smaller firm with nowhere near the same office space or staff size, he is eager to learn about the informal rules that are in effect at his new company. How could Sergio—or you, if you were in Sergio's shoes—be more comfortable in this new job while learning the ropes? One way is to keep in mind the following simple guidelines we use everyday to show courtesy to, and build relationships with, others:

■ Always say, "Excuse me. May I interrupt you for a moment?" before beginning a conversation with someone who is busy. You may be interrupting his or her train of thought. If you continually interrupt people, you will gain a reputation for being thoughtless and rude.

■ Never enter someone's space to wait for an appointment or visit to commence. Likewise, never borrow anything without asking (e.g., an item such as a tape dispenser, stapler, or file). Wait for the person to return, or find someone else from whom you can borrow the item. Nobody likes to return to a work area only to find that belongings have been moved or, worse yet, are missing.

■ Carry on conversations softly in open spaces such as cubicles. It is difficult for people in nearby areas to work when you are speaking loudly. Similarly, if you are meeting with guests, take them to an alternative place to talk (e.g., a conference room). That way, you won't be interrupting others.

■ Avoid gossip at all costs. If someone wishes to start a conversation with you about someone else, politely excuse yourself or diplomatically tell the person you prefer not to talk about the subject.

■ Be mindful of the workload and responsibilities of anyone who is assisting you, and avoid making excessive demands. Work together on setting priorities and goals, then stick to them if at all possible.

These general rules represent only a few of the basic courtesies you can show to your boss, colleagues, or assistant. When in doubt, remember: "Do unto others as you would have them do unto you."

Using Office Equipment.   Rules of conduct associated with equipment such as fax machines, E-mail, and telephones generally fall under the rubric of techno-life. As such, they will be discussed briefly later in this chapter and more completely in Chapter 12. However, it is appropriate to mention a few rules at this time regarding one piece of equipment that is often shared among people in everyday work life: the copy machine.

There are only a few basic guidelines to remember when it comes to photocopying; however, implementing them can make a positive difference in the relationships you are building with your colleagues. For example, if you are starting a long copy job, encourage people with shorter jobs to make their copies first. If you can interrupt a long run for someone with only one or two pages to copy, you should do so.

Second, if the copier jams or runs out of paper or toner during your job, take time to unjam the machine or replace the paper or toner before you walk away. If you don't know how, check with someone who does, or summon the person who normally maintains the equipment. Never leave the copy machine in disarray, thereby forcing the person behind you to fix the problem.

Finally, after you have completed a duplicating job, check the paper tray to see how much paper remains. It only takes a minute to add paper. Also, take the time to restore the number of copies to "one." Doing so will make photocopying easier and less aggravating for the person who follows.

Sharing Facilities.   When you share facilities in the workplace such as the kitchen and employee lounge, make sure you clean up after yourself. Always display appropriate table manners when dining with your colleagues.

Handling Appointments Appropriately

How many times have you found yourself trying to remember the time and date for a scheduled appointment? Maybe you agreed to meet a friend for coffee, a colleague for lunch, or a client to pitch your company's latest advertising proposal. However, you forgot to write yourself a reminder note.

With friends or colleagues, you probably would contact them by phone, remind them about your terrible memory, and reestablish the meeting time. However, with a client, the situation is trickier. With the amount of competition that exists today in the business world, one wrong move could cost your company millions of dollars.

To avoid the problem of memory lapses, which are common when your job calls for making and keeping appointments, you must create an appointment management system that works. For instance, an executive vice president with a small sportswear manufacturing firm might require a pocketsize calendar in which to note times and places of meetings. For a district manager who is responsible for several retail stores, a small electronic personal organizer might be more efficient. Finally, for a sales representative who spends more than 70 percent of the time on the road, a more elaborate system may be required. For instance, she might keep a record of appointments and travel expenses on a laptop computer with a program designed specifically for scheduling. Of course, all of these appointment management systems have one major requirement: They must be used consistently and well.

In addition to scheduling appointments in an organized fashion, smart business-people know that appointment etiquette requires preparation and follow-up. Michael Thomsett (1991), author of *The Little Black Book of Business Etiquette*, recommends that you adopt four rules for making and keeping appointments:

1. *Show up early rather than late.* Although you may be kept waiting, you will gain a reputation for promptness and professionalism.
2. *If you are late, apologize.* Sometimes, cars break down and other meetings run overtime. If you have a cellular phone, or access to a phone, call immediately and let the person with whom you have the appointment know you will be delayed.
3. *Be prepared to discuss all items on the agenda.* If you cannot prepare sufficiently, postpone the meeting and give as much advance notice as possible. If postponing isn't an option, prepare the best that you can.
4. *Always keep your promises.* Meetings generally involve taking action on agenda items, setting times for subsequent appointments, or preparing reports or other forms of written communication.

Thomsett recommends that you write a memo after the meeting confirming any actions that you will be taking. Then distribute your memo to everyone who was present at the meeting, and follow through on the promises that you made.

Receiving Guests

We have all heard the expression, "It's the little things that count." Nowhere does this expression apply more aptly than when you meet and greet business guests. For example, Sabath (1993) recommends the following courtesies when you invite visitors to gather at your office:

- Make sure the receptionist knows your guests' names and arrival times.
- Leave special instructions asking that you be notified immediately upon their arrival; if possible, greet them personally in the reception area.

- If you are unable to greet your guests in person, ask a staff member to welcome and escort them to your office.
- Above all, remember that time is money and never keep your visitors waiting.

As Gray (1993), author of *The Winning Image* notes, "Guests who leave after a five-minute wait are justified" (p. 161). If an unavoidable delay occurs, Gray recommends that you ask your secretary or receptionist to offer your visitors soft drinks or coffee, and a magazine or newspaper while they wait.

Again, when greeting your visitors, welcome them by name with a firm handshake. At meetings, offer your guests coffee, tea, or soda.

The Scout motto, "Be prepared," also applies when hosting business meetings. For example, you will want to make sure that you have enough chairs in your office to seat all of your guests, and that the seating arrangement is comfortable for everyone. If you have an administrative assistant or receptionist, request that your calls be held. (If you answer your own phone, turn on your answering machine during the meeting.) Gray (1993) also recommends that you be up-front with your guests, and let them know how much time is allotted for the meeting.

Once you have greeted your visitors, it is customary to begin with "small talk." For example, you might ask if your guest had trouble following your directions or locating your office building. Especially astute hosts make mental or written notes over time regarding the names of spouses or significant others, children, assistants, special events, or hobbies and interests of their clients. Think, for a moment, about how surprised you would be if an important person remembered and referred to one of the "little things" about your life.

Before a meeting ends, sum up the key points. Then, personally escort your visitors to the door and conclude the meeting with a handshake.

Public Life: Podium Etiquette

In Chapters 10 and 11, we will discuss how to develop and deliver a winning presentation. We also will explain how to maximize power, control emotions, develop a relationship with your audience, and increase your credibility. But what if you are a host rather than the speaker for an important occasion? How can you set the stage for delivery of a powerful, winning presentation by someone else?

In companies around the globe, outside speakers are often requested to make business presentations. If you are responsible for handling the arrangements, there are a number of things you can do to optimize the situation. To aid you in hosting outside presenters with grace and style, we offer you the checklist presented in Box 9.6.

The items in Box 9.6 are useful when it comes to the nuts and bolts of hosting a presentation. However, three specific rules of podium etiquette that will optimize your own credibility as a host were recommended by Sabath (1993):

- After introducing the speaker, wait until the person nears the podium. Then step back and welcome him or her with a handshake.

BOX 9.6

How Do You Measure Up?

A Checklist for Hosting Someone Else's Presentation

Directions: Consider using the following checklist whenever you are hosting someone else's presentation. Have you . . .

[ ] Requested *background information,* in the form of an introductory paragraph, from the speaker in advance?

[ ] Communicated with the speaker about the *audience, nature,* and *length* of the presentation?

[ ] Explained to the speaker *what the audience wants* to hear?

[ ] Inquired about the *correct spelling and pronunciation* of the speaker's name, including the title he or she prefers (e.g., Dr., Ms., Mrs., Mr.)?

[ ] Determined the speaker's *audiovisual equipment* needs?

[ ] Asked the speaker if a *rehearsal* is desired?

[ ] *Made reservations* for accommodations and sent directions?

[ ] Designated someone to be the *speaker's aide*?

[ ] Discussed *photo opportunities* or press times?

[ ] Arranged for the speaker to have *a time and place to rest* for at least an hour before the speech?

[ ] Created a *contract,* including fees to be reimbursed?

[ ] Asked the speaker if the speech can be *audio- or videotaped*?

[ ] Set up and tested the speaker's *A-V equipment*?

[ ] *Practiced your introduction* of the speaker so that it appears natural and conversational?

[ ] Written a *thank you note* within 48 hours of the presentation?

[ ] *Paid the speaker* promptly?

[ ] *Shared feedback* about the speech with the speaker?

Adapted from a discussion by B. Pachter and M. Brody (1995). *The Complete Business Etiquette Handbook* (Englewood Cliffs, NJ: Prentice-Hall), pp. 185–187.

■ Following the speech, return to the podium and extend your thanks to the person once again with another handshake and a verbal acknowledgment made through the microphone.

■ If several people will be speaking and you are to introduce each of them, thank the person who just spoke before presenting the next person (Sabath, 1993, p. 37).

As a speaker, you may be asked to introduce yourself prior to giving a presentation. We suggest that you keep your introduction brief and give background information that is relevant to your audience. For example, if you are speaking to a group of professional women, and are currently involved in a businesswomen's organization, mention this fact to your audience. Doing so creates common ground and heightens your credibility.

As you can see, podium etiquette isn't difficult to master. It just takes a little planning and common courtesy. In the next section, we will focus on the last area of business etiquette about which you should be aware: emerging rules and protocol associated with techno-life.

Techno-Life: Minding Your Electronic Manners

According to Joy Fox, head of Protocol International, a meeting planning and etiquette consulting firm in Canada, telephones, fax machines, and the latest computer technologies are creating new challenges and opportunities when it comes to business etiquette (Nigro, 1995, p. 77). For instance, consider the following questions: How many attempts should you make to return someone's telephone call? What is the most appropriate way to use someone's voice mail system? What courtesies should we afford others with regard to electronic mail?

These and other questions are emerging every day in small companies and Fortune 100 corporations alike. In fact, almost everyone has stories to tell about electronic mix-ups and technological confusion. Because technology affects our lives more and more as we approach the 21st century, we decided to include a brief discussion of electronic manners.

Telephone Manners

Businesses and professional reputations are built on effective communication. Because the telephone plays such a vital role in the way we communicate with others, you need to know what to say, how to say it, and a few key rules for optimizing telecommunications.

It all begins with a ringing telephone and what you say when you answer. According to Emily Post (1990), the best way to answer your phone is simply to say, "Hello, Deborah Gaut" or "Good afternoon, this is Deborah Gaut." Pachter and Brody (1995) agree and add to Post's list, "Deborah Gaut, Education Department." Their general rule of thumb is to keep your greeting to fewer than ten words. That way callers won't tune you out or become irritated with you (p. 116).

As we stated earlier, nonverbal communication carries more than 70 percent of a message. Given the loss of two key channels (i.e., sight and touch) when we use the telephone, vocal cues like pitch, tone, inflection, and rate of speech count more than in face-to-face interactions. That is why you should remember to smile whenever you answer a phone. A clear, pleasant voice says, "I am happy to talk with you," and "I am a consummate professional." Avoid rushing, even if you are rushed. Keep your voice even, and never raise your voice to a caller.

Answering Machines and Voice Mail.   More and more as we communicate with others by phone, we reach an answering machine or voice mail messaging system. For those of us who prefer person-to-person communication, the temptation is to talk with an answering machine or voice mail system as we would to a person. Additionally, older people who are uncomfortable with answering machines may speak to a recorder as if they are writing a letter. In fact, one of your author's parents finishes every voice mail recording that she leaves with the words, "Give us a call. Love, Mother."

Today's etiquette involves more than just "minding your p's and q's." Are you familiar with the rules of "netiquette?"

Interestingly, etiquette experts give very specific advice regarding person-to-machine communication. If you reach a recording device, leave your name, telephone number (including area or country codes), time and date of your call, and a brief message. To avoid playing an elaborate game of telephone tag, leave information regarding the best time to return your call, or make a telephone appointment for a call at a specific date and time. Then, make sure you are there to receive the call, or return the call again at the specified time.

Failing to return calls is one of the most common complaints you will hear in the business world. The general rule of thumb is to return a call within 24 hours unless you are out of town.

Experts also agree on the appropriate (and inappropriate) subject of messages that we leave. Messages dealing with personnel matters, trade secrets, apologies, reprimands, or performance reviews are taboo (Ramsey, 1996). So are frivolous, extraneous, or unnecessary messages. In fact, Emily Post (1990) recommends that you avoid leaving personal messages, with the exception of those that (1) confirm or cancel social plans, (2) welcome a person back after an illness, (3) extend congratulations on a job well done, or (4) offer best wishes for a happy birthday. According to Ms. Post, even birthday greetings may be inappropriate if the associate you are calling is also a friend. In this instance, she recommends that you call the person at home.

Other personal messages that you should avoid leaving on answering machines include information about relationships, personal problems, rumors, or gossip. In other words, if you wouldn't want your message on the cover of *Fortune* magazine, don't leave it on an answering machine.

With regard to receiving phone messages, Ramsey (1996) also offers some worth-while advice.

■ Keep recorded greetings simple and straightforward.

■ Change your greeting regularly to advise callers of your schedule and availability.

■ Check your messages at least twice a day.

■ Always listen to all of your messages.

■ If a caller's message is unclear, listen again.

■ Don't erase a message before you know what to do with it.

■ Respond to messages in a timely manner. Again, the rule of thumb is 24 hours (p. 12).

How many times should you attempt to return someone's telephone message? According to Joy Fox, "three calls and you're out" (Nigro, 1995, p. 77).

Cellular/Portable Phones.   Today, everywhere we go, we see people talking on cellular phones—from bicycle paths along the coast of Southern California to the crowded streets of New York. In fact, cellular and portable phones have become so prevalent that, in 1994, a trade association commissioned Judith Martin to write *Miss Manners' Guide to the Perfectly Proper Use of Cellular Telephones* (Samuels, 1994).

Because of the increasing pace of business, cellular and portable phones have become a necessity for many businesspeople. However, cellular phone etiquette often leaves much to be desired. To aid in polishing cellular phone skills, Brody (1995), president of Brody Communications, offered the following recommendations:

1. Inform the other party on the line that you're on your [cellular or portable] phone. In case you get cut off or fade in and out, they'll know the reason why.
2. Plan your call ahead of time. Have an agenda so you can keep your call brief, concise and, productive.
3. Don't try to take notes while you're driving. Rather, when you see a convenient place, pull over and jot down your notes or use a [tape recorder].
4. Preprogram your numbers if possible. Dialing while driving can be a dangerous sport.
5. Speak clearly, loudly, and try to reduce background noise as much as possible.
6. [If you are driving,] . . . anticipate your route. Don't begin a call a mile before you reach a tunnel, bridge, or any other obstacle that might interfere with reception. You'll wind up having to start over again.
7. If you must reach someone on a [cellular or portable] phone, find out first if it's OK . . . (pp. 14–15).

As with telephone messaging systems, you also should avoid talking about privileged information, or giving out credit card numbers over the phone. Electronic eavesdropping has become a multimillion dollar industry. Assume others are always listening, because they probably are.

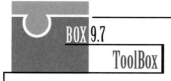

BOX 9.7

ToolBox   *Fax Etiquette*

1. Always use a cover sheet when you send a fax. Think of the cover sheet as you would a memo. Include (a) your own and the recipient's name, company address, phone number, and fax number; (b) the date; (c) the total number of pages you are sending; and (d) a brief note regarding the reason you are sending the fax.

2. Avoid sending unnecessary or complex graphics. Doing so ties up the fax machine, uses a lot of ink, and costs both companies time and money.

3. Be mindful that the reason you are using fax technology rather than another method of correspondence is that you require an immediate or same-day written response. For documents that are lengthy, use an overnight express service. (It is considered poor manners to tie up your and the recipient's fax machines for lengthy periods of time.) Additionally, should the recipient's fax machine run out of paper, your document may not be received in full.

4. For business correspondence being faxed outside your company type or word process the cover sheet and accompanying documents. (The only exceptions are one- or two-sentence notes on the cover sheet and initial price quotations, both of which may be handwritten.) Make sure to select a font type that is at least 12 points or higher for ease of reading.

5. To ensure that all pages of your document were received, you may want to make a quick phone call to the recipient.

6. Be courteous to colleagues who share the same fax machine. Avoid leaving your documents on or around the fax machine. If a faxed message comes in while you are sending yours out, place the incoming fax in the recipient's mail box or hand deliver it to his or her office.

Fax Mail and Cyber-Sensitivity

Fax (facsimile) technology has come a long way in the 1990s. As Maury Kauffman (1995), managing partner of the New Jersey–based Kauffman Group, has noted, fax machines are easy, cheap, fast, and everywhere. With such explosive growth, a few do's and don'ts may be in order.

Many companies have established their own rules guiding the use of fax machines. As Emily Post (1990) suggests, some companies prefer to train specific people to use fax machines, while others allow anyone to send a fax. Either way, we offer some basic guidelines in ToolBox 9.7 that you may find helpful.

E-mail etiquette, or cybersensitivity, is another major topic of discussion in the global workplace. However, as Ensman (1995) has noted, "Effective E-mail management follows E-mail etiquette—simple principles of courtesy and propriety [that] users should follow out of respect for their colleagues' time and energy" (p. 20). Some basic principles of E-mail etiquette that Ensman (1995) and Griaze (1993) recommend are:

- ■ Treat E-mail like business correspondence; basic rules of form and style still apply.
- ■ Check E-mail at least twice a day and answer in a timely fashion. If you can't answer right away, send a one-liner that says you received the message and will write later.

■ Avoid rambling—be concise and complete.

■ Limit each E-mail message to one topic.

■ Use upper- and lower-case letters and only essential punctuation.

■ Avoid blunt or insensitive statements as well as profanity.

■ When you're having on-line discussions with a number of people, forward all messages to all participants. Avoid sidebar discussions.

■ Observe the same chain of command that you would if you were sending memos.

■ Remember that E-mail is not entirely private. Avoid gossip, remarks about other individuals, or proprietary information.

■ Avoid "flaming," or sending angry missives in response to an idea to which you object.

■ If someone does you a favor, take a moment to say thank you, even if it's only for a quick response to your E-mail (Ensman, 1995, p. 20; Griaze, 1993, p. 77).

As technology continues to evolve, even more cybersensivity and new rules of etiquette will be required. However, as we stated earlier, etiquette is finding ways to make other people feel more comfortable. Remember this fact, and you will rarely go wrong, whether you are greeting guests in person or meeting them in cyberspace.

Case Study

"Snow White and the Seven Dwarves" Go to Dinner

Jan Flynn, Ph.D., Auburn University

The scenery was spectacular as the caravan of small cars wound its way up the steep Italian mountainside. High above, you could see the remains of a Roman fort built by Caesar hundreds of years before. That fort, or rather the restaurant that now called the fort home, was our destination.

Eight of us, seven men and one woman, had been working for two weeks in a small Italian town North of Milan. Our job was to check out a multimillion dollar piece of manufacturing equipment scheduled for delivery to our Georgia plant. To show their gratitude for our business, our hosts had planned this special evening.

From the minute we walked into the ancient structure housing the restaurant, it was obvious that this evening was special and had been planned with great care. Our hosts delighted in telling us about the history and significance of each food course. Appetizers, three pastas, salads, cheeses, and a wild pig had been prepared just for us . . . all in all, eight full courses. And each course was accompanied by a wine chosen to complement the food. Our hosts were very careful to let us know that we were being served the best of the best wines of one of Europe's great wine-producing regions.

One by one, the American guys in the group stopped drinking as the food kept coming and the wine kept flowing. This prompted one of the hosts to jokingly wonder "which one of the seven dwarves" was going to drop out next. He also remarked how pleased he was that "Snow White" was "holding up well" and seemed to have an appreciation for the quality of wine. At the end of the meal, only "Snow White" and one of the "dwarves" accepted a celebratory glass of the after-dinner drink called "grappa," this one peach-flavored in honor of the Georgia visitors.

Questions

1. What would you do in this situation if you were not a drinker? If you just simply didn't like wine? If you believed drinking alcohol is wrong?

2. Knowing just how important this business relationship was, and knowing how much work went into preparing this special dinner, what would you do if you were one of the American guests and could not eat all that was offered to you? Drink all that was offered?

3. How do you politely refuse food offered to you if you don't know what it is?

Summary

At one time or another, we have all felt embarrassed because we didn't know some basic (or not-so-basic) rule of social etiquette or protocol. For small businesses and Fortune 500 companies alike, the stakes are higher when such a situation arises. Increased global competition, a renewed emphasis on quality, and the role that proper manners play in the quality promise contribute now, more than ever, to a company's survival.

Training in business etiquette and protocol has become important to industry leaders around the world. The reasons are many; however, three important reasons are: (1) college graduates do not possess the necessary etiquette skills to succeed in today's business environments; (2) the roles of both technology and women are rapidly changing; and, (3) etiquette cuts across all four areas of business and professional communication: relational, work, public and techno-life.

Effectively managing first impressions, making your first ten words count, and using body language that communicates the desired message are three ways that you can optimize your relational life in the workplace. So, too, is understanding the rules of proper greetings and good-byes (e.g., shaking hands, making introductions, and using names and titles appropriately).

Rules of business etiquette and protocol are also important to your work life. For example, there are right and wrong ways for making entrances and exits, dealing with your colleagues' space, sharing office equipment, and using shared facilities. You also should know how to handle appointments effectively and receive guests with savvy and style.

Knowing how to handle arrangements for outside speakers is also important to your career. So, too, are introductions of guest speakers as well as of yourself. Whenever you introduce a guest, wait until he or she nears the podium, then step back and welcome him or her with a handshake. After the speech, return to the podium and extend your thanks once again with another handshake and a verbal acknowledgment through the microphone. If you must introduce yourself, the rule to remember is to make the introduction appropriate for the audience.

Techno-life is the area in which, perhaps, the greatest change is taking place with regard to etiquette and protocol. Emerging rules for the use of telephones, answering machines, voice mail, cellular phones, fax machines, and E-mail are just a few of the technologies that we addressed in this chapter.

As the global marketplace expands, business etiquette and protocol will play an even more vital role in the success of both individuals and companies. To learn more about the subject, we encourage you to visit your local library, favorite bookstore, or the world wide web, and check out the latest information. However, if you find yourself in a difficult situation and have no handbook handy, remember the "Do unto others" rule and our definition of etiquette. Etiquette is finding ways to make other people feel more comfortable. With these two thoughts in mind, you will rarely go wrong.

Knowledge Check

Key Concepts and Terms

(No new key terms presented.)

Putting It All Together

1. Why is knowledge of business etiquette critical for companies that plan to survive in the 21st century?

2. How can you make your first ten words count in a business conversation?

3. Briefly discuss the appropriate body language of a person who wants to make a positive first impression.

4. Identify four rules for making business introductions and provide an example of each.

5. Why is it important for you to respect your colleagues' space? Name at least three ways that you can do so.

6. You are hosting a meeting at your office with a very important client, who has the authority to award your company a multimillion dollar contract. You have no assistant, and the receptionist is out sick. How will you receive your guest? What steps will you take to ensure that the meeting is a success?

7. Write a self-introduction that you would give if you were making a presentation as part of the second interview for your dream job. Your audience will be comprised of three top executives from your dream company as well as the department head and supervisor under whom you will work if you get the job.

8. List at least five rules to remember when you are sending and receiving E-mail.

References

Baldridge, L. (1993). *Letitia Baldridge's new complete guide to executive manners.* New York: Rawson Associates.

Baridon, A. P., & Eyler, D. R. (1994). Workplace etiquette for men and women. *Training, 31*(12), 31–34, 36–37.

Brody, M. (1995). Car phones, and a few helpful tips, can help make you a real "wheeler dealer." *The American Salesman, 40*(8), 14–15.

Disbie, P. (1990, October 9). Executive etiquette: Young graduates just don't have it. *The Sacramento Union,* B1.

Ensman, R. G. (1995, November). E-mail etiquette: A primer. *The Secretary, 55*(9), 19–20.

Fast, J. (1970). *Body language.* New York: M. Evans.

Gray, J., Jr. (1993). *The winning image.* New York: American Management Association.

Griaze, L. (1993, November 29). Observing a little etiquette can only help E-mail users. *PC Week, 10*(47), 77.

Kauffman, M. (1995, February 20). There's no denying the fax. *Information Week, 515,* 92.

Mausehund, J., Dortch, R. N., Brown, P., & Bridges, C. (1995, December). Business etiquette: What your students don't know. *Business Communication Quarterly, 58*(4), 34–38.

McGarvey, R., & Smith, S. (1993, September). Etiquette 101. *Training, 30*(9), 51–54.

The new workplace requires new etiquette. (1995, July). *Personnel Journal, 74*(7), 22–23.

Nigro, D. (1995, June). Manners matter. *Meetings & Conventions, 30*(7), 76–80.

Pachter, B., & Brody, M. (1995). *The complete business etiquette handbook.* Englewood Cliffs, NJ: Prentice-Hall.

Phillips, L., & Phillips, W. (1990). *The concise guide to executive etiquette.* New York: Main Street Books.

Post, E. (1990). *Emily Post on business etiquette.* New York: HarperPerennial.

Ramsey, R. D. (1996, March). Voice mail etiquette. *Supervision,* 11–13.

Sabath, A. M. (1993). *Business etiquette in brief: The competitive edge for today's professional.* Holbrook, MA: Bob Adams, Inc.

Samuels, G. (1994, October 10). Cellular etiquette. *Forbes, 154*(8), 18.

Schaffer, B. F., Kelley, C. A., & Goette, M. (1993, July/August). Education in business etiquette: Attitudes of marketing professionals. *Journal of Education for Business, 68*(6), 330.

Thomsett, M. C. (1991). *The little black book of business etiquette.* New York: American Management Association.

Williams, T. (1994). *The personal touch.* New York: Warner Books.

Effective organizational communication involves more than achieving competence in face-to-face and group interactions. It also means gaining strength in managing the "public" aspects of corporate life, reflected in your organization's internal and external presentations. How well you represent yourself and the company in public presentations is vital to your professional success.

To help you achieve maximum competence in managing "public life" in your organization, Chapter 10 presents the types of formal business and professional communications you are expected to competently execute, the impact of your audience's predisposition on your message, three ways to approach an audience, and how to effectively target a message. We also identify the three major goals you need to set before launching any business communique and help you practice goal setting for oral presentations. We conclude Chapter 10 with a word about "stage fright" and how to manage communication apprehension.

From there, we turn to a discussion of how you can master the art of organizational presentations. Chapter 11 focuses specifically on organizing and effectively supporting a public presentation, based on clear goals that you have set for yourself at the outset. You will also learn how to achieve the image goals you have identified for yourself as a speaker, to confidently deliver messages that achieve your desired effect, and to develop captivating introductions and conclusions to wow your audiences. By the time you have completed these two chapters, you should have the necessary information to plan and present a compelling informative or persuasive presentation, and an entertainment speech that delights your audience.

The overriding premise of Unit Four is our firm belief that "the only way you can run faster is to run faster." In short, the only way to master "public life" is to practice your presentation skills. ∎

unit
4

Managing

Public Life in

the Workplace

Making Effective Business Presentations I:

Advance Work

**After studying this chapter,
you should be able to**

- Understand the distinctions among the four types of informative and two types of persuasive presentations.

- Know how to analyze your audience to determine the best approach to take before you plan your speech.

- Learn specific methods to conduct an effective audience analysis.

- Establish your presentation goals by knowing the differences among net effects goals, substance goals, and image goals.

- Comprehend the four major presentation formats; impromptu, extemporaneous, prepared manuscript, and memorization.

As associate vice president of investments with Prudential Securities, René Nourse has developed an investment practice working fairly exclusively with women. Her area of specialization came about after observing the financial crises women often face after divorce, or at the death of their partner. Additionally, she noted that, although women are making more money than ever before, they are still ill-prepared to handle finances and investments, primarily due to a lack of financial know-how. Prudential Securities recognized this problem as well, and, in conjunction with Nourse, developed a highly effective, educational investment seminar for women. The program is aptly named "Investment Planning for Women," and is a slide presentation that lasts about an hour. The seminar not only provides educational information, but also serves to affirm that women's investing needs are different from men's.

Although Prudential's "Investment Planning for Women" was only one year old at the time of this writing, the preliminary feedback has been positive. Seminar participants have said that they are comfortable with the material, enjoy being with other women, and especially appreciate the absence of a sales pitch (R. Nourse, personal communication, September 15, 1995).

What kinds of presentations will you have to make during the course of your professional career? How can you create compelling presentations that are custom-tailored for your audience and leave them wanting more, as René Nourse's audiences always do? The answers to these questions lie in understanding and mastering the keys to effective public speaking. This chapter will take you through the advance work required for winning presentations; Chapter 11 will focus on brainstorming, organizing, documenting, and delivering your message. Let's begin with a look at the many types of business presentations that are prerequisites for success in the workplace today.

The Many Faces of Business Presentations

Four types of informative presentations you will make at some time during your professional career are (1) status reports (or briefings), (2) introductions, welcomes, and acknowledgments of achievement, (3) short informative talks, and (4) long presentations. Persuasive presentations you invariably will make include (1) sales pitches and (2) motivational or inspirational talks. To give you a better idea about the nature of these presentations, let's take a closer look at each.

Status reports, or briefings, are short, concise updates on projects or tasks, which help keep a team, department, or unit on track. For instance, in many companies mem-

Status reports help keep a team on track.

bers of departments meet regularly to discuss current projects or activities. Such meetings allow the group to meet important deadlines and discuss any problems that are immediately at hand.

Introductions, welcomes and acknowledgments of achievement also play important roles in the business world. For example, when a new employee arrives in your unit, you may be asked to make an **introduction** of that person in a meeting, or take that person around and present him or her to your colleagues. The importance of completing this task effectively should not be overlooked; first impressions set the tone for interactions that follow. Impressive introductions provide an opportunity to get everyone on the right track and establish the new person's credibility at the outset.

Likewise you may be asked to **welcome** a visiting business executive. If your visitor is from another country, you may (or may not) be expected to select and properly present a gift. If you are a savvy business communicator, you will take this responsibility seriously. As noted by Pachter and Brody (1995), authors of *The Complete Business Etiquette Handbook,* "International visitors . . . bring their home country's gift-giving expectations with them, and may also bring presents. You want to appear gracious and not be caught off-guard, even if the situation is one that wouldn't require a gift if you were all North Americans" (p. 356). Whether or not your guest is from another country, welcomes require selecting the proper words and delivering them with style and finesse.

Awarding others for achievements in the company is another reason to sharpen your presentation skills. Supervisors and managers at all levels of business and industry conduct such activities on a regular basis. For example, promotions, retirements, and special employment anniversaries are formally honored by many companies. Many organizations also honor their employees through formal or informal "employee of the month" programs. How well you accomplish these tasks as a presenter speaks volumes about both you and the recipient.

Short informative talks are generally longer and involve presenting data to a group of people who either need or want that information. For example, if a new sexual harassment policy is being considered by your company, a human resource specialist may meet briefly with members from each department to announce, and answer questions about, the proposed policy. Similarly, your company's public relations director might hold a ten-minute press conference to lay out a new environmental plan that will benefit the company as well as the community.

Discussions of in-depth studies, problems, or projects that are currently being addressed in your company may take the form of long presentations. **Long presentations** are usually ten minutes or greater in length and include oral reports, state-of-the-company messages, and in-house training. Prior to long presentations, smart speakers circulate pertinent written materials in advance so that everyone in the audience will have an opportunity to peruse them. Then, during the actual presentation, speakers are free to discuss complex ideas in detail, and lead a discussion or debate regarding the issues (Bateman and Sigband, 1989, p. 361).

Oral presentations take two additional forms, with persuasion serving as the common denominator. **Sales pitches** generally involve selling an approach or idea to man-

> A speech is a solemn responsibility. The man who makes a bad thirty-minute speech to two hundred people wastes only a half hour of his own time. But he wastes one hundred hours of the audience's time—more than four days—which should be a hanging offense.
>
> —*Jenkin Lloyd Jones*

agement, staff, or a client. Your sales pitch may be as simple as selling your boss on a new $99 software program, or as complex as persuading a new client that the new advertising campaign you have developed is worth its $7 million price tag. In either instance, you must complete a substantial amount of homework to adequately develop and document your arguments.

Finally, you may be asked or required to give an **inspirational** or **motivational presentation,** the primary purpose of which is to inspire your listeners. Motivational presentations take a number of forms including staff pep talks, community luncheon addresses, after-dinner speeches, and impromptu meetings with disgruntled staff members.

As you can see, the list of presentations that you will make over the course of your professional life is virtually endless. Greatness for a public speaker takes practice and is cultivated one message at a time. We now turn to a discussion of the actual advance work required for a compelling and powerful presentation: analyzing your audience and the speaking occasion, setting your goals, and selecting the best format for your message.

Understanding Your Audience and the Speaking Occasion

When is the last time you studied Lincoln's "Gettysburg Address"? Was it during a ninth-grade civics class or a history class in college? One little-known fact about the president's famous speech on November 19, 1863, is that Lincoln was *not* the featured speaker that day. In fact, to dedicate the national cemetery at the Gettysburg battlefield, organizers brought in Edward Everett, a popular clergyman and former secretary of state. According to Dwyer (1994), the problem was that Lincoln was disliked and hated by many at the time. As commander-in-chief of the armed forces, Lincoln was held responsible by southerners and northerners alike for the wounded and dead being honored at Gettysburg that day. To make matters worse, many in the audience were wounded soldiers and families of soldiers who were dead and buried. Thus, Lincoln's invitation to speak was probably a matter of protocol rather than any statement about his popularity (p. 17).

Additionally, at the time he presented the speech, Lincoln was considered to be unsuccessful as a U.S. president; in fact, many people ignored his speech altogether. Only with time has the speech become a celebrated one (Einhorn, 1992).

With Lincoln's audience in mind, take a look at the text of his "Gettysburg Address" with fresh eyes. You will find his now-timeless message presented below. What a powerful message he ultimately communicated in just three paragraphs—in 243 words!

> Four score and seven years ago our fathers brought forth on this continent, a new nation, conceived in Liberty and dedicated to the proposition that all men are created equal.
>
> Now we are engaged in a great civil war, testing whether that nation or any nation so conceived and so dedicated can long endure. We are met on a great battlefield of

that war. We have come to dedicate a portion of that field, as a final resting place for those who here gave their lives that that nation might live. It is altogether fitting and proper that we should do this.

But in a larger sense, we cannot dedicate—we cannot consecrate—we cannot hallow—this ground. The brave men, living and dead, who struggled here, have consecrated it far above our poor power to add or detract. The world will little note, nor long remember what we say here, but it can never forget what they did here. It is for us, the living, rather to be dedicated here to the unfinished work which they who fought here have thus far so nobly advanced. It is rather for us to be here dedicated to the great task remaining before us—that from these honored dead we take increased devotion to that cause for which they gave the last full measure of devotion; that we here highly resolve that these dead shall not have died in vain; that this nation, under God, shall have a new birth of freedom; and that government of the people, by the people, for the people, shall not perish from the earth.

Perhaps the two most important contributors to the eventual success of Lincoln's famous oration were his ability to assess and empathize with the mood and predisposition of his audience, and his ability to understand the speaking occasion. No two variables affect the ultimate emotional impact of a message more than these. If this statement is true, how and where should you begin when you are developing an oral presentation? We would argue by clearly understanding your audience and the occasion for which you are speaking.

Identifying Your Audience

Your audience should determine almost every move you make as a speaker, from the selection of your specific topic to its delivery and follow-up. For example, think of the last political campaign speech that you heard at your college or university. Did the candidate use language appropriate for people your age? Did he or she ask you to donate money you couldn't possibly give as a student? Was the message dominated too heavily by either a feminist or male perspective? a partisan or bipartisan perspective? The answers to these questions were probably a function of the speaker's **demographic analysis** of the audience. Let's look at the demographic variables that you should always consider in developing a presentation.

Demographic Variables.   The age, economic status, and sex of your audience are three important demographic variables to consider when you plan a presentation. So, too, are your audience's ethnic or cultural identities, religious and political preferences, and significant group memberships. The reason that these variables are so important is that they directly influence how your message is perceived. In fact, they are so important that they should drive the arguments you make, the evidence you provide, and the examples and illustrations you use. For instance, if you have been asked to provide an inspirational message at your company's annual awards banquet, you will become a winning speaker if you develop your message with an eye toward your company's rich cultural diversity, commitment to a shared cause (e.g., environmental awareness), or other demographic variables that characterize your organization. (See Box 10.1 for sample questions.)

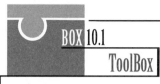

BOX 10.1

ToolBox   *How to Conduct a Demographic Audience Analysis*

Directions: Sprague and Stuart (1995, p. 34) offer the following questions to conduct a demographic audience analysis. You may add some of your own questions, depending upon the topic and your projected audience.

1. What is the average age of the audience members?

2. What is the age range?

3. What is the sexual breakdown of the audience?

4. What racial and ethnic groups are represented, in what proportions?

5. What is the socioeconomic composition of the group?

6. What occupations are represented?

7. What religious groups are represented?

8. What is the political orientation of the group?

9. How homogeneous (similar) or heterogeneous (diverse) are the audience members for each of the above characteristics?

At one time or another, we have all experienced the irritation and boredom that accompany a presentation that provides us with little new or useful information. Similarly, we have all attended presentations that were so far over our heads that we felt agitated and lost. When you prepare a presentation, you must also keep in mind the audience's knowledge level, and appropriately blend "old" and "new" information. The amount of familiar information to include should be gauged by asking the question, "How much of what the audience already knows is needed to help them understand what is new?" The amount of new information should also be dictated by the answer to this question as well as your listeners' overall interest level.

The audience's knowledge of you as the speaker also should influence the information you include. For example, if the audience knows nothing about you, you will need to provide them with data that help establish your credibility. That information might be presented by:

■ asking someone whom the audience knows and respects to introduce you,

■ personally establishing your own credentials during the introduction, or

■ providing the audience with enough background information during the presentation that they believe you are a knowledgeable speaker.

On the other hand, if you are perceived negatively by the audience before a presentation, you must do what you can to make up the initial loss, especially if you hope to make any progress with your listeners. Perhaps no more profound example of this statement exists than the credibility problems that emerged for three contemporary U.S. presidents: Richard Nixon after the Watergate scandal, George Bush after the Iran-Contra affair, and Bill Clinton as a function of his alleged involvement with Paula Jones and the Whitewater scandal.

> Talking and eloquence are not the same: to speak, and to speak well, are two things.
>
> —*Ben Jonson*

Psychological Predisposition.   Effective public speakers also consider the overall psychological predisposition of their audience. Of particular interest are the audience's beliefs, attitudes, values, and needs. Consider, for example, the following scenario.

You are the head of the accounting department in a large southern paper company. Employees in your department have heard rumors about possible changes in the company's organizational structure. You are planning a meeting for next week, but want to avoid discussing these tentative changes. Should you bring up this subject during the meeting anyway? Will your audience hear anything you say if you fail to address the proposed changes? Based on information you have about the audience's psychological predisposition, you may elect to deal briefly with the proposed changes in the company's organizational structure. Doing so will involve taking the risk that nothing else but the changes may be discussed. Doing so also will require an ability to keep control over the direction of the meeting. Whatever decision you make in a situation like this, consideration of these variables will increase your chances for successful communication in the long run.

Environmental/Physical Setting.   Another important variable you need to consider is the physical setting of your presentation. The size and location of the room in which you will speak makes a difference in the delivery of your presentation. For example, if the room is large, you may need a microphone to project your voice. You will need to check in advance to see if a microphone is provided, or if you need to bring one. You also may have to determine the type of seating arrangement that will be available. (In some instances, you may have little or no control over seating arrangement: at other times, you will have total control.) Always ask. As we discussed in Chapter 4, options include circular, rectangular, u-shaped, satellite, and classroom styles.

Another environmental factor to consider is whether or not you will be in close proximity to the audience. For example, will you be delivering your presentation at the same eye level as your audience, or will you be standing on a platform or stage? All of

The physical setting of a room affects the outcome of your presentation.

these factors play into the environmental/physical dimension of your message. The goal is to have as much control as possible over the environment.

Size of Your Audience. The fourth question you should ask when attempting to define your audience involves the size of the group to which you will be speaking. Knowing the size of your audience will allow you to select the best speaking format, to tailor your language appropriately, and to develop the appropriate visuals accompanying your presentation.

For example, using an extemporaneous format (i.e., outline only) and informal language style is more appropriate for a small audience, while using a prepared manuscript and more stylized language is more appropriate for a large audience. Knowing whether your audience is large or small also will help you develop more effective visuals (e.g., computer graphics using a laptop for smaller audiences, and overhead transparencies for larger audiences). You will learn more about the use of visuals in Appendix I.

Understanding the Speaking Occasion

When we began this section on audience analysis, we briefly addressed the obstacles that Abraham Lincoln faced the day he presented the "Gettysburg Address." Not only was he up against a hostile audience, but also he was relegated to the role of a "warm-up" speaker.

How can you, like Mr. Lincoln, maximize an occasion or situation in which you find yourself speaking? Communication expert Judi Brownell (1991, p. 42) offers some excellent advice: "Find out as much as possible about the events that surround your particular presentation and the speaking environment itself". Make sure you factor in:

■ the type, quality, and length of presentations that immediately precede [and follow] your speech,

■ the time of day,

■ the room arrangement and where key individuals will be sitting,

■ the availability of audiovisual equipment,

■ whether attendance at your presentation is voluntary or mandatory, and

■ the degree to which participants have prepared for the event (Brownell, p. 42).

By including an analysis of these variables as part of your research, you will be better prepared to give a presentation that is properly timed and adapted for the audience.

Accomplishing an Analysis of Your Audience and Occasion

How can you best gather the vital information you need about an audience and occasion and begin your trek down the road to more effective public speaking? Four major tools at your disposal are the telephone, abilities in power lunches and face to face, the personal computer, and the local library.

The Telephone. The telephone is perhaps the greatest audience analysis tool ever invented. This age-old device can be used to help you learn more about your audience (e.g., vital statistics about who and how many will attend) and to bounce ideas around with key people whom you want to win over before you give a presentation. In short, people are generally impressed with people who do their homework.

To illustrate, imagine yourself as an account executive for a large computer company in Dallas. Your assignment is to prepare a 30-minute presentation for the board of directors of an engineering firm with offices worldwide. You will make the presentation itself at the home office, which is located in Boston. Success on your part will mean the sale of 19 computer servers, along with a 10-year computer support contract. Success also will mean a promotion and salary increase for you.

How can the telephone help you develop a winning presentation? Whom should you call and, more importantly, what should you say? After doing some basic research about the audience and the people you want to interview, you might begin by phoning the chairperson to learn more about the composition of the board itself. How many people sit on the board? Are they paid members or volunteers? What is the ratio of women to men? What are their ages, overall education levels, and computer backgrounds? What is the average level of their knowledge about the specific servers being purchased? about your company? What is the general attitude of the board regarding the expenditure itself? What information would be most valued by the board during your brief 30-minute presentation? Will anyone other than board members be attending? (If possible, find out how many other companies will be making a similar pitch.)

While you are on the phone, determine the date, time, and place at which the presentation will be held, and as much information as you can about the room itself. How will the room be arranged? What necessary audiovisual equipment will be available? How can your computer equipment best be transported to the room? Will you need to bring your laptop computer with LCD screen?

Answers to these questions will provide you with much needed direction regarding the content, structure, and focus of your presentation. They also will net vital information as you develop your visuals.

Susan Silk (1994), founder and president of Media Strategy, Inc., recommends next asking for copies of recent newsletters and magazine articles about the group to develop a file of background data. As Silk notes, "All of this material will help you understand the important issues facing your audience. The background information enables you to carefully tailor your remarks to be relevant—and interesting—to the particular group" (p. 61).

Finally, if your phone call is carefully orchestrated, you will reap an additional benefit: credibility in the eyes of the chairperson before you arrive. In short, one or two well-placed phone calls can make all the difference in the success or failure of your presentation.

The Power Lunch and Other Face-to-Face Interviews.   The second tool you can put to good use in developing a winning presentation relates to your knowledge of excellent restaurants, preferably in each key city or town in which you work. Although, at first glance, such knowledge may seem superfluous to developing excellent presentation skills, some of the most important and influential presentations ever given were incubated, hatched, and discussed over a face-to-face "power lunch."

For example, during the time we were writing this book, one of your authors hosted just such a lunch to discuss the training needs of a potential client's company. The focus of her questions targeted the company's personnel structure (i.e., the potential audience). The client was so impressed with the lively discussion—not to mention the delicious food—that he committed verbally to a contract before the decadent chocolate dessert was served. By getting her client out of the office, your author was able to create an atmosphere that was conducive to an excellent discussion. Don't be afraid to develop a flair for power lunches (brunches, or cappuccino breaks) yourself. Such scenarios also can provide *you* with valuable information regarding your audience.

If you cannot meet face-to-face over a meal with the person you want to interview, do not despair. The key is to maximize a personal interview, no matter what the setting. Again, conduct as much research as you can in advance about your audience and interviewee. Then phone your interviewee and determine the best time and place to meet. If you are invited to his or her office, inquire if a meeting room or boardroom is available for your interview. That way, you can minimize distractions such as ringing phones and incoming faxes.

Be sure to prepare a list of questions before you arrive. Additionally, bring more questions with you than you hope to ask. Make sure to star those items that are most important and relevant to your research. Then, remember to ask your most important questions first (Grice & Skinner, 1993).

On the day of the interview, dress appropriately for the audience and occasion, and be sure to arrive on time. Introduce yourself, thank the person for meeting with you, restate the purpose of your visit, and reclarify the amount of time that he or she has given you for the interview. Once the interview begins, conduct yourself in a professional manner. Make every effort to relax your interviewee and ask questions clearly and concisely. At all costs, avoid being pushy or abrupt. Take notes efficiently and ask follow-up questions whenever necessary. When the interview is over, thank the person again, then follow up with a thank-you note within 48 hours (Grice & Skinner, 1993).

Your Personal Computer.   A third tool you can use to determine the best information to present to your audience is your own personal computer. How can you put your PC to work as an audience-analysis tool? You can do so by using it to develop a survey to be completed by members of your audience prior to your presentation, and to "surf the net or world wide web" for information. You also may E-mail (i.e., electronic mail) your network of friends and colleagues to request information or brainstorm ideas for your presentation. You will read more about using E-mail in Chapter 12.

Offering to conduct a formal survey prior to developing a one-day public speaking seminar is what cinched the deal for your author during the "power lunch" we mentioned earlier. The client quickly understood the value of a preliminary survey to custom tailoring the message for his company.

How do you go about developing a survey of your audience and occasion? The following six steps provide a guide for you to conduct an audience analysis survey.

1. Secure the appropriate approvals to conduct a survey.
2. Determine the specific target audience for your questions.
3. Decide the best format for gathering the information (e.g., by phone, fax, mail, E-mail, or in person).
4. Develop the questionnaire or survey instrument.

5. Physically administer the questionnaire yourself or have a key contact administer it for you.
6. Analyze and interpret the data.

A number of sources are available to teach you more specifics about developing and administering surveys. Check with your local librarian or on the Internet for the most current references available.

An audience analysis survey you might use prior to giving a two-hour workshop on the topic of public speaking is provided in Box 10.2.

A final note we need to add about audience/occasion surveys involves how you physically handle the data after you have gathered them. You must make every effort

---

BOX 10.2

ToolBox | *A Sample Audience Analysis Survey*

Directions: The following questions are designed to elicit specific information about an audience. You may adapt them in a number of ways, depending on the topic of your presentation, or add to them if you desire different (or more) information.

1. Over the last twelve months, how many public presentations (to more than five people) have you made?

    _____ none   _____ 4–6   _____ 11–12

    _____ 1–3   _____ 7–10   _____ more
    than 12

2. In general, how confident do you feel when you make a public presentation?

    _____ very confident

    _____ somewhat confident

    _____ not very confident

3. Have you ever had any formal public speaking training?

    _____ yes   _____ no

4. To what extent do you feel a public speaking workshop would aid you in presenting information more effectively? (Please circle number that best represents your perceptions: 1=low; 5=high.)

        1   2   3   4   5

5. Place an X beside each of the topics in the list that follows that you would like to know more about.

    _____ Overcoming "stage fright"

    _____ Setting public speaking goals

    _____ Audience analysis

    _____ How to use brainstorming as a public speaking tool

    _____ Organizing a public presentation effectively

    _____ How to present facts and figures without putting an audience to sleep

    _____ Delivering a message effectively

6. What other information, if any, would you like to have about making effective presentations?

    _____

    _____

7. Age at your last birthday (please place an X in the space provided).

    _____ 21–30   _____ 31–40   _____ 41–50

    _____ 51–60   _____ 61 or older

8. Your current job title: _____

    (This information will be kept confidential!)

to ensure the confidentiality or anonymity of your participants' responses. Depending on the nature and sensitivity of the information you request, you could jeopardize your respondents' job security or credibility if certain information leaks out. For that reason, avoid asking questions that could allow anyone, including yourself, to trace a given set of answers back to a specific individual. For example, avoid asking for names, social security numbers, job titles (if there are only a few), phone and fax numbers, and the like. Additionally, we suggest that you destroy paper questionnaires or erase computer disks, once you have used them to develop your presentation. In short, at all costs protect the security of those individuals who helped make your presentation a success.

As we suggested at the beginning of this section, your willingness to go the extra mile and develop a survey will go a long way in helping you develop a winning presentation. Not only can a survey help you assess your audience's demographic characteristics and interest level, it also will allow you to estimate their overall knowledge of, and predisposition toward, your topic. If you conduct a survey artfully and professionally, your credibility also will be enhanced.

Another way you can use a personal computer to gather information about your audience is by "surfing the net," especially on-line newspaper and magazine services. Although the Internet is presently a sea of unedited data, we predict that the future will be bright for using on-line information services to gather and retrieve data about any subject from anywhere in the world. See Chapter 11 for more Internet information and other communication technologies that are available to you for conducting research.

Your Local Library.   As information technology becomes available to more and more people everywhere, we will be better able to gather information about any subject (or audience) in a timely manner. Meanwhile, remember your local library. Included among the many valuable resources that are available, both on-line and in hard copy, are: books, magazines, journals, newspapers, government documents, dictionaries, encyclopedias, almanacs, yearbooks, and books of quotations, to name just a few.

To find the right news source about a person, company, or subject you are researching, a number of guides and indexes are available to you. Some of the most valuable indexes are presented in Table 10.1.

If your library is able to conduct computer database searches, ask about InfoTrac, Lexis-Nexis, and other computerized database services.

As you can see, audience analysis and researching a subject for a presentation are anything but boring these days! All you need is a research plan and answers to these four questions:

1. What information do I need?
2. Where can I go to find it?
3. What is the best method to use in gathering the information I need?
4. How do time constraints limit my research options? (Grice & Skinner, 1993)

Armed with answers to these questions and the information we have presented thus far, you are ready to begin.

Table 10.1 **Library Resources**

General Indexes	Specialized Indexes
Reader's Guide to Periodical Literature	American Statistics Index
	Business Periodicals Index
Public Affairs Information Service Bulletin	Education Index
	Hispanic American Periodicals Index
Magazine Index	Humanities Index
	Index to Legal Periodicals
	Index to Periodicals by and about Blacks
	Music Index
	Psychological Abstracts
	Social Sciences Index

Establishing Your Presentation Goals

Truly memorable presentations are rarely accidental; they are a culmination of well-conducted advance work, which begins with a comprehensive analysis of your audience and the speaking occasion and then moves to the establishment of your presentation goals. Clearly defining your goals before you make a presentation and "checking" them throughout the development process nets several benefits: a specific and clearly defined end result, a clear path to follow in order to achieve the desired result, and maximum use of your time and energy. To illustrate, consider the following scenario.

> Great wisdom is generous; petty wisdom is contentious. Great speech is impassioned, small speech cantankerous.
>
> —*Chuang-tzu*

Currently, Shannon works for a small computer software company whose primary market is the medical profession. She is developing a presentation to pitch to hospitals around the country regarding a new "breakthrough" line of computer software designed to aid doctors in the advanced diagnosis of cancer. Shannon knows that no competing software exists; her product defines the cutting edge. However, it is expensive, and hospitals of all sizes are spending less and less. Where should Shannon begin?

She could sit down and write her pitch from start to finish. However, such a session often ends in frustration—with a blank computer screen or a sea of crinkled paper. Instead, Shannon could begin with a set of succinct, precise statements about the exact feelings, thoughts, or behaviors that she wants to elicit from her audience. Does she want her audience to simply know about the software, or does she want them to purchase it? Does she want to heighten awareness about her company's monumental steps in developing the product? Is one of her goals to establish the company as the leader in the field? Knowing the exact responses you want from your audience will tell you if your presentation should be informative, persuasive, or both. By taking the time to answer the question, "What do I want to achieve?" you are establishing what Myles Martel (1989) calls your **net effects goals,** or the bottom-line behaviors you want from your audience.

Net Effects Goals

As we have stated, net effects goals identify the specific response, or responses, you want from your audience (for example, "I want my audience to learn how to choose the best presentation software to fit their needs," or "I want to persuade my audience to volunteer at least three hours per week with Habitat for Humanity"). Simply stated, net effects goals ultimately translate into your thesis statement as well as the major points of your presentation. (More later on developing thesis statements and main points from net effects goals in Chapter 11.)

According to Martel (1989, p. 9), net effects goals can be **positive** (seek a desired response), or **preventive** (discourage an unwanted response). They also can be **overt** (convey your intentions openly), or **covert** (disguise your true intentions). Generally, in a presentation, we want to achieve one or more of these goals.

To illustrate, return for a moment to the presentation that Shannon plans to make. The following are four different types of net effects goals (and corresponding examples) that Shannon wants to achieve with her message:

- ■ **Positive/Overt:**   To persuade hospitals to purchase our pioneering cancer software.

- ■ **Positive/Covert:**   To heighten my own profile with hospitals as a knowledgeable and responsive professional.

- ■ **Preventive/Overt:**   To persuade hospitals to avoid spending foundation dollars on developing similar software.

- ■ **Preventive/Covert:**   To establish the benefits of an ongoing relationship with our company and, in the process, discourage hospitals from purchasing software from potentially competitive companies in the future.

Substance Goals

Once you have established your net effects goals, the next step is to determine the best way to achieve your desired results. This step involves identifying your **substance goals,** or the way(s) you plan to achieve your net effects goals. For instance, "In order to teach my audience how to choose the best presentation software to fit their needs, I am going to *inform them about three major types of presentation software.*" According to Martel (1989), substance goals are established by asking yourself, "What 'specific . . . information, arguments, and actions' must I present or perform in order to bring about my desired net effects?" (p. 10).

Generally, substance goals are designed to accomplish four objectives: (1) inform, (2) convince, (3) inspire, and (4) move your audience to action (Martel, 1989, p. 10).

You do not necessarily need to develop substance goals to accomplish all four of these objectives. One or two substance goals per each net effect goal may be all you need. Figure 10.1 provides several sample substance goals that our friend, Shannon, might use to achieve each of her net effects goals.

Figure 10.1   **Examples of Substance Goals Developed to Achieve Desired Net Effects**

Net Effect Goal #1.   To persuade hospitals to purchase our pioneering cancer software.

(a) **Inform** audiences about the software by conducting a hands-on demonstration of its capabilities and user-friendliness.

(b) **Convince** boards that our software is on the cutting edge by presenting facts and evidence regarding its reliability.

(c) **Inspire** audiences with the story about the man whose life was saved when the software detected prostate cancer, despite three false negative tests that were the results of more conventional methods of diagnosis.

(d) **Move audiences to action** by discussing three plans the company offers to hospitals for purchasing the expensive software.

Net Effect Goal #2.   To heighten my own profile with hospitals as a knowledgeable and responsive professional.

(a) **Inform** audiences about my own mother's battle against breast cancer and the role my husband and I have played in caring for her.

(b) **Inspire** audiences with her story and the ways in which an early version of this software helped us diagnose and treat her cancer.

(c) Given my personal commitment to the early diagnosis and treatment of cancer, **convince** boards I will be there for them twenty-four hours a day, should their respective hospitals have a question or any problem with the software.

Net Effect Goal #3.   To persuade hospitals to avoid spending foundation dollars on developing similar software.

a) If appropriate, **inform** boards of my understanding that their respective foundations are looking into funding separate software research.

(b) **Convince** boards that our software will serve their respective hospitals' needs by demonstrating its full capabilities.

(c) **Move audiences to action** by offering to demonstrate the software to foundation trustees at a time that is convenient to them.

Net Effect Goal #4.   To establish the benefits of an ongoing relationship with our company and, in the process, discourage hospitals from purchasing software from competing companies in the future.

(a) **Inform** boards about our 24-hour hotline, which guarantees assistance within 90 seconds of a call.

(b) **Inform** audiences about a new research journal on the horizon: a joint publication of my company and the American Cancer Society designed to report the latest cancer research findings. (Provide ten complimentary copies to all hospitals that are clients of our company.)

(c) **Inform** audiences about future software upgrades that are planned and ways my company will work with hospitals to keep their systems constantly upgraded for a minimal cost.

To identify substance goals,

1. brainstorm the information, arguments, and actions that will be most informative or persuasive in bringing about each of your net effects goals;
2. place the information, arguments, and actions in the best order possible to achieve each net effects goal; and,
3. provide appropriate facts and evidence to support your arguments.

We will discuss each of these steps in greater detail in Chapter 11.

Image Goals

Once you have determined your net effects and substance goals, you have one more set of goals to establish: your image goals. According to Barker and Watson (1991), **image goals** involve the conscious selection of behaviors that optimize your perceived power, emotion control, relationship development with your audience, and credibility. As such, image goals are tied directly to how you make your presentation, from the clothes that you wear to your vocal delivery to your use of visuals. Because the achievement of image goals happens immediately prior to, during, and after your presentation, we also will discuss them more completely in Chapter 11. However, we previewed them at this time to show you how prepared you must be for a winning presentation.

Now that you have a clearer understanding of the importance of establishing net effects, substance, and image goals, let's turn to the third major element of effective presentation advance work: selecting the best format for your presentation.

Selecting the Best Format for Your Presentation

According to a recent survey of more than 100 executives from major North American companies, the dynamics of corporate presentations are shifting from showmanship to substance as mergers, takeovers, and corporate reengineering become the name of the game. As a result, in presentations around the globe, increased emphasis is being placed on attention to detail, ability to synthesize and relate complex information, and better organizational skills (Kane, 1992, p. 14). In fact, 68 percent of survey respondents reported that the presence or absence of these skills is having a greater and greater impact on their careers (Kane, p. 14).

If presentation success, indeed, is becoming "a yardstick for [career] advancement," as Kane and others report, you too need to be ready with a full array of tools at your disposal. In addition to effective goal-setting and analysis of audience and occasion, you also have four major presentation formats from which to choose: impromptu, extemporaneous, prepared manuscript, and memorization. Let's take a look at the definition, advantages, and disadvantages of each.

Impromptu

Impromptu presentations involve limited or no advance preparation. They usually emerge on the spur of the moment, out of the situation. For example, you are quietly chatting with the person beside you at a luncheon, only to hear over the public address system a request that you come to the podium and speak briefly to the audience. What should you do if this happens? First, think of a major point you would like to make with this particular audience. If you have time, quickly jot down that point on the paper napkin that is conveniently supporting your water glass, along with two or three subpoints you may want to make. Then, as you walk toward the podium, smile and think of something humorous or appropriate to say that will help you gain the audience's attention. Developing such an introduction not only will help you promote goodwill, but also will reduce the communication apprehension you probably will be feeling at the moment.

The obvious advantage of the impromptu format lies in its spontaneity. If you can think quickly on your feet, provide the requested information, and do so in a manner that befits the occasion, you will gain or increase your credibility with the audience instantaneously. Additionally, impromptu remarks are generally viewed as natural and conversational.

The primary disadvantages of impromptu speaking are that you have little time to prepare and can easily misstate your case or poorly word your message. Additionally, many people use this format believing that they can "wing it" through an important presentation, even though they may have had adequate time to prepare. We highly discourage this kind of thinking when it comes to public presentations of any kind. Even the most experienced speakers realize the importance of preparation and practice.

Extemporaneous

The second format that is available to you as a public speaker is **extemporaneous speaking** and involves the use of a skeleton outline to prompt your memory in a presentation. Usually that outline is in the form of key words or key phrases, which you fill in with details as you speak. Most of the public speaking you will do in the business setting involves this format.

The advantages of extemporaneous speaking are increased spontaneity and sincerity, the comfort provided by having an outline, the natural delivery style that results, and an ability to respond quickly to audience feedback. Additionally, working with an outline allows you the freedom to come and go from the lectern as you please.

The primary disadvantage of this format is that you may inadvertently eliminate details you had intended to cover, leaving your message devoid of necessary details. Additionally, properly timing such messages is difficult to accomplish. To avoid these obvious pitfalls, we suggest including critical details in the outline itself. We also recommend that you practice your message a minimum of three to five times aloud, or until you have achieved the level of precision and timing you desire.

Prepared Manuscript

A third format you can use when organizing a presentation involves the development of a complete manuscript to drive your message. Usually the **prepared manuscript** is worded verbatim, typed in large or bold type with double or triple spacing between lines, and coded to correspond with your use of visuals. Generally, this format is used when the exact words you select are critical to the success of your presentation (e.g., when you are speaking at a press conference or attempting damage control in a crisis situation). Furthermore, this format is useful when you are speaking on a topic about which you are unfamiliar, or in a large convention setting in which use of your audio-visuals is tied closely to your text.

Advantages of using this format include the reduced risk of misstating your message, the ability to use more precise and stylized language, and the insurance you are afforded regarding control of the timing and content of your message. In addition, if you wish to release a copy of your text to the media in advance, you can do so easily.

The primary disadvantage of using a prepared manuscript is that reading does little to enhance your perceived sincerity with an audience, unless you are an accomplished oral interpreter. Your ability to adapt readily to audience feedback also is reduced. For example, if you lose your audience at some point during the presentation, you will find it difficult to recover.

Memorization

The final format that is available to you involves **memorization** of a prepared manuscript and is usually used when precision, eloquence, and increased "sincerity" are a must. Generally, memorization is used for ceremonial occasions—for example, during the giving or receiving of an award. Advantages include the three associated with prepared manuscripts plus an ability to interact more freely with the audience if you are an accomplished speaker. Disadvantages include the less-than-conversational quality that often accompanies memorizing a written message and the amount of time that memorization requires. Unless you are adept as a speaker, your message also may suffer from the reduced flexibility that often goes with this particular format.

Now that you have learned how to complete the advance work that is necessary for a winning presentation, you are probably wondering about the actual delivery of your talk. Such concern is natural for all of us. In fact, some of the most celebrated speakers and entertainers in the world experience the phenomenon known as "stage fright," or communication apprehension.

A Word about "Stage Fright"

Elevated heart rate. Trembling hands. Dry mouth. Forgetfulness. Withdrawal. Nausea. Increased respiration (and perspiration!). What do all of these physiological responses have in common? They are all commonly associated with "stage fright," or communication apprehension, prior to giving a presentation. Research studies validate that most people would rather jump out of a plane, tangle with a snake, go to the dentist, or die than give a speech. What is your comfort level with speaking in public? Are you part of the "MTV generation" who enjoys performing in front of a crowd, or would you rather be a listener in the audience enjoying the performance? **Communication apprehension** is a common phenomenon associated with fear of public speaking. Before we discuss methods to alleviate communication apprehension, let us first examine its causes.

Causes of "Stage Fright"

The reason for your own anxiety about speaking may be deeply rooted in your past, or you may discover that you have no reason to be afraid to speak in public. However, if you have experienced communication apprehension, it probably was associated with one of the following causes:

■ *Skills Deficit.* Some people have never learned the skills associated with giving a presentation. They have not taken a course in public speaking, or have not sought advice on how to give a speech. Once you learn how to speak in front of an audience—from brainstorming to outlining to rehearsing—you are well on your way to conquering skills deficit.

■ *Negative Reinforcement.* Perhaps when you were younger, someone whom you respected made you feel uncomfortable when speaking out in public. Maybe you were reprimanded by your favorite teacher for being outspoken in a class when you were not called upon. As a result, your confidence level decreased, and you chose not to speak out in class again. This negative reinforcement made you feel self-conscious about speaking in public, which, in turn, led to an overall fear of public speaking. Turning negative self-statements into positive statements takes time and practice. To give you practice at turning negative self-statements into positive ones, complete the following exercise. The first example is provided for you.

Negative: "I can't speak in public because I don't know what I'm talking about."

Positive: I have prepared well for my speech. I have conducted my audience analysis, thoroughly researched my topic, and practiced my speech five times. I am enthusiastic about both my topic and delivering my presentation in front of class.

Negative: "I know I will forget part of my speech."

Positive: _____

_____

_____

Negative: "I am so stressed out that I will never be able to speak in public."

Positive: _____

_____

_____

Negative: "My voice is so monotonous. I will probably put everyone to sleep."

Positive: _____

_____

_____

■ *Fear of Failure.* Whenever people are evaluated, they tend to experience stress, which sometimes makes it difficult to perform in public. Some stress is positive because your adrenalin starts flowing, which gives you the extra boost you need in order to perform well. Any actor or television personality who is constantly in front of the camera will more than likely tell you that he or she tends to feel anxious prior to a performance.

Some apprehension is positive and can work for you; however, too much anxiety is detrimental. One technique that many seasoned speakers use before a presentation to prepare themselves mentally is called **visualization**. Visualization involves imagin-

*One major cause of communication appre-
hension is fear of failure.*

ing yourself in a business presentation from start to finish: thanking your department head for giving you the floor, introducing your report with a bit of humor, delivering your message point by point, concluding your report with a poignant quotation, and taking your seat feeling confident that you have prepared well and given an excellent presentation. World-class athletes, Academy Award winners, and winning toastmasters are only a few of the people who use visualization to complete a superb performance. You, too, can use this strategy to overcome communication apprehension and fear of failure, and to optimize a speaking occasion to your advantage.

Methods for Managing Communication Apprehension

No matter what drives communication apprehension for a speaker, learning to manage this form of anxiety is a lot like riding a bike. Think back to when you first learned how to ride your bike: the excitement you experienced when you finally rode a "two-wheeler" on your own, without any help from your mom, dad, or an older sibling. If you were like most children, you probably fell a couple of times along the way and felt somewhat shaky the first time on your own, but you did it! Learning how to ride your bike took time and practice, and, more than likely, you experienced some frustration along the way. Overcoming communication apprehension is a similar fete. It takes preparation, practice, and encouragement.

Methods for overcoming communication apprehension differ, depending on the reasons that cause your initial anxiety. We direct you to Box 10.3 for our best responses to six commonly asked questions about overcoming communication apprehension.

BOX 10.3

ToolBox

*Common Questions and Answers about
Overcoming Communication Apprehension*

Q: What if my mouth becomes so dry that I have a difficult time forming my words?

A: This is common with many first-time public speakers. What you are experiencing is called "cotton mouth" in general parlance, and is a physiological reaction to the stress of speaking in front of an audience. We suggest you have a warm drink (e.g., hot herbal tea) or room-temperature water prior to your presentation. (Avoid cold drinks; they constrict your vocal cords and make your voice sound "scratchy.") Also try taking a couple of deep breaths to relax yourself.

Q: What if I draw a blank and forget my place during my presentation?

A: Most speakers have notes in front of them while they are speaking. It's a good idea to look at your notes if you tend to forget your place, but remember: you are the "expert." In most cases, your listeners do not have as much information as you do on your topic. If you forget part of your message, ad lib or transition into the next part of your presentation. Keep in mind that, more than likely, no one but you will realize your blunder. Another technique you can use is to repeat the last line of the sentence before you drew a blank. Sometimes repeating key words will trigger the next thought and get you back on track. You also can color-code the main points on your notes to assist you if you lose your place.

Q: What if I tell a joke and nobody laughs?

A: Most of us don't have the timing of Robin Williams, Billy Crystal, or Ellen Degeneris when it comes to joke-telling. When you rehearse your presentation in front of a friend, colleague, or family member, try telling him the joke. Did he laugh or did he groan? This response should give you a good indication of how your listeners will react. Some people have the ability to use humor effectively. If

you are one of those people, use it to your advantage.

Q: I tend to talk too fast when I'm nervous. How can I slow the rate of my speech?

A: If you talk into a tape recorder during your rehearsal, you will be able to monitor your speech patterns. You may want to purposely talk fast into the tape recorder in order to experience how audience members will hear you. When you replay the tape and find that your presentation is less than understandable, you will probably remember to slow your speech rate the next time you make a presentation. Another idea that works is writing the words, "Slow down!" in red ink several times in the margin of your notes.

Q: I have a difficult time making eye contact with the audience. What can I do to alleviate this problem?

A: An effective technique you can use is to practice in the room where you will be speaking in advance of your presentation. While you are rehearsing, look directly at the eye level of the empty seats, and imagine the people who will be sitting in these chairs during your presentation. Another method is to place objects (e.g., large books, pets, or other objects) on a sofa during your practice sessions at home, and look directly at each object while you speak.

Q: How can I overcome a lack of self-confidence when speaking in public? I tend to feel embarrassed when everyone is looking at me.

A: Lack of self-confidence is a common problem among inexperienced presenters. If you research your audience, occasion, and topic well; set specific goals; research and outline your message; and rehearse your presentation in its entirety at least three times, you should be prepared. You also can practice the visualization technique that we mentioned earlier.

You may (or may not) experience more than one "symptom" of communication apprehension. However, no matter what form your symptoms take, a few additional guidelines that we recommend for overcoming apprehension are:

1. Practice, practice, practice. Nothing can take the place of rehearsing your message until you feel comfortable with your content and delivery.
2. Take a moment to compose yourself mentally and emotionally before you speak. As we said earlier, taking a few deep breaths also will help you relax.
3. Ask a friend to videotape and critique your presentation in advance. Observing yourself on videotape can help you assess your strengths and weaknesses prior to your actual presentation.
4. Always look for the friendly faces. As a speaker, you are always drawn to audience members who smile at you. A smile serves as positive reinforcement that your message has been met with approval from the audience.
5. Remain centered and quiet before your presentation, and focus on what you want your listeners to learn during your message. Try to eliminate all other thoughts in your mind, and focus completely on what you are going to say.

Communication apprehension, or "stage fright," can be overcome. All it takes is practice and a desire to improve. If you accept requests to speak on a regular basis, you can become more polished and professional in the public speaking arena. Like many other people, you may find that you enjoy public presentations after all, and may actually seek out speaking opportunities to further your career.

Case Study

The Mind Is a Terrible Thing to Lose: Overcoming Communication Apprehension

Deborah A. Gaut, President, Gaut & Associates

Normally, at this point in each chapter, we (your authors) present a case study that was created by a distinguished guest writer. However, something so terrifying happened to one of your authors on her first foray into the public speaking arena that we decided to write and present this case study ourselves.

In the late 1970s, Deborah was a graduate student at Auburn University and thought she had the world by the tail. At a mere age of 23, she was a graduate teaching assistant, had authored two chapters in a book, had published two or three articles in national journals, and was about to present her first academic paper at a major speech convention.

When she arrived at the convention hotel on the day before her presentation, she was feeling pretty good about herself. She had just put the finishing touches on her paper a few days before she arrived, and felt she knew the paper inside out—backwards and forwards. After all, she had written the paper, hadn't she?

Although Deborah had considered practicing her presentation in advance—after all, that's what she always warned her public speaking students to do—she decided that cruising the hotel and the beach sounded like much more fun. So she threw on a sweater (it was November in the Northeast), and off she went.

The morning of her presentation, Deborah felt very little communication apprehension. Her session was scheduled for the last day of the conference, and her mentor had assured her that only a few people would be in attendance. (As a result, she even decided to forgo checking out the room where she would be speaking!)

Much to her surprise, as she entered the room five minutes before her presentation, the crowd was "Standing Room Only!" To make matters worse, she began reading the name tags of the audience members as they entered the room. Many were top scholars in the communication field, whose work she had been studying since the moment she entered the graduate program.

The final blow was learning that she would be the last panelist to speak—behind four leading scholars in the field. She was the only graduate student on the panel and, needless to say, she began to feel panicky.

After the seemingly endless presentations of the four panelists who preceded her, at last, it was Deborah's turn. She looked up at the audience . . . and absolutely froze. She could remember NOTHING about the paper she had written, not even its topic. How was she ever going to make it through this terrifying experience?

Questions

1. What could Deborah have done prior to her presentation to reduce the chances that she would experience such debilitating communication apprehension?

2. Given that she didn't adequately prepare for her oral presentation, what techniques could Deborah have practiced (while the other panelists were presenting) in order to minimize the apprehension she was experiencing?

3. Obviously self-confidence contributes to the success of any presentation. In this instance, Deborah was overly confident, a state of mind that is equally as perilous as lack of self-confidence. What do you think Deborah should have learned about public speaking from this situation?

Summary

Business presentations play a major role in the life of every organization. Introductions, welcomes, recognitions, status reports, informative talks, and long presentations constitute the informative presentations you will make during your professional career. Persuasive messages that you will find yourself developing on a regular basis include proposal presentations, sales presentations, and motivational talks.

Analyzing your audience and the speaking occasion is the first order of business in developing an effective presentation. Understanding your audience means considering your listeners' demographics, psychological predispositions, and knowledge levels.

Don't forget to learn as much as you can about the physical environment and to estimate the size of your audience.

Four tools you can use to analyze your audience and the speaking occasion are the telephone, face-to-face interviews, your personal computer, and your local library. Once you have analyzed your audience and the occasion, you are ready to establish your presentation goals. Always begin with your net effects goals, or what you want from your audience. From there, you can determine how to best achieve those effects (substance goals), and the image you must project to be successful (image goals).

You also need to keep in mind the major presentation formats from which you can choose: impromptu, extemporaneous, prepared manuscript, and memorization.

Dealing with communication apprehension, or "stage fright," before your presentation is the final step required in advanced preparation. Common causes include skills deficits, past negative reinforcement, and fear of failure. Hopefully, the methods that we discussed in this chapter will help you better manage your own communication apprehension.

Advance work for presentations isn't difficult to accomplish; it simply requires that you think about what you want to achieve, how you want to achieve it, and how to best understand the audience you will address. Once you have established this important groundwork, you are ready to research, organize, and deliver your presentation.

Knowledge Check

Key Concepts and Terms

status reports
introduction
welcome
awarding others for
    achievements
short informative talks
long presentations
sales pitches

inspirational/motivational
    presentation
demographic analysis
net effects goals
positive net effects goals
preventive net effects goals
overt net effects goals
covert net effects goals

substance goals
image goals
impromptu presentations
extemporaneous speaking
prepared manuscript
memorization
communication apprehension
visualization

Putting It All Together

1. Why are proper welcomes and introductions important to the image and success of a company and its members?

2. Name at least six demographic variables that you should consider when analyzing an audience. Why are these variables important to consider?

3. How can a thorough analysis of environmental constraints and size of your audience aid you in making an effective presentation?

4. Briefly list and discuss four methods for conducting an audience analysis.

5. Why is it important for you to ensure confidentiality and anonymity if you conduct a written survey as part of your audience and occasion analysis?

6. Contrast net effects, substance, and image goals. Provide an example of each if you were developing a short informative presentation on the merits of public speaking training.

7. Name the four objectives of substance goals.

8. On what occasions would you best be served by memorizing a speech? What are the inherent dangers?

9. You are in a staff meeting and have just been asked to make an impromptu presentation (right now!) on the value of getting involved in your community's activities. You only have 30 seconds to come up with a witty introduction and three main points. Ready. Set. Go!

10. Based on our discussion, what methods of overcoming communication apprehension do you feel would best work for you and why?

References

Barker, L. L., & Watson, K. W. (1991). *Presentation skills.* Metairie, LA: Spectra, Inc.

Baskerville, D. M. (1994). Public speaking rule #1: Have no fear. *Black Enterprise, 24*(10), 76–83.

Bateman, D. N., & Sigband, N. B. (1989). *Communicating in business* (3rd ed.). Glenview, IL: Scott, Foresman and Company.

Brownell, J. (1991). Designing and delivering effective presentations. *The Cornell H.R.A. Quarterly, 32*(1), 41–45.

Dwyer, E. J. (1994). Lincoln's "Gettysburg address" and your presentation skills. *Training & Development, 48*(1), 17–19.

Einhorn, L. J. (1992). *Abraham Lincoln the orator: Penetrating the Lincoln legend.* Westport, CT: Greenwood Press.

Grice, G. L., & Skinner, J. F. (1993). *Mastering public speaking.* Englewood Cliffs, NJ: Prentice-Hall.

Kane, B. (1992). Business presentations for the nineties. *Training & Development, 46*(3), 14.

Martel, M. (1989). *The persuasive edge.* New York: Fawcett Columbine.

Pachter, B., & Brody, M. (1995). *Complete business etiquette handbook.* Englewood Cliffs, NJ: Prentice-Hall.

Silk, S. L. (1994). Making your speech memorable. *Association Management, 46*(1), 59–62.

Sprague, J., & Stuart, D. (1992). *The speaker's handbook,* 3rd ed. New York: Harcourt, Brace, Jovanovich.

Making Effective Business Presentations II:

Creating and Delivering a Compelling Message

After studying this chapter, you should be able to

- Brainstorm ideas and develop a logical sequence as you begin preparation of a presentation.

- Use seven different organizational patterns to mold and shape your message.

- Construct an outline and support your ideas with appropriate appeals and evidence.

- Gain your listeners' attention through effective introductions.

- Close your presentations with compelling conclusions.

- Apply the ethics litmus test to your message.

- Optimize your PERC-Quotient.

At United Airlines, the road to upward mobility requires mastering a number of communication skills. Chief among them is the ability to give presentations to management. For Marie T. Smith, a service director for the airline at New York's JFK International Airport, this fact of professional life posed a considerable problem early in her career. Smith was terrified of making public presentations. As she recalls, her first attempt in 1981 was a complete catastrophe. Despite extensive preparation, she stammered, forgot key portions of her message, and responded poorly to questions. As she recalled, "I was so terrified of making that presentation, I made myself a nervous wreck. . . .Once I got in that room, everything I'd rehearsed went out the window."

Promotions passed Smith by for several years before she got the training she needed to overcome her fear of public speaking. Since then, she has been promoted several times. Unfortunately Smith laments, "It took too many years and countless missed opportunities to get me here" (cited in Baskerville, 1994, p. 80).

273

More than ever, in companies around the world, employees like Marie Smith are making presentations on a regular basis. As Baskerville (1994) has noted, "Being able to convey crucial information credibly and convincingly before groups of all sizes has become as fundamental a job requirement as computer literacy. And being truly adept at it can propel you forward because public speaking gives you a visibility seldom achieved by sterling work alone" (p. 80).

On a scale of one to ten, how would you rate your current presentation skills? To what extent can you effectively organize and deliver an exciting and compelling oral presentation? In this chapter, you will learn how to feel confident about developing and presenting public messages and how to polish your organizational and delivery skills.

In Chapter 10, you were introduced to the many types of business presentations you will make during your career. You also learned tips and techniques for analyzing your audience, determining your presentation goals, and selecting the presentation format that is right for you. Finally, you learned more about how to manage communication apprehension. With this advance work behind you, you are ready to develop and organize your message. The place to begin is to develop your net effects, substance, and image goals, which we discussed in Chapter 10. Then set them aside. Next it is time to brainstorm the content of your message.

Brainstorming

Brainstorming is defined as the unrestrained, spontaneous development of ideas. Although there are many brainstorming methods available, the easiest and most useful one we have encountered is **mindmapping.** This technique involves the spontaneous "mapping" of information during a brainstorming session and allows an individual to freely jot down ideas without the limitations of linear thinking.

According to Mike Brown (personal communication, August 15, 1994), managing partner with Atheneum Learning Corporation of Los Angeles, mindmapping works well because it combines our creative right-brain processes with our more traditional, linear left-brain processes. As a result, the user can achieve greater creativity and remember the message better during the presentation. Further, Brown identifies two primary forms of mindmapping: open- and closed-ended. **Open-ended mindmapping** is used when the major topics of a presentation are not predetermined in any way. This provides maximum creative possibilities and is particularly useful for developing a top-level representation of the subject matter. For example, if you are giving a 30-minute presentation on a new robot that will be installed in your plant, you probably would be able to include any related topics of discussion that you wish. Thus, open-ended mindmapping involves brainstorming with no limiting or preexisting parameters.

Closed-ended mindmapping involves a slightly different process, in that your brainstorming session is affected at the onset by certain predetermined limitations. As Brown (1994) noted, "This technique is particularly useful for problem solving and helps focus the content of a presentation in a limited way." For instance, your boss asks you to make a presentation on a new approach to team building that you have implemented in your unit. Further, she asks that you discuss (1) how you came up with the idea, (2) how you went about implementing the novel approach, and (3) how produc-

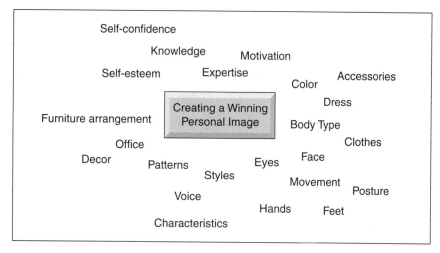

| **Figure 11.1** | Stage One of Open-Ended Mindmap on the Subject of Creating a Winning Image |

tivity and job satisfaction have been affected. As you can see, your brainstorming session would be limited before you begin by the parameters that your boss has placed on the presentation. As a result, your brainstorming session would be "closed" to alternative topics you otherwise might consider. Remember that, even with the use of closed-ended mindmaps, you will begin to develop, integrate, and intuit the subject in such a way that new and interesting connections or insights will occur. It is precisely this "ah ha!" phenomenon that can make your presentation stand out among the rest (M. Brown personal communication, August 15, 1994).

In either case, how would you begin a mindmapping session? First, start by writing a topic or key word(s) associated with your presentation in the center of a piece of paper, and draw a box around that word or words. For example, if the subject of your presentation is "Ways to Create a Winning Image," write the words "Creating a Winning Image" in the center of the page.

From there, jot down as many words as you can think of that are associated with building "winning images." Avoid attempting to censor or organize your thoughts in any way; organizing is the next stage of mindmapping. Simply write key associations anywhere on the page until you run out of things to write. Let your mind tell you where to go and stay in creative mode: avoid jumping to details or conclusions in the beginning. For instance, when we mindmapped the subject of image building after conducting some initial reading (Gray, 1993), the outcome looked something like the illustration presented in Figure 11.1.

Once you have brainstormed every key word you can think of, connect the words that seem to relate most closely to one another. Try using different-colored pencils to help you match up and discriminate among key words and concepts. Simply circle the words and connect similar concepts together with lines. Note that some concepts will emerge as major topic areas, others as subtopics within major topics. Figure 11.2 demonstrates how we related the key words that we brainstormed.

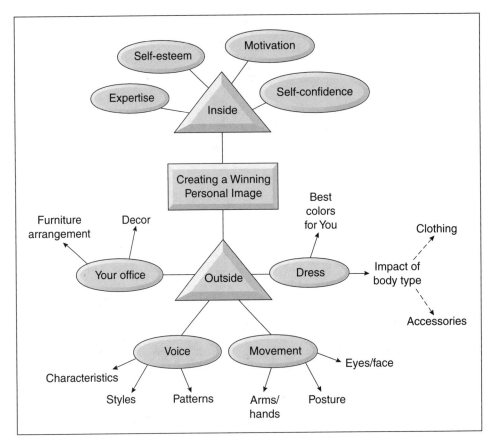

Figure 11.2   **Stage Two of Open-Ended Mindmap on the Subject of Creating a Winning Image**

What about closed-ended mindmapping? How does it work? In process, closed-ended mindmapping is very similar to open-ended mindmapping. The only difference is that you begin by placing the general subject area in the center of the page, and then surrounding it with the three or four predetermined topics that comprise your presentation. From there, you can brainstorm any other possible main topics and their corresponding subtopics. Simply jot them down around the main topics you have generated, and then connect the dots, so to speak.

As you can see, mindmapping is a fun and effective tool for the presenter, no matter what the subject matter might be. This tool allows you to create a graphic representation of the information that you have stored in long-term memory, and provides you with an initial assessment of the amount of research you will have to do. Now it's your turn. Take a moment and develop a mindmap in the space provided in Box 11.1. The subject of your would-be presentation is "How to Make a Lasting Impression during a Power Lunch." Just let your mind go and have fun. See how creative and free you can be as you go through the process.

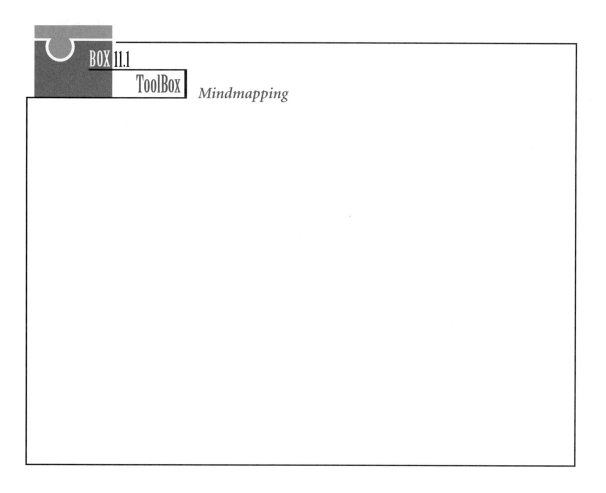

BOX 11.1

ToolBox *Mindmapping*

Brainstorming in any of its forms is an excellent tool for helping to determine the initial information you want to include in your presentation. From here you are ready to place your ideas into a logical sequence, and write the basic outline for your presentation. Before we discuss how to move from a mindmap to an outline, you need to know about three informative and four persuasive organizational patterns you can use to organize a message.

Developing Logical Sequences for Your Messages

All great presentations are quite simple when it comes to developing a logical sequence. Generally, informative messages reflect one of three patterns: chronological, spatial, or topical. Persuasive messages reflect one of four organizational patterns: cause-effect, problem-solution, climactic, or motivated sequence.

Chronological Pattern

The **chronological pattern** is simply that: a chronology or timeline around which you build your presentation. For example, you work for the National Aeronautical Space

Administration (NASA) in Houston, and have been asked by the Chamber of Commerce to make a 30-minute presentation to its members in honor of NASA's upcoming anniversary. You might elect to use the chronological pattern and begin with a discussion of the first unmanned space flight. From there you could take the audience on a visually stimulating trip through time, ending with the most recent advances in shuttle technology.

In contrast, if you are feeling particularly creative, you might begin by assuming the role of someone living on a space station in the year 2020, and move the audience in **reverse chronological order** back through time to the beginning of NASA's space program. Either way, you would be using "time" as the logical structure around which to build your presentation. The chronological and reverse chronological patterns are especially appropriate if your net effect goal is strictly to *inform* your audience about a given subject.

Spatial Pattern

Another great organizational pattern for informative presentations is the **spatial pattern.** Like a chronology, the name given to this pattern is self-explanatory and involves using "space," or geographical representation, as its underlying structure. Consider, for example, the following scenario. You are the chairperson of a major service committee with an international association. You have been asked to make a 15-minute report to the international executive committee at their next meeting regarding the results of a survey that your committee developed and administered. How would you organize your presentation, given that you are limited to 15 minutes? One way might be to structure your report on a region-by-region basis. You might begin with how members from the northwestern region (Region 1) responded to the survey and then proceed through the remaining five regions that were represented in the survey. In that way, the executive committee could get a clearer idea of how the membership responded regionally and how they might better serve the membership overall.

One way to organize your presentation is around geographical locations.

Topical Pattern

The **topical pattern** of organization involves taking three to five major topics that emerged from your brainstorming session and organizing them in an interesting and compelling way for your listeners. For example, consider the following situation. You are interviewing for a corporate-level job with Odetics, one of the "wackiest places to work in the United States today" (Levering & Moskowitz, 1994, p. 337). Odetics makes high-tech equipment such as robots, video security systems, and 80 percent of the digital tape recorders used in spacecraft (at the time of this writing).

Upon arriving at the interview, you learn that you will be given five minutes to prepare a three-minute introduction of yourself for 38 employees who have just completed their shift at the Anaheim corporate headquarters. At this very moment, they are waiting for you in the auditorium. Although they are tired, they also are curious about how you will introduce yourself. You know that your ability to be creative, think on your feet, and get the crowd's attention will play a critical role in the success or failure of your interview. Take just a moment, mindmap your own education and work experience, and identify three major topics to include in your presentation. Then decide the order in which you would present your three major topics. Use the space provided in Box 11.2, and be as creative as possible. Remember, Odetics is known for its commitment to innovation and creativity.

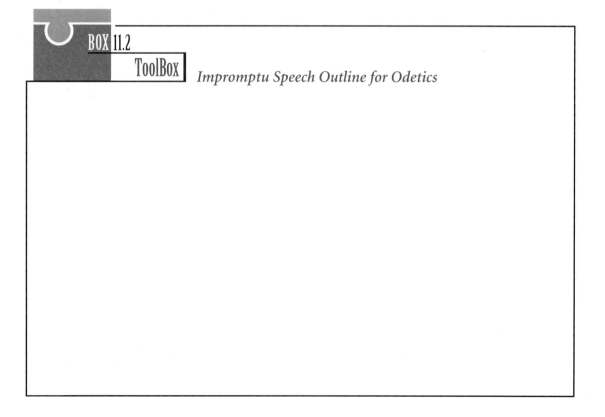

BOX 11.2

ToolBox *Impromptu Speech Outline for Odetics*

Thus far, we have discussed three patterns for organizing informative presentations: chronological, spatial, and topical. These patterns also can be used in combination to achieve the desired results. To illustrate, consider the following combination of the topical and spatial patterns.

As an up-and-coming junior executive for Xerox Corporation, you have been asked to make a 15-minute presentation via satellite to the company's North American field reps. They will be meeting simultaneously in seven regional meetings across the United States and Canada in early May. The subject of your presentation is the company's new reward system, which will be based on friendly sales competition among the regions.

After brainstorming the key information to be discussed, you decide to begin with a presentation of current sales figures on a region-by-region basis (Topic #1). By moving the audience geographically (or spatially) from region to region within this topic, you can provide them with a clear visual image of their "friendly" competition. From there, you will move to a discussion of the reward system itself, including a graphics-based illustration of how the system will work (Topic #2). To bring the presentation home to each sales representative, you conclude with an explanation of how the reward system can benefit each individual, his or her region, and the company overall (Topic #3). Since the system includes personal bonuses, regional awards, and company-wide recognition, the latter discussion will play a critical role in the success of your presentation. As you can see, combining the topical and spatial patterns would work well in this instance and can be easily accomplished for a number of other subject areas.

What about messages that are designed primarily to persuade? What organizational patterns are most persuasive? Think about what it takes for other people to change your attitudes, values, or beliefs. Certainly it takes more than the drop of a hat to make a lasting impression on any of us. Four persuasive patterns that you can use are: (1) cause-effect, (2) problem-solution, (3) climactic (or anti-climactic), and (4) Monroe's motivated sequence.

Cause-Effect Pattern

Effective persuasion involves presenting information in a truly persuasive fashion. One pattern of organization that has proven to be effective for persuasive messages is the **cause-effect pattern.** This approach involves the presentation of (1) the major causes of some event, (2) the effect(s) that have accrued as a result, and (3) the actions that must be taken to remedy or improve the situation. Using this structural pattern, you can easily develop a three-point presentation.

For example, you have been appointed as a new board member for a nonprofit organization that assists children with AIDS in your community. As a new member, you are especially interested in reversing the upward trend of AIDS cases in youth. At the next board meeting, you ask for 10 minutes to present the *causes* you believe are contributing to the increase, and the *effects* that this increase is having on the attitudes and morale of kids in your community. You could conclude with a brief discussion of three creative *ways* that the organization could work directly with kids to decrease the number of AIDS cases in children.

Problem-Solution Pattern

Another organizational pattern that has proven to be effective in persuasion is the **problem-solution pattern**. This pattern is similar to the cause-effect pattern in that it focuses on changing or improving a given situation or event. However, it differs in that the presenter first focuses on a description of the problem, then offers one or more viable solutions that would remedy that problem. For instance, you have accepted a new mid-management-level job with a company that has mounting problems. Going in, you know you must quickly diagnose the specific problems in your new unit, and work with the other members of the management team to develop solutions to those problems. By the time the first management meeting rolls around, you have discovered the department's greatest problem: flagging morale caused by rapid turnover at the management level. Using an open-ended brainstorming method to develop your five-minute presentation, you first lay out the factors that have contributed to the morale problem: rapid turnover at the management level, increased uncertainty regarding what is expected of employees on a day-to-day basis, and (as a result) job insecurity. Then you brainstorm solutions to the problem and arrive at three ideas that could be implemented immediately: instituting quality circles, hosting a brown bag lunch once a week to talk about problems, and establishing a recognition system for new ideas that are presented and used in your unit.

Using the problem-solution pattern when you actually make your presentation, you begin by describing the morale problem and the factors that have contributed (Point #1). You then discuss the three solutions that you have generated (Point #2), and conclude with a timeline for implementing your proposed ideas (Point #3).

Climactic Pattern

The third organizational pattern that can be particularly persuasive is the **climactic pattern.** To build a "climactic" argument, begin with a brainstorming session, and then organize your arguments from least to most persuasive. For example, you decide to talk with your boss about the reasons you should be awarded a raise. You might begin with a reminder about the promise he made to consider a raise after your first six months (least persuasive). Then, you might move to a list of your accomplishments over the last six months (more persuasive). You might conclude with information about an offer you received last week from a rival firm, which you would prefer not to accept. However, they have offered you a substantial increase in annual salary (most persuasive). As you can see, such a pattern would be more effective than simply beginning with your alternative job offer. By saving your biggest artillery for the final argument, you may be able to successfully negotiate a salary increase.

In certain circumstances, you may want to begin with your most important argument and then proceed with less persuasive arguments. This approach to organizing a message is termed the **anti-climactic pattern.** Generally, you should use an anti-climactic pattern when the audience is already favorably predisposed to your position. When an audience is either neutral or potentially hostile to your position, a climactic structure is usually more desirable and persuasive.

Motivated Sequence Pattern

The **motivated sequence pattern,** developed by Alan Monroe in the 1930s, is a fourth persuasive pattern you can use. Appropriate for problems that can be easily established, this method follows a predictable pattern of thinking that we all use: attention, need, satisfaction, visualization, and action. According to Monroe (1935; see also Gronbeck, Ehninger, & Monroe, 1988) a speaker must first gain the audience's attention in order to be persuasive, hence, the need for a definitive **attention** step. For example, assume that you want to persuade top management in your company to donate $500,000 to an organization that works with the homeless in your city. You might begin by "drawing a picture" in the minds of management of what life is like for a homeless child in your community. With vivid detail, you then might contrast that child's life with that of top management's children. The more visually oriented the description, the better. Remember, your sole purpose in this step is to maximize the audience's interest.

Once you have gained the audience's attention, you must establish some form of **need,** the second step of Monroe's motivated sequence pattern. Continuing your presentation on the plight of homeless children, you might present statistics on the number of homeless children in the streets of America, then in your state, and, finally, in the city in which you live. Again, the more attention you pay to detail, the more effective your presentation will be. Remember, you are attempting to reach your audience where they live.

Once you have established need in the mind of your listeners, you must provide them with a way to address that need. Here, the **satisfaction** step serves as your vehicle. In this step, you propose a way that the company can help solve the problem: by contributing $500,000 to help build a homeless shelter. You might talk about how far the charity has come thus far with the project, and how much money is still needed ($750,000). Again, by using colorful, vivid information that targets your company's top management, you will increase the chances for effective persuasion.

According to Monroe, however, you must not stop here. To bring about change, you must go two steps further. Monroe's **visualization** step is designed to help you intensify the audience's desire to implement your solution. For example, you might have top management imagine the smile on a homeless child's face, knowing that he or she would have a new home. You might also ask them to visualize how great they will feel, knowing that they have made a difference in the life of even a single homeless child.

Finally, you must ask the audience to take some form of specific **action.** In this step, you must be specific and tell the audience exactly what they must do. For instance, if you want the company to donate $500,000, ask them. If you want them also to volunteer their time, ask them. According to Monroe, you have a greater chance of achieving your net effects goal by asking for a specific action.

Developing Your Outline

Once you have mindmapped your ideas and decided which logical structure is best, you are ready to develop a rough draft of an outline for your presentation. Return for a moment to the goals and mindmap that you completed on "How to Make a Lasting Impression During a Power Lunch."

Based on your mindmap, first determine which of the seven organizational structures would serve your presentation best, given the pattern of information that emerges from the content of your mindmap. For example, you may have mindmapped the *chronology* of a perfect power lunch, or you may have brainstormed all of the *places* where you would host a power lunch.

Second, with your favored logical structure in mind, transfer your three to five major topics onto another page, this time in rough outline form (i.e., points #1, #2, #3 and so on). The criterion you should use to determine the three to five major topics you choose lies in the following question: Does this topic support my net effects, substance, and image goals? To aid you, Figures 11.3 (a and b) present an outline we first mindmapped, then developed and researched (Pachter & Brody, 1995; Gray, 1993) regarding effective power lunches.

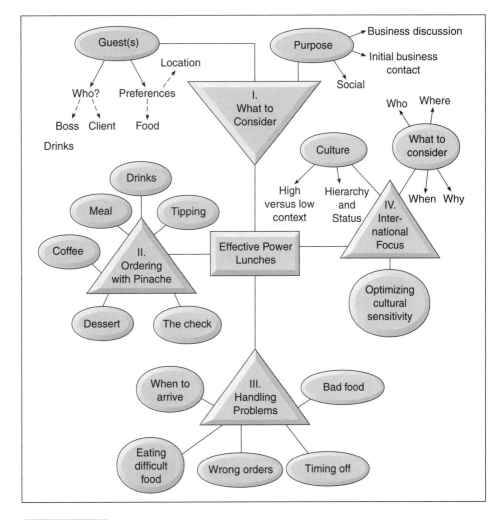

Figure 11.3a   Mindmap on the Subject of Effective Power Lunches

I.   What to Consider
   A. Guest(s)
      1. Who?
         a. Boss
         b. Client
      2. Preferences
         a. Type of Food
         b. Best location
   B. Purpose of lunch
      1. Social
      2. Initial business contact
      3. Business discussion
II. Ordering with Panache
   A. Drinks
   B. Meal
   C. Dessert
   D. Coffee

       E. Getting the check
       F. Tips on tipping
III. Handling Special Problems
   A. When to arrive
   B. Eating difficult food
   C. Wrong orders
   D. Timing of the meal is off
   E. Bad food
IV. International Focus (Cross-cultural issues)
   A. Culture of guest (or host)
      1. High versus low context cultures
      2. The role of hierarchy and status
   B. Optimizing cultural sensitivity
   C. What to consider
      1. Who will be dining
      2. Where lunch will take place
      3. Meal time—when will meal
         be served
      4. Why meal is taking place (purpose)

Figure 11.3b   **Outline That Emerged from Mindmap on the Subject of Effective Power Lunches**

As we said earlier, transfer major topics first, and leave room for your subtopics, or those ideas that are connected with lines to the major topics in your mindmap. Once you have transferred all of the major topic areas, move the subtopics into your outline. Now you have a rough outline for your presentation.

You will edit your rough outline many times as your presentation evolves. No matter how many revisions you make, think of the progress you will achieve if you (1) mindmap your presentation, (2) select an initial logical structure for your message, (3) make sure the topics that you include support your net effects, substance, and image goals, and (4) develop a rough-draft outline of your presentation. If you conduct this exercise *before you begin the formal research process,* your presentation will be well on the road to success.

Supporting Your Ideas: Generating Appeals and Gathering Evidence

Once you have developed a rough-draft outline, you are ready to develop your major points and provide evidence, or supporting documentation. Let's begin by looking at the three major points or appeals you can develop, based on the research that you conduct.

Types of Appeals

To begin, appeals are primarily used to support persuasive presentations, although they can be used to strengthen informative messages. Using the Aristotelian approach, speech experts agree on the three major influences of persuasion: appeals to logic (logos), appeals to emotion (pathos) and appeals based on your credibility as a speaker (ethos).

Logical appeals (logos) are arguments that are created to appeal to your audience's sense of reason. They are designed to engage your audience's mind and walk them through the reasoning underlying your presentation. To illustrate, consider the age-old dilemma of attempting to convince your significant other that the two of you ought to buy a car. In doing so, you might argue that the car you are considering—never mind that it's a Porsche Boxster—gets better gas mileage than your present car (5 mpg more!), has a safety record that is twice as good, and will provide you with a more dependable way to get back and forth to work, especially since your car has broken down four times this year. For many people, such logical appeals are all that you need to be persuasive.

Emotional appeals (pathos) are a second type of argument that you can make and are designed to touch the emotions of your audience. For example, if your significant other is unmoved by the three logical arguments you have made so far about the car, you might argue that (1) you have wanted a red Porsche since you were eighteen years old, (2) you have been saving your money for a fun car for more than five years, and (3) the two of you had so much fun on your honeymoon when you rented that fancy, red convertible and drove up the coast.

If these two types of appeals fail to accomplish your goal, you have one recourse left: an **appeal to** (your) **credibility** (ethos). In other words, you can argue that your significant other should be persuaded based on your knowledge, experience, trustworthiness, and so forth. Appeals of this nature must be carefully presented; otherwise you can come across as arrogant and lose your audience entirely. Continuing with our car purchase example, let's say that you thoroughly researched the Porsche Boxster. You have studied *Consumer Reports* and several leading automobile magazines, and have already obtained a rock-bottom quotation from the dealer before you usher your significant other to see the car. As you take a test drive, you might share all of the facts that you have gathered, subtly emphasizing all of the research you have completed. The more knowledgeable and believable you are in this instance, and the more information you easily share, the greater the chance that you will be persuasive. Such "arguments" would represent an appeal to your credibility as a persuasive speaker.

Appeals based on logic, emotion, and credibility serve as the foundation of every winning presentation, whether to one or a million people. The more persuasive and well-thought-out the appeals, the higher the probability that you will succeed in achieving your goal. To make your arguments really persuasive, however, you will need to provide evidence to document them. Let's take a look at several different forms your evidence can take.

Forms of Evidence

Think for a moment about the most memorable presentations you have heard. They were probably filled with colorful stories and examples, reinforced by compelling statistics, or supported by the testimony of experts you know and admire. Additionally, the most persuasive presentations are those in which difficult concepts are defined and explained, and striking comparisons or contrasts are offered. Informative presentations also use forms of evidence to support the main points as well as the net effects, substance, and image goals. All of us are capable of developing presentations that have impact. The secret is understanding the forms of evidence that really work, and conducting the necessary research to generate your evidence.

Stories.   Perhaps, one of the most awesome presentations we have heard concerned the topic of AIDS awareness. The speech was given by a young woman whose life was drastically altered when her husband of eleven months first told her he was gay; her world was shattered less than three years later when he contacted her and told her he was HIV-positive.*

Her speech began with a particularly vivid and colorful story, told in third person, about a young man and woman who were best friends and who fell in love. With gentle humor and a smile she walked the audience through the first eleven months of the marriage and, then, she related the shock on New Year's morning when the husband told his wife that he was gay. From there, she talked about the mourning period through which the young woman went, and how she pulled her life back together after the husband left. Her story climaxed with an account of the phone call the woman received three years later, when the man called to tell her he was HIV-positive, and that she must be tested.

At that point, the talented speaker made a most surprising move. Switching from third to first person, she then said, "When I picked up the phone that morning and heard what Jim had to say, I thought I was going to die. Once again, the man I once loved was radically shattering my life. . . .And, you know, if it happened to me, a good Mormon girl, it can happen to you.. That's why I'm here today . . . to drive home the point . . . it CAN happen to you!"

At that very moment during the introduction of her speech, you could have heard a pin drop in the audience. Noticeably shaken, people stared first at the speaker, then at one another. The story had served its purpose and reinforced the thesis of her presentation: If AIDS could touch her life, it could touch the audience's life, too.

Stories like the one this speaker told serve as excellent supporting evidence for a presentation. **Stories** are narratives, either true or fictitious, in prose or verse (Random House, 1991). Additionally, they may be told in the first or third person. First-person stories are those that draw on your own experiences about a subject, and can increase your credibility and persuasiveness as a speaker if used both creatively and judiciously. Equally powerful are third-person stories that relate a series of events in another per-

---

*This speech was presented by a student in a public speaking class. She prefers to remain anonymous. Names and a few facts concerning the story have been changed to protect her identity. The story is printed with the student's permission.

son's life. Generally, when you tell someone else's story, you speak from the point of view of a witness and use the story to illustrate a point you are trying to make.

Examples.   **Examples** are specific illustrations of some category of items, including people, places, objects, actions, experiences, or conditions (Grice & Skinner, 1993). Examples of famous leading men in contemporary film include Tom Cruise, Michael Douglas, Sylvester Stallone, and Arnold Schwartzenegger. Water polo, jet skiing, surfing, and sailing are examples of popular water sports.

Examples used in speeches may be brief or extended, depending on the extent to which you feel you must elaborate. Brief examples are short, specific instances like those in the previous paragraph. Extended examples are longer and allow you to create a more detailed picture of the category of items you are addressing.

Statistics.   Startling or compelling statistics are a third major source of support for your arguments. **Statistics** are collections of data that are used to make a point, clarify ideas, and make your presentation come to life. For example, in a speech to her local chapter of Women in Management, Sally used the following statistics from an article she had read in *Working Woman* to demonstrate progress by women in reducing the disparity between men's and women's salaries:

Sally: "Over the 15-year period that ended in 1993, pay for female executives and managers climbed approximately 18 percent, compared with a skimpy 2 percent gain for their male colleagues. Additionally, professional women gained over 15 percent versus a 3 percent climb for men in the same positions. These advances are even more impressive when you consider how poorly the rest of the workforce fared. Among blue-collar workers, for example, hourly wages dropped more than 14 percent for men and 6 percent for women. Wages for men and women in service jobs fell 11 percent and 4 percent, respectively" (adapted from Harris, 1995, p. 26).

Because your audience can process only so much information in the form of numbers, apply the following suggestions developed by public speaking experts Grice and Skinner (1993).

1. Use statistics judiciously and in combination with other forms of support. Bombarding your audience with statistics is less effective than using a few key statistics in combination with examples and explanations.
2. Round off statistics. A statistic of 51.6 percent has less impact and is more difficult to remember than "more than half." Likewise, your audience will better remember "two and a half million dollars" than a statistic like $2,496,532.68.
3. Use units of measure that are familiar to your audience. For example, if you are a trainer from the United States and giving a workshop in Canada on the valuation of property for appraisal purposes, you will have more impact if you calculate problems using the metric system of measurement (e.g., meters and kilometers) rather than the English system (e.g., feet and yards) still prevalent in the United States. Such examples will be more familiar, vivid, and appreciated by your audience.
4. Use visual aids to represent or clarify relationships among statistics. For example, you are a marathoner who is giving a speech to a group of gifted runners on a high school

track team, and you want to persuade them that anything is possible with effort and perseverance. To make the point, you decide to present results from the most recent Boston Marathon for both women and men. How can you make your point with maximum impact? One way to achieve your goal is to present the facts both orally and visually, with a slide, transparency, or flip chart (Grice & Skinner, pp. 159–60).

Expert Testimony.   A fourth way you can present supporting evidence for your arguments is through the use of **expert testimony,** generally in the form of a quotation or paraphrase from a credible source. Say that you are giving a presentation at a stockholders' meeting and are discussing your company's renewed commitment to managing human resources. You might begin your speech by incorporating the following quotation from best-selling authors, John Naisbitt and Patricia Aburdene, in their quintessential book, *Re-inventing the Corporation:*

> Business experts John Naisbitt and Patricia Aburdene once said, "In the new information society, human capital has replaced dollar capital as the strategic resource. People and profits are inexorably linked" (Naisbitt & Aburdene, 1985, p. 4). At Saunders and Sons, this simple statement has become the company's standard. Now let me tell you what we are doing about it. . . .

In this instance, you have borrowed not only the words but the credibility of the famous authors to support your position.

Expert testimony need not come from an outside source. Chances are good that, if you are asked to speak on some subject, you are considered to have credibility in your own right. As a speaker, you can recount your own experiences and have a positive impact if you can establish your credentials and experience prior to, or during the introduction of, a presentation. However, should you elect to use your own testimony as evidence, you must handle the situation with care.

How do you know whether or not to include specific testimony in a presentation? Again, Grice and Skinner (1993) offer some excellent advice in Box 11.3.

Definition and Explanation.   How many times have you sat through a highly technical presentation, only to find yourself lost at a critical juncture? How many times have you listened to a speech and heard terms with which you were unfamiliar? In those instances, you probably found yourself feeling overwhelmed and tuned out the speaker. On the other hand, chances are good that these situations could have been avoided if the speaker had offered definitions of complex words or phrases, or provided explanations to clarify difficult concepts. A **definition** is a formal statement regarding the meaning or significance of a word, phrase, and the like. Similarly, an **explanation** is the process of making concepts, ideas, causes, or reasons clear or intelligible (Random House, 1991). Definitions and explanations indirectly serve as evidence when difficult concepts or ideas are being presented.

Comparison and Contrast.   Comparison and contrast can serve you as a sixth form of evidence. **Comparison** is the process of depicting the likenesses between two items, whether they are persons, places, objects, or concepts. **Contrast** serves to illustrate the differences between two items. In either instance, the purpose is to inform or persuade your audience about the less familiar item. Thus, your audience must be familiar with

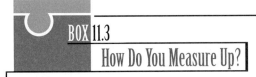

BOX 11.3

How Do You Measure Up?   *The Quality of a Source*

Directions: Ask yourself these five questions in order to determine the quality of a source:

1. Is the source competent or qualified to speak on the subject?

2. Is the source objective and unbiased? If he or she has a vested interest in sustaining a specific position, you may want to reconsider using them in the speech.

3. Does the source have special qualifications, such as an exceptional position, educational background, or experience in the area?

4. Is the source in the "mainstream" of thought, sharing the view of several experts?

5. Is the source either recent or timeless in what is being said? (The emphasis here is on timeliness of the information for the audience you are addressing, not necessarily on the age of the material!)

Source: Adapted from G. L. Grice and J. F. Skinner (1993). *Mastering Public Speaking* (Englewood Cliffs, NJ: Prentice-Hall), pp. 161–62. Printed with permission of the Publisher.

the item to which you are making the comparison or contrast in order to be effective. To illustrate, consider how well a *comparison* might work if you were attempting to persuade management to purchase a new computer system, especially if you had used that same system effectively in a job you held previously with a rival company. Moreover, *contrasting* the speed, efficiency, and user-friendliness of the proposed system with your current system might also serve as a compelling form of evidence.

Keep in mind that comparisons and contrasts may be literal or figurative in nature. While a **literal comparison** or contrast associates items that share actual similarities or differences, a **figurative comparison** or contrast depicts similarities or differences that may not exist in actuality. Generally, the latter contains an element of surprise and dares the audience to think in new ways about the person, place, object, or concept being described. Best-selling author Stephen King is a master of literal and figurative comparison, and generously sprinkles his novels with both to persuade us of the evil (or goodness) of his characters. Note how many subtle comparisons King uses to describe the Trashcan Man's world in the following brief excerpt from his novel, *The Stand:*

> Sometimes he [Trashcan Man] knew those voices weren't real, but sometimes he would cry out loud for them to stop only to realize that the only voice was his voice, hitting back at him from the houses and storefronts, bouncing off the cinderblock wall of the Scrubba-Dubba Car Wash where he used to work and where he now sat on the morning of June 30, eating a big sloppy sandwich of peanut butter and jelly and tomatoes and Gulden's Diablo mustard. No voice but his voice, hitting the houses and stores and being turned away like an unwanted guest and thus returning to his own ears (1978, p. 286).

Like King, you too can use comparisons and contrasts in novel ways to make your point in business presentations. All it takes is a little imagination and a commitment to making your presentations more colorful and compelling.

Introductions, Conclusions, and Transitions

Once you have polished your outline by filling in the appeals and evidence for each main point, you are ready to (1) develop the introduction and conclusion of your presentation and (2) develop your transitions from introduction to body, body to conclusion, and (within the body of your presentation) point to point.

Introductions That Grab an Audience's Attention

Whether you are giving an informative or persuasive presentation, your opening statement must grab the audience's attention. One of the funniest attention-getting devices that we have ever witnessed was delivered at a luncheon presentation by James C. Roddey, a Pittsburgh businessman and civic leader. After approaching the lectern and receiving a warm round of applause from the audience, Roddey began by saying, "Excuse me for a minute," and pulled out a small tape recorder from the inside pocket of his suit. After fumbling around with the recorder for a moment, he located the on-button and said in his most eloquent voice: "Mr. Speaker, distinguished senators, honored representatives, and welcomed guests." He then turned off the tape recorder and said, "That's for my mom. She's really impressed with this sort of thing." Then, as if he remembered at the last minute, he said, "Oh . . . and (after turning the tape recorder back on) Mr. Gore and Mrs. Hillary Clinton. . . . I'm delighted to see you here today." This simple, humorous, attention-getting device achieved exactly what Mr. Roddey hoped: first, head-scratching ("What in heaven's name was he doing?"); second, slow head-turning on the part of the audience to see if, perchance, Mr. Gore or Mrs. Clinton had entered the room; and third, laughter, the ultimate desired affect (J. C. Roddey, public speech, June 1994).

> A speech should be as long as a piece of string—long enough to wrap up the package.
>
> *—Anonymous*

Attention-getting devices such as this serve the first purpose of an introduction: to grab the audience's attention in some way. However, humor is only one way to achieve this desired effect. Other methods include the use of startling statistics, famous or powerful quotations, colorful stories or anecdotes that hit home with the audience, rhetorical or direct questions that cause your audience to think, or an acknowledgment or compliment for your audience.

Once you have commanded the attention of your audience, you are ready to state the purpose or topic of your speech, the second major goal of an introduction. Generally, your **purpose statement** takes the form of a simple declarative sentence that defines or delineates the main thrust of your presentation. An example might be, "Today, I plan to inform you of three ways that you can make a difference in the life of a homeless child, a child who lives right here in (your city) and who is struggling for survival."

Remember, in developing an effective purpose statement, you also must find a way to reveal to your audience that the topic is relevant or important to them. For instance, in the purpose statement we developed in the previous paragraph, we attempted to bring the subject home by focusing on homelessness in the audience's own city, rather than on homelessness in general. Add to the mix one or more well-timed slides of children that you took at a neighborhood shelter, and the impact will even be greater.

The third element of a well-rounded introduction is a preview of the main points you will be making. A **preview** is an advance delineation of the three to five main points in your presentation. Previews are usually provided in the introduction of a speech, unless (1) the audience is hostile toward either you or the topic before you begin, or (2) you want to maximize suspense in your presentation. In these instances, you wisely may elect to omit the preview; however, on most occasions, a preview is advisable.

Previews serve a number of purposes. First and foremost, they act as a road map for your audience. If your listeners know where you are taking them and the points of interest at which you plan to stop along the way, they will be better able to process the information you present throughout the speech. Second, previewing your main points helps your audience to remember them better. Indeed, research has shown that we remember things more accurately if we have heard them three to seven times. Using the repetition afforded by a preview serves an identical purpose. To recap: (1) tell the audience what you are going to tell them (in the preview), (2) tell them (via the main points), and (3) tell them what you told them (in the summary). You can increase the number of repetitions by adding a visual component, such as pictures, words, or graphics that reinforce your main points throughout the presentation.

To illustrate an effective preview, return for a moment to our thesis statement on the subject of homelessness: "Today, I plan to inform you of three ways that you can make a difference in the life of a homeless child . . . a child who lives right here in (your city) and who is struggling for survival." Although you might be tempted to list your "three ways" at the outset of the speech, you will have to say something compelling before you get the audience to draw the same conclusions. For instance, what three points (i.e., substance goals) could you develop if your net effect goals were to persuade your audience to: (1) volunteer just one hour per month to a reading program for kids at a local homeless shelter, (2) donate $10 per month to the shelter to help pay for food and clothing, and (3) sign a petition requesting the city to allocate additional funds to support the shelter? Three substance goals we might suggest are to *cite statistics* about growing homelessness among children in your hometown, *tell a compelling story* about an actual homeless child in the community, and *share information* about an innovative new program now being developed.

To convert your substance goals to a preview, you might say:

> Today, I plan to inform you of three ways that you can make a difference in the life of a homeless child . . . a child who lives right here in [your city's name] and who is struggling for survival. Before we get there, however, you need to know more about our city's homeless children. First, we'll talk for a moment about the growing number of children on our streets and the limited chances that they will ever be anything but homeless, unless we do something about it. Second, you'll hear about Angela, one of our own street children. Angela's just ten, but has been homeless since she was abandoned at age six. Finally, you'll hear about Hope House and some of the innovative programs the staff have started to shelter and protect our kids. I think you will find their message to be quite powerful!

As you can see, a preview such as this one has much to offer both a speaker and an audience. And you have saved your punch line until the last: what you want your audience to DO about the situation.

Conclusions That Make a Difference

The **conclusion** of your presentation should be designed to reiterate your main points, tie up any loose ends, and provide the audience with a sense of closure regarding your message. If one of your net effects goals is persuasion, your conclusion should also include your challenge to the audience, or your call to action. No matter how you elect to conclude a presentation, the key is to avoid presenting new information. Conclusions are designed to do just that: bring your presentation to a close.

So how might an ideal conclusion be structured? The best place to begin is with a summary of your main points, which will help the audience to better remember your message. Additionally, including a summary will let your audience know you are approaching your final remarks and that they will need to listen attentively for your call to action, especially if you are giving a persuasive presentation.

Once you have summarized your main points, find a way to provide your audience with some form of closure. Ways that you can do so include using a particularly salient quotation from someone whom the audience knows and admires, a humorous anecdote or story that brings your purpose statement home, a direct or rhetorical question designed to make the audience think, or a call to action if your presentation is designed to persuade. To illustrate, consider the following conclusion, which we might use in the speech regarding the plight of homeless children:

> To this point, you have heard about the growing number of children on the streets in our own hometown and the chances that they will remain homeless, unless we do something about it. Second, you've met Angela, one of our own precious children—a ten-year-old who has been homeless and destitute since she was six. Finally, you've learned about Hope House and some of their innovative programs to shelter and protect our kids. The question is what can we do to make a difference in the lives of children like Angela? What can we do to make a difference in the lives of our city's street children? One way you can help is to volunteer just one hour per month to a reading program for kids at Hope House. They are looking for people who care and who have a few minutes to share. If your schedule is packed, why not donate $10 or more per month to Hope House to help pay for food and clothing? One hundred percent of your donation will go to feeding and clothing kids like Angela. Finally, let me urge each of you to sign the petition at the back of the room on your way out. We plan to ask the city to allocate additional funds to support Hope House, and we need your support. As you can see, one small effort on our parts can make an incredible difference in the lives of our kids. Let's start now! Be a part of the solution. Just reach out and care!

The secret to an award-winning conclusion is to make the audience want to know more about your subject, or to follow through on the challenge or call to action you have offered them.

Transitions: Smoothing Out the Rough Edges

In putting together a winning presentation, you must consider another element of effective public speaking: how to smooth out the rough edges of your speech through the

A poor speaker quits talking when he is tired. A good speaker quits before the audience is tired.

—*Anonymous*

use of effective transitions. **Transitions** are words, phrases, or sentences that allow one idea to flow smoothly to the next. They must be strategically positioned between the introduction and body of your speech as well as between the body and the conclusion. Additionally, transitions should be used to bridge ideas and main points within the body of your presentation.

In developing an effective transition, complexity of the leap between points or ideas should be your guide. In some instances, a few words or a simple sentence will suffice. For example, signaling the three main points of your presentation with, "First . . . , Second . . . , Third . . . ," will help your audience to move easily from point to point. "Let's begin," "Another important idea," and "In conclusion," are other transitional phrases that serve as effective road signs for your audience.

If two ideas that you are presenting are not obviously linked or related to one another, you may need to develop two or more complex sentences that help make the connection clear. Remember, the goal of any transitional device is to help keep your audience on track throughout the presentation. By giving them signposts along the way, your presentation will be perceived as more organized and coherent. Additionally, your audience will be able to process your message and commit your main points to memory.

Ethicality of Your Message: The Litmus Test for Determining If You're Ready to Go

As we move into the 21st century, more and more companies are becoming concerned about the issue of ethicality in the workplace. In molding and developing your public

In molding and shaping your professional life, ethics should play a vital role.

BOX 11.4

ToolBox

Determining the Ethicality of a Message

Directions: We encourage you to apply the following ten questions on ethicality suggested by Nash (1990) as a final litmus test for every message you create.

1. In determining your position regarding a topic, have you adequately examined all related facts? weighted them accordingly? separated facts from present loyalties?

2. Have you carefully looked at the issues and facts to determine how an "opponent" might view them? taken your "opponent's" point of view into account as you have constructed your message?

3. Have you closely examined the history and context of all facts to ensure that none has been taken out of context?

4. To whom do you give your loyalties? self? family? race? sex? boss? company? society? Have these loyalties impacted your message in any way? If yes, how?

5. What is your intention in presenting the message? What are the probable consequences of

making this presentation? Could limitations of knowledge on your part lead to harm rather than good?

6. Whom could your message injure or adversely affect? Could you conduct a discussion with the potentially affected parties prior to the presentation?

7. Are you sure your position will be valid in the long term as well as the short term?

8. Could you present this message to your boss, spouse, children, society, or creator without any qualms?

9. What is the potential of your message if it is understood? misunderstood?

10. Under what conditions would you allow exceptions to your point of view?

Adapted from L. L. Nash (1990). "Ethics without the sermon." In W. M. Hoffman and J. M. Moore, *Business Ethics: Readings and Cases in Corporate Morality,* 2nd ed. (New York: McGraw-Hill).

life, professional image, and personal sense of self, ethicality in the messages you create should be utmost in importance.

Perhaps the best advice your authors have ever found on the subject is taken from Laura Nash in her 1990 treatise, "Ethics without the Sermon." Box 11.4 provides ten questions to help speakers determine the ethicality of their messages.

As you can see, these questions are thought provoking and can only serve to make your speech or presentation even more effective! By being sensitive to ethical issues associated with messages you create, you can increase the integrity associated with your presentations, enhance your credibility, and build a public life about which you can be proud. Indeed, ethicality is and should be the litmus test for every message we create.

Practice Makes Perfect

Once you have brainstormed, organized, documented, and reflected on the ethicality of your message, you are ready to practice your presentation. No amount of emphasis that we could place on rehearsing your presentation would ever be enough. Menzel and Carrell (1994) agree: The quality of speech performance correlates *positively* with time spent preparing visual aids, research outside the library (e.g., interviews, phone calls, surveys, etc.), preparation of speaking notes, time spent rehearsing silently, and time rehearsing out loud. Moreover, quality of performance correlates *significantly* with total preparation time and number of rehearsals.

How much practice is enough? The answer to this question depends on all of the variables previously listed, as well as the amount of anxiety you experience when you deliver an oral presentation. If you rehearse at least three times start-to-finish with your visuals, you should be well prepared. The reason you want to practice with AV materials is that they perform amazing tricks in front of audiences if you have never practiced with them. Pages of your flip chart will maliciously stick together; one of your slides will mysteriously turn upside down; and, your videotape will cue itself up somewhere in the middle. (You will find a more complete discussion about visuals in Appendix I.)

All of these unspeakable acts, in turn, will thwart your image goals, negatively affect your PERC-Quotient, and adversely affect the outcome of your message. It is to a discussion of your image goals, PERC-Quotient, and delivery of a message that we now turn.

Setting and Achieving Your Image Goals: Optimizing Your PERC-Quotient

How do you want to be perceived when you deliver a presentation? Accomplished and knowledgeable? Friendly and open? Powerful and inaccessible? The answers to these questions should depend on the audience, occasion, and purpose of your presentation. During an informative after-dinner presentation, you may want the audience to think you are affable, accessible, and funny. During a business meeting you may want to be perceived as powerful, credible, and in control. No matter what kind of message you create, setting and achieving specific image goals are the name of the game when it comes to effective delivery.

According to Kittie Watson and Larry Barker (1991), **image goals** are a speaker's personal, desired aims with regard to a specific audience, particularly those aims associated with:

- Power-Building,
- Emotion-Controlling (both the speaker's and those of the audience!),
- Relationship-Development with the speaker's listeners, and
- Credibility-Maintenance,

or better known as your PERC-Quotient.* Like net effects and substance goals, image goals should be determined in advance of a presentation. To achieve image goals, a speaker plans and works toward executing specific verbal and nonverbal behaviors.

For example, to increase perceived power with an audience, Watson and Barker (1991) recommend that you stand up straight, maintain good posture, and project

---

* Watson, K. W., and Barker, L. L. (1991). *Four keys to effective presentations* (Available from Spectra Communication Associates, 701 Jefferson Avenue, Metairie, LA 70001).

Power and credibility are two key elements in establishing your PERC-Quotient.

your voice with confidence. They also recommend looking your audience directly in the eye, using a slightly faster speaking rate than normal, using pauses for effect, and dressing for power.

To control your own emotions, the researchers recommend making a point NOT to be defensive—maintaining objectivity at all times, responding thoughtfully to criticism, attacking with moderation, and never taking yourself too seriously. To "control" your audience's emotions, make sure to avoid emotional triggers (i.e., words that you know will cause negativity in your audience), to use vivid and colorful examples or illustrations with people in them, and never to back your audience into a corner.

Watson and Barker (1991) recommend a number of behaviors to help develop a relationship with your audience. Smile and use pleasant facial expressions, use audience members' names (without favoring any one or two people), and avoid standing behind a lectern or table. In addition, try relating examples specifically to your audience's knowledge and interests, maintaining constant eye contact, and never turning your back on the audience if possible. Establishing a positive relationship also involves keeping your body language open (especially your arms and hands) and using personal examples.

Finally, how can you establish and maintain credibility with an audience? Watson and Barker (1991) suggest, again, maintaining constant eye contact, as well as using appropriate language for the audience and controlling your emotions and temper. They also advise that you refer to past accomplishments without appearing to brag, and refer to experts whom the audience admires. Finally, "stay in character" before, during, and after the presentation. Dress a bit more formally than your audience and make your movements deliberate and purposeful.

As we stated at the beginning of this chapter, the level at which you achieve skill in public presentations can have a tremendous impact on your professional career. Clearly, delivery skills are a cornerstone of effective business communication.

Case Study

Public Speaking Challenges for Persons with Disabilities

Henry J. Hanson, SR/WA, Hanson & Associates

After serving nearly thirty (30) years as a public employee in the fields of civil engineering, urban planning, and real estate or property management, I opted to assume the challenge of starting my own right-of-way and real estate training and consulting company. However, I was subject to at least one other rather distinctive circumstance. I am physically disabled as a result of contracting polio during my youth. Those of us who grew up with physical disabilities prior to the adoption of ADA, or the American Disability Act, have had to learn how to cope with and adapt to living in a society that made little or no provisions for the disabled. Thus, I learned how to communicate and negotiate for positions of employment suitable to my skills and training in a field that used to be generally limited to able-bodied males.

I possess a strong determination and desire not only to succeed but to excel in performing the duties of any task I undertake. This trait enables me to overcome the stigma of being labeled as "having a disability" and, therefore, as being unable to perform the required duties of certain positions. During my years in college and my employment with the government, I had to use a style of communication and negotiations that enabled me to pursue my chosen occupation. The occupations of civil engineering and surveying required the ability to gain access to, and be able to navigate to, remote undeveloped locations. As an urban planner, I was required to prepare and make presentations to both small and large audiences at public hearings and meetings at locations that were often inaccessible to anyone with a physical disability. As a right-of-way agent, I was required to meet and negotiate with property owners at their homes and at locations that were inaccessible to those with physical disabilities in order to acquire property rights needed for my employing agency.

As owner of my right-of-way and real estate training and consulting company, I have had to learn to adapt to a multitude of other professional negotiations and communications situations. For example, public speaking and consulting require different communication skills. As a professional public speaker, I am required to make arrangements for travel and accommodations throughout both the United States and Canada. Travel accommodations require communicating and negotiating for specialized transportation needs, such as renting vehicles equipped with hand controls. This always requires a lead time for the rental agency to arrange to have the vehicle ready upon arrival. What do you do when you arrive at your destination and discover that the vehicle you reserved is not ready or they have reserved it for the wrong date and canceled your reservation? Arranging air travel is similarly fraught with multiple renegotiations for seating and wheelchair handling. You learn, early on, that arriving at your destination only to find that your wheelchair has been left at the departing airport jetway gate is not simply a matter of inconvenience.

Arranging for facilities to make your presentations requires communicating and negotiating for a wheelchair-accessible room, special audiovisual equipment, special room layouts, and special hotel accommodations. What do you do when you check into a hotel, go to your room, and discover that their idea of "wheelchair accessible" means that you can get your wheelchair in the room and that maybe you have a remote TV control? You arrive at the facility where you are to make your presentation and discover that there are three or four steps to be negotiated. What do you do? You finally gain access to the room arranged for your presentation and discover that the speaker's platform or stage is up three steps or at the opposite end of the room, and the access isle is not wide enough for your wheelchair. What do you do? Arriving at facilities and rooms that are accessible does not eliminate your communication and negotiation needs. I am sure you are familiar with the speaker who controls his or her fears of public speaking by figuratively hiding behind a lectern. From a wheelchair, this would not be a figurative situation; you would literally be hiding behind that lectern. Blackboards and the newer whiteboards are usually set 80 to 90 centimeters (32 to 36 inches) from the floor. Similarly, flip chart stands are positioned for lecturers who stand during their presentations. Overhead projectors are placed on high stands. What do you do?

As a professional right-of-way and real estate consultant I am required to meet with clients and negotiate contracts for my services. Regardless of the advancements we have seen in awareness and accessibility provisions as mandated by ADA, we still live in a society attuned to giving preferential treatment to those individuals considered to be what is commonly known as "able-bodies." I still have to convince potential clients and employers that, regardless of my physical disability, I have the skill and ability to accomplish the necessary tasks and duties needed to successfully provide them with the highest level of professional service.

My decision to establish a firm to provide both training and consulting services was based on an understanding that there is a significant difference in the standards of perceived physical ability required for public speaking from those for providing consulting services. I use my skill and ability in preparing and presenting my training materials as a means of showcasing my experiences in actually performing right-of-way and real estate negotiations. The same communication skills needed to negotiate speaking facilities can be used to negotiate for meetings with potential clients. The skills needed to prepare and present training materials are the same skills needed to prepare and make presentations to a potential client. The skills needed to establish power, credibility, authority, and/or control to make the wheelchair disappear for an audience are the same skills needed in meeting and negotiating with potential clients.

Questions

1. You are the chairperson of a local arrangements committee, and you are working with a speaker who uses a wheelchair. What questions should you ask the speaker in advance regarding special arrangements that need to be made in order to ensure

a successful presentation? How can you make sure that the speaker encounters no surprises between the time of arrival in your city and his or her presentation?

2. What verbal and nonverbal messages can a public speaker who uses a wheelchair employ to establish power? control the emotions of the audience? establish a relationship with the audience? maximize credibility?

3. How might a speaker with a physical disability overcome the potential psychological barriers that exist between him or her and an audience? If you were a communication consultant working for a person with a disability, what suggestions would you make to him or her as a public speaker to "help make the wheelchair disappear"?

Summary

In describing the creation and delivery of your message, this chapter begins with brainstorming and ends with practicing your presentation. Open- and closed-ended mindmapping are two vehicles you can use to effectively brainstorm your message. Either way, mindmapping involves diagramming our thoughts in a visual, spatial manner, and then connecting the major and minor points that emerge.

Once you have brainstormed your message, you are ready to structure your points in a logical sequence. Chronological, spatial, and topical patterns are three logical sequences you can use with informative presentations. Cause-effect, problem-solution, climactic, and motivated sequence patterns are generally reserved for messages designed to persuade. Once you have selected the best pattern for your message, you are ready to outline your presentation. Begin with a rough draft, then research your message. Through research, the final draft of your presentation will emerge.

In developing supporting evidence for your message, you have several tools at your disposal. For example, you can use logical or emotional appeals, or you can appeal to your (or your company's) credibility. Actual forms of evidence you can use include stories or narratives; examples and illustrations; statistics; expert testimony; definitions and explanations; and comparisons and contrasts.

When developing the introduction to your presentation, there are several attention-getting devices you can use: startling statements, rhetorical questions, statistics, humor, or famous quotations. Don't forget that every good introduction has a thesis statement and a preview, unless the element of surprise is critical to the outcome of your presentation. In developing your conclusion, your goals are to summarize your main points, tie up any loose ends, and provide a sense of closure for your audience. As a result, you should avoid presenting new information in your conclusion. To bring your presentation to an effective close, try using humor, a famous quotation, or a rhetorical question. Challenges to action are the key to concluding powerful persuasive presentations.

After you have developed the three main parts of your speech, go back and work on smooth transitions. Transitions are bridges between and within the major and minor points of your message. At times, only a few words may be necessary to connect the ideas; at other times, a series of complex sentences may be required.

Next, you are ready to review your message and to apply the final litmus test: ethicality. Nash's "ten questions for determining the ethicality of a message" will serve you well in examining your motives and reasons for presenting information, and ultimately in building and maintaining a public life that is characterized by honesty and integrity.

Practice is key to successful oral communication. We recommend at least three to five complete rehearsals with visuals from start to finish. Remember, the two main keys to success are preparation and practice. Over time, you too can become an exceptional public speaker.

Knowledge Check

Key Concepts and Terms

brainstorming	attention	explanation
mindmapping	need	comparison
open-ended mindmapping	satisfaction	contrast
closed-ended mindmapping	visualization	literal comparison
chronological pattern	action	figurative comparison
reverse chronological order	logical appeals	attention-getting devices
spatial pattern	emotional appeals	purpose statement
topical pattern	appeal to credibility	preview
cause-effect pattern	stories	conclusion
problem-solution pattern	examples	transitions
climactic pattern	statistics	image goals
anti-climactic pattern	expert testimony	
motivated sequence pattern	definition	

Putting It All Together

1. Differentiate between open- and closed-ended mindmapping. Why is mindmapping a useful place to begin in organizing a presentation?

2. Develop two different speech outlines on the subject of your favorite hobbies or pastimes. The first should reflect the chronological pattern; the second should use a topical pattern. (Assume that the speech will be five minutes in length and audience members will be your classmates in a business and professional communication course.)

3. How do the cause-effect and problem-solution patterns of organization differ?

4. Assume that you work for your dream company and are attempting to persuade your boss (or partner) to upgrade your present (ancient!) computer hardware and software to the best on the market. Provide two examples each of appeals to logic, emotion, and credibility you would use to accomplish your goal.

5. You are developing a presentation and want to include some colorful stories and illustrations

as forms of evidence. To what sources could you turn for these two types of evidence?

6. Attention-getting devices are central to effective introductions. Develop the specific attention-getting device you would use if you were presenting the persuasive speech we mentioned earlier on homelessness in your home town. (Note: Don't just say what device you would use; actually develop the first few sentences of your introduction.)

7. You have been in your dream job for less than a year and have been asked to give an inspira-tional and motivational after-dinner speech at the annual awards banquet. Develop a list of specific image goals you would develop (i.e., a list of verbal and nonverbal behaviors you would use) to (1) balance power, (2) control your and the audience's emotions, (3) develop a warm relationship with the audience, and (4) maximize your credibility.

8. List and discuss at least three techniques you can use to manage your own communication apprehension. Why do you think these tech-niques can work for you?

References

Baskerville, D. M. (1994). Public speaking rule #1: Have no fear. *Black Enterprise 24*(10) 76–83.

Gray, J., Jr. (1993). *The winning image* (2nd ed.). New York: Amacom.

Grice, G. L., & Skinner, J. F. (1993). *Mastering pub-lic speaking.* Englewood Cliffs, NJ: Prentice-Hall.

Gronbeck, B. E., Ehninger, D., & Monroe, A. H. (1988). *Principles of speech communication,* 10th brief ed. Glenview, IL: Scott, Foresman.

Harris, D. (1995, January). Sixteenth annual salary survey 1995. *Working Woman,* 25–34.

King, S. (1978). *The stand.* New York: Doubleday.

Levering, R., & Moskowitz, M. (1994). *The 100 best companies to work for in America,* rev. ed. New York: Plume.

Monroe, A. H. (1935). *Principles and types of speech.* Chicago: Scott, Foresman.

Naisbitt, J., & Aburdene, P. (1985). *Re-inventing the corporation.* New York: Warner Books.

Menzel, K. E., & Carrell, L. J. (1994). The relation-ship between preparation and performance in public speaking. *Communication Education 43,* 17–26.

Nash, L. L. (1990). Ethics without the sermon. In W. M. Hoffman & J. M. Moore, *Business ethics: Readings and cases in corporate morality,* 2nd ed. New York: McGraw-Hill.

Pachter, B., & Brody, M. (1995). *Complete business etiquette handbook.* Englewood Cliffs, NJ: Prentice-Hall.

Random House Webster's college dictionary. (1991). New York: Random House.

Watson, K. W., & Barker, L. L. (1991). *Four keys to effective presentations.* Metairie, LA: Spectra, Inc.

Zenger, J. H., Musselwhite, E., Hurson, K., & Per-rin, C. (1994). *Leading teams: Mastering the new role.* Homewood, IL: Business One Irwin.

A s companies around the world approach the 21st century, communication technologies are playing a more prominent role in their everyday operations. From cellular phones, fax machines, and E-mail to electronic bulletin boards and virtual reality, such innovations pose a constant challenge for the professional who hopes to stay current in a field defined by constant change.

To increase your knowledge and understanding of the skills that you need to master "techno-life" in the 21st century, this unit takes a two-pronged approach. First, we provide you with information regarding how to employ key communication technologies. Then, we leap to the future and introduce you to new communication technologies on the horizon.

The final chapter of the book highlights some of the innovations you will encounter in the future. The focus of Chapter 12 is the mastery of key communication technologies and virtual offices of the future. Telephones, fax machines, E-mail, groupware, the Internet, and videoconferencing are a few of the many new capabilities in which you must gain some level of competence. All of these new technologies present a number of challenges to 21st century organizations and communities. We will provide strategies for coping with these new technological challenges.

Your virtual office of the future may consist of telecommuting, hoteling, or the mobile office. In the future, you may be working from your home or your car instead of the traditional office we know today. And let's not forget the human factor as we adapt to all of these new communication technologies.

Once you complete this unit, you will have gone as far as we can take you in a single book. Hopefully, you will have not only a clearer understanding of what it takes to master "techno-life," but also increased knowledge and skills regarding the use of various communication technologies, and the keen realization that with technology comes social, ethical and moral responsibility. ∎

unit 5

Managing Techno-Life in the Workplace

Successfully Managing Your Techno-Life

12

After studying this chapter,
you should be able to

- Identify four forces that are contributing to the changing role of information in the workplace.

- Understand why communication competence and life-long learning are the keys to successfully mastering techno-life.

- Identify eight communication technologies that are prevalent in U.S. business and industry.

- Distinguish among E-mail, groupware, the Internet, and intranets.

- Discuss the advantages and disadvantages of the eight communication technologies presented in this chapter.

- Explain the differences among telecommuting, hoteling, and the mobile office.

- Recognize the advantages and disadvantages of working in a home office.

- Comprehend the impact of communication technology on the 21st century workplace.

- Become more cognizant of business communication forecasts in the future.

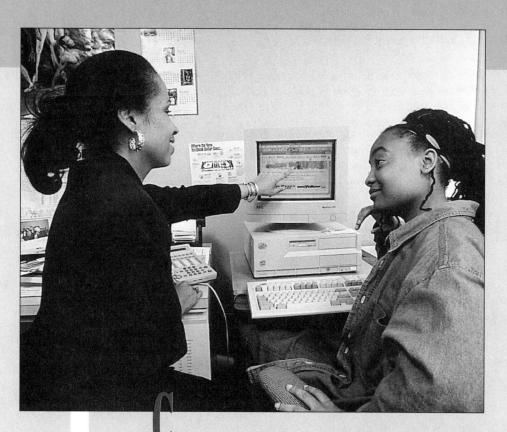

Cray Research, the current leading maker of supercomputers in the United States, has an interesting story to tell when it comes to defining the cutting edge of computer power. Prior to moving to its present location, Eagan, Minnesota, the company headquarters was based in Minneapolis. In front of its old headquarters stood a fountain that had been created by a local artist. The story goes that many of Cray's employees hated the fountain with a passion and displayed their feelings regularly by placing rubber ducks in it. The company's CEO accepted their prank in the spirit in which it was intended, and decided one day to begin a tradition called Ducky Days, a huge company picnic complete with outrageous duck awards, duck tug-of-war, duck hot dogs, and duck beer.

Later, when Cray Research moved to its offices in Eagan, the fountain (called the Octal) also was relocated. At the first company meeting after the move, the CEO came out dressed in a duck suit and introduced the fountain's architect, "who created the beloved Octal, which we couldn't bear to leave behind." The two gentlemen walked out on a deck overlooking the fountain that was being dedicated, pushed a detonator, and blew the fountain clear into the next century. Later when one of Cray's vice presidents was asked about the unusual "dedication ceremony," she responded in the following way:

> John [Rollwagen] believes that one of his roles as CEO is to create symbols because that is what people rally around. The burning of the fountain was symbolic of how we stay at the creative edge. The idea is you burn everything that went before and you keep starting over with a fresh sheet. You don't want to be pulled down by old thoughts that are no longer creative. (Levering & Moskowitz, 1994, p. 82)

Indeed, Cray's commitment to living and working on the cutting edge has bought the company two special benefits: leadership in designing, building, and selling the world's fastest and most powerful computers, and an ability to aid scientists in addressing such challenges as discovering the cure for AIDS and eliminating the hole in the ozone layer (p. 79). Interestingly, Cray Research designs and sells only one product: supercomputers. As a result, the company must be committed to quality and innovation when it comes to 21st century communication technology.

The Changing Role of Communication Technology in the Workplace

It is readily apparent to companies like Cray Research that information is a key resource for all organizations today. As a result of this fact, communication technology has become a significant contributor to the workplace. Jagdish Sheth (1994) identified four distinct forces that are contributing to the changing role of information technology in organizations: (1) intense competition, (2) globalization of business operations, (3) organizational changes, and (4) the technology revolution.

Intense Competition

As Sheth (1994) noted, intense competition is the first force that is driving companies to use state-of-the-art computer and automated technologies to stay ahead of their competitors and reduce operating costs. For example, in the telecommunications industry, AT&T has equipped employees with computerized billing, account management, and operator services—all of which result in significant savings for the customer. In turn, AT&T is recognized as a leader in the telecommunications field.

Globalization of Business Operations

Second, as industries become more global, communication technology is required to help companies bridge the barriers of distance and time. For example, businesses in the United States, Europe, and Japan have become highly interdependent through global competition, global mergers and acquisitions, and global business operations. Even

Being aware of proper international etiquette when dealing with people from other cultures contributes to your techno-life.

small companies are feeling the necessity, or lure, to "go global" and are using the world wide web to buy and sell goods, products, and services.

Organizational Changes

Third, companies are constantly reorganizing, a process that also requires cutting-edge communication technology. Mergers and acquisitions, downsizing and consolidation, market-driven reorganization, and crisis management are only a few of the realities that businesses will continue to face (Sheth, p. 9). As an illustration, communication technology has become a significant factor in the airline industry to integrate flight schedules, aircraft, crew, ground personnel, marketing, and computer systems of those companies that have merged or been consolidated.

The Technology Revolution

Fourth, we are experiencing a technological revolution that is driving the strategic importance of communication technology, and changing the way we conduct business in the process. As Sheth (1994) has noted, "[Communication] technologies have become distributed over time with respect to processing, memory and intelligence" (p. 13). As a result, multiple users of communication technology are now processing, storing, and switching information from one user to another. No longer is it necessary to have these capabilities contained in a centralized location. In addition, communication technologies are becoming increasingly integrated. Thus, companies are now transmitting, storing, processing, and distributing different forms of information (e.g., voice, data, video, and text) through a single integrated technology.

Communication Technology and You

As you will recall in your reading of Chapter 1, the U.S. Department of Labor identified several major competencies that you need in order to succeed in the workplace, no matter what occupation or industry you choose. Included among them were the ability to (1) identify, assimilate, and integrate information, and (2) select, use, and troubleshoot appropriate technology (Boyett & Boyett, 1995, pp. 164–165). Interestingly, the "Council of 55" were in considerable agreement in a survey they completed for the American Association of School Administrators in 1996. As this prominent group of thinkers, educators, and futurists noted, "Students will need to be skilled not only in accessing the vast array of information available through advanced technology, but in processing it as well" (Uchida, Cetron, and McKenzie, 1996, p. 3). Tom Curley, president and CEO of Gannett Company, James Renier, former chairman and CEO of Honeywell, Inc., and Michael Usdan, president of the Institute for Educational Leadership, were only a few of the Council members who agreed.

> The future influences the present just as much as the past.
>
> —*Friedrich Nietzsche*

As you can see, successfully developing and using communication technology is key to organizations and individuals who wish to achieve success in the workplace. However, one major challenge that all of us are facing is the fact that growth in the information industry is outpacing our ability to keep up. Every day, new computer hardware and software are being introduced in the market. Just about the time we think we have made a good hardware investment or mastered a word processing or spreadsheet program, a new or better version comes along, leaving us—yet again—feeling lost, bewildered, and overwhelmed.

Allow us to assure you that this problem will persist. The Information Age is no longer a name; it is a reality. To thrive and grow in the 21st century workplace, we must develop strategies for keeping the cutting edge in sight. Two ways that we recommend are: (1) to maximize your communication competence, and (2) to embrace the philosophy of learning as a life-long process.

Communication Competence and Life-Long Learning: The Keys to Successfully Managing Your Techno-Life

Communication Competence

Why do you need to gain communication competence, perhaps even more than technological competence? One answer to this question lies in the fact that technical skills last only about five years. If you question this fact, consider how quickly computer hardware and software become obsolete. Yesterday's portable computer is definitely tomorrow's "used car part."

A second answer lies in the fact that communication competence is significantly related to performance and productivity levels with new technologies. To test this hypothesis, Michael Papa (1989) conducted a study of 289 claims adjustors from two divisions of a large insurance company. Results of his study found that communicator competence was related to how well employees learned to perform with a new computer. Specifically, he found that communication competence is related to complex information processing tasks, especially "when a task is novel and its successful completion requires more conscious problem-solving skills" (p. 98).

Third, communication competence means the ability to select and use the most appropriate channel to communicate a message. With regard to techno-life, this means selecting and using the most appropriate communication technology (e.g., telephone, E-mail, or fax) for a given situation. Because this issue is so important to successfully managing your techno-life, we will discuss it more completely later in the chapter.

As we stated in Chapter 1, **communication competence** is best defined as the sensitivity, knowledge, skills, and values required to communicate effectively with others. Additionally, we presented you with the Puzzle Model of Business and Professional Life, and discussed the importance of mastering relational life, work life, public life, and techno-life. Unfortunately, the merit of basic communication competencies such as reading, writing, speaking, and listening are overlooked in the rush toward the latest technology. However, if you cultivate the many communication skills discussed in this text, you will be able to use any communication technology effectively, once you learn what it does, when to use it, and how it works.

The Philosophy of Life-Long Learning

Writer Henry Adams once said, "They know enough who know how to learn." Certainly no statement is more appropriate when it comes to communication technology. We

> It was not long ago that people thought that semiconductors were part-time orchestra leaders and microchips were very, very small snack foods.
>
> —*Geraldine Ferraro*

have all heard stories about a news reporter or writer who swears never to forsake grandmother's 1924 Olivetti typewriter. However, anyone under 18 years of age will roll his or her eyes in amazement if someone says, "I have no use for a computer or a cellular phone." Inherently, all human beings possess curiosity and an innate desire to learn more about their environments. These basic survival skills are especially critical in the 21st century workplace, where technology is constantly changing. Without a desire to keep up with the technology that is available in your workplace, rest assured that you will be left behind when it comes to raises and promotions. In short, if you fail to change with the times, your organization will change without you.

For example, consider the following scenario. Collette was a mid-level manager with a major long-distance telephone company for more than 17 years. She was happy in her job, knew what to do to get by, and had little interest in learning the new computer system, which was being installed in about a week. Collette only had three years to go before retirement, and, in her own words, "Using computers were what secretaries were for. . . ."

About a month after the new computer system was installed, Collette's company merged with a larger telephone system. Eighteen days later, the vice president called Collette into his office and presented her with her "walking papers." The major reason her boss fired Collette was that she had become too comfortable in her job. She had refused to participate in company training activities, and had been exceptionally vocal about the cost of the new computer system. The newly merged company planned to promote Sam, Collette's assistant, into the position. Although Sam and Collette were the same age and had the same amount of tenure, Sam constantly demonstrated a "life-long learning philosophy." He embraced every chance to learn with the passion of a 20-year-old. Not only had Sam already mastered much concerning the new system, he also was teaching his colleagues everything he knew.

Certainly, we could spend an entire chapter talking about communication competence and life-long learning as the keys to managing your techno-life. However, you probably are eager to learn more about the communication technologies you may need to manage, especially those that are prevalent in business organizations today.

> The world is moving so fast these days that the [person] who says it can't be done is generally interrupted by someone doing it.
>
> —Harry Emerson Fosdick

Communication Technology Today

> Wanted: Media Futurist. We're looking for a cutting-edge communication technologist to create courses and train employees to use new technologies in a Fortune 100 company. This individual will be working with top management to identify telecommunication trends affecting the organization, and to teach employees how to apply new technological skills. Qualified applicants should be familiar with state-of-the-art communication networks, digital video-distribution systems, and wireless communications. Previous experience with virtual reality a plus.

The media futurist position that you just read about and similar futuristic employment opportunities will be commonplace by the turn of the century. As more and more information technology becomes readily available, people will be "wired" electronically all over the world. Job-hunting will be as easy as turning on your computer and surfing the Internet for specific job opportunities, and then sending your resume on-line to your prospective employer. Already, technology is available to interview candidates via videoconference or computer, if both parties have compatible equipment.

Intelligent software. On-line information. Machines talking to machines. Smaller, faster computer chips. Worldwide satellite networks. Wireless communication devices. Transmitting digitized information to any medium, anytime, anywhere will become commonplace in the 21st century. The hallmark of the future workplace will be people and equipment teamed together in an open environment. Today, as well as in the future, we are no longer limited by space and time.

When you stop to think about the future and all the different channels of communication that are becoming available, it is overwhelming and, at times, incomprehensible. To assist you in assessing your own communication technology skills, you may want to ask yourself the following questions: (1) As a business person in the 21st century, what impact will communication technology have on me and my job? (2) What types of new communication technologies should I learn about in order to be successful in the business world? Once you have answered these questions, you may want to start thinking about areas of technology in which you need further training.

For the purposes of this chapter, **communication technologies** will be defined as those which "link distant individuals who might otherwise be unable or unlikely to communicate" (Rogers and Allbritton, 1995, p. 177). Therefore, our discussion will be limited to communication technologies that facilitate the one-to-one, one-to-group, and one-to-many exchanges that characterize interpersonal, small group, and mass communication.

Since the telephone is one of the most prevalent technologies we use in our techno-lives, we will begin with a discussion about teleconferencing. From there, we will move to facsimile (fax) and electronic communications, including E-mail, groupware, the Internet, and intranets. We will conclude our presentation of communication technologies with a brief discussion about video conferencing and business television.

Teleconferencing

At the most basic level, a **teleconference** (also termed a telephone conference call) is a meeting of a group of three or more people who agree to talk together via telephone at a designated time. Participants may use the phones in their respective offices, automobiles or hotel rooms. Since they require only a voice link-up, teleconferences are not as expensive as videoconferences. Teleconferences have become especially common in organizations that have multiple locations, or for companies that require decisions to be made by three or more people in different locales at a given time.

A primary advantage of teleconferences over other forms of communication is a savings in time and money. For example, consider the time and expense that would accrue if you were required to travel to Seattle from Tampa for a two-hour, face-to-face meeting. Or consider the time and expense that would be involved in bringing together an internationally recognized group of engineers from the United States, Japan, Belgium, Germany, and France. In short, if a face-to-face interaction plays little or no key role in the potential success of a meeting, teleconferencing provides a viable alternative.

On the other hand, teleconferences limit the amount of information you can receive through nonverbal cues. For instance, without the benefits that eye contact, facial expressions, and gestures afford, you may be missing important information. As Howard Armstrong (personal communication, May 1996), a highly respected right-of-way negotiator with Universal Field Services, has noted, "Technology shouldn't replace the personal touch. If your presence is necessary to close a major deal, traveling cross-country for a two-hour meeting is the only alternative."

Facsimile (Fax) Communications

According to Maury Kauffman (1995), author of *Computer-Based Fax Processing,* "Fax machines [are] the one true global communications standard" (p. 32). In fact, they are so standard that 93 million stand-alone fax machines were in place worldwide by 1996. Because fax machines are fast, inexpensive, and easy to use, they serve a major role in many organizations today. For instance, fax machines are used by companies to send everything from purchase orders, price quotations, restaurant menus, and lunch orders, to artwork, research questionnaires, and urgent memos. Fax technology is also used by many companies to keep in close contact with overseas clients.

Additionally, with the advent of "broadcast fax," marketers can reach hundreds of potential clients and customers through electronic direct mail (Walsh, 1988). By **broadcast fax,** we mean the ability to send multiple transmissions very quickly using fax technology and telephone lists that are organized like mailing lists. Documents are sent simultaneously using multiple telephone lines, or a single-line personal computer (PC) fax/modem and the Internet. (Note: PC fax/modems allow computer users to send and receive documents through their personal computers. We will talk more about PCs and the Internet later in this chapter.)

For example, using fax technology and a database of telephone numbers, many local chambers of commerce keep their members apprised of upcoming events such as important business shows. As another example, AmeriCares, a leading U.S. disaster re-lief organization, regularly uses broadcast fax to send an S.O.S. to companies and or-ganizations that can supply disaster relief (Norman, 1991).

Sending and receiving individual documents and marketing through broadcast fax are only two of many applications afforded by the fax machine. As fax technology be-comes more and more sophisticated, even more creative applications are emerging. For example, consider the concept of fax-on-demand. With **fax-on-demand** (FOD), a sim-ple telephone call allows an individual to request and receive information from a com-pany. By following the directions presented on a voice recording and pressing the correct keys on the phone, a caller can receive information in seconds once he or she has keyed in his or her fax number.

To illustrate, Gelman Sciences, based in Ann Arbor, Michigan, is a world leader in microfiltration products used in health-care facilities. As early as 1993, Gelman began a fax-on-demand service that offered customers a menu of more than 1,000 docu-ments. Accessible through a fax service bureau, the choice of documents included "product literature, data sheets, brochures, validation guides, technical papers, hands-on tips, facts, features, and technical articles. With fax-on-demand, Gelman could pro-vide valuable information immediately . . . ," and at a much lower cost than more traditional ways of distributing literature (Stambler, 1994, p. 78).

Other fax-on-demand applications include the ability to (1) retrieve reports; (2) handle information requests not directly related to sales; (3) provide documents from public relations, media relations, and product marketing departments of corpo-rations; (4) respond to information requests from the press and from current and po-tential investors; (5) order products to be delivered by next-day service; and, (6) alert members of cost clubs about special sales, to name just a few (Stambler, 1994).

As you can see, fax technology offers much to organizations as we approach the 21st century. Its primary advantages include savings in time, effort, and money. How-ever, as John Graham (1988), president of John R. Graham Inc., a Massachusetts-based public relations and advertising agency, notes, " . . . there's a darker side to fax and sev-eral pitfalls to avoid" (p. 9).

First, faxing messages should never replace personal contact, or the discussion and rapport that a phone call or meeting affords. Second, fax technology seems to engender greater sloppiness than direct or overnight mail, in the form of quickly scribbled, handwritten notes. If making a positive nonverbal impression is one of the major purposes of your communication, we encourage you to type or word process your faxed message.

Third, there is a growing prevalence of "junk fax ads," or unsolicited fax ads being sent to potential customers. We encourage you to think carefully if you are in a position to use broadcast fax. Junk fax ads use ink, paper, and time at the expense of (often) unwilling or uninterested recipients. Additionally, although sending broadcast faxes late at night may reduce the cost for you, doing so may anger the recipient whose home office is located directly across the hall from his or her bedroom—especially if the fax arrives at 5:30 A.M. on Saturday.

Electronic Mail (E-mail)

According to a survey of companies conducted by your authors, 88.7 percent of companies currently use, or will employ, electronic mail (or E-mail) by the turn of the century (Perrigo and Gaut, 1994). To lend credence to our survey, consider that, in 1995, 95 billion E-mail messages were sent in the United States alone—a number that exceeded the number of ordinary messages sent through the U.S. mail (Fulton, 1996, p. 24). At Microsoft, the software giant cofounded by Bill Gates, employees send a total of 200 million E-mail messages to each other per month. In fact, E-mail is so prevalent at Microsoft that Gates spends several hours each day communicating by E-mail (Rogers and Allbritton, 1995, p. 182).

As you will recall in Chapter 9, **E-mail** is a type of interactive technology that serves to interconnect participants by computer and telephone lines or local area networks (LANS). As such, E-mail is a type of mediated interpersonal communication that involves:

- **mutual discourse,** or "the degree to which a particular communication act is based on a prior series of communication acts";
- an **exchange of roles,** or the ability of users A and B to empathize with one another; and,

Techno-savvy means being familiar with Internet and E-mail communication systems.

■ **control,** or "the degree to which a user can choose the timing, content, and sequence of a communication act, search for alternatives, enter message content into storage, etc." (Rogers & Allbritton, 1995, pp. 178–179).

What distinguishes E-mail from other forms of interpersonal communication is the physical distance between users, and the ability of interactive communication systems to overcome differences between people like race, gender, social status, and appearance.

[With E-mail] a person... can say 'Help' to 10,000 people.... The next morning he may have 15 answers to the problem.

—*Tekla S. Perry (1992)*
Senior Editor,
IEEE Spectrum

For example, in Santa Monica, California, the Public Electronic Network (PEN) allows several thousand participants to exchange information. Through PEN, an extraordinary interpersonal phenomenon has taken place over the past eight to ten years. In 1989, an E-mail conference was established to bring together Santa Monica's 2,000 plus homeless people, public officials, local business people, and the city's 90,000 "homed" residents. Because the city's homeless could access PEN at public terminals in city libraries, at city hall, and at other public sites, these four groups of people were able to establish the SHWASHLOCK Project (a project that allows the homeless to shower, wash clothing, and lock up their possessions). Out of SHWASHLOCK came a number of positive outcomes, including an increase in the employment level. Through the project, the homeless could improve their appearance and compete more effectively for jobs (Rogers & Allbritton, 1995).

Whether you are a novice or a bona fide computer guru, the advantages of E-mail are numerous:

■ the ability to avoid elaborate games of telephone tag and time zone differences;

■ the flexibility to assemble multifunctional teams without stressful transfers of personnel or expensive temporary assignments;

■ the possibility of uncovering hidden expertise in companies by sending "does anybody know" requests throughout an electronic mail network;

■ the capability to tap into international expertise and debate complex technical issues (or chat) with the best minds in the world;

■ the lack of intrusiveness of E-mail as opposed to a telephone call (i.e., you can access E-mail at a time that is convenient for you);

■ the record-keeping function of E-mail (Note: an electronic record is kept from almost every conversation.);

■ the ability to distribute meeting notes to interested parties both in and outside a core team; and,

■ the economy associated with E-mail (In U.S. dollars, the average letter costs $.51, a fax averages $1.66, and a two-page E-mail between two people worldwide costs approximately $.22.) (Perry, 1992).

Of course, like all technology, E-mail also has its limitations. First, E-mail mailboxes easily fill up with messages and can keep you from doing your real work, or from having a personal life. For example, one of our university colleagues often spends two hours each night (from 11:00 P.M. to 1:00 A.M.) responding to her E-mail.

Second, without the nuance that face-to-face nonverbal communication affords, E-mail messages can be misinterpreted and create needless conflict. Third, as Perry (1992) has noted, there is always the temptation to **flame** someone, or "to dash off an angry message or ill-conceived reply to a message" (p. 28). Flaming is much easier to do when you are on your computer than when you are responding orally or in a formal letter (p. 28).

Additionally, people have been fired for sending E-mail messages that they thought were "private." Further, like junk fax mail, junk E-mail is beginning to proliferate. Finally, there is a growing concern that electronic communication may be lowering the quality of our writing and "desensitizing us to egregious grammatical gaffes" (McGoon, 1996, p. 23). Although some people argue that the informal atmosphere of cyberspace is one of its attractions, Cliff McGoon, a San Francisco–based business writer and consultant, makes an excellent point:

> . . . would you write a printed memo to your boss with typos in it? To what earthly purpose? How can someone on the other end of an E-mail message know that you're really an intelligent person, . . . if your writing contains misspellings, poor punctuation and no format? Can't online E-mail writing be both fast and good? (1996, p. 23).

Although E-mail, indeed, has these limitations, its use is becoming more and more prevalent in organizations around the world. Thus, we encourage you to take the plunge now if you have yet to do so and have access to a computer, a modem, and an on-line service like America Online, Prodigy, CompuServe, Delphi, NETCOM, or GEnie. For tips on E-mail and other cybersensitive etiquette, we refer you to Chapter 9.

Groupware

Another example of a communication technology that enables people to work together on-line is called groupware. **Groupware** is a category of software that goes a step beyond E-mail and allows two or more people in remote sites to work in groups and share information via computer. At present, groupware products generally offer consumers one or more applications: knowledge sharing, group calendaring and scheduling, real-time meetings, bulletin boards, group document handling, and work-flow tracking (Field, 1996).

At first blush, people sometimes confuse groupware with E-mail. However, as Dave Hoffman (1995), managing partner for Andersen Consulting in Chicago, has noted,

> While E-mail is imbedded in groupware products, it is confined to passing messages and documents to one or many users, promoting point-to-point communications. But groupware can become a powerful strategic weapon when creatively applied (p. 78).

For example, one of Andersen's clients, an insurance brokerage firm, is currently using groupware to support a global knowledge-sharing system. Brokers in Europe and the United States collaborate on proposals and policy reviews, and bring the best thinking of the firm to its clients. (Hoffman, p. 78).

Other opportunities and possible applications for groupware include creating mission and vision statements, strategic planning, building teams, developing training programs, resolving conflicts, restructuring organizations, improving and redesigning work processes, surveying employees, and implementing focus groups ("When and Where to Use Groupware," 1995, p. 36).

The benefits of groupware to people and organizations are numerous, including (1) convenience of use and ease in scheduling; (2) greater responsiveness to clients as a function of the ability to reduce turnaround time for decisions and meetings; (3) the ability of group members to share knowledge before conducting initial or further research on a project; (4) improved delivery of client reports and other information from different viewpoints; (5) closer partnerships between companies and clients as a function of collaborating on solutions to problems; (6) the creation of "borderless teams," a plus for telecommuters or employees who travel frequently; and, (7) the opportunity to bring out more introverted staff members who are communication-apprehensive about speaking in meetings (Strom, 1995).

Disadvantages that users encounter with groupware products include the present start-up investment required to purchase the software, hardware, and requisite consulting and training; a possible lack of security and confidentiality with regard to sensitive documents; and, the tendency to pick up a phone and call rather than enter text, especially for new PC users.

Communication problems similar to those we discussed for fax and E-mail also arise, especially regarding the absence of nonverbal communication. Additionally, as William Snizek, Alumni Distinguished Professor of Sociology at Virginia Polytechnic Institute, has noted, dramatic differences exist between electronic meetings and those in which all parties are in the same room. Although electronic meetings have the advantages of convenience and ease in scheduling, they often are "devoid of spontaneity and intensity" (1996, p. 17). To underscore this point, Snizek offered the following analogy:

> The sense of organizational membership that one experiences from continually taking part in virtual meetings, whether by E-mail or conference calls, is not unlike the feeling of congregational membership one achieves from watching a televised religious service. Meetings, like religious services, are quite different when experienced in person, rather than through an electronic medium (p. 17).

In short, if a meeting is designed solely to communicate and inform, electronic meetings are entirely appropriate. However, if the purpose of a meeting includes creating a sense of community, a face-to-face meeting is essential.

Finally, since working in any kind of discussion group has its own share of potential problems, working in groups on-line can also be tricky. To help you avoid some common electronic problems and pitfalls, we refer you to Box 12.1.

The Internet

The Internet is one of the hottest communications technologies available today, and allows all three types of communication we have addressed in this text: one-to-one, one-to-group, and one-to-many. So vast and all-encompassing is the Internet that a totally new and global social fabric of life has been created.

The **Internet,** or Net, is a highly decentralized network of previously existing computer networks that allows people to share information along high-speed data lines.

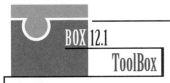

BOX 12.1
ToolBox
Groupware Tips

Whenever you are asked to use groupware—especially to share knowledge—keep in mind the following suggestions from Alice Bredin (1996), author of *The Virtual Office Survival Handbook.*

1. Agree as a team how often members should check databases. (Note whether A.M. or P.M. checks are best.)

2. Limit the length of entries in groupware and encourage use of E-mail for one-to-one communication, to cut down on clutter in the system.

3. Assign someone the role of database manager. This person is responsible for editing, filtering,

and categorizing comments in the database. This person keeps the discussion on track and makes sure it is logical and easy to follow.

4. Provide shared address books, either electronic or on paper, so that participants in a discussion know whom they are talking to.

5. Do not use a discussion database as E-mail. . . . It should be used to make general comments, post responses to issues in the database, and provide information to the discussion at large.

6. As a remote user, be sure to replicate databases before and after using them (pp. 233–234).

The Internet allows users to access information from all over the world. Included among its many capabilities are:

- Telnet—allows you to access directories, library files, and databases at libraries, universities, government agencies, and private systems around the globe;

- FTP (File Transfer Protocol)—allows you to download or upload files from directories and archives;

- Listserv—allows you to access lists of people, programs, documents, books, other lists, and the like; allows a list of people to receive E-mail;

- E-mail—allows you to have one-to-one, asynchronous communication with other computer users;

- Servers—special programs that allow you to search for, read, download, or have mailed to you programs, pictures, sound and music files, documents, books, listings, directories, and so forth;

- News groups—allow real, synchronous communication in the form of "forums" and "chat-rooms"; allow one-to-many communications among people covering just about any topic imaginable; and,

- Files On-line—includes full-text copies of classical literature, research papers, cookbooks, bartender's manuals, or just about any other document that you can dream of (Johnson, 1993).

Who are Internet users? Internet users include virtually everyone who has a computer with the capability to link up to the Internet. Like the Net, its users know no boundaries. They are a mixture of every demographic variable imaginable. However, what Internet users have in common is an interest in computers as a channel of communication.

One way to access information from the Internet is through "web sites." A **web site** is a server that uses programming protocol to transmit information graphically. To locate specific information about a company, product, service, or individual, you use browser software such as Netscape, which allows you to read material you have accessed on a site that conforms to Web protocol. Many people (the president of the United States), organizations (Jerry's Cajun Restaurant in Pensacola, Florida), cities (Paris, London, Rome), and so forth have web sites on the Internet. For example, if you are looking for information about London, England, you can connect to a web site using a computer modem and browser software, and download information (i.e., graphics, audio, and text) from the site. You also can access information about London's calendar of events and weather conditions, and can even book your travel reservations.

Information on web sites is changed fairly frequently, depending on the nature of the company or product. You can access many web sites 24 hours a day, although some sites are on-line only a few hours a day, especially if the server is down.

Because of the Internet's capability to allow people to post and read messages on public bulletin boards or forums, to chat live back and forth with other users in real time, to send and receive information via E-mail, and to retrieve information about virtually any topic in the world, this incredible interactive communication technology is becoming a mainstay in many organizations. Thus, we encourage you to conduct "hands-on" research on the Internet, and to learn more about its many applications.

If you have yet to "surf the Net" and want to know more, consider attending a workshop at a local community college or university, observing a training program offered by a local computer consulting firm, or reading pertinent books and magazines at your favorite bookstore. Again, we urge you to learn as much as you can about the Internet. Your ability to work on-line may give you just the edge you need to get and keep a job in the 21st century workplace.

Intranets

Intranets, or internal, single-company networks, are in use in many companies and businesses. In fact, according to the Business Research Group in Newton, Massachusetts, intranets are the future of intraorganizational communication. For instance, 23 percent of the decision makers at 169 medium-size and large companies already have implemented (or plan to implement) intranets. Another 20 percent are studying the prospect (Carr, 1996, p. 61).

According to Melanie Berger, author of "The Other Net," an **intranet** is

> . . . an internal company network that looks and feels like the Internet, because it uses the same tools, such as browsers like Netscape Navigator, and standards that people use on the Net. Most intranets, however, are not connected in any way to the Internet. Instead they're company networks that link employees through their PCs. (1996, p. 26)

Like other communication technologies, intranets are used by employees to send E-mail and collaborate as groups. However, currently, their most frequent use is to make accessible to employees important electronic documents like manuals, sales data, news about competitors, and product specifications.

Intranets offer organizations a number of benefits: (1) cost savings over more conventional databases and groupware; (2) access to information and graphics by all users no matter what type of computer platform they use; (3) communication among geographically dispersed sites that is cheaper and easier to deploy than groupware; (4) a streamlined, safe introduction to the Internet; and, (5) enhanced productivity due to ease in learning and navigation (Carr, 1996; Berger, 1996).

For example, at the time of this writing, Northrup Grumman was in the process of developing an intranet for the U.S. Air Force that should save in excess of $800 million across 20 years of use. By linking the Contractor's Integrated Technology Information Service to Northrup's intranet via a web browser, air force personnel in three different locations will be able to reengineer components of different planes and place the redesigned components out for bid. They will be able to do so by viewing and manipulating a variety of information, (e.g., technical data, engineering drawings, and component specifications) in ways they never have before (Carr, 1996).

Limitations of intranets include the fact that they are still in the development stage; security issues linger; and, some groupware capabilities are unavailable at this time. Because the communication problems associated with E-mail and groupware are identical to those of intranets, we refer you to our earlier discussion of those two topics.

Videoconferencing and Business Television

Two technological innovations that have changed the face of regional, national, and global business are videoconferencing and business television. A **videoconference** is a two-way (or multipoint) interactive meeting through video link-ups at two or more sites. Audio and video signals are transmitted via local and long distance telephone lines, direct cable connections, microwave ground base stations, or satellites. Although videoconferencing has been used for some time by Fortune 500 companies and the fed-

Videoconferencing allows companies to save time and money when they are making decisions with people at off-site locations.

eral government, the decrease in transmission and equipment costs has allowed smaller companies to adopt videoconferencing technology. In terms of use, videoconferencing is especially suited for involving people at off-site locations in decision making; developing new products, services, or plans; executing complex projects; and, conducting management meetings at the global level. In instances in which time and money can be saved, videoconferencing also is used to conduct employment interviews.

In contrast, **business television** (BTV) is comprised of a one-way video broadcast from a single source to one or more audiences. Although interaction can take place using BTV if audience members phone in questions, BTV presentations are generally not structured for dialogue (Maltz, 1989). Presently BTV is used by the largest of the major corporations, government agencies, and independent producers to provide business television services to the corporate world. However, again, as BTV becomes more affordable, this technology will be used by smaller companies as well. BTV is particularly useful for employee and motivational training, the introduction of new products and services, merchandising changes, rollouts of new advertising campaigns, and business or industry updates ("Videoconferencing: A Strategic Business Tool in an Information Age," 1995).

As an illustration of how videoconferencing technology can be used to help businesses become more efficient, consider Management Recruiters International (MRI), a Cleveland-based executive recruitment firm. At a price below $20,000, MRI purchased a full-featured video conferencing system that transmits video signals over telephone lines. Prior to making this seemingly costly investment, the firm arranged 90,000 trips per year to match individual job candidates with their corporate clients. At an average cost of $1,650 per interview, the annual cost of travel was $148,500,000. By relying on videoconferencing instead of travel to get their candidates to interviews, MRI saved its clients more than $135 million annually in recruiting expenses, not to mention the savings in time (Matthes, 1993).

In recent years, traditional videoconferencing technology has been usurped by Internet videoconferencing. Desktop computers are equipped with a camera, microphone, and videoconferencing circuit board, which allow multiple PC users to videoconference. If you have yet to take part in this particular type of meeting, perhaps you will by the year 2005.

Two advantages of videoconferencing and business television are savings in both time and travel costs. They also allow people from all over the world to link with one another simultaneously, thereby aiding in the development of corporate culture and propagation of company values. ("Videoconferencing: A Strategic Business Tool in an Information Age," 1995). From the perspective of a communication student or scholar, a third major advantage is that participants can receive both audio and visual images—both verbal and nonverbal communication. Aside from greater communication fidelity and sheer enjoyment, two related results accrue: 50 percent increased comprehension, and retention, over printed material alone—particularly in training situations (Flanagan, 1994).

The primary disadvantage of videoconferencing and BTV is the lack of human touch, in this case actual face-to-face communication. No matter how sophisticated technology gets, many people feel more comfortable shaking hands with those with whom they do business.

BOX 12.2

ToolBox — *Eight Basic Rules for Videoconferencing*

Consider the following eight guidelines suggested by Patrick Flanagan* whenever you participate in a videoconference or BTV broadcast.

1. *Be on time and stick to the agenda.* Meetings held via these two related technologies tend to be more productive because of strict time limitations. Virtually every minute spent during the meeting translates into dollars, given that the company must purchase time—generally, by the minute.

2. *Introduce yourself and wait your turn.* If you need to or want to interject a point, say your name and look up to see if you're on or off camera. Once the camera is positioned on you, you may talk.

3. *Use a normal tone of voice and speak clearly.* Since microphones are sensitive, you should also avoid drumming your fingers or tapping your pen on the table. Doing so wreaks havoc with the audio.

4. *Prepare graphics, but make them easy to understand.* Use large fonts and limit charts to bar and pie formats. Write horizontally and make visuals clear and easy to view.

5. *Realize that video speed can be disconcerting.* In contrast to watching television (30 frames per second), viewing video at 15 frames per second can make images appear as if they are swimming. For that reason, avoid moving around or using your hands a great deal. Over time, you will adapt to viewing (and making presentations!) in light of the slower video speed.

6. *Rely less on gestures.* If you are an extremely animated speaker, you may require a wider camera angle in which to work. However, asking for such a favor may call undue attention to yourself. Instead, you may want to depend more on your facial expressions and voice than your hands to communicate your message effectively.

7. *Appearance counts.* You are on television now, so make sure your dress is appropriate. Wear primary colors and avoid stripes, dots, or checks at all costs. Remove shiny jewelry or jewelry that "jingles"; it reflects light and the sound may be picked up on your microphone! In short, dress simply but in a businesslike manner.

8. *Anticipate problems and be considerate.* Mail or fax copies of your presentation materials to other participants in advance. Follow up after the meeting or program with a report, minutes, or a "to do" list. Doing so will add closure to the meeting.

*Reprinted by permission of the publisher, from *Management Review*, February 1994 ©1994. American Management Association, New York. All rights reserved.

Another disadvantage of videoconferencing and BTV is the start-up costs associated with purchasing the requisite equipment. However, as more and more companies use these technologies as tools, the costs should begin to drop and make the equipment more affordable.

As with any new technological device, including the six we discussed earlier, a new set of communication rules must be established and learned in order to master videoconferencing and BTV. To get you started in the area of videoconferencing, consider the guidelines outlined by Patrick Flanagan (1994) and presented in Box 12.2.

In this section, we have discussed eight different communication technologies that are dramatically affecting the way we conduct business. Also emerging as a driving force in organizations today is the creation of alternatives for the traditional office environment. As we noted in Chapter 1, the environment in which we communicate is as important as the other major elements of communication (i.e., the source, message, channel, receiver, and feedback). For that reason, we now turn to a discussion of several types of virtual offices—perhaps, the primary business communication environments of the 21st century.

Humans, Technology, and the Virtual Office

Managing techno-life involves more than mastering specific communication technologies. Mastering techno-life also involves accomplishing your work in a number of different environments, termed "virtual offices" in the technology literature.

According to Alice Bredin, author of The Virtual Office Survival Handbook, a **virtual office** is "any worksite outside of the traditional office in which people still do the work associated with a traditional office" (1996, p. 1). The term "virtual" in virtual office implies the use of technology in some form for the worker to establish contact with his or her traditional office. As we indicated earlier, the virtual office is fast becoming the "norm" for the workplace environment.

Jay Chiat, managing partner of the advertising agency Chiat/Day in Venice, California, is the self-proclaimed inventor of the term "virtual office." While on a ski slope

Marlboro, NY—Comic book creator/comedian Scott Lobdell uses a portable laptop computer to write while sitting on the porch of his parent's home during a visit.

in Colorado one day, Chiat thought about all the time he and his employees wasted commuting to the office to retrieve their messages and to open mail. He wanted his employees to spend more time with their clients, so he came up with the idea of assigning employees to individual team projects. He also created a new way to approach the office environment. Chiat described his new office strategy as follows:

> Since team members change with each new project, they no longer need private offices and assigned desks. Instead, each employee is given a locker in which to keep personal items. When employees come into the office, they . . . check in with a "concierge" who doles out phones and computers, and assigns each person a space as needed. The office consists of large meeting rooms, with long conference tables [to conduct business]. Computer terminals are scattered throughout the office. Any employee can log on and access E-mail messages or the Internet. Even the mail is scanned into the computer network every day (Ogilvie, 1994, p. 31).

Types of Virtual Offices

The traditional office to which employees commute via car, bus, or subway and work a standard Monday-through-Friday, 8:00–5:00 job is no longer the only work option. Many different types of virtual offices exist in the global workplace today. Included among the most common are telecommuting, the mobile office, hoteling, and the home office. In the following pages, we will briefly discuss each type of virtual office as well as the advantages and disadvantages of each.

Telecommuting.   **Telecommuting** is "the practice of working at home, or at a satellite location near the home, where you can use computer and telecommunications technology in lieu of physically travelling to a central workplace. The goal of telecommuting is to move workplaces to the most convenient location for the worker" (Cooper, 1996, p. 10).

> Just as a cafeteria offers a variety of foods to suit individual tastes, the workplace is evolving toward a model for which alternative work options will be the norm.
>
> —*Greengard (1994)*

The advantages of telecommuting are a more flexible work environment, fewer distractions, a feeling of empowerment, and overall increased satisfaction with your professional and personal life. The disadvantages are a tendency to overwork and a feeling of isolation. You also must be an excellent time manager.

For example, Raul was the type of person who was able to manage his time well. He was a single parent who had the responsibility of driving his children to and from school every day. Because his parental duties took him away from work during the day, Raul came to realize that his peak performance work time was in the evening. By choosing telecommuting as his "virtual office," Raul was able to be an attentive parent, which, in turn, allowed him to be more productive at his work. As a result, Raul's morale improved; so did his self-concept and his perceptions of the company for which he worked.

What does the future of telecommuting hold? According to Michael Bell, director of corporate real estate for Dun & Bradstreet Corporation, "[As a function of telecommuting . . .], space needs will decline. Dedicated private offices will diminish. . . . The office will look more like a college building than an office building, dominated by meeting rooms, think tanks, conference areas, training areas and group work areas" (Cooper, 1996, p. 19).

Hoteling.   The term used for work arrangements in which corporate employees use desks on an as-needed basis is **hoteling.** The expression is quite appropriate because it is exactly what it sounds like: when you need a desk, you reserve one (Bredin, 1996, p. 8).

With hoteling, your "desk" may be situated at a home office or located somewhere on the road. If you are on the road and travel to a satellite location of your company, you usually will be provided with a cubicle, a telephone, electrical outlets, and some office supplies. You are responsible for supplying your own computer, fax machine, modem, or other technology necessary to do the job. Hoteling works well for people whose jobs require them to travel constantly (e.g., auditors, salespeople, and regional managers, to name a few). The disadvantages of hoteling are that you have no assigned office on a long-term basis, and storage can be problematic.

To illustrate, Taylor is an auditor for one of the "big six" accounting firms. He travels for his company approximately 80 percent of the time. Taylor carries his laptop computer with him and is able to link to his corporate office in New Orleans any time of day or night, no matter where he is located. Taylor is able to keep the corporate office informed by turning in his audit reports via on-line computer. He also carries a fax machine with him to send hard copies of his audit reports back to headquarters.

The Mobile Office.   A **mobile office** is comprised of communication technologies that travel with you to assist you in conducting business. Your "office" may be located in your car or briefcase and, therefore, is accessible if you spend a lot of time on the road. A mobile office allows you to complete your work from your car without returning to a central office location.

Hoteling and the mobile office are similar in some ways but the distinction can be confusing at times. The primary difference is that hoteling involves reserving temporary space in advance, whereas a mobile office always travels with you.

One of the advantages of a mobile office is the ability to spend more time with your clients; you can talk with them on the phone at any time while you are driving. Employees who work from a mobile office have incredible freedom and flexibility. In fact, some mobile offices have fax machines and computers hooked up in the car so orders can be processed in a timely manner.

One disadvantage of the mobile office is that you are working while you are driving, which can be dangerous. Additionally, instead of working you could be listening to your favorite CD, radio station, or book on tape in order to reduce stress. Another downside is that working while driving can be both stressful and isolating.

For example, Hiromi owns her own public relations business and travels extensively within a three-state area. When she is on the road, Hiromi conducts most of her business from her mobile office. She has a cell phone and fax machine in her car so she can talk with her clients day or night. When she arrives at home, Hiromi can relax because she knows she has taken care of her clients' immediate needs.

BOX 12.3

ToolBox *Tips for Creating a Functional Home Office in Any Environment*

To create a home office that will optimize your effectiveness and efficiency, keep in mind the following suggestions from Alice Bredin, author of *The Virtual Office Survival Handbook*:

- Set up your office space in a room that is well-ventilated and well-lit.
- Establish your office away from the busiest areas.
- Clear all old clutter out of that space.

- Establish a dedicated work area for you and, if possible, allow space for a coworker or client.
- Organize your supplies so they are easily within reach.
- Create a "paper only" trash can in case you have to retrieve something you have inadvertently thrown away.

Adapted from A. Bredin (1996). *The Virtual Office Survival Handbook* (New York: John Wiley & Sons), pp. 72–74.

The Home Office. Another type of virtual office that works well as an alternative to the traditional office is a home office. A **home office** might be a small dorm room connected to the world by a PC; a desk in an apartment you share with two roommates after graduation; a portion of a kitchen counter or family room in a small house you share with a spouse or significant other; or a fully equipped office that is located in your home and used exclusively by you for no other purpose than your work. Ideally, in each of these instances, your home office will occupy a specific space where all of your work-related papers and office technology are located. No matter where you live, Alice Bredin (1996), author of *The Virtual Office Survival Handbook,* offers some excellent advice for setting up a home office in Box 12.3.

If you decide that you want to make your home office your primary site for conducting business, and your employer agrees to the arrangement, you will want to make your office as pleasant and inviting as possible, especially if you will be meeting clients. To maximize the user-friendliness of your home office in this instance, consider the ideas presented in ToolBox 12.4 on page 326.

Perhaps, the biggest advantage of working in a home office is that you are in control of your own time. This means fewer meetings to attend and virtually no commute time to and from the office (short of walking from one room to the next, of course!). According to a study conducted by AT&T Home Business Resources, 80 percent of people who work at home say they are more productive at home than they are in a traditional office (Bredin, 1996, p. 6).

Additionally, in cases where employees have the option to work in a home or other virtual office, productivity generally increases because they have had a voice in how and where they will work. Additionally, reduced commuting time allows workers to spend more time with their clients, which results in higher customer satisfaction.

Fourth, in some cases, a home (or other virtual) office improves the overall quality of an employee's work life. Having the flexibility to choose work hours means hav-

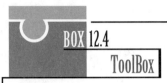

BOX 12.4

ToolBox — *Maximizing the User-Friendliness of Your Home Office*

If you plan to have your home office serve as your primary office, and you plan to work with clients in your home, you will want to make your work space as inviting as possible for both you and them. To do so, consider the following suggestions for setting up a home office.

- Begin with a realistic budget and make a list of office equipment you will need. Then think about how and where you will arrange your office within your allotted space.

- Buy a desk, chair, bookcase, filing cabinet, and supply cabinet that correspond to the decor of your home.

- Equip your office with the communication technologies you need in order to conduct

business efficiently, e.g., telephone, answering machine, personal computer, printer, fax, modem, and copy machine. Design your office so that you have maximum productivity at your fingertips.

- Choose a pleasant color for your walls, something that makes you think creatively.

- Make sure you have appropriate lighting. You may need a desktop lamp for close vision.

- Bring in a comfortable chair for chatting with clients or other business associates.

- Select artwork for the walls that makes a statement about you.

- Use attractive containers to hold supplies so your desk is uncluttered.

ing the flexibility to choose free time. For example, working moms or dads can get up and check a crying baby at any time during their workday. Similarly, for sales representatives with clients in other countries and time zones, a home office allows them to work on the client's schedule.

Although working out of a home office offers a number of advantages, several disadvantages also exist. First, there are distractions that you will encounter while you work that you would not experience in a traditional office. For example, friends and relatives may think they can call you any time during the week to chit-chat. Thus, part of the discipline of working at home requires informing friends and family that you prefer to talk with them after business hours unless an emergency occurs.

Another disadvantage of working at home is attempting to define when your workday begins and ends. If self-discipline isn't your strong suit, you will need to set specific beginning and ending times for your workday (e.g., 9:00 A.M. to 5:00 P.M. on Monday through Thursday) and stick to them.

Loneliness is another drawback of working at home, or in any virtual office for that matter. If you are used to working in a traditional office and enjoy interacting face-to-face with many people every day, you may want to think twice about working in a home office.

Additionally, boundaries between work and personal life often become blurred; as a result, techno-life can create a lot of stress. Finally, for the organization, management is required to develop new criteria for evaluating employee performance. This task is often difficult because the employee is rarely on site.

Three Tips for Maximizing Techno-life Competencies

Ultimately, managing techno-life is about more than communication technologies and where we use them; it is about effective human communication. This statement brings us back full circle to our model of communication, and to three tips about human communication that will help you to more successfully manage your techno-life.

Tip #1: Select the Appropriate Channel

As you will recall from the communication model we presented in Chapter 1, both a sender and a receiver are required to produce shared meaning. However, their mere presence isn't enough; each must select the best channel (medium) of communication to adapt to the other person's needs or preferences, and to optimize the chances for successful communication. Certainly this axiom of communication holds true for our relational, work, and public lives. However, it is especially salient for our techno-lives.

For example, Brianna, a sales executive for a cable television station, uses E-mail as her primary channel of communication with her coworkers. However, Dan, her regional manager, prefers to use his cell phone instead of E-mail to get the latest sales figures from the sales execs. Because Brianna knows Dan is continuously updating sales information for the corporate office—and rarely takes the time to check his E-mail—she carries her cell phone with her at all times. If Dan wants a hard copy of the sales figures for any given day, week, or month, Brianna also faxes information to him since she knows he carries a fax machine wherever he travels. In this situation, Brianna uses the cell phone or fax machine rather than E-mail in order to accommodate her supervisor's preferred channels of communication.

Tip #2: Be Sensitive to Others' Abilities

Think about the number of bookstores and software companies that sell computer guides entitled *(Fill-in-Software Name) for Dummies*. Indeed, we each have our own apprehension and learning curve when it comes to adapting to new technology. For

Always be sensitive to others' abilities to use communication technology and do not assume they have the same knowledge and skills as you do.

that reason, you should always be sensitive to others' abilities to use communication technology before assuming that they have the same abilities and skill levels as you.

To illustrate, Andreas and Julie were asked to develop a new web site for their company. While Andreas was adept as a web master, Julie was still trying to learn and felt frustrated because Andreas was light years ahead of her in designing web pages. Andreas was enthusiastic about the assignment and, at first, didn't want to take time to teach Julie about web technology. When Julie discussed the fact that she needed to learn more about it before they could continue, Andreas realized that he needed to take the time to teach her. Because Andreas was sensitive to the discrepancy in their skill levels, they were able to complete the assignment on time, and Julie learned more about creating web sites.

Tip #3: Realize the Importance of the Personal Touch

Sometimes the old-fashioned personal touch is required for effective communication. Being sensitive to this fact and acting accordingly are requisite if you truly wish to successfully manage your techno-life. For instance, consider the following example.

Tom, a computer analyst with a small accounting firm, decided to send an E-mail birthday greeting to Gayle, a friend who worked in the human resources department. Tom knew that Gayle checked her E-mail daily, and thought he would surprise her by having an E-mail birthday greeting waiting for her when she arrived at the office. Much to Tom's amazement, Gayle was disappointed that she didn't receive a "real" birthday card from him, as she had so many times in the past. Even though Gayle appreciated the fact that Tom remembered her birthday, she would have preferred a more "personal touch": a paper card that she could save, hold in her hand, and read over and over again.

Selecting the appropriate channel, being sensitive to others' abilities, and realizing the importance of the personal touch all contribute to successfully managing the four aspects of the Puzzle Model of Business and Professional Life. Indeed, they are key to effective human communication no matter what technological developments are yet to unfold. What will the workplace of tomorrow look like when it comes to business and professional communication? How will our communication with others be affected? To round out this chapter, we thought we would give you a glimpse of the workplace of tomorrow.

Technolife in the Year 2005: What Will It Look Like?

Perhaps one of the most sought-after prognosticators of the business future is John Naisbitt, best-selling author and management consultant. In his article, "A Brief History of the Future," Naisbitt discusses a "media merger" where "telephones, faxes, televisions and personal computers will merge into multimedia telecenters, which will link households and businesses to a seamless, global network of networks' " (1992, p.13). All of this technology will process information at lightning speed, and will simultaneously send and receive high-resolution images, computer data, and the human voice.

Naisbitt also speculates that each person will have a mobile, global telephone number, accessible anytime day or night, which will serve as a link to thousands of services around the globe. This telecommunications linkage via the telephone will allow you to set up a conference call—voice, image, and video—with your family members or management team, whether they are in the next room or in another city around the world (p. 13).

Another pundit who forecasts future technology is Bill Gates, founder and CEO of Microsoft Corporation. "We are now crossing a technology threshold that will forever change the way we learn, work, socialize, and shop. It will affect all of us and businesses of every type in ways far more pervasive than most people recognize" (1995, p. 21). Gates says that the future communication infrastructure will allow us to transfer information around the office or around the world with ease. Fiber-optic cable and other advances in wireless technology will increase the performance and capacity of data communications (p. 20).

According to Gates, by 2005, many companies also will require customized business applications. For example, a field salesperson will use voice recognition (i.e., giving voice commands to an interactive system) by talking into a microphone system in the car. The system will automatically organize the work, file, and initiate follow-up activities while the salesperson is calling on the next customer (1995, p. 20).

One company in the forefront of the technological revolution in the telecommunications industry is Motorola. Motorola has a reputation as a leader in developing innovative, futuristic technological communication devices. To take you into the future of telecommunications, Bob Growney, general manager of Motorola Inc.'s Paging & Wireless Group, envisions " . . . a completely wireless communication device about the size of your wallet. It would unfold to reveal a screen for sending and receiving text, handwritten messages, or graphics, and also have a voice system for making telephone calls—like a telephone and notepad all in one" (Stevens, 1994, p. 32). Portable multifunction personal digital assistants similar to the one just described are already available.

Communication in 2005 will be technological in nature as well as extremely fast-paced. In fact, Nicholas Negroponte, director of the MIT Media Lab and an Internet pioneer, believes that the communication technology revolution has changed our relational and work lives forever. As he noted,

> Information is universally accessible [anytime, anywhere]. . . .Early in the next millennium your right and left cuff links or earrings may communicate with each other by low-orbiting satellites and have more computer power than your present PC. Your telephone won't ring indiscriminately; it will receive, sort, and perhaps respond to your incoming calls like a well-trained English butler. Mass media will be redefined by systems for transmitting and receiving personalized information. . . . (Negroponte, 1995, p. 8)

At the time of this writing, Negroponte's example is futuristic; however, the technology is in place for this scenario to become a reality.

A Final Note

You may be familiar with, or even possess, a "dream catcher." A dream catcher, circular in shape, looks like a spider web and is crafted artistically from wood, feathers, stones, shells, and leather. Native Americans introduced us to dream catchers long ago.

It is believed these dream catchers capture both good and bad dreams and funnel the good dreams through the center hole to the sleeper. The bad dreams become enmeshed in the intricate webbing and perish in the light of day. Because it is believed that dreams can change or direct one's path in life, dreams attain a magical status (Uchida, et al., 1996, p. 68).

At this point, you might be asking yourself, "What do dream catchers have to do with technology? For that matter, how do they relate to business and professional communication?" Throughout this textbook, we have presented you with a myriad of information about communication skills and competencies that are essential for your success in the 21st century workplace. We also have discussed many communication behaviors and situations that you should avoid. By studying this text and implementing the suggestions and recommendations, you will grow more and more into the role of a professional communicator. In turn, we believe you can ultimately become your own "dream catcher."

As this text comes to a close, we would like to hear your thoughts about this book. If you have any great ideas, suggestions, or recommendations for future editions, please let us know. Our E-mail addresses are

dgaut@gulf.net and eperrigo@uwf.edu.

If you don't have specific recommendations, but want to share your thoughts about the future of business and professional communication, please feel free to write us. As author Charles Kettering so insightfully noted, "We should all be concerned about the future because we will have to spend the rest of our lives there."

Case Study

Using Communication Technology to Enhance Productivity at Hewlett-Packard

Dan Knasel, Regional Sales Representative

When sales quotas are rising and the price of computer equipment is falling, how can a sales representative continue to survive and obtain quota performance? The answer lies in becoming more efficient and effective. But how can a sales rep increase total sales dollars in a market where the price per unit is decreasing? For Hewlett-Packard, the answer was communication technology.

Factors Inhibiting Productivity

For HP, four factors were inhibiting their sales representatives' productivity:

■ traveling to and from accounts, to sales and product training, and to corporate update meetings;

■ due to ever-changing product technology, the all-consuming and complicated process of maintaining current literature;

- lack of availability of updated presentation materials at all times; and
- the need for accurate orders, the timely delivery of products, and the necessity of faxing information.

Questions

1. What communication technologies would you recommend to Hewlett Packard to address each of the aforementioned problems?
2. How would you deploy the necessary tools to the thousands of reps who comprise HP's sales staff?
3. What incentives would you use to encourage HP's sales reps to use the new technologies that you recommend?
4. How would you train sales reps at varying levels of personal computer literacy to use the recommended technologies?
5. What are the advantages and disadvantages associated with the communication technologies you would recommend to HP?

Summary

Techno-life is that part of your business and professional life associated with mastering technology, particularly communication technology. For the purposes of this chapter, we defined communication technology as "technologies that link distant individuals who might otherwise be unable or unlikely to communicate." Four forces that are changing the role of information in the workplace include: intense competition, globalization of business operations, organizational changes, and the technology revolution. The two keys to successfully managing your techno-life are communication competence and life-long learning.

In this chapter, we discussed eight major communication technologies in the workplace with which you may need to be familiar: teleconferencing, fax communications, E-mail, groupware, the Internet, intranets, videoconferencing, and business television. Included in our discussion were definitions and uses of each. Additionally, we addressed their advantages and disadvantages, and provided you with several Tool-Boxes offering tips and techniques that may prove to be useful in your working life.

In the workplace of the future, you will have many alternative offices available to you. Virtual offices such as in telecommuting, hoteling, and the mobile office will continue to flourish at the beginning of the next century. Many people also will choose to work from a home office, which is another type of virtual office. Benefits and common pitfalls of working in each of these environments were addressed.

A major component in implementing communication technology is the human factor. Selecting the appropriate channel, being sensitive to others' abilities, and realizing the importance of the personal touch all contribute to the creation and acceptability of communication technologies.

Finally, we provided you with a framework for communication in the year 2005. You can better prepare yourself for the 21st century workplace by knowing what is expected of you and by continuously updating your technological skills.

Knowledge Check

Key Concepts and Terms

communication competence	exchange of roles	videoconference
communication technologies	control	business television
teleconference	flame	virtual office
broadcast fax	groupware	telecommuting
fax-on-demand	Internet	hoteling
E-mail	web site	mobile office
mutual discourse	intranet	home office

Putting It All Together

1. Distinguish among the four forces that are driving the strategic importance of information technology.

2. Why are competence and life-long learning two major keys to mastering techno-life?

3. E-mail has been called "mediated interpersonal communication" by some communication researchers. How is E-mail like face-to-face communication? How does it differ?

4. Briefly discuss the benefits of groupware for an organization.

5. Name and briefly describe six capabilities of the Internet as a communication technology.

6. Explain the components of a virtual office and provide three examples.

7. What are some advantages and disadvantages of a home office?

8. According to Naisbitt and Gates, what will communication in 2005 look like?

References

Armstrong, H. (1996, May 13). Personal Communication.

Berger, M. (1996, September). The other 'net.' *Sales & Marketing Management, SMT Supplement,* 26–29.

Boyett, J. H., & Boyett, J. T. (1995). *Beyond Workplace 2000: Essential strategies for the new American corporation.* New York: Dutton.

Bredin, A. (1996). *The virtual office survival handbook.* New York: John Wiley & Sons.

Carr, J. (1996, February 19). Intranets deliver. *Infoworld,* 61–63.

Cooper, R. C. (1996, February). Telecommuting: The good, the bad and the particulars. *Supervision, 57*(2), 10–19.

Field, A. (1996, September 17). Groupthink. *Inc., 18*(13), 38–44.

Flanagan, P. (1994, February). Videoconferencing changes the corporate meeting. *Management Review, 7.*

Fulton, K. (1996, March/April). A tour of our uncertain future. *Columbia Journalism Review, 34*(6), 19–26.

Gates, W. H. (1995, January). Opportunities technology will bring by 2005. *Journal of Business Strategy, 16*(1), 19–21.

Graham, J. R. (1988, November 7). Avoid being snared by the fax trap. *Marketing News, 22*(23), 9.

Greengard, S. (1994, September). Making the virtual office a reality. *Personnel Journal, 73*(9),66–77.

Hoffman, D. E. (1995, April). Groupware is more than just glorified E-mail. *Best's Review, 95*(12), 78.

Johnson, N. B. (1993). *A guide to accessing the global internet by E-mail* [On-line]. Available: PRODIGY ID BVHKO6C.

Kauffman, M. (1995, February 20). There's no denying the fax. *Informationweek, 32.*

Levering, R., & Moskowitz, M. (1994). *The 100 best companies to work for in America.* New York: Penguin/Plume.

Maltz, M. (1989, August). Applications drive videoconferencing choices. *Video Systems, 52–55,* 58–60.

Matthes, K. (1993, May). Videoconferences can change the way you do business. *HR Focus, 70*(5), 23.

McGoon, C. (1996, January/February). Speed vs. accuracy in cyberspace. *Communication World,* 22–25.

Naisbitt, J. (1992, September). A brief history of the future. *Across the Board, 29*(9), 13–14.

Negroponte, N. (1995). *Being digital.* New York: Vintage Books, a division of Random House.

Norman, S. (1991, April). Fax processing adds new communication dimensions for AmeriCares. *Telemarketing Magazine, 9*(10), 32–33.

Ogilvie, H. (1994, September/October). Virtual office. *Journal of Business Strategy, 15*(4), 27–31.

Papa, M. (1989, Fall). Communicator competence and employee performance with new technology: A case study. *The Southern Communication Journal, 55*(1), 87–99.

Perrigo, E., & Gaut, D. (1994, Winter). Is academia in sync with the business world? *Journal of Career Planning and Employment,* 58–60.

Perry, T. S. (1992, October). E-mail at work. *IEEE Spectrum, 29*(10), 24–28.

Rogers, E. M., & Allbritton, M. M. (1995, April). Interactive communication technologies in business organizations. *The Journal of Business Communication, 32*(2), 177–195.

Sheth, J. N. (1994). Strategic importance of information technology. In *Advances in Telecommunications Management 4.* Greenwich, CT: JAI Press, Inc., 3–16.

Snizek, W. E. (1995, September). Virtual offices: Some neglected considerations. *Communications of the ACM, 38*(9), 15–17.

Stambler, S. (1994, January 15). A matter of fax. *CIO,* 78, 82, 84.

Stevens, T. (1994, January). The smart office. *Industry Week, 243*(2), 31–34.

Strom, D. (1995, June 5). How do you implement groupware? *Forbes ASAP,* 95–97.

Uchida, D., Cetron, M., & McKenzie, F. (1996). *Preparing students for the 21st century.* Arlington, VA: American Association of School Administrators.

"Videoconferencing: A strategic business tool in an information age." (1995, March). *Chain Store Age Executive, 71*(3), B9-B11.

Walsh, J. (1988, November 7). Fax to the max: How marketers are finding ways to use facsimile. *Marketing News, 22*(23), 1, 8–9.

"When and where to use groupware." (1995, November). *Training & Development, 49*(11), 36.

I

The Visual Impact of Your Message

We live in a visually oriented world. From the moment we get up in the morning until we go to sleep at night, we are continuously bombarded with visual stimulation. Television. Billboards. The environment. Colors. Shapes. Textures. All of these familiar sights contribute to the visual images of our daily life.

How do visual images affect the delivery of your presentation? Chances are, when you hear a presentation, you may not remember everything the speaker says, but more than likely you will recall the visuals that illustrated the points the speaker made. A **visual** is any prop used to assist the speaker when giving a presentation. The visual impact of your message can make the difference between delivering a memorable, dynamic presentation and offering one that is dull and uninteresting.

Purposes of Visuals

There are many reasons why you should add visuals to your presentation. In the following paragraphs, we will discuss four advantages of using visuals to add impact to your message.

To Clarify Your Message. You can make your message clearer by displaying the information you are presenting visually. For example, if you are talking about historical events, you can depict a timeline graphically that outlines the beginning and ending dates pertaining to your topics. Through the timeline, your audience can see a visual image of the details you are discussing.

To Add Interest. Visuals enliven presentations by adding interest to your message. Just as photographs, charts, and cartoons enhance the written word in textbooks, visuals add interest to the spoken word.

To Establish Credibility.   Presenters who prepare professional visuals are more credible in the eyes of the audience. If you have taken the time to develop visuals, you have demonstrated that you are well prepared. As a result, your professionalism will be reinforced.

To Optimize the Chance Your Audience Will Remember Your Message.   Studies have shown that if listeners see *and* hear information, they will remember the material presented for a longer period of time. For example, suppose you are giving a verbal description of the aftereffects of a hurricane or earthquake. Actual pictures or photographs of hurricane or earthquake damage are powerful, descriptive, and leave a lasting impression.

Using visuals takes a considerable amount of planning and preparation. To begin, you must first determine the type of visual that would best fit your topic and size of audience.

Types of Visuals

Objects.   Objects are the actual, physical props that you have on hand during your presentation. For example, if you were giving a persuasive presentation comparing which soap detergent was better from an environmental perspective, you might bring in the actual soap detergent containers and read the labels aloud in front of the audience. Doing so establishes credibility and lets your audience know you have done your research.

Poster Boards.   Poster boards are heavy pieces of cardboard or foam-core board on which you place key words, diagrams, or charts relating to your topic. When using poster boards, make sure they are all the same size with consistent lettering. You may hand-letter the information on your poster boards with markers or use press-on letters for a more professional appearance. You will need an easel to display poster boards.

Flip Charts.   Flip charts range in size from small tabletop versions to 30" × 40". The most common are large tablets of paper placed on an easel in front of an audience. In meetings, flip charts can be used to keep up with ideas or information that is generated. They add color, movement, and interest to a training program if you prepare them in advance. To create a professional-looking flip chart, use dark colors and wide magic markers. If you use watercolor markers, the lettering will not bleed through as you move from page to page. If you use permanent markers, make sure to leave one or two blank pages between each chart as you prepare them. Again, you will need an easel to display your flip chart.

Transparencies.   Transparencies enlarge printed information or images on a clear or lightly tinted sheet of acetate. Transparencies are usually prepared in advance of your presentation, and are inexpensive and easy to produce. You can make professional-looking transparencies by avoiding brightly colored acetates, using dark lettering, and reproducing the information on a color printer. However, as Holcombe and Stein (1996), authors of *Presentations for Decision Makers,* warn, you should reserve bright colors or lettering for items you want to highlight or emphasize. In short, never use color simply for the sake of using color.

To keep the transparencies from sticking to one another or from sliding off the projector, use ready-made cardboard frames. (You can find them at your nearest office supply store). Frames allow you to block out extra light and to make notes inconspicuously on the frames themselves. You will need an overhead projector to display transparencies.

Videotapes and Laser Discs.   Videotapes and laser discs can enhance your presentation, but they both require special equipment. For maximum impact, Robert Pike, author of the *Creative Training Techniques Handbook,* recommends that you use a television monitor that has "one diagonal inch of viewing screen for each participant" (1994, p. 44). In other words, if you are speaking to 20 participants, a 20-inch monitor will be sufficient. However, for audiences of 75 or more, Pike recommends that you use a video projector.

Another item to include on your checklist if you use a videotape or laser disc is to cue up your tape or disc before the presentation. It is important to use only those portions of the videotape or laser disc that are pertinent to your topic. You may find that you need to edit your videotape in order to make your presentation more effective.

Remember to conduct an audio check immediately before your presentation to ensure that your sound levels are appropriate. As a final note, make sure you know how to use all equipment prior to your presentation. The "Practice! Practice! Practice!" rule especially holds when you advance to presentations with a multimedia component.

Computer-Generated Graphics.   If you have access to a computer and one of the latest presentation software packages (e.g., PowerPoint), you can create professional-looking **computer-generated graphics** such as charts, graphs, diagrams, and maps. Additionally, with software programs like PC Storyboard, you can display your visuals in a sequence, and create video-like transitions using wipes, fades, and dissolves. With additional equipment you can turn your graphics into 35mm slides, handouts, and transparencies of visuals (Pike, 1994, p. 47).

In short, the world of professional presentations is virtually at your fingertips, with the help of a computer and adherence to the following seven basic rules of graphic design: Make sure each visual is clear, readable, relevant, interesting, simple, accurate, and communicates a single idea (Pike, p. 54). Once it's time to present your computer-generated visuals, you will need a computer, preferably a laptop, and a television monitor or overhead projector.

Multimedia.   Multimedia involves the use of several different types of audiovisual equipment simultaneously. More specifically, **multimedia** is the combination of text, high-quality graphics, audio, animation, photographic images, and video into a single interactive presentation that is driven by computer technology. For instance, a multimedia presentation may be as simple as displaying color graphics on a television monitor with accompanying sound, or using multiple television monitors, each projecting its own unique images.

As with computer-generated graphics, remember the seven rules of graphic design when creating a multimedia presentation. Further, make sure your equipment is suitable for the size of your audience.

Basic Rules for Creating Effective Visuals

Just as a builder needs a blueprint for building a house, a presenter also needs some ground rules for constructing effective visuals. The following rules will help you create impressive visuals no matter what medium or media you choose.

- Always practice the KIS-C rule (Keep It Simple and Clear).
- Make sure your visuals are large enough for everyone to see. Use at least a 24-point font size when you are creating text on transparencies. Also, use upper- and lower-case letters rather than "all caps." On poster boards and flip charts, letters should be at least 3" in height if the room in which you are presenting is the standard classroom size (i.e., holds 25 to 30 people comfortably). To hold audience interest in long meetings or training programs, we also suggest that you use alternating colored markers as you move from line to line on posters and flip charts.
- Ensure that all visuals are professional and consistent in appearance.
- Select visuals that are well suited for your subject, audience, occasion, and environment.
- Use color whenever possible.

Strategies for Using Visuals

Grice and Skinner (1993, p. 276) offer some excellent tips for using visuals before and during your presentation.

BEFORE:

- Practice using your visuals as you rehearse your presentation. Remember, practice makes perfect.
- Arrive early to set up your visuals.
- Carry back-up supplies with you. For example, if you will be using an overhead projector, make sure you have an extra light bulb and extension cord with you in case you need them.
- Ensure easy viewing by all audience members.
- Arrange for safe transportation of your visuals. Never store visuals in the baggage compartment of a plane. (Murphy's law says they will go to the Bahamas even though you are going to Atlanta.)

DURING:

- Reveal visuals only when you are ready.
- Stand close to your visual when referring to it.
- Refrain from talking *to* your visual during your presentation.

- Conceal your visual after you have made your point.
- Use the hand closest to your visual to point.
- Never stand between your visual and your audience.
- Use handouts with caution. If you must use them, we recommend that you wait to distribute them until after your presentation.

Visuals that are prepared well in advance and are introduced at the appropriate time will greatly enhance your presentation. When you use electronic equipment, make sure you give yourself plenty of set-up time. Carry back-up visuals if you are using electronic equipment in case of equipment failure. If you are using computer-generated graphics, make sure the equipment is working and that the outlets in the room where you present are wired for such presentations.

To illustrate, Mark was giving a computer-generated presentation using the Internet. The day he presented the information in class, he found out the room was not wired correctly and he could not use the Internet. Luckily, Mark had paper copies of his presentation as back-up, so he handed them out to class members and conducted his presentation from his handout.

Professional visuals can create a lasting impression and make a positive impact on your audience, if used appropriately. Effective use of visuals requires planning, preparation, and practice.

Knowledge Check

Key Concepts and Terms

visual	flip charts	computer-generated graphics
objects	transparencies	multimedia
poster boards		

References

Grice, G. L., & Skinner, J. F. (1993). *Mastering public speaking.* Englewood Cliffs, NJ: Prentice-Hall.

Holcombe, M. W., & Stein, J. K. (1996). *Presentations for decision makers,* 3rd ed. New York: Van Nostrand Reinhold.

Pike, R. W. (1994). *Creative training techniques handbook,* 2nd ed. Minneapolis: Lakewood Books.

Case Study Solutions

Chapter 1   *Merger of Network USA and A+ Communications*

How the Case Was Actually Handled

Management groups from both companies were challenged to work together. They began by creating massive "to-do" lists and a common dialogue. A team composed of eight employees from each company was formed to smooth the transition process, quell rumors, answer questions, and make recommendations on combined company policies. Additionally, the transition team published an informative monthly newsletter that contained answers to employee questions (where possible), information regarding each company, and progress that was being made in reorganizing departments. Two toll-free numbers were installed—one for employees to leave questions on, and one through which answers were provided.

Finally, the newly formed upper management encouraged sales leaders and department managers to make decisions quickly and intelligently. Going into the last quarter before the merger, A+Network, Inc., needed to be more successful than ever.

David Sims
Network USA
Pensacola, Florida

Chapter 2   *Listening in a Chemical Plant: Career Management in the New Team Environment*

How the Case Was Actually Handled

The consultant held six coaching sessions with the engineer over a three-month period. At the second session, she asked him to begin observing successful peers and comparing his behavior and appearance to theirs. She videotaped the third session. By the fourth session, the engineer was clearly aware of communication behaviors that contributed to his being "misunderstood" and was ready to make behavior changes. With the exception of minor changes in appearance (getting a good haircut), these changes involved developing active listening habits.

The consultant first advised the engineer to practice looking like a good listener, that is, to improve his attending behaviors: maintain eye contact, develop a neutral tone of voice and facial expression, observe others' personal space, and adopt a listening posture—open body position with a slight forward lean.

Next, the consultant pointed out that whatever a speaker is saying is true for him or her at that moment. As a consequence, those who immediately disagree are perceived as negative, hostile, or "not listening." Obviously, anyone who really listened would understand. Anyone who really understood would agree! Since people at the plant generally had difficulty dealing with conflict, those who opposed projects and practices were thought of as difficult, "poor listeners."

The engineer then understood the effect of constantly focusing on obstacles to plant operations in an effort to do his job protecting the environment. He agreed to work on enhancing his response behaviors: to practice withholding judgment until he heard and understood all issues, to point out areas of agreement with speakers, and to offer solutions instead of harping on problems. He also began to prioritize his environmental concerns and to choose his battles carefully so that his coworkers would begin to perceive him as helpful instead of as a roadblock.

Finally, the two discussed listening preferences. The engineer conceded that his dominant preference was content-oriented, and that he exhibited many of the negative traits of the content-oriented preference. He was determined to practice being flexible in listening, especially to avoid overwhelming others with intimidating questions.

By the sixth session, the engineer was moved to a new position with expanded responsibilities. He felt that his career was back on track and that the coaching had indeed helped him become an active listener and be "better understood."

Patrice Johnson
Spectra, Inc.
New Orleans, LA

Chapter 3   *Coaching and Counseling Employees at Marriott International*

How the Case Was Actually Handled

In order to remedy the situation immediately, a two-step process was put into place. First, Donna conducted one-on-one meetings with each staff member who voiced a concern. Since Walter is the overall manager and is knowledgeable about the situation, he attended the meetings as an observer. Second, Donna called a work group meeting. The purpose of the meeting was threefold: (1) to cover topics discussed in the one-on-one meetings, (2) to explain the rationale for the intended changes, and (3) to allow group members to offer feedback.

It was important for Donna to convey to each staff member that change is difficult for everyone and that even though it takes time to adjust to new ways of doing things, progress is being made. Also, Donna reemphasized the expectations she had for each employee and discussed ways in which she could help her staff members reach those expectations. Donna also informed her employees that more time was needed to fully implement the changes. After the changes were properly tested and evaluated, Donna let the staff know that additional changes needed to be made. She also reassured staff members that they would be included in future problem identification and resolutions.

Steve Siler
Marriott Corporation
Washington, D.C.

Chapter 4   *Teambuilding in Turbulent Times*

How the Case Was Actually Handled

The CIO realized that the absence of new goals, clear ways to contribute to those goals, and tools to successfully stay on target were creating anxiety and fear at the workplace. He also realized that there were no easy answers to those concerns because of the pace and direction of change.

As a result, the CIO worked with a local organizational development consulting firm to design a flexible, high-participation and high-involvement intervention strategy. He felt the key was to help people feel more a part of the changes they were experiencing and to shape outcomes based less on fear and more on information and courage. The last quarter of 1994, specially trained internal facilitators met with small groups of employees to listen to their concerns. These concerns were communicated back to the CIO, and he acknowledged their significance in an employee-wide meeting shortly after the information was synthesized and reviewed. He then set up five 8-person teams to deal with the most pertinent and emotional of the issues. These included many areas of focus traditionally reserved for senior managers such as management behaviors, communication, training and education, rewards and recognition, and staffing and workflow. Over a period of eight months, the leaders, members, and sponsors (senior-level managers) of these teams were trained in the team concept and coached in how to deploy problem-clarification and problem-solving processes. They learned how to identify a meaningful team charge, communicate with each other about roles needed within the team and who would play which roles, and mechanisms to get work done while also performing the "back-home job." Most importantly, all those involved looked ahead to the future. They made decisions as teams about how they could work—as individuals, as a work group, as a true team, and with other teams—to model those new behaviors. They also used a team-effectiveness tool to measure their results as they learned how to operate more as a flexible set of diverse individuals than a collection of rigid individuals. Each team member reached out to the rest of his or her organization to better understand root causes of beliefs and assumptions and to explore alternatives to the past. Eventually, all teams presented their findings, including recommendations, to management and peers. Implementation teams were formed and recommendations were built into ongoing business plans. Currently, intact work groups seeded by experienced members of the special teams (called bridge teams) are being trained and developed to take responsibility for outcomes and be part of the leadership they seek.

The organization recently reported that it weathered a new acquisition with much less stress, fewer transition dollars, and many more helpful ideas than could have been expected two years ago. The "bridge" concept is now being explored as a viable option for building true teams throughout the rest of the business.

Debra Jacobs
Jacobs Consulting Group, Inc.
Charlotte, North Carolina

Chapter 5   *Managing Diversity*

How the Case Was Actually Handled

In order to address the issue of interdepartmental diversity, the public service director created a game called "Believe It Or Not." The premise of the game was to create the most horrible day in the life of a newspaper. Role-playing was the primary teaching method used. Participants were placed in roles that were directly opposite their own. For example, the publisher reversed roles with a news reporter, the executive editor with the marketing director, and so forth. Participants were given a synopsis of the day featuring the major problems arising in each department, along with decisions that needed to be made. Solutions to problems were required to be realistic. The game concluded with a mock operational committee meeting, during which leaders reported their solutions to the assigned publisher.

The group enjoyed the activity. They expressed satisfaction with the role-reversal exercise and a new understanding of the challenges their counterparts faced in their respective departments.

Sheila Reed
Pensacola News Journal
Pensacola, Florida

Chapter 6   *Tackling Corporate America as a Recent College Graduate*

How the Case Was Actually Handled

1. Realizing that I would be competing with many students for an internship with a record company, I designed a record jacket with a photo of myself on the cover. The back of the jacket cover listed highlights of my background, fashioned to look like song titles. After the cellophane that surrounded the record jacket was unwrapped, my resume was neatly tucked inside. To add interest, the typeface on the jacket cover matched my resume. Needless to say, the interviewers were impressed.

2. Be prepared! First of all, review your background qualifications for the potential interview. What do you have to offer a prospective employer? Why should this firm choose to hire you over someone else? Second, research the companies in which you are interested. Let them know what you know about the organization and why you are interested in their company. Third, when you arrive for the interview, make sure you are dressed appropriately. If they should offer you the job immediately, your appearance gives the interviewer the impression that you "fit in" with the image of the company.

3. In most cases, as a result of your internship, your supervisor will have given you a written evaluation about your progress during your internship. Perhaps your supervisor has even mentioned that, if a position was available within the department, he or she would hire you. At this time, it is appropriate to ask your supervisor for a letter of recommendation for future reference. Your supervisor may know of an upcoming job opening within the company and may forward your resume to the appropriate person.

> Melissa Crooke
> Sony Music Entertainment, Inc.
> New York, New York

Chapter 7   *Leadership and the Management of Strategic Change at Shell Internationale Petroleum Maatschappij B.V. (Holland)*

How the Case Was Actually Handled

In order to overcome barriers, purchasing employed a new plan. The key elements were:

- A specific cost improvement target was recommended to senior corporate management. The size of the target was challenging, but obtainable, and was consistent with improvement demonstrated by outside companies.

- Corporate management endorsed the target, and communicated it down the hierarchy to managing directors of the operating companies. In turn, directors were asked to build the target into their business plans, or justify reasons for not doing so.

- Purchasing offered their services to operating companies in analyzing expenditure patterns, identifying specific improvement opportunities, and facilitating cross-functional teamwork. However, ownership of the improvement target remained firmly with the operating companies.

The new tactic triggered renewed support for the purchasing strategy. It fit well within a corporate culture that was "top down" driven and "target oriented." Purchasing became a facilitator, and not the owner, of the strategy.

> John R. Lickvar
> Shell Internationale Petroleum
> The Hague, Netherlands

Chapter 8   *How to Reduce Stress in a New Job*

How the Case Was Actually Handled

1. To reduce stress, Theressa knew she had to manage her time well. She got to work early to plan out her day and week before the telephone started ringing and faxes started coming in. Additionally, she stayed late to work on projects, to finish anything that was left undone during normal business hours, and to write down any unfinished business that needed immediate attention the next day. Since Theressa knew that physical activity also reduces stress, she brought her athletic shoes to work and went for a 30-minute walk every day during lunch. Doing so allowed Theressa to think more clearly, especially on high-stress days.

2. As a new employee, Theressa consulted with her manager before making any business decisions. Even though she felt capable of prioritizing tasks and meetings based on her job description, she knew her manager had her own agenda about what was most important. To reduce the chances for unnecessary stress and conflict, Theressa knew that communication was the key. She provided her manager with present and future weekly calendars, her work schedule, upcoming projects, and any potential conflicts with future agendas.

3. This was obviously a stressful situation since Theressa knew she would be judged on her knowledge of the subject, her presentation skills, and how thoroughly she addressed the subject matter. To reduce stress, she began by communicating the vice president's request to her manager, who then gave her extra time to prepare for the upcoming presentation. Theressa then contacted the vice president to determine the purpose of the presentation, the intended audience, where the presentation would be held, and the approximate length of time that she would speak. Once she learned the answers to these questions, Theressa's stress level was reduced because she knew exactly what was expected of her.

> Jim Knasel
> AT&T
> Chicago, Illinois

Chapter 9   *"Snow White and the Seven Dwarves" Go to Dinner*

How the Case Was Actually Handled

1. Your Italian hosts went to great lengths to make sure your meal was prepared to perfection. Even if you could not eat all of the meal, you at least should taste several bites of food to let them know how much you appreciate their kindness.

2. Two of the group members did not drink at all due to religious beliefs. Their hosts acknowledged their beliefs, and understood the situation completely. Another way to handle the situation would be to take a couple of sips of wine and graciously decline after you feel you have had enough to drink. Most Europeans take great pride in the selection of wine offered during a meal.

If you don't care to drink, say so without hesitation, but also without judgment for those who do wish to drink. Realize that wine is the foundation of celebration in many cultures and, as such, is offered as a sign of great respect. The better the wine, the higher the level of respect. Realize, accept, and appreciate the honor, even if you don't accept or appreciate the wine.

3. One of the ways you can handle this situation is by engaging in a discussion with your host about the type of food, what region of the country it is from, and how it is prepared. Doing so will show interest in the food and give you an idea about the taste before you put it in your mouth. If you find you don't care for the food, wash it down with liquid and then go on to the next course.

Jan Flynn, Ph.D.
Auburn University
Auburn, Alabama

Chapter 10   *The Mind is a Terrible Thing to Lose: Overcoming Communication Apprehension*

How the Case Was Actually Handled

Deborah's first mistake was breaking the first law of public speaking: Practice! Practice! Practice! The only thing that saved her during the oral presentation was that she had taken the time to read through the paper one more time the night before, and to underline in red the most important passages. In fact, Deborah was so apprehensive by the time it was her turn to present, she didn't even recognize the words that were written on the page. She simply read verbatim every sentence that was underscored in red.

After making a mad dash for the door and running to her room in tears after the session, Deborah remembered all the advice she had given to her public speaking students that very term. She should have practiced her presentation numerous times until she was comfortable giving it. While the other panelists were taking their turns, she should have used the time wisely to compose herself. She should have breathed slowly and deeply to help reduce the physical symptoms of her apprehension. She also should have used the time to visualize herself being successful, and should have avoided the debilitating effects of negative self-statements (e.g., "I can't believe my adviser said nobody would be here." "I'm going to bomb!" "My career in the communication field is over and I haven't even graduated yet!")

To this day, Deborah avoids the pitfalls of too much self-confidence, and practices every major presentation she gives at least three to five times, start-to-finish. When she speaks before audiences that are exceptionally large (to date, her largest is 900), she has been known to practice her message 25 or 30 times. (She has even been known to rehearse during early morning runs and while brushing her teeth!)

Additionally, Deborah always arrives early to the room in which she is presenting, makes sure her A/V equipment is working and her visuals are ready to go, and runs through her introduction (or speech in entirety if the message is short) in front of an imaginary audience. She also takes time to mentally compose herself moments before each presentation and avoids negative self-statements if she feels them coming on.

Indeed, Deborah learned that communication apprehension can be your best friend or greatest enemy. The adrenalin rush that goes with it can serve to debilitate or energize you as a speaker, depending on how you focus your mind and physical energy!

Deborah A. Gaut
Gaut & Associates
Pensacola, Florida

Chapter 11 *Public Speaking Challenges for Persons with Disabilities*

How the Case Was Actually Handled

1. Most able-bodied individuals have difficulty in determining how to broach the subject of special needs to someone with a disability. Physical disabilities should not be any more difficult to discuss than any other need that a potential speaker might recognize. When you, as the arrangement committee representative, contact a potential speaker who uses a wheelchair and you begin the process of negotiating a contract, openly request what special provisions or arrangements the speaker will need. Public speakers who have disabilities are aware of their situations and will usually approach the subject if you don't. After determining the speaker's needs, imagine that you are the speaker and visit (or revisit) the site where the speaker will be presenting his or her program. Check to make sure that the facility is accessible via wheelchair. Accessibility should be not only at the doors into the building and into the room, but also to and from the parking lot, bathroom facilities, dining areas, and other pertinent locations. Check the hotel accommodations if the speaker is staying over.

   Also make sure to check with the speaker about type, height, and location of visual aids and room layout preferences. If you or your committee is not providing the visual aids, negotiate with A/V suppliers to insure that aids can be made to accommodate the speaker's needs.

   When you contact the speaker about the program and special needs, offer to arrange to meet the speaker upon his or her arrival and to provide transportation to and from the airport if needed. Make sure to find out if the speaker has any transportation needs. The severity of the speaker's physical disability often will determine the extent of any special needs that he or she may have. Most speakers with physical disabilities will gladly provide the information you need to make the program a pleasant and successful occasion.

2. The first line of attack that those of us who use wheelchairs can use to establish control, power, and credibility is to stop thinking that we need to establish these types of credentials any differently than anyone else. We have to get past our own prejudicial ideas that others are going to perceive us as having a physical disability, and concentrate on the importance of our abilities.

   When you accept a speaking assignment, you need to make sure that you arrive at the location early, not only to scout out the facilities but to get ready to greet participants or guests at the door. We do not want to make the mistake of missing the one chance we have to make a good first impression. Greet listeners as you would a close friend by being open, friendly, and approachable. When you are ready to begin and are being introduced, or while introducing yourself, it is often helpful to establish control, power, and credibility by providing the audience with a brief summary of your experience and credentials. The ability to stage a commanding public presence is not an inherent ability, but rather a learned and practiced attribute garnered by those who have spent the time to develop it. The big difference is that it is easier for a tall, attractive, athletic, well-dressed person to develop this ability that it is for an overweight, average-looking, rumpled person with a disability requiring a wheelchair for mobility.

Regardless of who a speaker might be, he or she has to develop a relationship with the audience by bringing himself or herself to a peer level with that audience. This is where the speaker who uses a wheelchair has the advantage. We can often be literally at the same level as those seated in the audience. It is easier to establish a friendly, open, and approachable relationship when you are at an eye-to-eye level with those around you. However, you need to ensure that you are visually within reach of the entire audience. Just like all successful public speakers, we have to practice both our verbal and nonverbal skills.

3. Like an ostrich that hides by sticking its head in the sand, we often fail to recognize that there are many psychological barriers that exist between those with physical disabilities and the so called "able-bodied" members of our society. Teachers have ascendancy over students in school due purely to the fact that, by standing, they establish a physical height authority over those students. It is easier to rule from on high than it is from the bottom of a trench.

Another barrier is the tendency of all of us to have guilt feelings about those who we feel are less fortunate than us. Those feelings of guilt are often characterized by the belief that we have to make special allowances for the less fortunate. Special allowances may take the form of being overly sensitive and attentive to physical needs. We also have a tendency to expect less from those with physical disabilities. Individuals with disabilities can help break down these psychological barriers by recognizing their existence and attacking the barriers head on.

You can overcome the need of others to expect less from you by letting them know how much you are going to expect of them. You can reduce or eliminate guilt feelings by being explicit about what assistance you will accept and what you reserve for yourself. By asking participants to help rearrange a room layout, you can lessen those unspoken guilt feelings. This is nothing more than what an able-bodied speaker might ask. Politely refusing to take cuts in a lunch line or to let someone else carry your lunch tray lets others know that you do not need special treatment for situations within your control and ability.

We help others "make the wheelchair disappear" when we, as users, stop seeing it as a mental crutch and start thinking of it as an alternative choice of mobility available to the lucky few who still have alternatives.

Henry J. Hanson, SR/WA
Hanson & Associates
Tucson, Arizona

Chapter 12

Using Communication Technology to Enhance Productivity at Hewlett-Packard

How the Case Was Actually Handled

Hewlett-Packard responded to their sales representatives' needs in the following ways.

1. Satellite stations were installed at most sales offices to allow sales reps to receive corporate television broadcasts (BTV). System Response Units (SRUs) are placed in front of each participant, which allows real-time, immediate feedback to presenters and other BTV participants. The SRUs measure 8" by 8" and have five buttons (A,B,C,D and speaker). Presenters can ask true/false or multiple-choice questions. The feedback data are immediately represented on the video screen in a graphical question. If a sales rep wishes to ask a question, he or she simply presses the speaker button and, when prompted by the presenter, speaks into the built-in microphone.

2. All sales reps were equipped with personal computers, printers, and networking hook-ups to link with corporate data bases. A simple graphic interface was used to give the sales team the ability to quickly order, fax, print literature, access competitive information, and display cutting-edge visual presentations.

Dan Knasel
Hewlett-Packard
Grand Rapids, Michigan

Index

Aaron, C., 135, 137
Aburdene, P., 138, 288
Accommodation, 210
Achievement, 186
A+ Communications, 26–27
Action, 282
Action-oriented listeners, 46
Adams, H., 309
Adams, J., 36
AEIOU Method, 212
Agendas, meeting, 107–108, 109, 112
AIDA principle, 151–153
Alexander, J. W., 189
Allbritton, M. M., 311, 313, 314
American Association of School Administrators, 308
Americans with Disabilities Act (ADA) of 1993, 135–136, 137–138
AmeriCares, 312
Amiable style, 67
Analytical style, 67
Andersen Consulting, 315
Anderson, R., 64
Anderson, S., 79
Andrews, L. V., 182
Androgyny, 181
Angelou, M., 130, 180
Answering machines, 236–238
Anti-climatic pattern, 281
Appeals, 285
Appeals to credibility, 285
Appearance, 222
Appointments, 231, 232–233
Ardrey, R., 207
Armstrong, H., 311
Assessing, 38
Atheneum Learning Corporation, 274
AT&T, 213–214, 306, 325
Attending, 36–37
Attention, 42, 282
Attention-getting devices, 290
Autocratic leadership style, 176, 178–179

Avoidance, 210
Awarding others for achievements, 249

Bailey, J., 112
Bailey, R., 143
Baldridge, L., 217–218
Bamford, J., 162
Barge, J. K., 176
Baridon, A. P., 219
Barker, L. L., 34, 37, 44–45, 46–47, 262, 295–296
Barry, D., 121
Baskerville, D. M., 273–274
Bate, B., 126
Baterman, D. N., 249
Bell, M., 323–324
Ben & Jerry's Homemade, 9–10, 74, 96–97
Bennis, W., 173, 175, 183–184
Berger, M., 318, 319
Berko, R., 164
Birth order, 179–180
Blanchard, K., 211–212
Blohowiak, D., 188
Body language, 135, 224, 236, 316
Body position, 42
The Body Shop, 7–8
Bolton, D. G., 67
Bolton, R., 67
Borisoff, D., 44
Bostrom, R., 34
Boundaries, 7–10, 326
Boyett, J. E., 4, 5, 7
Boyett, J. H., 4, 5, 7, 308
Braiker, H., 77
Brainstorming, 102–103, 274–277
Breakpoint, 100
Bredin, A., 317, 322, 324, 325
Bridges, C., 220
Broadcast fax, 312–313
Brody, M., 219, 223, 224, 227–230, 235, 236, 238, 249, 283
Brotherton, P., 165
Brown, M., 274–275
Brown, P., 220
Brownell, J., 35, 36, 163, 254

Bunker, B. A., 128
Burke, J. E., 18
Bush, G., 252
Business Research Group, 318
Business television (BTV), 320–322

Campbell, J. K., 183
Carlson, J., 8
Carr, C., 183
Carr, J., 318–319
Carrell, L. J., 295
Carter, J., 180, 199
Carty, M., 96
Caudron, S., 74, 75
Cause-effect pattern, 280
Cellular/portable phones, 238
Certainty, 71
Cetron, M., 308, 330
Channel, 22, 327
Chase Manhattan Bank, 132–133
Chiat, J., 322–323
Chiat/Day, 322–323
Chronological pattern, 277–278
Chronological (paper) resume, 149–150, 151
Chuang-tzu, 259
Chung, R. K., 64
Climactic pattern, 281
Clinton, B., 77, 199, 252
Closed communication, 69
Closed-ended mindmapping, 274–277
Coaching interviews, 164–165
Coakley, C. G., 34, 36, 49
Cochlea, 35
Coercive power, 182
Cohen, B., 9
Colby, L., 164
Collaboration, 210
Committees, 95
Communication apprehension, 264–268
causes of, 264–266
managing, 266–268
Communication climate, 68–71

Communication competence, 21, 308–309
Communication process, 20–25
Communication styles, 66–68
Communication technologies, 310–322
business television (BTV), 320–322
e-mail, 239–240, 256, 313–315
fax (facsimile), 239, 311–313
groupware, 315–316, 317, 319
Internet, 316–318
intranets, 318–319
teleconferencing, 311
telephone, 219, 236–238, 254–255, 311
videoconferencing, 319–322
virtual office and company, 64–66, 303, 322–326
Comparison, 288–289
Competition, 209
Complex cyclic path, 99–100
Compromise, 103, 106, 210
Computer(s)
as audience analysis tools, 256–258
electronic resumes and, 149
e-mail, 239–240, 256, 313–315
visuals generated by, 336
See also Communication technologies
Computer-generated graphics, 336
Conclusions, 292
Conflict, 205–213, 219
benefits of, 213
causes of, 206–208
defined, 205
management of, 209–213
symptoms of, 208–209
Conlin, J., 8
Consensus, 103

Content-oriented listeners, 46
Context, 24–25
Contrast, 288–289
Control, 314
Control orientation, 70
Conversations, 60–61, 222–224, 231–232, 234
Cooper, R. C., 323–324
Corporate culture, 9
Corporate Performance Center, 187–188
Corporate vision, 7–10, 189–190
Counseling interviews, 164–165
Cover letters, 150–153
Covert goals, 260
Covey, S., 199, 203–204, 209, 212–213
Cray Research, 305–306
Crichton, M., 78
Crooke, M., 166–167
Cross-functional teams, 96–97
Curley, T., 308

Daily, B., 124–125
Daley, R. J., 217
Day, C., 43
Deal, T., 9, 17
DeBats, D., 74
Decision-making, group, 99–100
Decoding, 21
Defensive communication, 69
Definitions, 288
Democratic leadership style, 176, 179
Demographic analysis, 251–252
Demographic variables
  and audience analysis, 251–252
  diversity and, 129–130
  groups and, 97–99
Departments, 95
Description, 69–70
Dewey, J., 101
DiGaetani, J. L., 51
Disabled coworkers, 135–137, 297–298
Disbie, P., 218
Diversity, 118–139
  barriers to, 131–132
  coworkers with disabilities and, 135–137, 297–298
  defined, 130
  demographic variables and, 129–130

future of, 137–138
gender and, 121–129
implementing diversity programs, 132–135
implications of workforce, 130
language of sensitivity and, 137
Dortch, R. N., 220
Downward communication, 62
Dress, 222
Driving style, 66–67
Dubrin, A., 72
Dulek, R. E., 48
Dun & Bradstreet Corporation, 323–324
Dwyer, E. J., 250

Eastman Kodak Company, 74, 119–120
Effect of message, 23
Ehninger, D., 282
Einhorn, L. J., 250–251
Eisenhower, D. D., 158
Electronic resumes, 149
Elevators, 230
Ellis, D. G., 100, 177
E-mail (electronic mail), 313–315
  in audience analysis, 256
  etiquette for using, 239–240
Emotional appeals, 285
Empathy, 70–71
Employment applications, 154
Employment interviews, 19–20, 153–162
  group, 160–162
  interviewee preparation, 156–160
  interviewer preparation, 153–156
Empowered organizations, 183–184
Empowerment, 183–184
Encoding, 21
Ensman, R. G., 239–240
Entrances, 229–230
Environment, of presentation, 253–254
Equality, 71
Error, 22
Escalators, 230
Ethics, 293–294
Etiquette, 216–242
  appointments, 231, 232–233
  blunders and, 219, 229
  body language and, 224

conversations, 60–61, 222–224, 231–232, 234
e-mail, 239–240
entrances, 229–230
Etiquette IQ Test, 220
exits, 229–230
fax (facsimile), 239
first impressions and, 221–224, 225
good-byes, 225–226
greetings, 219, 225–226
handshake, 225–226, 229, 234–235
importance of, 218–221
introductions, 226–228, 234–235, 249, 290–291
names, 228, 229
podium, 234–236
receiving guests, 233–234
shared office equipment, 232
telephone, 219, 236–238
titles, 228
work space, 231–232
Evaluation, 69–70
Examples, 287
Exchange of roles, 313
Exit interviews, 165–166
Exits, 229–230
Expectations, 203–204
Expert power, 182
Expert testimony, 288
Explanations, 288
Expressive style, 67
Extemporaneous speaking, 263
Eye contact, 42, 131, 162
Eyler, D. R., 219

Faltemeir, S., 105
Fast, J., 222
Fax (facsimile) communications, 239, 311–313
Fax-on-demand (FOD), 312
Fayol, H., 13
Federal Express, 171–172
Feedback, 22
Ferraro, G., 309
Fidgeting, 42
Field, A., 315
Fielden, J. S., 48
Field of experience, 21
Figurative comparison, 289
Finch, M., 124–125
First impressions, 221–224, 225
Fisher, A., 78
Fisher, B. A., 100, 177
Fisher, D., 93, 94
Flaming, 240, 315
Flanagan, P., 320–322
Flextime, 133

Flip charts, 335
Floor hoggers, 92–93
Flynn, G., 136–137
Flynn, J., 240–241
Formal communication, 62–63
Formal groups, 94, 95–97
Fosdick, H. E., 310
Fox, J., 236, 238
Freeman-Evans, T., 130
French, J. R., 182
Friedan, B., 59
Friendliness, 82–83
Fulton, K., 313
Functional resume, 150, 152

Galagen, P. A., 119
Gannett Company, Inc., 138
Gates, B., 9, 313, 329
Gaut, D. A., 6, 11, 13, 37, 268–269, 313
Gelman Sciences, 312
Gender issues, 121–129
  feminine communication style, 122–123, 126
  leadership style and, 181
  listening and, 44
  masculine communication style, 122–123, 126
  nonsexist/inclusive language, 123–129
  sexual discrimination, 79
  sexual harassment, 77–80
Gender roles, 121
Gendron, G., 187
Gershenfeld, M., 99
Gibb, J. R., 69, 70, 71
Globalization, 306–307
Goette, M., 218
Golen, S., 43
Goodall, Jr., H. L., 144, 157
Good-byes, 225–226
Gorman, B., 155
Gossip, 232
Graham, J. R., 312
Gray, Jr., J., 234, 275, 283
Green, F. B., 97
Green, K. D., 188
Greenfield, J., 9
Greengard, S., 323
Greeting, 219, 225–226
Griaze, L., 239–240
Grice, G. L., 256, 258, 287–288, 289, 337–338
Griffith, H. W., 199
Gronbeck, B. E., 282
Group employment interviews, 160–162
Groups, 88–104
  advantages of, 90–92

decision-making by, 99–100
defined, 90
demographic variables affecting, 97–99
disadvantages of, 92–94
formal, 94, 95–97
informal, 94–95, 97
meetings and, 107–112
problem solving and, 92, 96, 100–101
teams, 90, 96–97, 104–107
See also Teams
Group structural characteristics, 99
Group task characteristics, 99
Groupthink, 93–94
Groupware, 315–316, 317, 319
Grove, A., 16
Growney, B., 329
Guests, receiving, 233–234
Gutner, T., 33

Hackman, M. Z., 174, 177, 179
Hales, D., 200
Hales, R., 200
Handshakes, 225–226, 229, 234–235
Handy, C., 206–208
Hanson, H. L., 297–298
Hauser, M. F., 36
Hearing, 35–36
Helfgott, D., 81
Herman Miller, Inc., 183
Hershey Foods, 8
Hewlett-Packard, 330–331
Hidden agendas, 70
Hill, A., 77–78
Hilliard-Jones, A., 130, 132–133
Hitt, W. D., 185, 189
Hoffman, D. E., 315
Holcombe, M. W., 335–336
Holmes, Jr., O. W., 25
Home offices, 325–326
Horizontal communication, 63
Horizontal organization, 64–66
Hostile work environment, 79
Hoteling, 324
Hot spots, 203–204, 209
Hudson, V. C., 218
Human behavior approach, 8, 15–17
Humor, 73–76, 267, 290
Hurson, K., 96, 105

Ideology, 207
Image goals, 262, 295–297
Impatience, 40, 41–42, 46–47
Impromptu presentations, 262–263
Inclusive language, 123–129
Informal communication, 63–64
Informal groups, 94–95, 97
Informational interviews, 162–163
Information overload, 41
Ingram, R., 129, 137–138
Inherent risk, 48–49
Inspirational presentations, 250
Integrated approach, 8–9, 17–18
Intel, 15–16
International Business Machines, 129–130
Internet, 316–318
Interpersonal communication, 58–85
communication climate, 68–71
communication styles, 66–68
conversations in, 60–61, 222–224, 231–232, 234
defining, 60–61
formal, 62–63
friendliness and, 82–83
horizontal organization, 64–66
humor in, 73–76
informal, 63–64
mentoring and, 81–82
networking and, 80–81
office politics and, 71–73
romantic relationships and, 76–77
sexual harassment and, 77–80
vertical approach, 64–66
Interpretation, 38
Interruptions, 40, 125–127
Interviewing, 153–166
in audience analysis, 255–256
coaching or counseling interviews, 164–165
defined, 144
employment interviews and, 19–20, 153–162
exit interviews, 165–166
informational interviews, 162–163
performance appraisal interviews, 163–164
Intrafunctional teams, 96

Intranets, 318–319
Intrapersonal noise, 23
Introductions
personal, 226–228
presentation, 234–235, 249, 290–291
Introspection, 201, 209

Jacobs, D., 113–114
Janis, I. L., 93
Job-sharing, 133
Johnson, C. E., 174, 177, 179
Johnson, M., 182
Johnson, N. B., 317
Johnson, P. M., 54–55
Johnson & Johnson, 17–18
Jokes, 75–76, 267, 290
Jones, J. L., 249
Jones, P., 9, 77, 252
Jonson, B., 252
Jordan, M., 182
Jorgensen, B., 133

Kahaner, L., 9
Kahn, R., 17
Kane, B., 262
Katz, D., 17
Katzenbach, J. R., 104
Kauffman, M., 239, 311–312
Keffeler, J. B., 63
Kelley, C. A., 218
Kennedy, A., 9, 17
Kennedy, G., 148, 150
Kennedy, J. F., 217
Kennedy, J. L., 149
Kettering, C., 330
King, S., 289
Knapp, M. L., 23
Knasel, D., 330–331
Knasel, J., 213
Kotter, J. P., 174
Kouzes, J. M., 173
Kreps, G., 213

Laissez-faire leadership style, 176–177, 179
Land's End, 63–64
Larson, C. E., 101
Laser discs, 336
Leadership, 170–193
defined, 173
developing competencies in, 184–190
effective, 174–176
future and, 190
management versus, 173–174
and power, 182–184
styles of, 176–181
Lee, C., 172
Legitimate power, 182
Leman, K., 179–180

Leonardo da Vinci, 180
Leveling, 127
Levering, R., 16, 18, 59, 64, 96–97, 172, 183, 279, 305–306
Library research, 258–259
Lickvar, J. R., 191–192
Life-long learning, 309–310
Lightner, C., 184–185
Likert, R., 15
Lincoln, A., 250–251, 254
Listening, 4, 5, 32–56, 219
assessing effectiveness of, 44–49
barriers to effective, 40–43
benefits of effective, 34–35
defined, 35–36
gender differences and, 44
hearing versus, 35–36
improving, 49–52
in meetings, 111
model of, 36–40
Literal comparison, 289
Littlejohn, S. W., 99
Logical appeals, 285
Long, P., 75
Long presentations, 249

MADD (Mothers Against Drunk Driving), 184–185
Mainiero, L., 76
Malec, W., 33–34
Maltz, M., 320
Management, leadership versus, 173–174
Management Recruiters International (MRI), 320
Manske, F. A., Jr., 173
Marcus, S., 189
Marriott International, 83–84
Marshall Field's Inc., 130
Martel, M., 260–261
Martin, J., 238
Mathematics skills, 4, 5
Matthes, K., 320
Mausehund, J., 220
Mayo, E., 15
McConnell, J., 190
McDevitt, Kaye, 136–137
McFarland, L., 190
McGarvey, R., 217–219
McGoon, C., 315
McGregor, D., 15
McKenzie, F., 308, 330
McPhee, R. D., 99
Media Strategy, Inc., 255

Meetings, 107–112
  agendas for, 107–108, 109, 112
  managing, 107–111
  participating in, 112
  presentations, 137
  rooms for, 109–111
Memorization, 264
Mentoring, 81–82
Menzel, K. E., 295
Merrill, A. R., 199, 209
Merrill, D. W., 66
Merrill, R., 199, 209
Message, 20–21, 48, 334
Metamessages, 125
Microsoft Corporation, 8–9, 313, 329
Millar, F. E., 21
Mindmapping, 274–277
Mobile offices, 324
Modeling, 186
Monroe, A. H., 282
Moore, G., 16
Moskowitz, M., 16, 18, 59, 64, 96–97, 172, 183, 279, 305–306
Motivated sequence pattern, 282
Motivational presentations, 250
Motorola Inc., 89–90, 329
Multimedia, 336
Musselwhite, E., 96, 105
Mutual discourse, 313

Naisbitt, J., 138, 288, 328–329
Names, 228, 229
Nanus, B., 173
Napier, R., 99
Nash, L. L., 294
National Association of Colleges and Employers (NACE), 11–13, 144, 154
Need, 282
Negroponte, N., 329
Nelton, S., 181
Net effects goals, 260, 261
Networking, 80–81
Network USA, 26–27
Neutrality, 70–71
Nieman-Marcus, 189
Nietzsche, F., 308
Nigro, D., 236, 238
Nixon, J. C., 40
Nixon, R., 252
Noise, 23
Nonsexist language, 123–129
Nonverbal behavior, 135, 224, 236, 316

Norman, S., 312
Northrop Grumman, 319
Nourse, R., 247–248
Noyce, R., 16

Objective task characteristics, 99
Objects, 335
Odetics, 279
Office equipment, 232
Office politics, 71–73
Ogilvie, H., 323
Open communication, 69
Open-ended mindmapping, 274–277
Organizational fit, 19–20, 178–179
Orientation to work, 8, 13–20
Ouchi, W., 17
Outlines, presentation, 282–284
Overt goals, 260

Pachter, B., 219, 223, 224, 227–230, 235, 236, 249, 283
Packwood, R., 77
Papa, M., 309
Peale, N. V., 211
Pearce, W. B., 60, 61
Pearson, J. C., 98, 127
People-oriented listeners, 46
Perceiving, 38
PERC-Quotient, 295
Performance appraisal interviews, 163–164
Perrigo, E., 6, 11, 13, 181, 313
Perrin, C., 96, 105
Perry, T. S., 314, 315
Personal touch, 328
Peters, T. J., 9, 34
Petrini, C., 137
Peurifoy, R. Z., 199, 202, 204–205
Phillips, L., 226
Phillips, W., 226
Photocopying, 232
Physical setting, of presentation, 253–254
Physical stress, 198
Pike, R. W., 336
Plutarch, 209
Poole, M. S., 99, 100, 205–209
Portable/cellular phones, 238
Positive goals, 260
Posner, B. Z., 173
Post, E., 236, 237, 239
Poster boards, 335

Powell, C., 67
Power, 182–184
  empowerment and, 183–184
  sources of, 182–183
Power differential, 48
Power lunches, 255–256
Prepared manuscripts, 263–264
Presentations, 246–300
  appeals in, 285
  audience analysis for, 250–259
  brainstorming for, 274–277
  conclusions, 292
  ethicality of, 293–294
  evidence in, 286–289
  format for, 262–264
  goals of, 259–262
  image goals for, 295–297
  introductions, 234–235, 249, 290–291
  logical sequences for, 277–282
  outlines of, 282–284
  podium etiquette, 234–236
  practicing, 267, 268, 294–295
  speaking occasion for, 254–259
  stage fright and, 264–268
  transitions, 292–293
  types of, 248–250
  visuals and, 334–338
  workers with disabilities and, 137
Preventive goals, 260
Previews, 291
Problem orientation, 70
Problem-solution pattern, 281
Problem solving
  conflict and, 211–212
  groups and, 92, 96, 100–101
Problem-solving teams, 96
Protocol International, 236
Provisionalism, 71
Prudential Securities, 247–248
Pseudolistening, 42
Psychological predisposition, 253
Psychological stress, 198
Public Electronic Network (PEN), 314
Public life, 10–11, 13
Punctuality, 219
Purdy, M., 44
Purpose statement, 290

Putnam, L. L., 205–209
Puzzle Model of Business and Professional Life, 6–13, 309

Quid pro quo harassment, 79

Ramirez, I., 148, 150
Ramsey, R. E., 237, 238
Rapport talk, 122–123
Rasberry, R. W., 43
Raven, B., 182
Ray, R., 164
Reading skills, 4, 5
Receiver, 22
Reed, S. K., 138
Referent power, 182
Reflective thinking, 101–104
Reid, R. H., 66
Relational activities, 100
Relational life, 10, 12
Relational noise, 23
Relationship, 23–24, 48. *See also* Interpersonal communication
Renier, J., 308
Report talk, 122–123
Research
  audience analysis, 251–259
  and evidence for presentations, 286–289
  library, 258–259
  telephone, 254–255
Responding, 38
Resumes, 144–150
  electronic, 149
  formats of, 149–150
  structure of, 147
  topics excluded from, 146
  topics included in, 144–146
Reverse chronological order, 278
Reward power, 182
Rockwell International Corporation, 133
Roddey, J. C., 290
Roddick, A., 7–8
Rogers, E. M., 311, 313, 314
Rogers, L. E., 21
Romantic relationships, 76–77
Roosevelt, F. D., 180
Roth, J., 100
Rudman, C., 125–127

Sabath, A. M., 222, 225–226, 233–235
Saint-Exupery, A. de, 68
Sales pitches, 249–250

Samuels, G., 238
Satisfaction, 282
Sayre, J. M., 36
Scandinavian Airlines, 8
Schaffer, B. F., 218
Schwarzkopf, H. N., 186–187
Schweitzer, A., 172
Scientific management approach, 8, 13–14
Secretary's Commission on Achieving Necessary Skills (SCANS), 4–5, 10
Seibert, J. H., 34
Seibold, D. R., 99
Self-confidence, 186
Self-directed teams, 97
Self-motivation, 186
Senn, L., 190
Sensitivity, 48, 137
Sexual discrimination, 79
Sexual harassment, 77–80
Seyle, H., 198
Seymour, D. T., 188
Shared meaning/reality, 22–23
Sheehy, B., 187–188
Shell International Petroleum, 191–192
Sheth, J. N., 306–307
Shockley-Zalabak, P., 14, 15, 17, 18
Short informative talks, 249
Sigband, N. B., 249
Siler, S., 83–84
Silk, S. L., 255
Sims, D., 26–27
Single-question procedure, 101
Situation, 24–25
Situational noise, 23
Skinner, J. F., 256, 258, 287–288, 289, 337–338
Small groups, 90. *See also* Groups
Small talk, 223, 234
Smith, A. C., 97
Smith, D. K., 104
Smith, F., 171–172
Smith, M. T., 273
Smith, S., 217–219
Snizek, W. E., 316
Social loafing, 92
Solution-oriented decision making, 100
Sorenson, R., 148, 150

Source, 21
Southwest Airlines, 143
Spatial patterns, 278
Speaking skills, 4, 5
and hearing-impaired individuals, 137
improving, 52–54
podium etiquette, 234–236
See also Presentations
Spielberg, S., 197–199
Spontaneity, 70
Sprague, J., 252
Stage fright, 264–268
causes of, 264–266
managing, 266–268
Stairs, 230
Stambler, S., 312
Standard unitary decision-making, 99–100
Statham, A., 127
Statistics, 287–288
Status reports, 248–249
Steil, L. K., 34, 44–45
Stein, J. K., 335–336
Stereotypes, 131, 181
Stevens, T., 329
Stories, 286–287
Strategies, 70
Stress, 198–205, 219, 326
causes of, 198–199
defined, 198
management of, 204–205
positive and negative responses to, 199–204
symptoms of, 201–202
Stress interviews, 155–156
Strom, D., 316
Stuart, D., 252
Substance goals, 260–262
Subtle sexual harassment, 79
Sun Tzu, 197
Superiority, 71
Supportive communication, 69
Swift, A. T., 73–74
Swift, W. B., 73–74
Swinney, S., 92
Sypher, B. D., 34

Tannen, D., 44, 78, 121, 122, 181
Targeted resume, 150
Task forces, 95–96
Task-process activities, 100
Taylor, F. W., 13

Teams, 90, 104–107
defined, 104
groupware and, 315–316, 317, 319
types of, 96–97
See also Groups
Techno-life, 11, 13, 303–332
communication competence and, 308–309
communication technologies in, 238–240, 310–322
etiquette of, 236–240
future of, 328–329
life-long learning and, 309–310
maximizing competencies for, 327–328
role of communication technology and, 306–308
Technological revolution, 307–308
Telecommuting, 323–324
Teleconferencing, 311
Telephone
as audience analysis tool, 254–255
etiquette for using, 236–238
teleconferencing and, 311
Tennessee Valley Authority (TVA), 33
Territory, 207–208
Thank-you notes, 256
Thinking-speaking time differential, 40
Thomas, C., 77–78
Thomas, K. W., 209
Thomsett, M. C., 233
Thornton, B., 213
Time-oriented listeners, 46–47
Titles, 228
Todd-Mancillas, W., 98
Topical patterns, 279–280
Topic-focus activities, 100
Transitions, 292–293
Transparencies, 335–336
Turner, L. H., 98, 104, 127

Uchida, D., 308, 330
United Airlines, 273
UNUM Life Insurance Company of America, 136–137

Upward communication, 62–63
Ury, W., 198
Usdan, M., 308

Values, 203–204
Vanderbilt, A., 229
Vangelisti, A., 23
Vertical approach, 64–66
Videoconferencing, 319–322
Videotapes, 336
Virtual company, 64–66
Virtual office, 303, 322–326
Vision, 7–10, 189–190
Visitors, receiving, 233–234
Visualization, 265–267, 282
Visuals, 334–338
purpose of, 334–335
rules for effective, 337
types of, 335–337
using, 337
Voice mail, 236–238
Voice projection, 54
Voting, 103–104

Walsh, J., 312
Waterman, Jr., R. H., 9
Watson, K. W., 34, 36–39, 44–45, 46–47, 262, 295–296
Wattleton, F., 179
Weber, M., 13
Web sites, 318
Weiland, R., 89
Welcomes, 234–235, 249
West, J. F., 40
West, R. L., 127
White, B., 59
Wilde, L., 75
Williams, T., 223
Wilson, G. L., 59, 144, 157
Wisinski, J., 209–210, 212
Wolvin, A. D., 34, 36, 49, 164
Wood, J. T., 121, 181
Workers with disabilities, 135–137, 297–298
Work life, 10, 12–13
Wright, W., 180
Writing skills, 4, 5

Xerox Corporation, 280

Zellner, W., 143
Zenger, J. H., 96, 105

Photo Credits:

Page 8: Howard Dratch/The Image Works; **Pages 3 and 16:** John Coletti; **Page 24:** Bruce Ayers/Tony Stone Images; **Pages 33 and 39:** Sarah Putnam/ Stock Boston; **Page 41:** Bob Daemmrich/Stock Boston; **Page 47:** John Coletti; **Page 68:** J. L. Atlan/Sygma; **Pages 59 and 73:** Bachmann/Photo Researchers, Inc.; **Page 74:** Will Hart; **Page 82:** John Coletti; **Pages 89 and 91:** John Coletti; **Page 102:** Robert Harbison; **Page 108:** Peter Vanderwarker/Stock Boston; **Page 120:** Will Faller; **Pages 119 and 125:** Shaffer Photography; **Page 131:** Will Hart; **Page 136:** Bob Daemmrich/Stock Boston; **Page 150:** Michael Newman/ PhotoEdit; **Pages 143 and 154:** John Coletti; **Page 161:** Michael Newman/ PhotoEdit; **Pages 171 and 175:** AP/J. Scott Applewhite/Wide World Photos; **Page 178:** John Coletti; **Page 180:** Jim Pickerell; **Page 200:** (left) Jon Levy/ The Gamma Liaison Network, (right) AP/Greg Gibson/Wide World Photos; **Page 206:** AP/Bill Waugh/Wide World Photos; **Pages 197 and 211:** John Coletti; **Pages 217 and 221:** Sarah Putnam/The Picture Cube, Inc.; **Page 231:** Mike Malyszko/FPG International; **Page 237:** Timothy Shonnard/Tony Stone Images; **Page 248:** John Coletti; **Page 253:** Shaffer Photography; **Pages 247 and 266:** Will Hart; **Pages 273 and 278:** Will Hart; **Page 293:** Shaffer Photography; **Page 296:** Reuters/Rick Wilking/Archive Photos; **Page 307:** Robert A. Isaacs; **Page 313:** Michael Newman/PhotoEdit; **Page 319:** Cindy Charles/PhotoEdit; **Page 322:** McLaughlin/The Image Works; **Pages 305 and 327:** Will Hart.